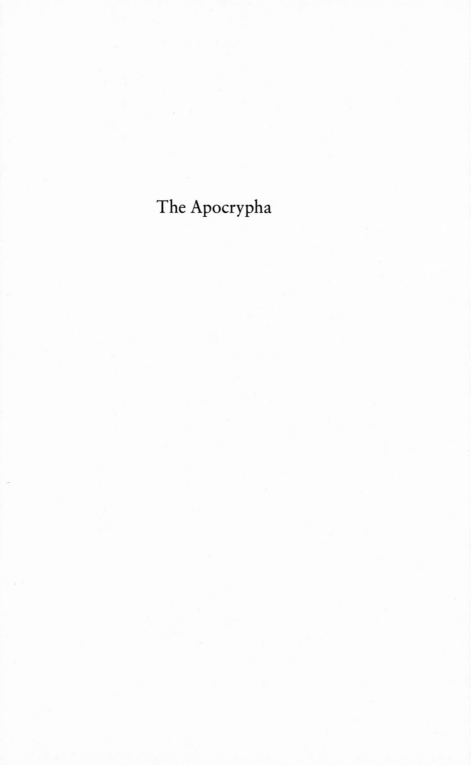

The Apocrypha

The Apocrypha

The Deuterocanonical Books of the Old Testament

GOD'S WORD Translation

BakerBooks

a division of Baker Publishing Group
Grand Rapids, Michigan

© 2009 Baker Publishing Group

GOD'S WORD®
© 1995 by God's Word to the Nations
Used by permission of Baker Publishing Group. All rights reserved.

Published by Baker Books
A division of Baker Publishing Group
P.O. Box 6287, Grand Rapids, MI, 49516-6287
www.bakerbooks.com

Library of Congress Cataloging-in-Publication Data
Bible. O.T. Apocrypha. English. GWN. 2009.
        The Apocrypha : the Deuterocanonical Books of the Old Testament /
    [Eugene W. Bunkowske, editor].
          p. cm.
        ISBN 978-0-8010-7220-8 (cloth)
        I. Bunkowske, Eugene W. II. Title.
    BS1692 2009
    229'.05208—dc22   2009007619

A portion of the purchase price of your new Bible has been provided to God's Word to the Nations. This mission society is being used by the Holy Spirit to promote and support a movement among God's people to be active participants in his mission "to seek and save people who are lost" (Luke 19:10).

13   14   15   16   17   18   19   8   7   6   5   4   3   2

Contents

Introduction

The Old Testament Scriptures were written in the Hebrew language (except for a few sections, which were written in Aramaic). As the Greek language and culture spread due to the conquests of Alexander the Great, the need arose for a Greek translation of the Hebrew scriptures. So the Hebrew Bible was translated into the Greek language resulting in an authoritative Greek version of the Old Testament. This Greek version of the Old Testament is commonly called the Septuagint. The Septuagint contained some writings which were not found in the Hebrew Bible. These additional writings were interspersed among the Old Testament books. They are generally referred to as "the Apocrypha."

In this translation, the word *apocrypha* is used to designate the following writings: Tobit, Judith, Esther (the Greek version), Wisdom, Sirach, Baruch, the Letter of Jeremiah, The Prayer of Azariah and the Song of the Three Young Men, Susanna, Bel and the Snake, First Maccabees, and Second Maccabees.

The term *apocrypha* comes from the Greek language and means "things that are hidden." Over the centuries, the term *apocrypha* has been used in two distinct ways. Those who viewed these writings as Holy Scripture considered these writings to have been "hidden" in the sense that the writings were reserved for highly educated believers. However, others believed these writings deserved to be hidden because of secondary, questionable, or heretical content. So the term came to be used in both an honorable and a derogatory sense.

During the time of the reformation, Martin Luther's German translation of the Bible contained these writings in an appendix located at the end of the Old Testament. Luther gave them the title "Apocrypha" and wrote that these writings are "books which are not held equal to the Holy Scriptures but yet are profitable and good to read." Afterward, most Protestant Bible translations (including the King James version) followed Luther by separating these books from the rest of Holy Scripture and giving them the designation "Apocrypha." Even today Protestants do not consider these books to be part of the canon of Holy Scripture.

On April 8, 1546 at the Council of Trent, the Roman Catholic Church officially declared the Apocrypha to be inspired, authoritative, and equal with the books of the Old Testament. At this council, the books of the Apocrypha were given the designation "Deuterocanonical." This designation indicates that these books are part of the canon of Holy Scripture and that their canonical status was decided at a later date than the other Old Testament books, which are called *protocanonical*.

Despite the two different opinions on the degree of authority that should be given to these books, most Christians agree that these books are valuable. Because these books were written in the intertestamental period, they provide helpful information regarding the life and thought of the Jewish people during an important period of Jewish history. These books offer insight into Jewish history, beliefs, and religious practices immediately prior to the birth of Jesus. People who read them will be better able to understand the political, cultural, ethical, and religious background of Jesus' contemporaries. Also, these books are valuable because they emphasize the fact that God protects and guides his chosen people, and they encourage God's people to follow his teachings and trust his promises.

Tobit

Tobit's Background

1 ¹This book tells the story of Tobit. Tobit was the son of Tobiel, the grandson of Hananiel, and a descendant of Aduel, Gabael, Raphael, and Raguel. Raguel belonged to the family of Asiel, who was from the tribe of Naphtali. ²When Shalmaneser was king of Assyria, Tobit was taken as a prisoner from the city of Thisbe. Thisbe is located north of the city of Asser, south of the city of Kedesh in the territory of Naphtali in northern Galilee, and northwest of the city of Phogor.

Tobit Tells About His Life

³I, Tobit, have always been faithful to God's teachings and have lived my life in a way that God approves of. I've given many gifts to poor people from my nation, people who were brought as prisoners with me to the city of Nineveh in the country of Assyria. ⁴When I was a young man, I lived in the country of Israel. The entire tribe of my ancestor Naphtali rebelled against the dynasty of my ancestor David and against the city of Jerusalem. Jerusalem was the city that had been chosen from among all the tribes of Israel as the ˻only˼ place people could offer sacrifices. The temple, where God is present, was dedicated in Jerusalem and was built to last throughout every generation.

⁵All my family, including all the relatives of my ancestor Naphtali, began sacrificing on every mountain in Galilee. They sacrificed to the statue of a calf that Israel's King Jeroboam had set up in the city of Dan. ⁶I was the only one from my family who regularly went to Jerusalem for the religious festivals that everyone in Israel is required to attend because of God's enduring command. I would take the first produce from my harvest, the firstborn animals from my flock, one-tenth of my cattle, and the first wool sheared from my sheep, and I would hurry to Jerusalem. ⁷I would give these things to the priests, the descendants of Aaron, at the altar.

Then I would give one-tenth of my grain, wine, olive oil, pomegranates, figs, and other fruit to Levi's descendants who serve in Jerusalem. Every year, except the seventh year, I would also take a tenth of my money and spend it in Jerusalem. ⁸In fact, in the third year I would bring the money and give it to orphans, widows, and converts to Israel's religion. We would use the money for a meal, exactly as Moses' Teachings command and exactly as my great-grandmother Deborah*a* taught me. She taught me because I became an orphan after my father died.

⁹When I grew up, I married ⌊Anna,⌋ a woman from my father's side of the family. We became the parents of a son, whom I named Tobias.

¹⁰After I was captured and brought to Assyria, I was taken to the city of Nineveh. The whole tribe of Naphtali, including all my family, began eating food that non-Jewish people eat. ¹¹But I was careful not to eat that food. ¹²Since I have always kept God foremost in my thoughts, ¹³the Most High allowed me to make a good impression on Shalmaneser and become Shalmaneser's purchasing agent. ¹⁴So until Shalmaneser's death, I used to make purchasing trips for him to the country of Media. Once, while I was in Media, I deposited a large sum of money with my friend Gabael, the son of Gabri. ¹⁵But when Shalmaneser died and his son Sennacherib succeeded him as king, the roads in Media became unsafe, and I couldn't travel there anymore.

¹⁶During the time that Shalmaneser was king, I gave many gifts to those who were poor among my people. ¹⁷I gave my food to those who were hungry and my clothes to those who didn't have enough to wear. If I saw that the dead body of one of my people had been thrown outside the wall of Nineveh, I would bury it.

¹⁸I also buried those who were killed by King Sennacherib. Because Sennacherib insulted the king of heaven, the king of heaven punished him when he quickly retreated from Judea. So Sennacherib killed many Israelites because he was angry. I secretly removed these bodies and buried them. When Sennacherib looked for these bodies, he couldn't find them.

¹⁹Then someone from Nineveh informed the king that I was the one burying these people. When I found out that the king knew about me and wanted to kill me, I had to go into hiding. I was afraid and ran away. ²⁰After that, all my possessions were taken away. I had nothing left. Everything that belonged to me was taken to the royal treasury. All I had left was my wife Anna and my son Tobias.

²¹But less than 40 days later, Sennacherib was assassinated by two of his sons. They escaped to the mountains of Ararat, and another son, Esarhaddon, succeeded Sennacherib as king. Esarhaddon appointed Ahikar, my brother Hanael's son, as the chief financial officer of his kingdom. Ahikar eventually took control of the entire administration. ²²In fact, Ahikar had been the chief of security, the keeper of the king's seal, an

---

a 1:8 Some manuscripts read "my grandmother Deborah."

accountant, and the chief financial officer for King Sennacherib of Assyria. So Esarhaddon kept Ahikar in office. Ahikar was a close relative, my nephew. He interceded for me, and as a result, I was allowed to return to Nineveh.

2 ¹After Esarhaddon became king, I returned home. I was reunited with my wife Anna and my son Tobias. At the Festival of Pentecost (the Festival of Weeks) a wonderful dinner was prepared for me, and I sat down to eat. ²A lot of food was set on the table. So I said to my son Tobias, "Son, find some poor person from our people to share this dinner with me. Make sure he is one of the prisoners taken to Nineveh and a person who always keeps God foremost in his thoughts. I'll wait for you to return, Son."

³So Tobias left to look for a poor person among our people. But he came back, shouting, "Father!"

I asked, "What is it, Son?"

He answered, "Father, one of our people has been murdered! His body is still lying in the marketplace where he was strangled."

⁴I jumped up and left the dinner table before I had even tasted my food. I removed the body from the street and laid it in one of my guest rooms. I left it there until sunset, when I could bury it. ⁵When I returned, I washed myself and ate my food in sorrow. ⁶I remembered what the prophet Amos had spoken against Bethel:

"Your festivals will be turned into funerals
    and all your songs into funeral songs."

⁷Then I began to cry.

After the sun had set, I went outside, dug a grave, and buried the man. ⁸My neighbors laughed at me. They said to each other, "He's still not afraid! People have already tried to kill him for burying the dead, and he ran away. Now he's back at it again, doing the same thing."

Tobit Loses His Sight

⁹That same night I washed, went into my yard, and slept by the wall. Because it was hot outside, I didn't cover my face. ¹⁰I didn't realize that, above me, sparrows were perched on the wall. Their warm droppings fell into my eyes and caused a white film to develop on them. I went to doctors for treatment. But the more medication they gave me, the worse my eyesight became until I lost my sight entirely. For four years I couldn't see. All my relatives felt sorry for me, and Ahikar supported me for two years until he went to the province of Elam.

¹¹At that time my wife Anna earned money by making arts and crafts like some women do. ¹²She would take what she made to her customers, and they would pay her for it. On the seventh day of the month of Dys-

trus, she cut off from the loom a piece of cloth she had woven and took
it to her customers. They paid her in full for it, and gave her a young
goat from their flocks to take home.

¹³ When my wife came home, the goat began to cry. So I called my wife
and asked her, "Where did you get this little goat? You didn't steal it, did
you? Give it back to its owners. We have no right to eat anything that's
stolen."

¹⁴ But my wife said to me, "The little goat was given to me as a gift."
But I didn't believe her and told her to give it back to its owners. I became
very angry with her over this. Then she replied, "Where have your gifts to
the poor gotten you? You've done many things to gain God's approval.
Where have they gotten you? Certainly, people can see that you have
nothing to show for them!"

Tobit Prays in His Distress

3 ¹ I was very sad, so I groaned and started to cry. Then I began to
pray:

² "Lord, you are right.
　　Everything you do is right.
　You are merciful and faithful in everything you do.
　　You judge the world.
³ Lord, remember me, and treat me kindly.
　　Don't punish me because of my sins
　　　or because of the sins that my ancestors and I are unaware of.

⁴ "We have certainly disobeyed your commands.
　　So you allowed us to be looted, captured, and killed
　　　and to be ridiculed, slandered, and insulted
　　　　among every nation where we have been scattered.
⁵ Your many judgments are true.
　　Treat us as our sins deserve,
　　　because we haven't done what you commanded
　　　　or been faithful to you.

⁶ "Do whatever you like with me.
　　Let me die.
　　　Free me from life on earth
　　　　so that my body can become dust.
　　I'd rather be dead than alive,
　　　because I've had to listen to insults that aren't true,
　　　　and I'm very sad.
　　Lord, free me from this distress.
　　　Free me to go to my eternal home.
　　　　Don't ignore me, Lord.

I'd rather die than have to see so much distress in my life
and listen to insults."

Sarah Prays in Her Distress

⁷On the same day in the city of Ecbatana in Media, Sarah, the daughter
of Raguel, also happened to hear insults that were made about her by one
of her father's female servants. ⁸Sarah had been married seven times. But
a wicked demon named Asmodeus killed each of her husbands before
she could sleep with them. The servant said to Sarah, "You're the woman
who kills her husbands! You've already been married seven times, and
you still don't have a new last name.ᵃ ⁹You have no right to punish us
just because your husbands have died. Why don't you go and join them?
I hope that I never have to see a son or daughter of yours!"

¹⁰Sarah was so sad that day that she began to cry. She went upstairs
and intended to hang herself. But she had second thoughts. She thought,
"I don't want anyone to insult my father and say to him, 'You had only
one daughter. You loved her, but she hung herself because of the wicked
things she did.' Then, because of me, my elderly father would go to his
grave full of grief. I'd better not hang myself. Instead, I'll pray to the Lord
and ask him to let me die so that I won't have to listen to insults for the
rest of my life."

¹¹At that time, she stretched out her hands toward the window and
prayed:

"God, we praise you because you are merciful.
    People will praise your name forever.
        Everything you've made will praise you forever.
¹²Lord, I'm looking to you for help.
¹³   Free me from this earth
        so that I won't have to listen to insults any longer.
¹⁴Master, you know that I'm pure
        and that I haven't had sex with any man.
¹⁵I haven't disgraced my name or my father's name
    in this country where I've been taken as a prisoner.
I'm my father's only child.
    He has no other child to be his heir.
    He doesn't have any relatives that I can marry.
I've already suffered the loss of seven husbands.
    Why should I go on living?
Lord, if you don't want to take my life,
    at least listen to how I'm being insulted."

ᵃ 3:8 Some manuscripts read "and you haven't satisfied the sexual desires of any of your
husbands."

God Answers Tobit's and Sarah's Prayers

¹⁶At that very moment, God, in his glory, heard the prayers of Tobit and Sarah. ¹⁷So God sent the angel Raphael to heal both of them. Raphael would heal Tobit by removing the white film from his eyes so that he could see again. Raphael would heal Sarah, Raguel's daughter, by arranging for her to marry Tobias, Tobit's son. (Tobias had the right to marry her before anyone else did.) Also, Raphael would free Sarah from the wicked demon Asmodeus.

At the same time that Tobit went back into his house from the yard, Sarah, Raguel's daughter, went downstairs.

Tobit Gives His Son Instructions

4 ¹That same day Tobit remembered the money that he had deposited with Gabael in the city of Rages in the country of Media. ²He thought, "Now that I've asked the Lord to let me die, I should let my son Tobias know about the money." ³So he sent for his son Tobias. When Tobias arrived, Tobit said to him, "When I die, make sure that I have a proper burial. Honor your mother, and don't leave her as long as she lives. Do whatever she wants, and don't do anything to upset her. ⁴Son, remember that she faced many dangers for you while she was pregnant. When she dies, bury her next to me.

⁵"Son, keep the Lord foremost in your thoughts every day. Never be willing to sin or disobey his commands. Do what God approves of every day of your life. Don't get involved in anything wicked, ⁶because those who are faithful to God's teachings will be successful in everything they do.

⁷"Give gifts from your possessions to all those poor people who do what God approves of.ᵃ Never refuse to give gifts to poor people. Never ignore anyone who is poor, and God will never ignore you. ⁸Your gifts to the poor should be based on how much you have. But even if you don't have very much, don't be afraid to give something to the poor. ⁹When you do this, you will be saving up for any future crisis that you may have. ¹⁰In fact, giving gifts to the poor will save you from death and keep you from going into the darkness. ¹¹The Most High considers gifts given to the poor as the best kind of offering.

¹²"Son, keep away from every kind of sexual sin. Most importantly, marry a woman who is a descendant of one of your own ancestors. Never marry a woman who doesn't come from our people, because we are the descendants of the prophets. Son, remember that all our earliest ancestors—Noah, Abraham, Isaac, and Jacob—married women from their own people. They were blessed with children, and their descendants will inherit the land of Israel. ¹³So, Son, love your own people. Don't be so

---

ᵃ 4:7 Tobit 4:7b-19a is not found in some manuscripts and translations.

arrogant that you refuse to marry a woman from your own people. This kind of arrogance causes problems and a lot of disorder. In the same way, laziness leads to loss and severe poverty, because laziness causes famine.

¹⁴ "Never keep overnight the pay you owe your hired workers. Instead, pay them every day. If you serve God by doing this, he will reward you. Son, be careful in everything you do, and always show self control. ¹⁵Don't do to people anything that you would hate them to do to you.

"Never drink so much wine that you become drunk. Drunkenness must not be a part of your life.

¹⁶ "Give some of your food to people who are hungry, and give some of your clothes to people who don't have enough to wear. Give whatever you have left over to the poor. Never refuse to give gifts to poor people. ¹⁷Place food on the graves of people who have God's approval, but don't give any food to sinners.

¹⁸ "Seek advice from every wise person, and don't take any useful advice lightly.

¹⁹ "Take every opportunity to praise the Lord God. Ask him to help you lead a decent life and to make you successful in everything you do and plan. None of the nations have ⌐God's⌐ plan. The Lord is the only one who can give a good plan to a nation. The Lord can bring anyone he wants to the deepest part of hell. Son, remember these instructions. Never forget them.

²⁰ "Finally, Son, I need to tell you that I once deposited a large sum of money with Gabael, the son of Gabri, in the city of Rages in Media. ²¹Son, don't be afraid now that we have become poor. If you fear God, avoid every kind of sin, and do what the Lord your God considers good, you will be very rich."

Tobias Plans a Trip to Media

5 ¹Tobias said to his father Tobit, "I'll do everything that you've told me. ²But how can I get the money from Gabael? He doesn't know me, and I don't know him. What kind of identification can I give him to prove who I am so that he'll believe me and give me the money? Besides, I don't even know what roads to take to get to Media."

³Tobit answered, "Twenty years ago, when I deposited the money, Gabael and I divided the receipt between the two of us. Each of us has one half of the receipt, and I left his half with the money. Son, find a man you can trust to go with you. We'll pay him when you return. Just get the money back from Gabael."

Tobias Meets the Angel Raphael

⁴So Tobias left to find someone who knew the way to Media and who would go with him. Soon after he left the house, he met the angel

Raphael, who was standing in front of him. But Tobias didn't realize that Raphael was one of God's angels. ⁵So Tobias asked him, "Where are you from, young man?"

Raphael answered, "I'm an Israelite and a relative of yours. I've come here to find work."

Tobias asked him, "Do you know the way to Media?"

⁶Raphael replied, "Yes. I've been there many times. I know the way there and all the roads. I've often traveled to Media. I used to stay with one of our relatives, Gabael. He lives in the city of Rages in Media. The trip from the city of Ecbatana to Rages takes two days, because Rages is located in the mountains and Ecbatana is in the middle of the plain."

⁷Then Tobias said to Raphael, "Wait for me while I go into the house and tell my father. I want you to go to Media with me, and I'll pay you."

⁸Raphael replied, "Alright, I'll wait for you. But don't take too long."

⁹So Tobias went into the house and told his father, "I've just met a man who is an Israelite and a relative of ours."

His father replied, "Invite the man in! I want to find out about his family, what tribe he's from, and if I can trust him to go with you."

¹⁰Then Tobias went outside and invited Raphael to come into the house. He said, "My father has invited you to come in." So Raphael went into the house to meet Tobias' father. Tobit greeted him first.

Then Raphael replied, "A very good day to you, sir!"

But Tobit responded, "How can I have a good day? I've lost my eyesight. I can't see anymore. Instead, I lie in darkness like those who are dead and can no longer see. Although I'm still alive, I'm as good as dead. I can hear people talking, but I can't see them."

But the young man said, "Cheer up! God is going to heal you soon. So cheer up!"

Then Tobit said to him, "My son Tobias wants to go to Media. Can you go with him as his guide? I'll pay you, my friend."

The young man answered, "I can go with him, and I know how to get there. I've often gone to Media and have crossed all its plains. I'm familiar with its mountains and all of its roads."

¹¹Then Tobit asked him, "My friend, tell me what family and tribe you come from."

¹²The young man replied, "Why do you want to know my tribe?"

Tobit answered, "My friend, I want to make sure whose son you are and what your name is."

¹³The young man said, "My name is Azariah. I'm the son of the older Hananiah, one of your relatives."

¹⁴Then Tobit said to him, "Welcome! May God keep you safe and protect you, my friend. Don't be upset with me for wanting to be sure about your family background. You are a relative who is from a good and honorable family. I knew Hananiah and Nathan, the two sons of the older Shemeliah. They used to go with me to Jerusalem and worship with me there. Nothing could ever make them unfaithful to God. Your relatives are good people, and you come from a good background. You're certainly welcome here!"

¹⁵Then Tobit added, "I'll pay both of you a regular day's wage plus expenses. So go with my son. ¹⁶I'll even give you a bonus in addition to your wages."

Raphael replied, "I'll go with him. Don't worry. The roads are safe, so we'll have no problem getting there and back."

¹⁷Tobit responded, "May God bless you, my friend."

Then Tobit said to his son, "Pack what you need for the trip, and leave with your friend. May God in heaven bring you there and back safely. May one of God's angels go with both of you to keep you safe."

Before Tobias left the house to go to Media, he kissed his father and mother goodbye. Tobit wished him a safe trip, ¹⁸but Anna began to cry.

She said to Tobit, "How can you send my son away? Hasn't he always taken care of us? ¹⁹Money isn't everything! For our son's sake, forget about the money. ²⁰We should be content with the life the Lord has given us."

²¹But Tobit said to her, "Don't talk like that! Our son will get there and back with no problem. You'll see! He'll come back safe and sound. ²²So don't talk like that! Don't worry, my dear. One of God's angels will go with him. He'll have a successful trip and return safe and sound." ¹Then Anna stopped crying.

Tobias Begins His Trip

6 ²Tobias left, and the angel went with him. Tobias' dog also went with them. The three of them traveled that first day. When night came, they camped by the Tigris River. ³Tobias went to wash his feet in the river. Suddenly, a huge fish jumped out of the water and tried to bite off one of his feet. Tobias yelled, ⁴and the angel said to him, "Grab the fish, and hold it tightly!"

So Tobias grabbed the fish and pulled it up on the riverbank. ⁵Then the angel said, "Cut the fish open, and take out its gall bladder, heart, and liver. Keep them, but throw the intestines away. The gall bladder, heart, and liver can be used as medicines."

⁶So Tobias cut the fish open and kept the gall bladder, heart, and liver. Then he roasted some of the fish and ate it. He preserved the rest of the fish with salt so that he could take it with them.

The three of them continued to travel together. When they were near Media, ⁷Tobias asked the angel, "Azariah, my friend, how can the fish's heart, liver, and especially its gall bladder be used as medicines?"

⁸Azariah replied, "The fish's heart and liver can be used to get rid of demons or evil spirits that are tormenting someone. If the heart and liver are burned in that person's presence, the smoke will chase the demons away forever. ⁹The fish's gall bladder can be used on a person's eyes. If a person's eyes are covered with layers of white film, rub the fish's gall bladder on that person's eyes and blow on them. Then that person will be able to see again."

¹⁰When they arrived in Media and were close to the city of Ecbatana, ¹¹Raphael said, "Tobias, my friend."

"What?" Tobias replied.

Raphael continued, "We're going to stay at Raguel's house tonight. He's your relative, and he has a daughter named Sarah. ¹²He doesn't have any other children. You are her closest relative. So you have the right to marry her before anyone else does. You also have the right to inherit her father's possessions. In addition, the girl is sensible, brave, and very beautiful, and her father is an honorable man. ¹³You have every right to marry her. So listen to me, my friend. Tonight I'll talk with her father, and we can make arrangements so that she can become your wife. When we return from the city of Rages, we'll celebrate the marriage. I know that Raguel cannot keep her from marrying you or promise her in marriage to another man. If he does, he deserves the death penalty according to the laws in the Book of Moses. He knows that you have the right to marry his daughter before anyone else does. Listen to me. Tonight we'll talk about the girl and arrange her engagement to you. Then, when we return from Rages, we'll bring her back with us to your house."

¹⁴But Tobias objected, "Azariah, my friend. I've heard that she has already been married seven times and that each of her husbands died in the bedroom. I've heard that on the very night of the wedding, when they went into her bedroom, they died. People say that a demon killed these men. ¹⁵The demon doesn't hurt her, but it kills every husband who tries to sleep with her. I'm an only child. I'm afraid that if I die, my father and mother would die of grief. They don't have another son to bury them."

¹⁶Then Raphael said to Tobias, "Don't you remember your father's instructions? Don't you remember that he told you to marry a woman from his side of the family? Now listen to me, my friend. Don't even think about this demon! Marry Sarah. I know that she will become your wife tonight. ¹⁷When you enter the bedroom, take along the fish's heart and some of its liver. Put them on some burning incense. An odor will spread in the bedroom. ¹⁸As soon as the demon smells it, he will quickly

leave and never come back again. When you're ready to sleep with her, both of you must first stand and pray. Ask the Lord of heaven to show you mercy and keep you safe. Don't be afraid. God set Sarah apart for you before the world was created. You will save her ˻from the demon˼, and she will go ˻home˼ with you. I'm sure that you and Sarah will have children, and they will be precious to you. So don't talk like that!"

When Tobias heard everything that Raphael said, especially that Sarah was related to him through his father's side of the family, he fell in love with her and was determined to marry her.

Tobias Marries Sarah

7 ¹When they arrived in the city of Ecbatana, Tobias said, "Azariah, my friend, take me to Raguel our relative right away." So Azariah took Tobias to Raguel's house.

They found Raguel sitting beside the entrance to his yard. They greeted Raguel first, and he replied, "Welcome, friends! I'm glad to see you! How are you?"

Then he took them into his house ²and said to his wife Edna, "This young man looks a lot like my relative Tobit."

³Edna asked them, "Where are you from?"

They answered, "We're descendants of Naphtali. We were taken to Nineveh as prisoners."

⁴She said to them, "Do you know our relative Tobit?"

"Yes! We do," they replied.

Then she asked them, "How is he?"

⁵"He's alive and well," they responded.

Then Tobias stated, "He's my father!" ⁶At that, Raguel jumped up, kissed Tobias, and began to cry.

⁷He said to Tobias, "May God bless you, my son. Your father is a good and honorable man. What a shame that such an honest man who gives to the poor should become blind." Raguel hugged his relative Tobias and began to cry again. ⁸Then Edna also began to cry about Tobit, and so did their daughter Sarah. ⁹After that, Raguel slaughtered a ram from his flock and gave his guests a warm welcome.

After Tobias and Raphael had washed up and had taken their place to eat, Tobias said to Raphael, "Azariah, my friend, ask Raguel to let me marry Sarah."

¹⁰Raguel overheard what Tobias said and replied, "Have something to eat and drink, and have a good time tonight. You're the only person who has the right to marry my daughter Sarah. I don't have the right to let her marry anyone else because you are my closest relative. However, let me be very truthful with you, my son. ¹¹I've already allowed her to marry seven men who were related to us. Each of them died on his wedding

night when he went into her bedroom. Don't worry. The Lord will work everything out. So have something to eat and drink."

But Tobias said, "I won't eat or drink anything until you settle this with me."

So Raguel said, "Alright! That's what I'll do. I will allow her to marry you according to the laws in the Book of Moses. This marriage has been arranged in heaven. Take her as your wife. From now on you belong to her, and she belongs to you. Starting today, she is yours forever. My son, may the Lord bless you tonight and give you his mercy and peace."

¹²Then Raguel called his daughter Sarah. When she came to him, he took her hand, gave it to Tobias, and said, "Take Sarah to be your wife according to Moses' Teachings, according to the laws written in his book. She is yours. Take her safely to your father's home. May the God of heaven bless you with his peace."

¹³Raguel called his wife and told her to bring him some paper. On the paper he wrote out the marriage contract, stating that Sarah became Tobias' wife according to the laws in Moses' Teachings. ¹⁴After this, they began to eat and drink.

¹⁵Raguel said to Edna, "My dear, get the other bedroom ready, and take Sarah there."

¹⁶So Edna got the bedroom ready as Raguel had told her and brought Sarah there. Sarah began to cry.ᵃ But then Edna wiped the tears away and said to Sarah, ¹⁷"Cheer up, my daughter! The Lord of heaven will make you happy since you've had so much sorrow. Cheer up, my daughter!" Then Edna left the room.

The Demon Leaves

8 ¹When they had finished eating and drinking, they were ready for bed. Raguel and Edna led Tobias from the dining room into the bedroom. ²Tobias remembered what Raphael had told him. So he took the fish's liver and heart out of the bag where he had been keeping them, and he put them on some burning incense. ³The smell from the fish kept the demon away. In fact, it made the demon run off to southern Egypt. Raphael followed the demon there and immediately tied up his hands and feet.

The Wedding Prayer of Tobias

⁴After Sarah's parents had left the room and had closed the door, Tobias got out of bed and said to Sarah, "Get up, my dear! We have to

---

ᵃ 7:16 Some Greek manuscripts; other Greek manuscripts read "Edna cried about her daughter."

pray. We must ask our Lord to show us mercy and keep us safe." ⁵So Sarah
got up, and together they began to pray, asking God to keep them safe.
Tobias prayed:

"God of our ancestors, we praise you.
　Your people will praise your name forever.
　　Heaven and all creation will praise you forever.
⁶You made Adam, and you made his wife Eve to help
　　and support him.
　From these two people, the human race began.
　You said, 'It is not good for the man to be alone.
　　We must make a helper who is like him.'
⁷I'm not marrying my dear wife because I want
　　a physical relationship.
　I'm marrying her because I want a true marriage relationship.
　　Show us your mercy so that we can grow old together."

⁸Then together they both said, "Amen! Amen!" ⁹and slept through the
night.

Raguel Digs a Grave for Tobias

Meanwhile, Raguel got up and called his servants. Together they went
outside to dig a grave ¹⁰because Raguel thought, "More than likely, Tobias
will die, and people will laugh at us and insult us." ¹¹After they finished
digging the grave, Raguel went back inside the house. ¹²He told his wife,
"Send one of the female servants into the bedroom to see if Tobias is still
alive. If he's dead, we've got to bury him before anyone finds out." ¹³So
they lit a lamp, opened the door, and sent a servant into the bedroom.
She found Tobias and Sarah sound asleep together. ¹⁴Then the servant left
and told Raguel and Edna that Tobias was still alive and that everything
was fine. ¹⁵So Raguel and Edna praised the God of heaven. They said,

"God, we praise you because all your blessings are pure.
　People will praise you forever.
¹⁶We praise you because you have made us happy.
　Things turned out better than we expected.
　　You have shown us how merciful you can be.
¹⁷We praise you because you have shown mercy
　　to these two children. Each is an only child.
　Master, show them your mercy, and keep them safe.
　　Fill their lives with happiness and kindness."

¹⁸Then Raguel ordered his servants to fill in the grave before sunrise.

Preparations for the Wedding Reception

[19] After this, Raguel told his wife to bake a lot of bread. Then he went out to his herd, brought back two oxen and four rams, and ordered his servants to slaughter them. So the servants began to prepare ˻for the wedding reception˼. [20] Then he told Tobias,[a] "You can't leave for two weeks. Stay here, and have something to eat and drink with me. It will make my daughter happy. After all, she has been very depressed. [21] Then you may take half of everything that I own and return safely to your father. The other half of my possessions will be yours when my wife and I die. You can count on that, my son. I'm your father now, and Edna is your mother. From now on, we'll be one, big, happy family. You can count on that too, my son!"

Raphael Gets the Money From Gabael

9 [1] Then Tobias said to Raphael, [2] "Azariah, my friend, take four servants and two camels, and go to the city of Rages. Go to Gabael's house. Give him the receipt for the deposit, and get the money. Then bring him back with you for the wedding reception. [3] You know that my father will be counting the days until I get back. If I'm even one day late, he'll become very worried. [4] You saw how Raguel made me take an oath. I can't break my promise."

[5] So Raphael took four servants and two camels, went to Rages in Media, and stayed with Gabael. Raphael gave him the receipt. He also told him that Tobit's son Tobias had gotten married and that Tobias had invited him to the wedding reception. Gabael quickly checked the money bags to make sure they were still sealed and counted them.[b]

[6] They both got up early in the morning and left for the wedding reception. When they went inside Raguel's house, they found Tobias sitting at the dinner table. Tobias jumped up, greeted Gabael, and cried. Gabael praised Tobias, saying, "You're an honorable and good person. You're just like your father, who is honorable, good, honest, and generous. May the Lord give blessings from heaven to you, your wife, and your in-laws. Praise God! I've seen Tobias, who looks like my cousin Tobit."

Tobit and Anna Become Worried

10 [1] Meanwhile, day after day, Tobit was keeping track of the days that were needed for Tobias to get to Rages and back. When the expected time had passed and his son hadn't come back, [2] he thought,

---

[a] 8:20 Or "Then he made Tobias take this oath:" See 9:4.
[b] 9:5 Some manuscripts read ". . . sealed and loaded them on the camels."

"Maybe he's been detained there. Or maybe Gabael has died, and no one is there to give him the money." ³Then he began to worry.

⁴Tobit's wife Anna said, "My son's dead. He's never coming back." Then she began to cry and mourn for her son. She said, ⁵"My son, my pride and joy! This is terrible. I never should have let you take that trip."

⁶But Tobit replied, "Dear, be quiet, and don't talk like that. Tobias is alright. I'm sure there's a good reason why he's late. Besides, the man who went with him is one of our relatives. He can be trusted. So don't worry about Tobias, dear. He'll be home any minute."

⁷Then Anna responded, "Don't tell me to be quiet! And stop lying to me! My son is dead."

Every day Anna would rush outside to the road that Tobias had taken, and she would watch for her son. No one could talk her out of doing this. When the sun would set, she would go back home, cry and mourn all night long, and not get any sleep.

Tobias Begins His Trip Home

The two-week wedding reception that Raguel had promised to have for his daughter ended. So Tobias approached Raguel and said, "Let me go back home. I'm sure that my father and mother think that they'll never see me again. I'm begging you, Raguel. Let me go so that I can return to my father. I've already told you how ˻worried˼ he was when I left him."

⁸But Raguel said to Tobias, "Don't go, my son. Stay with me. I'll send messengers to your father to tell him everything that's happened to you."

⁹But Tobias insisted, "No! I'm begging you. Let me go back to my father."

¹⁰So Raguel gave Tobias his daughter Sarah, half of all his possessions, male and female slaves, oxen and sheep, donkeys and camels, clothes, money, and household items. ¹¹Then Raguel sent them on their way. He hugged Tobias and said, "Goodbye, my son. Have a safe trip. May the Lord of heaven make you and your wife Sarah successful, and may I live long enough to see your children." ¹²Then Raguel said to his daughter Sarah, "Live with your in-laws, because from now on they are your parents as much as your mother and I. May the Lord go with you, my daughter. I hope to hear nothing but good news about you while I'm still alive." When he had finished saying goodbye, he sent them on their way.

Before they left, Edna said to Tobias, "My dear son, may the Lord bring you safely home. I hope I'll live long enough to see the children that you and my daughter Sarah will have. With the Lord as my witness, I now give my daughter to you. Don't ever upset her as long as you live. May the Lord go with you, my son. From now on, I'm your mother, and

Sarah is your dear wife. May all of us be successful as long as we live."
Then she kissed both of them and sent them on their way.

¹³So Tobias left Raguel's home. He was healthy and happy, and he
praised the Lord of heaven and earth. He praised the Lord, the king who
rules everything, because the Lord had made his trip successful. Then
⌐Raphael⌐ said to Tobias, "If you honor Raguel and Edna as long as they
live, you will be successful."

Tobias Arrives Home

11 ¹When they were close to the city of Kaserin, which was near Nineveh, ²Raphael said, "You know what condition your father was in
when we left him. ³Let's run ahead of your wife and get the house ready
before everyone gets there." ⁴As the two went on together, Raphael said
to Tobias, "Have the fish's gall bladder ready." The dog followed them.

⁵As usual, Anna was sitting along the road and watching for her son.
⁶When she saw Tobias coming, she shouted to his father, "Your son is
coming, and so is the man who went with him!"

⁷Before Tobias approached his father, Raphael said to him, "I know
that your father will get his sight back. ⁸Spread the fish's gall bladder on
your father's eyes. This medicine will make the white film on his eyes
shrink and peel off. Then your father will be able to see again."

⁹Anna ran up to her son, hugged him, and said, "Now that I've seen
you again, my child, I don't care anymore if I die." And she began to
cry.

Tobit Regains His Sight

¹⁰Tobit got up and stumbled through the entrance to his yard ⌐toward
Tobias⌐. Tobias went up to him ¹¹and had the fish's gall bladder ready. He
held his father firmly, blew into his eyes, and said, "Cheer up, Father."
Then Tobias spread the medicine on his father's eyes. ¹²Next, using both
hands, Tobias peeled the white film from his father's eyes.

¹³Tobit hugged Tobias ¹⁴and began to cry. He shouted, "My son, my
pride and joy! I can see you again!" Then Tobit said,

> "Praise God!
> Praise his mighty name!
> Praise all his holy angels!
> > May his mighty name be ⌐praised⌐ among us.
> > May all his angels be praised forever.
> ¹⁵   He punished me with blindness,
> >   but now I can see my son Tobias!"

Tobias was happy as he went inside the house, and he praised God
loudly. He told his father that his trip had been successful and that he

had brought the money back. He also told him that he had married Raguel's daughter Sarah and that she was on her way and was very close to Nineveh.

[16] So Tobit left the house to meet his daughter-in-law at the entrance to Nineveh. He was happy, and he praised God. When the citizens of Nineveh saw him walking briskly without anyone leading him, they were amazed. [17] In front of everyone, Tobit acknowledged that God had shown him mercy and had restored his sight.

Tobit walked up to Sarah, the wife of his son Tobias, and greeted her: "Welcome to Nineveh, my daughter! Praise God because he has brought you to us. God has blessed your father Raguel, my son Tobias, and you, my daughter. What a joy and blessing it is to welcome you into your new family!"

So that day all the Jewish people in Nineveh were joyful. [18] Also, Ahikar and Nadab, Tobit's nephews, were there to share in his happiness.[a]

Raphael Reveals Who He Is

12 [1] When the wedding reception in Nineveh was over, Tobit called for his son Tobias. He said to him, "Son, make sure you pay the man who went with you, and give him a bonus."

[2] Tobias asked, "Father, how much should I pay him? I wouldn't mind giving him half of everything he helped me bring back. [3] After all, he brought me back safely, cured my wife, and helped me get the money. He also cured you. What kind of a bonus should I give him?"

[4] Tobit answered, "Son, he deserves half of everything he brought back."

[5] So Tobias called for Raphael and said, "Take half of everything you brought back, and have a safe trip home."

[6] Then Raphael took both of them aside and spoke to them privately. He said to them, "Praise God! Tell everyone you see about the good things that God has done for you. Then they, too, will sing hymns to praise his name. Honor him by letting everyone know what he has done. Don't hesitate to tell people about him. [7] Keeping a king's secret is good, but honoring God by making known what he has done is even better. If you do good, nothing bad will happen to you. [8] Praying sincerely is good. Giving away money that was made honestly is better than getting money that was made dishonestly. Giving gifts is better than storing up gold. [9] Giving to the poor will save you from death and cleanse you from every sin. Life will be satisfying for those who give to the poor. [10] But those who sin and do wrong are their own worst enemies.

---

[a] 11:18 Some manuscripts add verse 19: "People joyously celebrated Tobias' wedding for one week."

¹¹ "I'll tell you the whole truth. I won't keep anything from you. I've already told you that keeping a king's secret is good, but that honoring God by making known what he has done is even better. ¹²Tobit, when you and Sarah prayed, I brought your prayers to the Lord, in his glory, so that he would remember them. I did the same thing whenever you would bury the dead. ¹³When you immediately got up and left the dinner table to bury that dead man, I was sent to test you. ¹⁴At the same time, God sent me to heal you and your daughter-in-law Sarah. ¹⁵I am Raphael! I'm one of the seven angels who stands in front of the Lord, in his glory, and serves him."

¹⁶Both Tobit and Tobias were terrified and fell facedown on the ground. ¹⁷But Raphael said to them, "Don't be afraid! God's peace is yours. Praise God forever. ¹⁸I didn't come to you because I wanted to, but because God wanted me to. So praise God as long as you live. Sing praises to him. ¹⁹You thought you saw me eat. But I didn't really eat anything. It only looked as though I were eating. ²⁰Get up, praise the Lord, and acknowledge him. Now I'm going to the one who sent me. Write down everything that has happened to you." Then Raphael disappeared.

²¹Tobit and Tobias got up, but they couldn't see Raphael anymore. ²²Then they began to sing hymns of praise to God and to acknowledge him for the spectacular things he had done, especially for sending his angel Raphael to appear to them.

Tobit's Psalm of Praise

13 ¹Then Tobit said,

"Praise the God who lives forever
    and whose kingdom never ends.
²He punishes and shows mercy.
He can bring people down to hell, the lowest part of the earth,
    and he can bring people back from that place of total ruin.
        Nothing can escape his power.
³You people of Israel,
    acknowledge him among the nations
        where he has scattered you.
⁴He has shown you his greatness even among the nations.
Honor him in the presence of every living creature
    because he is our Lord.
        He is our God.
        He is our Father.
        He is God forever.
⁵He will punish you for every wicked thing you do
    but will show mercy to all of you
        wherever you've been scattered among all the nations.

⁶If you turn your every thought and your entire life over to him
　　and do what he considers right,
then he will turn to you
　　and always pay attention to you.
Look at everything he has done for you.
Thank him loudly.
Praise the Lord, who does what's right.
　　Honor the king who rules forever.*a*
I'll acknowledge him in the country where I'm a prisoner.
I'll tell about his power and greatness to a sinful nation.
You sinners, turn your lives around, and do what God approves of.
　　Who knows? Maybe he will be kind to you and show you mercy.
⁷I will honor my God.
The king of heaven and his greatness will fill me with joy.

⁸"May all people acknowledge him in Jerusalem.

⁹"Jerusalem, you are the holy city.
　　God will punish you for the things your people have done,
　　　　but he will again show mercy to the people
　　　　　　who do what he approves of.
¹⁰Acknowledge the Lord as he deserves.
Praise the king who rules forever.
　　His tent will be rebuilt for you as you rejoice.
May he cheer up your prisoners
　　and show your suffering people his love forever.

¹¹"Jerusalem, you are a bright light that will shine
　　　　throughout the earth.
People from many faraway nations will come to you.
Those who live in the most remote areas of the earth will come
　　　　to you
　　because of your holy name.
They will have gifts in their hands for the king of heaven.
Generation after generation will joyfully praise you,
　　and your name—the name of the chosen city—
　　　　will endure forever.
¹²Everyone who says harsh things against you will be cursed.
Everyone who destroys you, tears down your walls,
　　knocks down your towers, or burns your houses will be cursed.
　　　　But everyone who respects*b* you will be blessed forever.

---

a 13:6 Tobit 13:6i-10b is not found in some manuscripts.

b 13:12 Some manuscripts read "everyone who loves you." Other manuscripts read "everyone who rebuilds you."

¹³So rejoice with the people who do what God approves of,
　　because they will be gathered together
　　　and will praise the Lord, who rules this world.
¹⁴Blessed are those who love you, Jerusalem,
　　and blessed are those who rejoice when you're at peace.
　Blessed are all those who feel sorry when you're punished
　　because they will rejoice with you
　　　and see all your happiness forever.

¹⁵"I praise the Lord, the mighty king,
¹⁶　　because Jerusalem will be rebuilt
　　　and his temple will be rebuilt for the city forever.
　I will be happy if the rest of my descendants are still alive
　　to see Jerusalem's glory and acknowledge the king of heaven.

　"Jerusalem's gates will be rebuilt with sapphires and emeralds,
　　and its walls will be rebuilt with precious stones.
　Jerusalem's towers will be rebuilt with gold,
　　and its fortifications with pure gold.
¹⁷Jerusalem's streets will be paved with rubies
　　and with stones from the country of Ophir.
¹⁸People will sing joyful songs from Jerusalem's gates,
　　and all those who live in Jerusalem's houses will sing,
　　　'Hallelujah! Praise the God of Israel!'
　All the people of Jerusalem will praise his holy name forever
　　and ever."

¹Then Tobit's psalm of praise came to an end.

Tobit's Death

14 ²Tobit died peacefully when he was 112 years old. He was given an honorable burial in Nineveh. He was 62 years old when he lost his eyesight. After he regained his sight, he lived a good life, gave to the poor, and continued to praise God and to acknowledge God's greatness.

³Before Tobit died, he called for his son Tobias and Tobias' seven sons.[a] He said, "Son, take your children ⁴ and go quickly to the country of Media because I believe what God said about the city of Nineveh through the prophet Nahum. Everything that Nahum said will happen to Assyria and Nineveh. Everything that was spoken by Israel's prophets, whom God had sent, will happen. Not one single thing that they said will fail to come true. Everything will take place at its appointed time. So you will be safer in Media than in Assyria or Babylon. I know and believe that everything God has said will certainly come true. Not one

---

[a] 14:3 Latin; Greek omits "and Tobias' seven sons."

single prediction that the prophets made will ever be wrong. All of our people who live in Israel will be scattered and taken from that good land as prisoners. The entire land of Israel will be deserted. Even the cities of Samaria and Jerusalem will be deserted. God's temple will be painful to look at for some time, because it will be burned down.

⁵ "But God will have mercy on his people again. God will bring them back to the land of Israel. They will rebuild the temple, but it won't be like the first one until the right time comes. Then, when the time is right, all the people will return from the places where they were prisoners. They will be in their glory when they rebuild Jerusalem, and God's temple will be rebuilt in Jerusalem as Israel's prophets predicted. ⁶Then every nation in the world will be converted and will worship God sincerely. All the nations will abandon their false gods, who used lies to lead them astray. ⁷Instead, they will praise the eternal God in a way that he approves of. At that time, all the Israelites who will be saved, who truly keep God foremost in their thoughts, will be gathered together. They will go to Jerusalem and live safely in the land of Abraham forever, and God will give them that land. Those who sincerely love God will be happy, but those who sin and do wicked things will disappear from the earth.ᵃ

⁹ "My children, listen to my instructions: Serve God sincerely, and do what pleases him. Tell your children to do what is right, to give to the poor, to keep God foremost in their thoughts, and to sincerely praise his name with all their might whenever they have the opportunity.

"Son, leave Nineveh. Don't stay here. ¹⁰On the day you bury your mother, get out of this city. Don't even stay here a single night. I have seen a lot of wickedness in this city and a lot of the dishonesty that goes on here, and people don't have any sense of shame. Remember what Nadab did to Ahikar, the man who brought him up. Didn't Nadab think he could kill Ahikar and get away with it? But Nadab ended up in a grave.ᵇ God repaid him directly for the dishonorable thing he had done. Ahikar lived to see the light of day, but Nadab went into eternal darkness. Because Ahikar gave to the poor, he escaped the deadly trap that Nadab had set for him. But Nadab fell into his own trap and destroyed himself.

¹¹ "My children, see what giving to the poor accomplishes. And look at what wrongdoing accomplishes. Wrongdoing brings death! But I'm having a hard time breathing now."

Then they laid Tobit on his bed. He died and was given an honorable burial.

ᵃ 14:7 Some manuscripts add verse 8: "Son, leave Nineveh because what the prophet Jonah said will certainly come true."

ᵇ 14:10 Or "Didn't Ahikar have to hide to save his life because Nadab tried to kill him?"

The Last Events in Tobias' Life

¹²When Tobias' mother died, he buried her next to his father. Then he and his wife left for Media and lived in the city of Ecbatana with Raguel, his father-in-law. ¹³He treated his wife's parents honorably in their old age and buried them in Ecbatana in Media. He inherited the property of both Raguel and Tobit, his father.

¹⁴Tobias died when he was 117 years old. He was a highly respected man. ¹⁵Before Tobias died, he heard about the destruction of Nineveh. Also, he saw King Ahikar's prisoners being led into Media. Tobias praised God for everything God had done to the people of Nineveh and Assyria. He was happy that Nineveh had been destroyed before he died. He praised the Lord God as long as he lived.

Judith

King Nebuchadnezzar Goes to War Against King Arphaxad

1 ¹When King Nebuchadnezzar, who ruled Assyria from the magnificent city of Nineveh, was in his twelfth year as king, Arphaxad ruled the Medes from the city of Ecbatana. ²Arphaxad had built a wall around Ecbatana. The wall was made from stone blocks that were 4½ feet wide and 9 feet long. The wall was 105 feet high and 75 feet wide. ³At the city gates he built towers that were 90 feet wide at the base and 150 feet high. ⁴He made the gates 105 feet high and 60 feet wide so that his powerful army could march out with the infantry in battle formation.

⁵At that time, King Nebuchadnezzar went to war against King Arphaxad in the Great Plain in the region of Ragau. ⁶All the people who lived in the mountains, all those who lived along the Euphrates, Tigris, and Hydaspes Rivers, and all those who lived on the plain ruled by Arioch, king of the Elymeans, joined forces with King Arphaxad to oppose King Nebuchadnezzar. Many nations joined forces with Cheleoud's descendants*a* to fight King Nebuchadnezzar.

⁷Then King Nebuchadnezzar of Assyria sent messengers ˻to order others to join forces with him against King Arphaxad˼. He sent messengers to all the people who lived in Persia and in the west: to Cilicia and Damascus, Lebanon and Antilebanon, to all the people who lived along the coast, ⁸and to the people who lived in Carmel and Gilead. He also sent messengers to northern Galilee, to the large plain named Esdraelon, ⁹to everyone who lived in the cities of Samaria, and to the people who lived west of the Jordan River as far as the cities of Jerusalem, Betane, Chelous, and Kadesh. The messengers were also sent as far as the River of Egypt, Tahpanhes, Rameses, and the whole region of Goshen. ¹⁰They went to all the people who lived in Egypt, even to those who lived beyond Tanis and Memphis as far as the border of Ethiopia.

¹¹But everyone who lived in those areas despised the orders of King Nebuchadnezzar of Assyria. They refused to join him in the war because

---

a 1:6 Greek meaning of "Cheleoud's descendants" uncertain.

they weren't afraid of him. They didn't think that he was anyone special. So they disgraced his messengers by sending them back empty-handed. ¹²Nebuchadnezzar became very angry with this entire region. So he swore an oath by his throne and kingdom. He swore that he would punish the entire region by killing all the people who lived in Cilicia, Damascus and Syria, Moab, Ammon, Judea, and Egypt, as far as the region of the two seas.

¹³In Nebuchadnezzar's seventeenth year as king, he led his army against King Arphaxad. He defeated King Arphaxad in battle and destroyed his cavalry and chariots—his entire army. ¹⁴Then Nebuchadnezzar took possession of the cities that Arphaxad had controlled. When he came to Ecbatana, he took control of its towers, looted its marketplaces, and disgraced that beautiful city. ¹⁵He captured Arphaxad in the mountains of Ragau and killed him that same day with a spear.

¹⁶Then Nebuchadnezzar and his entire army returned to Nineveh with all the loot. His army was very large and was made up of soldiers from many nations. In Nineveh, Nebuchadnezzar and his army rested and feasted for four months.

King Nebuchadnezzar Plans a War Against the West

2 ¹King Nebuchadnezzar of Assyria had promised to punish the entire western region. On the twenty-second day of the first month of Nebuchadnezzar's eighteenth year as king, the subject of this punishment came up in the palace. ²King Nebuchadnezzar called a meeting of all his advisers and top officials to present his secret plan to them. He personally told them how the people in that region had openly disobeyed him. ³So they decided to destroy everyone who had not obeyed the king's orders.

⁴When King Nebuchadnezzar of Assyria had finished presenting his plan, he called Holofernes. Holofernes was the highest-ranking general in Nebuchadnezzar's army and was second in rank to the king. Nebuchadnezzar told him, ⁵"This is what I, Nebuchadnezzar, the great king and the lord of the whole world, say: Leave here, and take with you strong, confident soldiers: 120,000 from the infantry and 12,000 from the cavalry. ⁶Attack all the people in the western region, because they have disobeyed my orders. ⁷Tell the people there to be ready to surrender unconditionally because I'm furious and I'm going to attack them. My army will cover their whole territory and will loot everything they own. ⁸I will fill the ravines with their wounded. All the streams and rivers will overflow with dead bodies. ⁹Then I will capture the people ⌐who are still alive⌐ and lead them away to the ends of the earth.

¹⁰"Holofernes, first invade their territory, and take possession of it for me. Make them surrender to you, and hold them for me until the time comes for me to punish them. ¹¹Throughout the entire region under your

command, slaughter those who refuse to obey you, and loot their property. [12]As I live and by the power of my kingdom, I will do everything I have promised. [13]Holofernes, don't make any mistakes in what I, your lord, have ordered you to do. Carry out my orders exactly as I have told you, and do it quickly."

[14]So Holofernes left Nebuchadnezzar and summoned all the commanders, generals, and officers of the Assyrian army. [15]He picked the best soldiers for his army as Nebuchadnezzar had ordered: 120,000 infantrymen and 12,000 archers, who rode horses. [16]He organized them as all great armies are organized for war. [17]He took along a large number of camels, donkeys, and mules to carry their supplies, and he took countless sheep, oxen, and goats for food. [18]He also had plenty of rations for every soldier and a very large amount of gold and silver from the royal palace.

Holofernes Leads His Army Against the West

[19]Then Holofernes and his entire army set out to go ahead of King Nebuchadnezzar and to cover the entire western region with their chariots, cavalry, and best infantrymen. [20]Many other people went along with the army. They looked like a swarm of locusts or like the dust on the earth. No one was able to count the people because there were so many.

[21]Three days after the army left Nineveh, it arrived in the plain of Bectileth. The army moved from Bectileth and camped at the mountains to the north of Cilicia. [22]From there Holofernes took his entire army—his infantry, cavalry, and chariots—and advanced to the mountain region. [23]He destroyed Put and Lud and looted all the possessions of the Rassisites and the Ishmaelites who lived on the edge of the desert, south of Cheleon.[a]

[24]Then Holofernes followed the Euphrates River, went through Mesopotamia, and leveled every fortified city along the Abron River until he came to the sea. [25]He took possession of the territory of Cilicia and massacred everyone who opposed him. Then he advanced to the southern territory of Japheth, which bordered Arabia. [26]He surrounded all the Midianites, set their tents on fire, and took the sheep from their pens. [27]He went down into the plain of Damascus during the wheat harvest. He set every field on fire, destroyed the flocks and herds, looted the cities, stripped the land, and killed all the young men.

[28]So the people who lived in the cities along the coast (in Sidon and Tyre, in Sur and Ocina, and all who lived in Jamnia) were overcome with fear and trembling because of Holofernes. The people who lived in the cities of Azotus and Ashkelon were also very afraid of him.

---

[a] 2:23 Greek meaning uncertain.

The West Surrenders to Nebuchadnezzar

3 ¹The people in the west sent messengers to Holofernes to ask for peace. They said, ²"We are the servants of the great king, Nebuchadnezzar. We bow on the ground in front of you. Treat us as you please. ³Our buildings, all our land, all our wheat fields, our flocks and herds, and all the sheep pens where we camp are at your service. Use them as you please. ⁴Our cities and all the people who live in them are also at your service. Come and visit them whenever you want."

Holofernes Continues To Destroy the West

⁵After the messengers went to Holofernes and asked him for peace, ⁶Holofernes went down to the coast with his army. He stationed troops in the fortified cities and took the best men from those cities to be soldiers in his army. ⁷The people along the coast and all the people in the surrounding territories welcomed Holofernes. They presented him with flowers and danced to the beat of drums. ⁸Yet, Holofernes completely destroyed all their worship sites*a* and cut down their poles dedicated to the goddess Asherah. He even destroyed all the gods in the land. He did this so that all the nations would worship only Nebuchadnezzar and so that all people, regardless of their languages and the tribes they belonged to, would pray to Nebuchadnezzar as god.

⁹Then Holofernes traveled through the plain of Esdraelon and passed near the city of Dothan. Dothan borders the huge mountain range in Judea. ¹⁰He camped between the cities of Geba and Scythopolis and stayed there for an entire month in order to collect all the supplies his army needed.

The Israelites Prepare for War

4 ¹The Israelites who lived in Judea heard that Holofernes, the highest-ranking general under King Nebuchadnezzar of Assyria, had looted and destroyed all the other nations' temples. ²So they were terrified of Holofernes and were worried about Jerusalem and the temple of the Lord their God. ³They had recently returned from exile. All the people of Judea had just reunited and rededicated the holy utensils, the altar, and the temple, which had been dishonored. ⁴So the Israelites sent messengers to every region—to Samaria, Kona, Beth Horon, Belmain, and Jericho, to Choba and Aesora, and to the valley of Salem. ⁵They quickly stationed troops on all the high hills, fortified the villages there, and stored up food in order to prepare for war. (They were able to store food because they had recently harvested their fields.)

---

a 3:8 Syriac; Greek "territories."

⁶Joakim, who was the chief priest in Jerusalem at the time, wrote to the people in the cities of Bethulia and Betomesthaim, which borders Esdraelon along the plain near Dothan. ⁷He told them to occupy the mountain passes because the enemy would use these passes to enter Judea. He also told the people that they would easily be able to stop the enemy from advancing through the passes since the passes were only wide enough for two men to enter at a time. ⁸So the Israelites followed the orders that they received from the chief priest Joakim and the council, which represented all the people of Israel and was in session in Jerusalem.

⁹With intense devotion the men of Israel prayed loudly to God and humbled themselves. ¹⁰They, their wives, their children, and their cattle wore sackcloth. Every foreign resident, hired worker, and slave also wore sackcloth. ¹¹Every man, woman, and child living in Jerusalem bowed in front of the temple. They covered their heads with ashes and spread out their sackcloth in the Lord's presence. ¹²They even covered the altar with sackcloth. With intense devotion all of them prayed loudly together to the God of Israel. They didn't want their children or wives to be captured and carried off like loot or the towns they had inherited to be destroyed. They also didn't want foreigners to dishonor and disgrace the holy place by making it an object of ridicule. ¹³The Lord heard their prayers and saw their distress.

The people fasted for many days throughout Judea. In Jerusalem they fasted in front of the holy place of the Lord Almighty. ¹⁴The chief priest Joakim and all the priests who served the Lord wore sackcloth. They sacrificed the daily burnt offerings, the offerings made to fulfill vows, and the freewill offerings from the people. ¹⁵They put ashes on their turbans and prayed as loudly as they could for the Lord to be kind to all the people of Israel.

Holofernes Summons All the Rulers

5 ¹Holofernes, the highest-ranking general in the Assyrian army, received a report that the Israelites had prepared for war by closing off the mountain passes, fortifying all the high hills, and setting traps in the plains. ²This made Holofernes very angry. He summoned all the rulers in Moab, the leaders in Ammon, and all the governors on the coast to his headquarters. ³He said to them, "Canaanites, give me a report. Who are these people living in the mountains? Which cities do they live in? How big is their army? What do they rely on for their power and strength? Does their king lead their army? ⁴Why are they the only people in the west to turn their backs on me and refuse to come out and meet me?"

Achior's Speech

⁵Then Achior, the governor of all the Ammonites, said to him, "Sir, please listen to me. I'll tell you the truth about the Israelites, these people who live in the mountains near your camp. I won't lie to you. ⁶These people are descendants of the Chaldeans. ⁷But because they didn't want to follow the gods of their ancestors, who lived in Chaldea, they moved to Mesopotamia. ⁸(They had abandoned the religion of their ancestors and had begun to worship the God of heaven, the God they had come to know. They were forced to leave because they had rejected the gods of Chaldea. So they went to Mesopotamia, where they lived for a long time.)

⁹"Later, their God told them to leave Mesopotamia and go to Canaan. They settled in Canaan, became very wealthy, and accumulated a lot of livestock. ¹⁰However, when a famine spread throughout Canaan, they went to Egypt and stayed there as long as they had food. While in Egypt, they became so numerous that they couldn't be counted. ¹¹So the king of Egypt became hostile toward them. He was shrewd in the way he took advantage of them by forcing them to make bricks. The Egyptians humiliated them by making them slaves. ¹²But the Israelites prayed to their God, and their God struck the entire land of Egypt with plagues for which there were no cures. So the Egyptians forced them out of Egypt. ¹³Then God dried up the Red Sea in front of the Israelites ¹⁴and brought them all the way to Sinai and Kadesh Barnea.

"The Israelites forced out all the people who lived in the desert ¹⁵and began to live in Amorite territory. They were so strong that they destroyed all the people who lived in the city of Heshbon. They crossed the Jordan River, took possession of all the mountains, ¹⁶and forced out the Canaanites, Perizzites, Jebusites, Shechemites, and all the Girgashites, all of whom had lived in Canaan for a long time.

¹⁷"As long as they didn't sin in the sight of their God, they prospered because their God, who hates any kind of wickedness, was with them. ¹⁸But whenever they rebelled against the way God had arranged for them to live, they were defeated in many wars. Eventually, they were led away as prisoners to a foreign country, the temple of their God was leveled, and their enemies took control of their cities. ¹⁹But now that they have returned to their God, they have come back from the places where they were scattered. They have again taken possession of Jerusalem, where they have their holy place, and have settled in the mountains, where no one was living.

²⁰"Sir, maybe these people are sinning against their God without knowing it. If we can find out that they are sinning, then we can attack them and force them to fight. ²¹But, sir, if these people aren't guilty of any sin, then I'd advise you not to attack them. I'm afraid that their Lord and

God might defend them and that we will be disgraced in front of the whole world."

Reaction to Achior's Speech

²²When Achior had finished speaking, all the people standing around the headquarters began to complain. Holofernes' top officials and all those from the coast and from Moab demanded that Achior be put to death. ²³They said, "We're not afraid of the Israelites! They don't have a strong army. Their army isn't strong enough to put up a fight. ²⁴General Holofernes, let's attack them. Your powerful army will wipe them out."

Holofernes' Speech

6 ¹When the crowd standing around the headquarters became quiet, Holofernes, the highest-ranking general in the Assyrian army, spoke to Achior*ᵃ* in front of all the rulers from Moab and all the foreigners. He said, ²"Achior, who do you and your mercenaries from Ephraim think you are? You've prophesied among us today. You've told us not to fight against the people of Israel because their God will defend them. Is there any other god besides Nebuchadnezzar? Nebuchadnezzar will send his forces and wipe the people of Israel off the face of the earth. Their God can't save them. ³But we are King Nebuchadnezzar's servants. We will destroy the people of Israel as if they were only one man. They won't be able to withstand our powerful cavalry. ⁴Our cavalry alone can beat them. The mountains will be drenched with their blood. The fields will be filled with their dead bodies. Nothing will be left of them after our attack. We will totally destroy them. This is what King Nebuchadnezzar, the lord of the whole world, predicts. When Nebuchadnezzar predicts something, his prediction comes true.

⁵"As for you, Achior, you Ammonite mercenary, you've spoken to me for the last time. You won't see me again until I punish these people who came out of Egypt. ⁶When the battle is over, my army and my advisers will kill you with their swords. You will die with Israel's wounded.

⁷"My servants are now going to take you into the mountains and leave you in a city located in one of the passes. ⁸You will die there along with the Israelites. ⁹If you really believe that their cities won't be captured, then don't look so depressed. I have spoken, and not a word of what I've said will fail to come true."

Achior Arrives at the City of Bethulia

¹⁰Then Holofernes ordered the servants who were at the headquarters to arrest Achior, take him to the city of Bethulia, and hand him over to

---

ᵃ 6:1 Some Greek manuscripts add "and to all the people from Moab."

the Israelites. ¹¹So his servants arrested Achior and led him out of the camp into the plain. From the plain they took Achior into the mountains as far as the spring that was below the city of Bethulia.

¹²When the men of Bethulia saw them coming, they grabbed their weapons and ran out of the city to the top of the mountain. All the men used their slings to hurl stones at Holofernes' servants and kept the servants from coming up the pass. ¹³So Holofernes' servants took cover at the foot of the mountain. Then they tied up Achior, left him there, and returned to the general.

¹⁴Later, some Israelites came down from Bethulia and found Achior. They untied him, brought him back to the city, and made him stand in front of the city leaders. ¹⁵At that time the leaders were Uzziah (who was the son of Micah and was from the tribe of Simeon), Chabris (who was the son of Gothoniel), and Charmis (who was the son of Melchiel). ¹⁶They summoned all the older leaders of the city. All the women and young people also ran to the assembly. The leaders made Achior stand in the middle of all the people. Then Uzziah questioned him about what had happened. ¹⁷Achior told them what had happened at Holofernes' headquarters. He told them everything that he had said in the presence of the Assyrian leaders and everything that Holofernes had bragged he would do to the people of Israel.

¹⁸Then the people bowed to worship God and prayed loudly, ¹⁹"Lord God of heaven, notice the arrogance of the Assyrians. Show mercy to our people because the Assyrians are humiliating them. Be kind to your holy people today."

²⁰Then the people comforted Achior and praised him highly. ²¹When the assembly was over, Uzziah took Achior home with him and served dinner to the older leaders. All night long they prayed to the God of Israel for help.

Holofernes Goes to War Against Bethulia

7 ¹The next day, Holofernes gave an order to his entire army and to all the soldiers who had become his allies. He ordered them to march to the city of Bethulia, to seize the passes that led into the mountains, and to go to war against the Israelites. ²So on that day, all the soldiers marched to Bethulia. The Assyrian army had 170,000 soldiers in the infantry and 12,000 in the cavalry. This didn't include the soldiers who were in charge of supplies. The entire army was extremely large. ³The army set up camp by the spring in the valley near Bethulia. The camp was so wide that it covered the area from Dothan to Balbaim, and it was so long that it extended from Bethulia to Cyamon, which faces Esdraelon.

⁴When the Israelites saw the size of the Assyrian army, they were worried. They said to each other, "This army is going to eat everything

in the entire region. The high mountains, the ravines, and the hills don't have enough food to feed all those soldiers." ⁵Even though all the people of Bethulia were worried, they grabbed their weapons, started signal fires on the watchtowers, and remained on guard all that night.

⁶The next day, Holofernes led out his entire cavalry so that the people of Bethulia could see it. ⁷He inspected the passes that led to their city and the spring that supplied their water. He took possession of the spring, stationed soldiers there to guard it, and returned to his army.

⁸Then all the rulers of Edom,ᵃ all the governors of the Moabites, and the commanders from the coast went to Holofernes and said, ⁹"You're our general. Please listen to us so that your army won't suffer any casualties. ¹⁰These Israelite people don't rely on their weapons to protect them. Instead, they rely on the height of the mountains where they live, because the climb to the top of their mountains is very difficult. ¹¹So, General, don't use regular battle formations to fight them. In this way, not one soldier in your army will be killed. ¹²Stay in your camp, and keep every soldier in your army there. Let some of us take possession of the spring that is at the bottom of the mountain, ¹³because that's where all the people who live in Bethulia get their water. Then, when they're about to die of thirst, they'll surrender. We'll go up the neighboring mountaintops with our troops and camp there to prevent anyone from getting out of the city. ¹⁴Men, women, and children will starve to death. Before the war ever begins, they will be lying all over the streets. ¹⁵This is how you can pay them back for rebelling against you and for refusing to come out and meet you peacefully."

¹⁶What they said pleased Holofernes and all his advisers. So Holofernes gave orders to do as they suggested. ¹⁷A company of Ammonite soldiers, together with 5,000 Assyrians, moved out and camped in the valley. They took possession of the spring where the Israelites got their water. ¹⁸Soldiers from Edom and Ammon went into the mountains and camped facing Dothan. They sent some of their troops to the southeast toward the city of Egrebel. Egrebel is near Chusi, which is beside the Mochmur River. The rest of the Assyrian army camped on the plain and covered all of it. The tents and supplies also covered a large area since there were so many of them.

¹⁹The Israelites prayed loudly to the Lord their God because they lost their courage when they saw that all their enemies had surrounded them and that there was no way to escape. ²⁰The entire Assyrian army—infantry, chariots, and cavalry—surrounded them for 34 days. By that time everyone who lived in Bethulia had run out of water. ²¹The cisterns were going dry. Because the people had to ration their water, they couldn't quench their

---

ᵃ 7:8 Or "Esau." Esau was the son of Isaac and the ancestor of the people of Edom.

thirst. ²²Their children had no energy. Women and young people were fainting from thirst and were collapsing in the entrances to the city and in the city streets because they had become so weak.

²³ Then everyone, including the young people, the women, and the children, gathered around Uzziah and the city leaders. They shouted at the older leaders, ²⁴"You made a big mistake when you didn't make peace with the Assyrians. May God decide whether you were right or wrong. ²⁵We don't have anyone to help us now. God has handed us over to them. They will find us lying on the ground and dying of thirst. ²⁶Get the Assyrians right away! Surrender to Holofernes and his entire army, and let them loot the city. ²⁷We would be better off as captives. They will make us slaves, but at least we will be alive, and we won't have to see our infants die and our wives and children breathe their last breath. ²⁸God is punishing us for our sins and for the sins of our ancestors. Heaven, earth, and our God, the Lord of our ancestors, are our witnesses. We beg you: Please do today what we have asked."

²⁹Everyone in the assembly began to cry together and pray loudly to the Lord God. ³⁰Then Uzziah said to them, "Cheer up, brothers and sisters! Let's hold out for five more days. By then the Lord our God will show us his mercy. He won't abandon us forever. ³¹But if five days go by and we don't get any help, I'll do as you say."

³²Then Uzziah made the men take their positions on the walls and towers of their city, and he sent the women and children home. The people in the city felt depressed.

A Description of Judith

8 ¹At that time, Judith heard what was happening at the assembly. Judith was the daughter of Merari. Merari was the son of Ox, the grandson of Joseph, the great-grandson of Oziel, and a descendant of Elkiah, Ananias, Gideon, Raphain, Ahitub, Elijah, Hilkiah, Eliab, Nathanael, Salamiel, Sarasadai, and Israel. ²Judith had been married to Manasseh, who belonged to her tribe and family. He died during the barley harvest. ³While Manasseh was supervising workers who were tying up bundles of barley in the field, he suffered sunstroke and was forced to stay in bed. Later, he died in his hometown, Bethulia, and was buried in the family tomb in the field between Dothan and Balamon.

⁴Judith had been a widow for three years and four months. ⁵She built a shelter for herself on the roof of her house. She wore sackcloth around her waist and always dressed as a widow. ⁶She fasted every day that she had been a widow except for Fridays, the weekly days of worship, the New Moon Festivals, the day before the New Moon Festivals, and the annual festivals of the people of Israel.

[7]She was very attractive and had a beautiful figure. She managed all the money, slaves, livestock, and fields that her husband Manasseh had left her. [8]No one ever said anything bad about her, because she was a God-fearing woman.

Judith Meets With the Leaders of Bethulia

[9]Judith heard about the horrible things that the people had said to their leader Uzziah because they were discouraged by the lack of water. She also heard about everything that Uzziah had said to the people, especially how he had promised under oath to surrender to the Assyrians after five days. [10]So she sent a female slave, whom she had put in charge of all her possessions, to invite Uzziah, Chabris, and Charmis (the older leaders of the city) to her home.

[11]When the leaders arrived, Judith said to them, "Leaders of the people of Bethulia, please listen to me. What you said in front of the people today wasn't right. You made a promise to God. You promised that you would surrender to our enemies if the Lord didn't help us within five days. [12]Who do you think you are? You are testing God and taking the place of God in human affairs. [13]Today you're putting the Lord Almighty on trial. Can't you understand that? [14]You can't discover how deep human feelings go or even grasp how the human mind works. So how will you ever figure out God, who made everything? How will you ever understand the way his mind works or comprehend the way he thinks?

"Friends, don't ever make the Lord our God angry. [15]What if he doesn't want to help us within five days? He has the right to protect us whenever he pleases or to destroy us in front of our enemies. [16]Stop dictating to the Lord our God what he should do, as if he were forced to do it. You can't force God to make promises like you can humans or talk him out of something like you can other people. [17]Instead, while we wait for him to save us, pray to him so that he will help us. He will listen to us if we pray for what pleases him.

[18]"At no point in our recent past or at the present time have we had any tribe, family, town, or city that worships gods made by humans as our ancestors did. [19]That's why our ancestors were overwhelmed with disasters and were handed over to their enemies, who killed them in battle and looted their properties. [20]But we don't acknowledge any god except the Lord. So we can be sure that he won't ignore us or anyone from our nation. [21]If we are captured, all Judea will be captured. Our holy place will be looted, and the Lord will make us pay with our lives for allowing it to be dishonored. [22]Wherever we are scattered among the nations, he will hold us responsible for the slaughter of our people and for the capture and destruction of the land we've inherited. We will be despised and disgraced by those who own us. [23]Our slavery won't have a

happy ending. Instead, the Lord our God will make our slavery end in disgrace. ²⁴"Friends, today we must set an example for our people because their lives depend on us. Also, what happens to the holy place, especially the temple and the altar, depends on us. ²⁵Furthermore, we must thank the Lord our God because he is testing us as he tested our ancestors. ²⁶Remember everything he did with Abraham. Remember how he tested Isaac, and remember what happened to Jacob while he was working as a shepherd for his uncle Laban in Syrian Mesopotamia. ²⁷The Lord isn't putting us through a severe trial as he did our ancestors. He isn't punishing us. Instead, the Lord disciplines those who are close to him in order to warn them."

²⁸Then Uzziah said to her, "Everything you've said is true. No one can possibly disagree with you. ²⁹Today is not the first time you have shown your wisdom. Ever since you were young, people have recognized that you are good at understanding things. ³⁰However, the people were so thirsty that they forced us to make a promise to them and to take an oath that we cannot break. ³¹Since you're a very religious woman, pray for us today. Ask the Lord to send rain to fill our cisterns. Then we won't faint from thirst any longer."

³²Then Judith said to them, "Listen to me. I'm going to do something that our people will never forget. ³³Be at the city gate tonight so that I can leave with my female slave. Before the day arrives, the day on which you have promised to surrender to our enemies, the Lord will use me to rescue Israel. ³⁴But don't try to find out what I'm doing. I won't tell you until I've finished what I'm going to do."

³⁵Uzziah and the leaders said to her, "May the Lord God go with you and guide you so that you can punish our enemies." ³⁶The men left Judith's rooftop shelter and went back to their positions on the city walls and towers.

Judith's Prayer

9 ¹When the evening incense was being offered at God's temple in Jerusalem, Judith bowed, put ashes on her head, and uncovered the sackcloth she was wearing ˻around her waist˼.

Then she prayed loudly to the Lord, ²"Lord God of my ancestor Simeon, you gave Simeon a sword with which to punish the foreigners who had raped a virgin and dishonored her. She was ashamed and disgraced because they humiliated her by having sexual intercourse with her. You had said that something like this must never happen. Yet, they did it anyway. ³So you allowed their leaders to be slaughtered. You allowed the bed on which they had committed this terrible sin to become soaked with their blood. You killed servants and princes alike. ⁴You allowed their wives to become captives and their daughters to become slaves. You let their possessions be divided among the people you loved, the people who were devoted to you. Your people couldn't stand having a mixed bloodline, so they prayed to you for help. God, my God, I am a widow. Listen to me too.

⁵ "You made those things happen as well as what happened before and after. You know what's happening now and what will happen in the future. Everything you have planned to do has happened. ⁶The things you have planned offer themselves to you and say, 'Here we are!' Everything you've determined in advance is ready.

⁷ "Look how the Assyrians have grown in power. They take pride in their horses and riders. They brag about the strength of their infantry and trust their shields, spears, bows, and slings. They don't realize that you are the Lord who defeats armies. The Lord is your name. ⁸Use your power to break their strength. In your anger overthrow their government because they plan to dishonor your holy place. They plan to disgrace the tent where your glorious name lives and break off the horns of your altar with their weapons. ⁹Look at how arrogant they are! Unleash your anger on them. Give me, a widow, the strength to carry out my plan. ¹⁰By the deceitful things I say, kill the slaves with their leaders and the leaders with their servants. Give me, a woman, the power to destroy their pride.

¹¹ "Your strength doesn't depend on a large army. Your might doesn't depend on people in power. Instead, you are the God of humble people. You help oppressed people and support weak people. You protect those who are discouraged and save those who have no hope. ¹²Please, God of my father, God of Israel's inheritance, Lord of heaven and earth, Creator of the oceans, King of all creation, please listen to my prayer. ¹³Let what I say deceive those who have planned to do cruel things to us. They plan to do away with your promise,ᵃ your holy temple (which you have given to your children), and Mount Zion. Let my words injure and wound my enemies. ¹⁴Make every tribe in your entire nation know and understand that you are God, the all-powerful and mighty God, and that you are the only God who defends the people of Israel."

Judith Goes to the Assyrian Camp

10 ¹When Judith had finished praying loudly to the God of Israel, ²she stood up from where she had been kneeling. She called her female slave and went down into the house where she spent her time on the weekly days of worship and on festival days. ³She took off the sackcloth and the widow's clothes she was wearing and bathed. Then she put on expensive perfume, brushed her hair, tied a ribbon in it, and put on

ᵃ 9:13 Or "They plan to destroy your covenant."

the clothes that she used to wear on joyful occasions while her husband Manasseh was still alive. ⁴She put on her sandals, anklets, bracelets, rings, earrings, and all her other jewelry. Judith spent a lot of time putting on her make-up so that she would be attractive to all the men who would see her. ⁵She had her slave carry a bottle of wine, a jar of oil, and a bag filled with roasted grain, dried fig cakes, and bread. The slave also carried dishes that Judith had wrapped up.

⁶Then the two women went to the city gate of Bethulia. There they met Uzziah and two of the city's older leaders, Chabris and Charmis. ⁷When these men saw Judith wearing make-up and dressy clothes, they were stunned by her beauty. They said to her, ⁸"May the God of our ancestors be kind to you and make your plans succeed. Then Jerusalem will be honored and the people of Israel will brag." When Judith heard what the men said, she bowed to God.

⁹Judith said, "Order someone to open the city gate so that I can do what you said." So they ordered some young men to open the gate for her as she requested. ¹⁰When the gate was opened, Judith and her slave left the city. The men of the city watched her go down the mountain and through the valley until they couldn't see her anymore.

¹¹The two women were going straight through the valley when an Assyrian patrol met them. ¹²The soldiers in the patrol arrested Judith and questioned her, "What is your nationality? Where are you coming from, and where are you going?"

Judith answered, "I'm a Hebrew. I'm running away from my people because you're going to destroy them. ¹³I'm on my way to see Holofernes, the general of your army, to give him some reliable information. I'll show him a way that he can take possession of the entire mountain region without a single man dying."

¹⁴As the soldiers listened to what she said, they couldn't take their eyes off of her. When they saw how beautiful she was, they said to her, ¹⁵"You've saved your life by hurrying to see our general. Go at once to his tent. Some of us will escort you there and introduce you to him. ¹⁶When you stand in his presence, don't be afraid. Instead, tell him what you've just told us, and he'll treat you well." ¹⁷Then they chose 100 men to go with Judith and her slave. The men took the two women to Holofernes' tent.

¹⁸The entire camp became excited as the news of Judith's arrival spread from tent to tent. While some of the men who escorted Judith were telling Holofernes about her, soldiers gathered around her as she stood outside his tent. ¹⁹The soldiers were stunned by her beauty and wondered about the people of Israel because of her. They said to each other, "How can we hate people who have women like this? We better not leave any of their men alive. If we let any of them get away, they could outsmart the whole world."

Judith Meets Holofernes

20 Then Holofernes' bodyguards and all his advisers came out and led Judith into Holofernes' tent. 21 Holofernes was resting on his bed under a purple mosquito net that had gold, emeralds, and other precious stones woven into it. 22 When they told him about Judith, he went to the front part of the tent. Silver lamps were carried in front of him. 23 When Holofernes and his advisers saw Judith, all of them were stunned by her beauty. Judith bowed on the ground in front of Holofernes but his servants made her get up.

11 1 Then Holofernes said to Judith, "Cheer up! Don't be afraid, because I've never hurt anyone who chose to serve Nebuchadnezzar, king of the whole world. 2 If your people who live in the mountains hadn't despised me, I wouldn't have declared war on them. Certainly, they have brought this on themselves. 3 So tell me, why have you run away from your people and come over to our side? You're safe now. Cheer up! You'll live through the night and for a long time to come. 4 No one will hurt you. Instead, people will treat you well, as they do the other servants of King Nebuchadnezzar."

5 Judith answered him, "Let me speak to you. You'll be happy to hear what I have to say. I won't give you any false information tonight. 6 If you follow my advice, God will accomplish something through you, and you won't fail to carry out God's plan. 7 I swear by the life and power of Nebuchadnezzar, who is king of the whole world and who sent you to enforce his policies on everyone. I swear that, because of you, not only people but also wild animals, cattle, and birds will serve him. Nebuchadnezzar and his administration will rule them. 8 We have heard about your wisdom and about the wonderful things you have done. The whole world knows that you are the bravest, most experienced, and most brilliant general in the entire kingdom.

9 "We heard what Achior said to your council, because the people of Bethulia spared him. Achior told the people of Bethulia everything he said to you. 10 General Holofernes, don't ignore what Achior said. Keep it in mind because it's true. No one can punish my people or defeat them in war unless they sin against their God.

11 "But now they're about to be caught in a sin. As soon as they disobey God's law, they will make him angry. So you're not going to fail or be unsuccessful, because they are going to die. 12 Since they have run out of food and water is scarce, they have planned to kill their livestock and eat everything that God has forbidden in his laws. 13 They have decided to eat the first grain harvested and to use the wine and oil that have been set apart as holy. These things have been dedicated to the priests who serve God in Jerusalem. Even touching these holy things is not allowed. 14 The

people in Jerusalem have already been eating these things. The people of Bethulia have sent messengers to Jerusalem because they want to get permission from the council in Jerusalem to do the same thing. [15]On the day they get permission and eat what they want, God will allow you to destroy them.

[16]"So when I found out about all this, I ran away from them. God has sent me to do some important things with you that will shock the whole world whenever people hear about them. [17]I'm a God-fearing woman, and I worship the God of heaven day and night. So, General, I'll stay here with you. But I must go into the valley every night and pray to God. He will tell me when my people have sinned. [18]Then I'll report to you so that you can attack them with your entire army. None of them will be able to stand up against your attack. [19]Then I'll lead you through Judea all the way to Jerusalem. I'll place your throne in the center of the city, and you will lead the people, who are like sheep without a shepherd. Dogs won't even growl at you. God told me these things so that I would know about them in advance, and he sent me to report them to you."

[20]Holofernes and all his advisers liked what Judith said. They were stunned by her wisdom and said, [21]"No other woman in the whole world looks so beautiful or speaks so intelligently."

[22]Then Holofernes said to her, "God has done well to send you to our army so that we will have the power to win the battle and destroy those who despise King Nebuchadnezzar. [23]You are both beautiful and eloquent. So if you do as you've said, your God will be my God. Furthermore, you will live in the palace of King Nebuchadnezzar and be famous throughout the world."

Judith's Conduct in the Assyrian Camp

12 [1]Then Holofernes commanded his servants to bring Judith into his dining area and ordered them to serve her some of his own food and wine. [2]But Judith said, "I'm afraid I would be committing a sin if I ate any of your food. I'm sure that the food I brought with me will be enough for me to eat."

[3]Holofernes asked, "But if your food runs out, where can we get you more? None of your people are here with us."

[4]Judith replied, "General, I swear that my food won't run out before the Lord uses me to do what he has planned."

[5]Then Holofernes' advisers took Judith to her tent, where she slept until midnight. Just before dawn, she got up [6]and sent this message to Holofernes: "General, allow me to go out of the camp to pray." [7]So Holofernes ordered his bodyguards not to stop her. Judith stayed in the camp for three days. Each night she would go into the valley of Bethulia and bathe at the spring near the place where Holofernes had stationed

soldiers. [8]When she had finished bathing, she would pray to the Lord God of Israel to guide her so that his people could be proud of themselves again. [9]After she had purified herself, she would return to the camp and stay in her tent until she ate her evening meal.

Holofernes Has a Party

[10]On the fourth day that Judith was in the camp, Holofernes had a party. The party was for his servants only. He didn't invite any of his officers to attend. [11]Holofernes said to Bagoas, the eunuch in charge of his personal affairs, "Go to the Hebrew woman's tent. Since you take care of her, persuade her to come and have something to eat and drink with us. [12]It will really look bad if I let an attractive woman like this go without sleeping with her. If I can't get her into bed with me, she'll make fun of me."

[13]So Bagoas left Holofernes, went to Judith, and said, "Since you are such a beautiful woman, come quickly to the general's tent. He wants to honor you. He wants you to drink some wine with us, to enjoy yourself, and to become like the Assyrian women who serve Nebuchadnezzar in his palace."

[14]Judith replied, "How can I refuse the general's invitation? I'll do whatever he wants at once. Now I'll have something to brag about until the day I die."

[15]So Judith put on a gorgeous dress and all her jewelry. Her slave went ahead of her to spread lambskins on the ground in front of Holofernes. (Earlier, Bagoas had given Judith lambskins to sit on when she ate.)

[16]Then Judith went into Holofernes' tent and sat down. When Holofernes saw her, he became aroused. He had an uncontrollable desire to have sex with her and had been looking for an opportunity to seduce her from the first day he had seen her. [17]So Holofernes said to Judith, "Have a drink, and have some fun with us!"

[18]Judith replied, "I'll have a drink, General, because today has turned out to be the best day of my life." [19]Then, in front of Holofernes, she ate and drank what her slave had prepared for her. [20]Holofernes was so captivated by her that he drank a lot of wine, more than he had ever drunk on any one day in his entire life.

13 [1]When evening came, Holofernes' servants quickly left. Bagoas closed the tent from the outside to keep Holofernes' servants from coming in. The servants went to bed because the party had lasted a long time and everyone was very tired. [2]So Judith was left alone in the tent with Holofernes, who had passed out on his bed because he was so drunk.

[3]Judith had told her slave to stand outside the bedroom and wait for her to come out. Judith told her that she would be going out to pray as she had done on the other nights. She had told Bagoas the same thing.

Judith Cuts Off Holofernes' Head

[4] So everyone had left. No one else was in the bedroom. Then Judith stood beside Holofernes' bed and offered this silent prayer: "Lord, you are the all-powerful God. Protect me in what I'm going to do for the honor of Jerusalem. [5] Now is the time to help your people and to carry out my plan to destroy the enemies who have attacked us."

[6] Judith went to the bedpost near Holofernes' head and took down his sword. [7] She grabbed the hair on his head and prayed, "Give me strength now, Lord God of Israel!" [8] Then she struck his neck twice with all her might and cut off his head. [9] She rolled his body off the bed and pulled down the mosquito net from the bedposts. After this, she came out of the bedroom and gave Holofernes' head to her slave, [10] who put it in the food bag.

Judith Returns to Bethulia

Then the two women left together to pray as they always did. They went through the camp, around the valley, and up the mountain to the gate of Bethulia. [11] From a distance Judith called out to the guards at the gate, "Open the gate! Open the gate! God, our God, is still with us. He has shown his strength in Israel and his power against our enemies today."

[12] When the people in the city heard Judith's voice, they hurried to the city gate and summoned their leaders. [13] All the people, from the least important to the most important, came running because they couldn't believe that Judith had come back. They opened the gate and welcomed the two women. Then they started a fire so that they could see, and they gathered around the women. [14] Judith shouted, "Praise God! Praise him! Praise God! He still shows his mercy to the people of Israel. He has used me to destroy our enemies tonight."

[15] Then Judith pulled Holofernes' head out of the bag and showed it to them. She said, "Look! Here's the head of Holofernes, the general of the Assyrian army! And here's the mosquito net under which he lay drunk! The Lord has used a woman to kill him. [16] I swear by the Lord, who lives and has protected me, that my good looks seduced Holofernes and led to his destruction. I swear that Holofernes didn't commit any sin that dishonored or shamed me."

[17] All the people were amazed. They bowed to worship God and said together, "We praise you, our God, because today you have treated your people's enemies with contempt."

[18] Then Uzziah said to Judith, "My dear friend, the Most High God has blessed you more than any other woman on earth. Praise the Lord God, who created heaven and earth! He has guided you so that you could cut off the head of our enemies' leader. [19] People will never forget to praise

you when they remember God's power.*ª ²⁰May God honor you and bless you forever because you risked your life when our people were being humiliated. You did the right thing in God's sight by taking revenge on our enemies."

Everyone who was there said, "Amen! Amen!"

Judith's Advice

14 ¹Then Judith said to the people, "Friends, listen to me! Take Holofernes' head, and hang it on the city wall. ²At daybreak, when the sun comes up, every able-bodied man should grab his weapons. Pick an officer for the men, and go out of the city. Pretend you're going down to the plain to attack the Assyrian outpost. But don't actually go down. ³The Assyrian soldiers will grab their weapons and hurry into the camp to alert their officers. The officers will rush into Holofernes' tent, but they won't find him. Then they will panic, and all the Assyrian soldiers will run for their lives. ⁴You and everyone who lives in Israel should chase them and kill them as they retreat. ⁵But before you do all this, bring Achior the Ammonite to me. I want Achior to identify the man who insulted both him and the people of Israel and who sent him here to die."

Achior Is Converted

⁶So some people brought Achior from Uzziah's house. When Achior arrived and saw a man in the people's assembly holding Holofernes' head, he fainted and fell flat on his face. ⁷When the people picked Achior up, he fell at Judith's feet out of respect for her and said, "People in every home in Judah will praise you, but people in other nations will become terrified when they hear your name. ⁸Tell me everything you've done during the last few days."

With people all around her, Judith told Achior everything she had done from the time she left Bethulia until that very moment. ⁹When she finished, the people shouted and filled the city with cheering. ¹⁰Achior saw everything that the God of Israel had done, and he became a firm believer in God. So he was circumcised and became a member of the people of Israel. He's still a member today.

Bagoas Finds Holofernes' Headless Body

¹¹At dawn the people hung Holofernes' head on the wall. Then all the men grabbed their weapons and went out in groups to the mountain passes. ¹²When the Assyrian soldiers saw them, they sent a message to their officers. Their officers went to inform the generals, captains, and

---

ª 13:19 Some manuscripts read "People will never forget your confidence in God when they remember God's power."

all the other leaders. ¹³The officers went to Holofernes' tent and said to
Bagoas, the man in charge of Holofernes' personal affairs, "Wake up the
general! The Hebrew slaves have become bold enough to come down to
attack us, even though they can't win."

¹⁴Bagoas thought that Holofernes was sleeping with Judith. So he
shook the curtains at the entrance to Holofernes' tent. ¹⁵But when no one
answered, Bagoas opened the curtains, went into Holofernes' bedroom,
and found Holofernes' headless body lying over a footstool. ¹⁶Bagoas
screamed. He cried, groaned, and yelled as he tore his clothes in grief.
¹⁷Then he went to the tent where Judith had been staying. When he didn't
find her there, he rushed out to the soldiers and shouted, ¹⁸"The slaves
have tricked us! A Hebrew woman has brought disgrace on King Nebuchadnezzar's entire kingdom. Look! Holofernes is lying on the ground
with his head cut off!"

¹⁹When the leaders of the Assyrian army heard this, they tore their
clothes in grief. They were terrified, and their shouting and yelling echoed
throughout the camp.

The Israelites Chase the Assyrian Army

15 ¹When the soldiers in the tents heard about what had happened
to Holofernes, they were shocked. ²Overcome with fear and trembling, they scattered in every direction. They used all the roads through
the mountains and the plain in their attempt to escape. No one waited for
anyone else. ³The soldiers who had camped in the hills around Bethulia
also ran away. Then the Israelite soldiers ran after them.

⁴Uzziah sent messengers to the cities of Betomesthaim, Choba, and
Kola and to every region in Israel to tell the people what had happened.
He wanted everyone to chase the Assyrians and destroy them. ⁵When the
Israelites heard about this, they all joined together and attacked the Assyrians. They continued to kill the Assyrians all the way to Choba. The
men from Jerusalem and the surrounding mountains also joined the fight
because they had been told what had happened in the Assyrian camp.
The men in Gilead and Galilee continued to slaughter the Assyrians all
the way to the borders of Damascus.

⁶Meanwhile, the rest of the people of Bethulia went to the Assyrian
camp and made themselves very rich by looting it. ⁷When the Israelite
soldiers returned from the slaughter, they took what was left. Even the
people from the cities and villages in the mountains and on the plain got
a lot of the loot because there was so much of it.

The Victory Celebration in Bethulia

⁸Then the chief priest Joakim and the council, which represented the
Israelites who lived in Jerusalem, went to Bethulia to see the good things

that the Lord had done for Israel. They also came to see Judith and to wish her well. [9]When they met Judith, all of them praised her and said, "You've brought honor to Jerusalem! You've given Israel something to brag about, and our nation is very proud of you. [10]You've done all this by yourself. You've done good things for Israel, and God is pleased with what you've done. May you be praised in the presence of the Almighty Lord forever!"

And all the people said, "Amen!"

[11]All the people looted the Assyrian camp for 30 days. They gave Judith Holofernes' tent, all his silver dinnerware, beds, bowls, and furniture. Judith loaded some of these things on her mule. Then she hitched up her wagons and piled everything else on them.

[12]All the women of Israel gathered to see her. They praised her, and some of them performed a dance to honor her. Judith took branches and gave them to the women who were with her. [13]She and those who were with her were wearing wreaths made of olive leaves on their heads. She went in front of all the people and led all the women in a dance. All the men of Israel followed fully armed. They, too, wore wreaths on their heads and sang hymns of praise.

Judith's Song of Praise

[14]Judith gave thanks to God in front of all the people of Israel, and all the people loudly sang this song of praise with her.

16 [1]Judith sang:

> Start singing to my God.
> Sing to my Lord.
>> Use tambourines and cymbals.
>>> Please him with a psalm of praise.
>>> Honor him, and pray in his name.
> [2]The Lord is a God who defeats armies.
>> He rescued me from those who were pursuing me.
>> He brought me back into his camp
>>> and allowed me to stand in front of his people.
> [3]The Assyrians came down from the northern mountains.
>> Their soldiers couldn't be counted.
>>> They were so numerous that they blocked up the rivers.
>>> Their cavalry covered the hills.
> [4]They said they would burn up my territory,
>> kill my young men in battle,
>>> smash my nursing infants on the ground,
>>>> capture my children,
>>>> and carry off my young women.

⁵The Lord Almighty used a woman to trick them.
⁶   Young men didn't kill the Assyrians' mighty general.
       Large monsters didn't strike him down.
          Huge giants didn't attack him.
But Judith, Merari's daughter, used her beauty
    to cut off his head.
⁷She brought honor to the suffering people of Israel
    by taking off her widow's clothes
       and by putting on perfume.
⁸She deceived the general
    by tying a ribbon in her hair
       and by wearing expensive clothes.
⁹Her sandals caught his eye.
Her beauty captivated him.
    But a sword cut through his neck!
¹⁰The Persians trembled at her daring.
The Medes were terrified by her boldness.

¹¹At one time, my humble people cried.
My weak people were afraid; they were terrified.
    They shouted to God,
       and the Assyrians retreated.
¹²The descendants of slaves stabbed them
    and wounded them like runaway slaves.
The Lord's army destroyed them.

¹³I will sing a new hymn of praise to my God.
Lord, you are great and glorious.
    Your strength is awesome, and no one can defeat you.
¹⁴Let all your creation serve you.
    You spoke, and everything came into existence.
    You sent your Spirit, and he formed everything.
       No one can oppose what you say.

¹⁵Mountains will be shaken off their foundations
    into the oceans.
Rocks will melt like wax when you look at them, Lord.
    But you will continue to show mercy to those who fear you.
¹⁶Fragrant offerings mean little to you.
Pieces of fat given as whole burnt offerings mean even less.
    But those who fear you, Lord, are always important to you.

¹⁷How horrible it will be for the nations that attack my people!
    The Lord Almighty will punish the people of those nations
       on judgment day.

He will send fire and worms into their bodies,
and they will cry in pain forever.

The Victory Celebration in Jerusalem

[18] When the people arrived in Jerusalem, they worshiped God. As soon as they purified themselves, they sacrificed their burnt offerings and free-will offerings, and they presented their gifts. [19] Judith dedicated to God all of Holofernes' possessions, which the people had given her. She even dedicated the mosquito net that she had taken from Holofernes' bedroom as an offering to God. [20] For three months the people celebrated in Jerusalem in front of the holy place, and Judith stayed there with them.

The End of Judith's Life

[21] After the celebration was over, all the people returned home. Judith went back to the city of Bethulia and lived there on her estate. For the rest of her life, she was honored throughout the country. [22] Many men desired her. But after her husband Manasseh was dead and buried, she never had sex for the rest of her life. [23] She became very famous and lived in her husband's house until she was 105 years old. She set her female slave free. Judith died in Bethulia and was buried in the same cave as her husband Manasseh. [24] The people of Israel mourned for her for seven days. Before she died, she divided her property between her closest relatives and Manasseh's closest relatives. [25] No one ever terrorized the Israelites again during Judith's lifetime or for a long time after her death.

Esther

(The Greek Version)

ADDITION A*a*

Mordecai's Dream

¹On the first day of the month of Nisan, in the second year that Artaxerxes the Great was king, Mordecai had a dream. Mordecai was from the tribe of Benjamin and was a descendant of Jair, Shimei, and Kish. ²Mordecai was a Jew who lived in the Persian city of Susa and was an important man who served in the king's court. ³He was ˻a descendant of˼ the prisoners that King Nebuchadnezzar of Babylon had taken from Jerusalem along with King Jeconiah of Judea.

⁴Mordecai dreamed about noise, confusion, thunder, earthquakes, and disturbances on the earth. ⁵Then two large serpents appeared. Both of them made loud noises and were ready to fight. ⁶So every nation prepared for war against a nation of innocent people. ⁷This was a dark and gloomy day with suffering and distress. People were being mistreated, and there were serious disturbances on the earth. ⁸All the people from the innocent nation were terrified. They were so afraid of the disasters that threatened them that they were prepared to die. ⁹So they prayed to God for help. Because of their prayer, a wide, overflowing river came from a small spring. ¹⁰Light appeared as the sun rose. Humble people were honored, and they destroyed those who held important positions.

¹¹Then Mordecai woke up. In this dream he had seen what God was planning to do. He thought about the dream all day, because he wanted to know what every detail of the dream meant.

Mordecai Saves the King's Life

¹²Mordecai was resting in the courtyard with Gabatha and Tharra. They were two of the king's eunuchs who guarded the courtyard. ¹³Mordecai

---

a Addition A:1-17 is chapters 11:2–12:6 in some translations.

overheard them talking, noticed that they were nervous, and found out that they were preparing to assassinate King Artaxerxes. So Mordecai told the king about their plot. ¹⁴The king interrogated the two eunuchs. After they had confessed, they were led away to be executed. ¹⁵The king wrote these things in his official records. Mordecai also wrote an account of what had happened. ¹⁶Then the king appointed Mordecai to serve in his court, and he rewarded Mordecai for what he had done.

¹⁷Haman, who was the son of Hammedatha and was a Bougaean, held an important position in the king's court. Haman looked for a way to harm Mordecai and his people because of what Mordecai had done to the king's two eunuchs.

Queen Vashti Disobeys King Artaxerxes

1 ¹After this, the following events took place when Artaxerxes was king. This was the same Artaxerxes who ruled over 127 provinces from ⌊India to Sudan⌋. ²In the third year that King Artaxerxes ruled in the city of Susa, ³he held a banquet. The banquet was for his friends, for people from other nations, for important Persians and Medes, and for the governors of the provinces. ⁴For 180 days he showed them the wealth of his kingdom and what a magnificent celebration that wealth could provide. ⁵After that, when the days of celebration were over, the king had a wine party. This party was for the people from other nations who lived in the fortress ⌊at Susa⌋. It lasted for six days and was held in the courtyard of the royal palace.

⁶The courtyard was decorated with curtains made of fine linen and cotton. The curtains were hung on cords made of purple linen. The cords were attached to gold and silver blocks that were mounted on pillars made of marble and other stones. Gold and silver couches were placed in the courtyard, which was paved with emeralds, pearl-like stones, and marble. The couches had covers on them. The covers were embroidered with flower designs and with roses around their borders. ⁷The drinking cups were made of gold and silver. A miniature cup was on display. It was made from a ruby and was worth millions of dollars. There was plenty of sweet wine like the king usually drank. ⁸This party wasn't like previous parties. But that's the way the king wanted it. He had told the waiters to do whatever he and his guests wanted.

⁹Queen Vashti also had a party for the women. It was held in King Artaxerxes' palace.

¹⁰On the seventh day, the king was feeling happy ⌊because he had been drinking⌋. So he told Haman, Bazan, Tharra, Boraze, Zatholtha, Abataza, and Tharaba, the seven eunuchs who advised King Artaxerxes, ¹¹to bring the queen to him. He wanted to make her the queen officially by

placing the crown on her head. She was a beautiful woman, so he wanted
to show off her beauty to all the governors and to the people from the
other nations. [12]But Queen Vashti disobeyed him and refused to go with
the eunuchs. This upset the king, and he became angry.

[13]The king told his friends what Vashti had done. He asked them to
make an official ruling on how to handle this situation. [14]Arkesaeus, Sar-
sathaeus, and Malesear, who were governors of the Persians and Medes,
came to the king. They were his closest and most important officials.
[15]They told the king what must be done to Queen Vashti according to
their laws because she had disobeyed the order that the king had given
her through the eunuchs.

[16]Then Muchaeus said to the king and the governors, "Queen Vashti
has done something wrong, not only against the king but also against
all the king's governors and officials." [17](Muchaeus had told them what
the king had done and how she defied the king.)[a] [18]"Today the governors'
wives in Persia and Media will hear what the queen did to the king.
They will also be bold enough to dishonor their husbands in the same
way that Queen Vashti defied King Artaxerxes. [19]So if you approve, Your
Majesty, issue a royal decree that can never be repealed. Write, according
to the laws of the Medes and Persians, that the queen may never come
into your presence again, Your Majesty. Furthermore, Your Majesty,
you should give her royal position to another woman who is better than
she. [20]Whatever law you issue must be spread throughout your kingdom.
Then all wives will honor their husbands, whether their husbands are
rich or poor."

[21]The king and the governors liked this idea. So the king did as
Muchaeus had suggested. [22]He sent the decree throughout his kingdom
to every province in its own language. He did this so that every husband
would be respected in his own house.

Esther Becomes Queen

2 [1]After this, the king got over his anger and forgot about Vashti. He
forgot what she had done and how he had condemned her. [2]Then the
king's advisers said, "Your Majesty, conduct a search for young women
who are pure and beautiful. [3]Appoint officials in every province of your
kingdom to choose beautiful young virgins and bring them to your wom-
en's quarters in the city of Susa. Place them in the care of the eunuch
who is in charge of women and give them cosmetics and whatever else
they might need. [4]Then let the woman who pleases you, Your Majesty,
become queen instead of Vashti."

---

[a] 1:17 The last part of verse 17 has been placed in verse 18 to express the complex Greek
sentence structure more clearly in English.

The king liked this suggestion, so that's what he did.

⁵A Jew named Mordecai lived in the city of Susa. He was from the tribe of Benjamin and was a descendant of Jair, Shimei, and Kish. ⁶He had been taken as a prisoner from Jerusalem when King Nebuchadnezzar of Babylon had captured that city. ⁷He had adopted a child named Esther. She was the daughter of his father's brother Aminadab. When Esther's parents died, Mordecai raised her as his own child until she was an adult.ᵃ She was a beautiful young woman.

⁸When the king issued his decree, many young women were gathered together ⌐and brought⌐ to the city of Susa. There they were placed under the supervision of Gai, who was in charge of women. Esther also was brought to Gai. ⁹Gai liked her, and she was his favorite. So he quickly provided her with cosmetics, her portion of food, and seven female servants assigned to her from the palace. Gai treated Esther and her female servants better ⌐than the others⌐ in the women's quarters.

¹⁰Esther had not revealed her race or what country she was from, because Mordecai had told her not to tell anyone. ¹¹Every day Mordecai would walk in the courtyard of the women's quarters to find out what was happening to Esther.

¹²Each young woman was given twelve months of beauty treatment before she went to the king. The time of this treatment was spent as follows: For six months the young women used oil of myrrh, and for another six months they used perfumes and other cosmetics. ¹³Then a young woman would go to the king. She would be given anything that she wanted to take along with her from the women's quarters to the king's palace. ¹⁴In the evening the young woman would go to the king's palace, and in the morning she would leave and go to the other quarters for women. (Gai, the king's eunuch, was in charge of these women also.) That young woman would never go to the king again unless she was summoned by name.

¹⁵The time came for Esther to go to the king. (Esther was the daughter of Aminadab, the brother of Mordecai's father). She did everything that Gai, the eunuch in charge of women, had told her to do. Esther was the favorite of everyone who saw her. ¹⁶She went to King Artaxerxes in the month of Adar, the twelfth month, in the seventh year that he was king. ¹⁷The king fell in love with Esther and favored her more than all the other virgins. So the king put the queen's crown on her head. ¹⁸Then the king had a wine party for all his friends and officers to celebrate his marriage to Esther. The party lasted seven days. He even stopped collecting taxes from those who were under his rule.

ᵃ 2:7 Or "raised her to be his wife."

Mordecai Saves the King's Life

¹⁹ Meanwhile, Mordecai was serving in the king's court. ²⁰Esther still had not revealed what country she was from. Mordecai had told her to fear God and to do what God demanded, just as she did when she lived with him. So Esther didn't change the way she lived.

²¹ Two of the king's eunuchs, his chief bodyguards, were upset because Mordecai was promoted. So they searched for a way to assassinate King Artaxerxes. ²²But Mordecai found out about this and told Esther. Then Esther informed the king about the plot. ²³The king interrogated the two eunuchs and had their dead bodies hung on poles. To honor Mordecai, the king ordered a record of Mordecai's loyalty to be written and placed in the royal library.

Haman's Plot To Destroy the Jews

3 ¹After this, King Artaxerxes honored Haman by promoting him to the position of prime minister over all the king's other officials. (Haman was the son of Hammedatha and was a Bougaean.) ²Everyone in the king's court would bow to Haman, because this is what the king had ordered them to do. But Mordecai wouldn't bow to Haman.

³ Then the members of the king's court asked Mordecai why he was ignoring the king's order. ⁴They asked him this every day, but Mordecai didn't pay any attention to them. So they informed Haman that Mordecai was disobeying the king's order and that Mordecai had told them that he was a Jew.

⁵ When Haman found out that Mordecai wouldn't bow to him, he became furious. ⁶So he plotted to destroy every Jew in Artaxerxes' kingdom.

⁷ In Artaxerxes' twelfth year as king, Haman reached a decision. He threw dice every day for months to determine on what day he would destroy Mordecai's people. Based on the dice he threw, Haman chose the fourteenth day of the month of Adar.

⁸ Then Haman said to King Artaxerxes, "There are people from a certain nation scattered among the other nations throughout your kingdom. Their laws are different from those of every other nation, and they ignore your laws. So it's not in your best interest to tolerate them, Your Majesty. ⁹If you approve, give the order to destroy them. ⌊For this⌋ I will give you 750,000 pounds of silver."

¹⁰ The king removed his signet ring and gave it to Haman so that Haman could put a seal on the order written against the Jews. ¹¹The king told Haman, "Keep your silver, and do whatever you want to the people from that nation."

Haman Prepares To Destroy the Jews

¹²On the thirteenth day of the first month, the king summoned his scribes. In the king's name, they wrote everything that Haman ordered them to write. They wrote to the chief officers ⌐of the cities⌐ and to the governors of the nations in each of the 127 provinces from India to Sudan. Each nation was addressed in its own language. ¹³Messengers carried Haman's order throughout Artaxerxes' kingdom. The chief officers and the governors were ordered to destroy the Jews on a single day in the twelfth month, the month of Adar, and to seize their property.

ADDITION B*a*

A Copy of Haman's Order To Destroy the Jews

¹This is a copy of ⌐Haman's⌐ order:

King Artaxerxes the Great sends the following order to the governors of the 127 provinces from India to Sudan and to the officials under their authority:

²I have become the ruler of many nations and have conquered the entire world. Yet, I haven't abused my authority. I always act with fairness and kindness. So I have promised that my people will live in peace forever, that my kingdom will be civilized, that travel from one end of my kingdom to the other will be safe, and that the law and order which everyone wants will be restored. ³When I asked my officials how I could accomplish this goal, Haman pointed something out to us. Haman is famous among us for his sound judgment. He has proved himself by his constant good will and unfailing loyalty, and he has won the second-highest position in the kingdom. ⁴Haman pointed out to us that a group of hostile people is mixed throughout the nations of the world. These people have laws that are contrary to those of every nation, and they continually ignore the king's

---

a Addition B:1-7 is chapter 13:1-7 in some translations.

orders. So it has been impossible for us to unify the administration of the kingdom perfectly as we intended. [5]Therefore, we want to state clearly that these people, more than any others, are in constant opposition to all humanity. They have a strange way of living because of their laws, they hate our government, and they commit the worst crimes ˩against it˩. So it's impossible for our kingdom to become stable.

[6]Therefore, we order you to destroy the people that Haman mentioned in this order. Haman is in charge of these matters. (He is like a second father to us.) All these people, including women and children, must be destroyed by their enemies' swords. Don't spare anyone or show them any mercy. This order must be carried out this year, on the fourteenth day of the twelfth month, the month of Adar. [7]In this way those who have been hostile for so long will die violently in a single day. Then our government will be completely stable and undisturbed in the future.

3 (CONTINUED)

[14]Copies of the order were distributed in every province. Every nation was ordered to be ready for that day. [15]The news also spread quickly to the city of Susa. While the king and Haman were drinking together, the people in the city of Susa were worried.

4 [1]When Mordecai found out what was happening, he tore his clothes in grief, put on sackcloth, and sprinkled ashes on himself. Then he ran through the main street of the city shouting, "An innocent nation is going to be destroyed!" [2]He went as far as the king's gate and stopped there, because people who had ashes on and were wearing sackcloth weren't allowed to enter the courtyard.

[3]In every province where the king's order was distributed, the Jews cried loudly and mourned. They put on sackcloth and sprinkled themselves with ashes.

Esther's Problem

[4]Queen Esther's eunuchs and female servants came and told her ˩about Mordecai˩. She became upset when she heard what was happening. So she sent clothes for Mordecai to put on in place of his sackcloth. But Mordecai refused to accept the clothes. [5]Then Esther summoned Hachrathaeus, one of the eunuchs who served her. She sent him to Mordecai to find out exactly what had happened.[a]

---

[a] 4:5 Some manuscripts add verse 6: "So Hachrathaeus went to Mordecai, who was on the main street of the city in front of the city gate."

⁷Mordecai informed Hachrathaeus about what was happening. Mordecai told him how Haman had promised to give the king 750,000 pounds of silver in order to destroy the Jews. ⁸He also gave Hachrathaeus a copy of the order to destroy the Jews that had been distributed in Susa. He told Hachrathaeus to show it to Esther and to tell her to plead with the king and beg him to help her people. He also said to Hachrathaeus, "Remind Esther of her humble background when she was brought up in my care. Since Haman, who is second only to the king, has sentenced our people to death, tell Esther to pray to the Lord. Then tell her to speak to the king for our people and save us from death."

⁹So Hachrathaeus returned to Esther and told her all these things.

¹⁰Esther told Hachrathaeus, "Go to Mordecai and tell him, ¹¹"Everyone in the kingdom knows that any man or woman who goes to the king's inner court without being summoned will die. A person is safe only if the king holds out his golden scepter. I haven't been summoned by the king for 30 days now.'" ¹²So Hachrathaeus told Mordecai everything that Esther had said.

¹³Mordecai told Hachrathaeus to go back to her and say, "Esther, don't think that you are safer than all the other Jews in the kingdom. ¹⁴The fact is, if you ignore this opportunity, help and protection will come to the Jews from somewhere else. However, you and your father's family will die. And who knows, maybe you have become queen just for a time like this."

¹⁵Then Esther gave the messenger this reply to take back to Mordecai: ¹⁶"Assemble all the Jews who are in Susa. Hold a fast for me. Don't eat or drink anything for three days and nights. My female servants and I will also go without food. After that, although it's against the law, I'll go to the king, even if I must die."

¹⁷So Mordecai did everything that Esther told him to do.

ADDITION C*ᵃ*

Mordecai's Prayer

¹Then Mordecai remembered everything that the Lord had done, and he prayed, ²"Lord, Lord, you are the king who rules everything. The

---

ᵃ Addition C:1-30 is chapters 13:8–14:19 in some translations.

universe is under your control. No one can stop you when you want to save Israel. ³You made heaven and earth and every wonderful thing under heaven. ⁴You are Lord of everything. No one can oppose you, Lord.

⁵ "You know everything, Lord. You know that when I refused to bow to that arrogant man Haman, I didn't refuse because I was rude or arrogant or because I wanted to be famous. ⁶You know that I would have been willing to kiss his feet to save Israel. ⁷But I refused to bow so that I wouldn't honor any man more than I honor you, God. I won't bow to anyone except you, my Lord. I won't act arrogantly.

⁸ "And now, Lord God and King, the God of Abraham, spare your people. Our enemies are looking for a way to ruin us. They want to destroy those who have belonged to you from the beginning. ⁹Don't overlook the group of people you reclaimed from Egypt. ¹⁰Hear my prayer. Have mercy on the people who belong to you. Turn our sorrow into joy. Then we will still be alive to sing hymns of praise to your name, Lord. Don't destroy the people who praise you."

¹¹ All the people of Israel cried loudly because they could see that they were about to die.

Esther's Prayer

¹² Queen Esther turned to the Lord for help because she was afraid that she was about to die. ¹³She took off her beautiful robes and put on clothes that showed her suffering and sorrow. Instead of putting on expensive perfumes, she put ashes and manure on her head. She did everything she could to humble herself by changing her beautiful appearance. She even left her hair uncombed and let it cover her body. ¹⁴Then she prayed to the Lord God of Israel, "My Lord, our king, you alone are God. I'm alone and have no one to help me but you. ¹⁵Help me, because I'm in great danger. ¹⁶Lord, ever since I was born, I heard from my father's family that you chose Israel from all the nations. I heard that you chose our ancestors from the people who preceded them to be yours forever and that you did everything for them you promised.

¹⁷ "We sinned against you, and you handed us over to our enemies ¹⁸because we honored their gods. You were right in doing that, Lord. ¹⁹But our enemies are not satisfied with making slavery bitter for us. Instead, they have made an agreement with their false gods. ²⁰They want to do away with what you promised and to destroy the people who belong to you. They want people to stop praising you. They want to dishonor your temple and to extinguish the fire on your altar. ²¹They want the nations to praise the excellent qualities of their false gods and to admire a human king forever.

²² "Lord, don't surrender your scepter to gods that don't exist. Don't let our enemies laugh at our misfortune. Instead, turn their plan against

them, and make an example out of the man who started all this against us. ²³Remember us, Lord. Make your presence known to us during this time of suffering. Give me courage, King of the gods, since you have power over every ruler. ²⁴Help me to say the right things when I appear in the presence of the lion, King Artaxerxes. Change the king's mind so that he will hate the man who is fighting against us and will put an end to that man and to those who agree with him. ²⁵Use your power to save us, and help me. I am alone and have no one to help me but you, Lord.

"You know everything. ²⁶You know that I hate to receive honor from people who don't follow our teachings. I despise being married to an uncircumcised man or to anyone from another race. ²⁷You know the pressure I'm under. You know that I hate ˌthe crown,ˌ the symbol of my high position. You know that I wear it only when I make public appearances, never in private. I hate it like a menstrual rag. ²⁸I've never eaten at Haman's table, and I've never honored the king's parties ˌby attending themˌ. I've never drunk the wine offered to the gods. ²⁹I haven't been happy from the day that I was brought here until now. The only happiness I've had is because of you, Lord God of Abraham. ³⁰God, you are more powerful than anyone. Listen to your people, who are in despair. Save us from the power of evil people, and save me from what I fear."

ADDITION D^{*a*}

Esther Brings Her Request to the King

¹Three days later Queen Esther finished praying. She took off the clothes in which she had humbly prayed, and she put on her beautiful robes. ²She looked absolutely beautiful. After she had prayed again to her God and Savior, who watches everyone, she took two female servants with her. ³She leaned gently on one servant for support. ⁴The other servant followed her and carried the train of her long robe. ⁵Esther's face was radiant. She was lovely and appeared to be cheerful, even though her heart was pounding because she was afraid. ⁶After she had gone through all the doors, she stood in front of the king. The king was sitting on his royal throne. He was wearing his royal robes, which were decorated with gold and precious stones. The sight of him was awe-inspiring. ⁷Then the

---

^{*a*} Addition D:1-16 is chapter 15:1-16 in some translations.

king looked up. His face was radiant with royal splendor, but he was very angry as he looked at her. The queen staggered, turned pale, fainted, and collapsed on the female servant who was escorting her.

⁸Then God changed the king's mood, and the king became gentle. The king was upset by what had happened. So he quickly got up from his throne and held Esther in his arms until she revived. He reassured her with comforting words and said, ⁹"What's the matter, Esther? I'm your husband. Don't be afraid. ¹⁰You won't die. Our law applies only to common people. ¹¹You may come here."

¹²Then the king raised his golden scepter, touched Esther's neck with it, hugged her, and said, "You may talk to me."

¹³Esther said to him, "Sir, when I saw you, you looked like one of God's angels. I was terrified when I saw your awe-inspiring majesty. ¹⁴Sir, your appearance is stunning. You look kind."

¹⁵While Esther was speaking, she fainted. ¹⁶Then the king was worried, and all his advisers worked to revive her.

5 ᵃ³The king asked her, "What do you want, Esther? What's your request? Whatever you want is yours, up to half of my kingdom."

⁴So Esther answered, "Today is a special day for me. Please, Your Majesty, come with Haman to a dinner that I'll prepare today."

⁵Then the king said, "Bring Haman right away so that we can do what Esther wants." So they both went to the dinner that Esther had invited them to.

⁶While they were drinking wine, the king asked Esther, "What's the matter, Queen Esther? Whatever you want is yours."

⁷Esther answered, "This is what I want. This is my request. ⁸If I am your favorite, Your Majesty, come with Haman to a dinner that I will prepare for you tomorrow. I'll give you an answer tomorrow."

Meanwhile, Haman Is Disgraced Because of Mordecai

⁹When Haman left the king, he was very happy and feeling good. But when Haman saw Mordecai the Jew in the courtyard, he became furious. ¹⁰He went home and sent for his friends and his wife Zosara.

¹¹Haman told them how rich he was, how the king had honored him, and how the king had promoted him to the position of prime minister. ¹²Haman went on to say, "The queen didn't invite anyone to dinner with the king except me. I've even been invited again tomorrow. ¹³But none of these things make me happy as long as I see Mordecai the Jew in the courtyard."

ᵃ In chapter 5, verses 1-2 of the Hebrew version of Esther are replaced by Addition D in the Greek version.

¹⁴His wife Zosara and his friends said to him, "Have a pole set up, 75 feet high. In the morning ask the king to have Mordecai's dead body hung on it. Then go to dinner with the king, and enjoy yourself."

Haman liked the idea, so he had the pole set up.

6 ¹That night the Lord wouldn't let the king sleep. So the king told his secretary to bring the official daily records and read them to him. ²The secretary came across an entry that described how Mordecai had told the king about two of the king's eunuchs who were guards and who were trying to assassinate King Artaxerxes.

³The king asked, "Did we ever honor Mordecai or reward him for this?"

The king's advisers answered, "Nothing was done for him."

⁴While the king was inquiring about Mordecai's loyalty, Haman showed up in the courtyard. The king asked, "Who's in the courtyard?" (Haman had come to ask the king to hang Mordecai's dead body on the pole that was already set up.)

⁵The king's advisers answered, "Haman."

The king said, "Call him in here."

⁶Then the king asked Haman, "What should I do for a man whom I want to honor?"

Haman thought, "Who would the king want to honor more than me?" ⁷So Haman told the king, "This is what you should do for the man you want to honor, Your Majesty. ⁸Your servants should bring a robe made of fine linen that you have worn and a horse that you have ridden. ⁹Both of these things should be given to one of your distinguished officials, Your Majesty. That official should put the robe on the man you're honoring, help him mount the horse, and lead him through the main street of the city, shouting, 'This is what will happen to everyone whom the king honors.'"

¹⁰Then the king said to Haman, "Good idea! Do exactly what you've said for Mordecai the Jew, who serves in my court. Don't leave out anything you've said."

¹¹So Haman got the robe and the horse. He put the robe on Mordecai, helped him mount the horse, and led him through the main street of the city, shouting, "This is what will happen to everyone whom the king wants to honor."

¹²After that, Mordecai went back to the courtyard, but Haman returned home in despair with his head covered. ¹³He told his wife Zosara and his friends everything that had happened to him. His friends and his wife told him, "If Mordecai is of Jewish descent, and you've been humiliated in front of him, you will certainly lose ⌐your position⌐. You will never be able to defend yourself, because the living God is with him."

¹⁴While they were still talking, the eunuchs arrived to take Haman to the dinner that Esther had prepared.

Esther Brings About Haman's Downfall

7 ¹So the king and Haman went to have dinner with Queen Esther. ²On that second day, while they were drinking wine, the king asked, "What's the matter, Queen Esther? What do you want? What is your request? Whatever you want is yours, up to half of my kingdom."

³Then Queen Esther answered, "If I'm your favorite, Your Majesty, spare my life and the lives of my people. ⁴I've heard that my people and I have been sold. We will be destroyed, our property will be seized, and we and our children will become slaves. Our enemy doesn't deserve to be a member of your court, Your Majesty."

⁵Then the king asked, "Who dared to do such a thing?"

⁶Esther said, "This evil man Haman is the enemy!" At this, Haman became panic-stricken in the presence of the king and queen.

⁷The king got up from the dinner and went into the garden. Haman saw that he was in deep trouble, so he began to beg the queen for his life. ⁸When the king returned from the garden, Haman had thrown himself on the queen's couch and was pleading with the queen. Then the king said, "Are you even going to rape my wife in my palace?" Haman was shocked when he heard this.

⁹Then Bugathan, one of the eunuchs, said to the king, "Did you know that Haman has already set up a pole for Mordecai? Mordecai is the man who gave you the information that saved your life, Your Majesty. The pole is 75 feet high and is at Haman's house."

The king said, "Hang Haman on it!"

¹⁰So Haman was hung on the pole that he had set up for Mordecai. Then the king got over his anger.

8 ¹On that same day King Artaxerxes gave Esther all the property of Haman, the enemy. The king summoned Mordecai because she had told the king that Mordecai was related to her. ²Then the king took off his signet ring, which he had taken away from Haman, and he gave it to Mordecai. Esther put Mordecai in charge of everything that had belonged to Haman.

Esther Brings Her Request to the King

³Then Esther spoke to the king again. She threw herself at his feet and begged him to stop the evil plot that Haman had planned against the Jews. ⁴The king held out his golden scepter to Esther, and Esther got up and stood in front of the king. ⁵She said, "Your Majesty, if you approve and if I'm your favorite, cancel the order that Haman wrote to destroy

the Jews in your kingdom. ⁶How can I bear to see my people mistreated? How will I escape if the people from my country are destroyed?"

⁷The king said to Esther, "I've given all of Haman's property to you, and I've hung him on a pole because he intended to kill the Jews. Is there anything else that you want? ⁸Write what you think is best, and sign my name to it. Seal it with my signet ring, because whatever is written with my permission and is sealed with my ring cannot be canceled."

Mordecai Uses His Position To Save the Jews

⁹That same year, on the twenty-third day of Nisan, the first month, the scribes were summoned. Everything that Mordecai ordered was written to the Jews and to the administrators and governors of the 127 provinces from India to Sudan. Each province received the order in its own language.

¹⁰The order was written with the king's authority, sealed with his ring, and sent by messengers. ¹¹The king told the Jews in every city to live by their own laws and to defend themselves. The Jews were also told to treat their opponents and enemies however they wished. ¹²They could do this throughout Artaxerxes' kingdom on one day, the thirteenth day of Adar, the twelfth month.

ADDITION E *ᵃ*

A Copy of Mordecai's Order To Save the Jews

¹This is a copy of ⌐Mordecai's⌐ order:

From King Artaxerxes the Great.
To the governors of the 127 provinces from India to Sudan and
    to our loyal people.
Greetings!

²Many people often become arrogant when they are honored through the rich generosity of those who support them. ³Since they are not able to handle prosperity, they look for ways to hurt the people of our country. They even plot against those who support them ⁴and make others feel that there is no need to

---

ᵃ Addition E:1-24 is chapter 16:1-14 in some translations.

be thankful when people give them their support. Instead, they get carried away by the praise of those who don't know what goodness is. They even think that they will escape from a God who always sees everything and who won't tolerate evil.

⁵Many times people get appointed to positions of authority because they have friends in public office. These friends are tricked into becoming accessories to the murders of innocent people, and they become involved in other tragic events. ⁶All this is due to people who lie unexpectedly and who use twisted reasoning to persuade people ⌐to act⌐ against the sincere intent of their rulers.

⁷It is possible for those who want to investigate this matter to see examples of this. They can see this not so much from our ancient history but from investigating the terrible things that have been done recently by those who are in power. ⁸In the future I will devote myself to making my kingdom quiet and peaceful for everyone. ⁹I will do this by changing my methods and by always using careful consideration to judge whatever comes to my attention.

¹⁰Let me give you an example. Haman, who was Hammedatha's son and a Macedonian, was a foreigner who became our guest. He wasn't a Persian. Therefore, he was not as kind as we have been, ¹¹but he fully enjoyed the kindness we have shown toward people from every nation. In fact, people called him "Father," and they continually bowed to him because he was second only to the king. ¹²However, he was unable to control his arrogance. He tried to murder me and take away my kingdom. ¹³Using clever strategies, he asked to destroy Mordecai, a man who saved my life and who has continually supported me. He also asked to destroy Esther, my innocent royal partner. He even wanted to destroy all the people from Mordecai and Esther's nation. ¹⁴In this way he thought that he could catch us with our guard down and give the Persian kingdom to the Macedonians.

¹⁵However, I find that the Jews, whom this very evil man wanted to destroy, are not criminals. There's really nothing wrong with their laws. ¹⁶They are children of the living God who is the Most High God, the Almighty. He has guided the kingdom for us and for our ancestors in a very successful way.

¹⁷So I advise you not to follow the order that Haman, the son of Hammedatha, sent to you. ¹⁸He and everyone in his family have been hung on poles at the city gates of Susa. God, who rules everything, has quickly given Haman the punishment that he deserves.

¹⁹Distribute copies of this order in every province. Allow the Jews to live by their own customs. ²⁰Also, help them so that they can defend themselves against those who attack them on the thirteenth day of Adar, the twelfth month. ²¹God, who rules everything, has turned that day—the day intended for the destruction of his chosen people—into a day of celebration.

²²Therefore, include this special day among your festivals, and observe it joyfully. ²³Now and in the future, this day will remind you and loyal Persians how you were saved. It will be a reminder that people who plot against us will be destroyed.

²⁴Every city or province that doesn't follow this order will be destroyed by my armies and burned to the ground. No human will ever go there again. Even wild animals and birds will hate that place forever.

8 (CONTINUED)
¹³Distribute copies of this order throughout the kingdom. Also, all the Jews must be ready to fight against their enemies on that day.

¹⁴Messengers on horses left quickly to carry out the king's order. The order was also distributed in Susa.

¹⁵When Mordecai left ˌthe kingˌ, he was wearing a robe which indicated royalty and a gold crown with a royal band of purple linen around it. The people in Susa were very happy when they saw him.

¹⁶So light and joy came to the Jews. ¹⁷Throughout the country, the order was distributed, and the Jews drank and celebrated happily. Many people who were not Jewish were circumcised and lived like the Jews because they were afraid of them.

The Jews Defend Themselves

9 ¹On the thirteenth day of Adar, the twelfth month, the king's order was carried out.

²On that same day the enemies of the Jews were destroyed. People couldn't stand up to the Jews because they were afraid of them. ³The governors of the provinces, the princes, and the royal scribes respected the Jews, because they were afraid of Mordecai ⁴and because the king ordered all the people throughout the kingdom to honor him.ᵃ

⁶In the city of Susa, the Jews killed 500 men and seized their property.ᵇ ⁷These men included Pharsannestain, Delphon, Phasga, ⁸Pharadatha, Barea, Sarbacha, ⁹Marmasima, Aruphaeus, Arsaeus, and Zabuthaeus.

ᵃ 9:4 Some manuscripts add verse 5: "Then the Jews attacked all their enemies. They killed them, destroyed them, and did whatever they pleased to those who hated them."

ᵇ 9:6 The last part of verse 10 has been placed in verse 6 to express the complex Greek paragraph structure more clearly in English.

[10]They were the ten sons of Haman, who was Hammedatha's son and a Bougaean. Haman was the enemy of the Jews.

[11]On that same day the number of people killed in Susa was reported to the king. [12]So the king said to Esther, "In the city of Susa, the Jews have killed 500 men. What do you suppose they have done in the rest of the provinces? Is there anything else that you want? It, too, will be yours." [13]Esther said to the king, "Allow the Jews to do the same thing tomorrow. They can hang Haman's ten sons on poles." [14]The king agreed to this. He handed over the bodies of Haman's sons to the Jews of the city so that they could hang them on poles.

[15]The Jews in Susa assembled on the fourteenth day of the month of Adar and killed 300 men, but they didn't seize any of their property. [16]The other Jews in the kingdom also assembled to defend themselves. They killed 15,000 of their enemies on the thirteenth day of Adar, but they didn't seize any of their property. [17]On the fourteenth day of the same month, when the fighting was over, they celebrated joyfully.

[18]Because the Jews in Susa didn't stop fighting when they assembled on the fourteenth, they celebrated on the fifteenth. [19]That's why the Jews who are scattered in the outlying provinces celebrate the fourteenth day of the month of Adar as a holiday. On that day they send gifts of food to each other. However, the Jews who live in the large cities celebrate the fifteenth day of the month of Adar as a holiday. They, too, send gifts of food to each other.

The Festival of Purim Is Established by Esther and Mordecai

[20]Mordecai wrote these things down in a book. He sent it throughout Artaxerxes' kingdom to all the Jews, whether they lived near or far away. [21]He wrote the book to establish the fourteenth and fifteenth days of the month of Adar as holidays for the Jews to celebrate. [22]On these days the Jews stopped fighting their enemies. The Jews were told to celebrate throughout the month of Adar. In the month of Adar their sorrow and despair turned into a joyous holiday. The Jews were told to observe these holidays as a time for feasting and celebration. They were to send gifts of food to their friends and to the poor.

[23]The Jews accepted everything that Mordecai had written to them. [24]Mordecai wrote how Haman, who was Hammedatha's son and a Macedonian, fought against them, how he issued a decree, and how he threw dice to determine when to destroy them. [25]Mordecai also wrote how Haman had gone to the king and had asked to hang Mordecai on a pole. Every evil thing that Haman attempted to do to the Jews was done to him. He and his sons were hung on poles.

[26]Because of everything that Mordecai wrote in this book, because of everything that had happened to the Jews to make them suffer, and espe-

cially because of the throwing of dice, the Jews call these days *Purim.* (In the Jewish language, *Purim* means *dice.*) ²⁷So Mordecai established ˌthe festival of Purimˌ. The Jews accepted it, and it became a tradition for themselves, for their descendants, and for anyone who would join them. They would celebrate this festival exactly as Mordecai had told them to. In every city, family, and country the Jews would remember these days of Purim and celebrate them from one generation to the next. ²⁸Their descendants must never forget these days of Purim and must celebrate them every year forever.

²⁹So Queen Esther, who was Aminadab's daughter, and Mordecai the Jew wrote down everything they had done. They permanently established the festival of Purim through their book.ᵃ ³¹Both Mordecai and Queen Esther took the responsibility for establishing this festival. Then, after they risked their own lives, they carried out their plans. ³²Esther established the festival of Purim forever by her order. She had a record of the festival written ˌin a bookˌ so that the festival would be remembered.

Mordecai's Greatness

10¹The king wrote about his reign over land and sea. ²He also wrote about his strength, bravery, riches, and the glory of his kingdom. These things are recorded in the history of the kings of the Persians and Medes. ³Mordecai was appointed as successor to King Artaxerxes. Mordecai was an important man in the kingdom, and the Jews respected him. He was loved by his entire nation for the way he lived.

ADDITION F ᵇ

Mordecai Remembers and Interprets His Dream

¹Then Mordecai said, "God has caused all these things to happen. ²I remember the dream I had about these things. Everything in that dream has come true. ³The small spring that became a river is Esther, whom the king married and made his queen. She was the light, the sun, and the large river that flowed. ⁴The two serpents are Haman and me. ⁵The nations are all the people who assembled to destroy the Jews. ⁶My nation

---

ᵃ 9:29 Some manuscripts add verse 30: "Mordecai sent official documents granting peace and security to all the Jews in the 127 provinces of Artaxerxes' kingdom."

ᵇ Addition F:1-11 is chapters 10:4–11:1 in some translations.

is Israel. Israel is the nation that prayed to God for help and was saved. The Lord saved his people, rescued us from all these disasters, and performed spectacular miracles and wonders that never happened among other nations. [7]That's why God created two destinies: one for his people and one for all the other nations. [8]These two destinies came together at the right time on the right day, when God determined the future of all the nations. [9]God remembered the people who belong to him and declared them innocent. [10]These days, the fourteenth and the fifteenth days of the month of Adar, will be observed by his people Israel. Throughout every generation, the people of Israel will assemble in the presence of God, and they will celebrate."

Postscript

[11]In the fourth year of the reign of Ptolemy and Cleopatra, a man named Dositheus, who said that he was a Levitical priest, brought this book about Purim ⌞to Egypt⌟. He was accompanied by his son Ptolemy. They said that this book was genuine and that Lysimachus translated it. Lysimachus was the son of Ptolemy and lived in Jerusalem.

Wisdom

An Appeal to the Rulers of the World

1 ¹Love justice, you rulers of the world.
  Consider that the Lord is good.
  Be sincere in your search for him.
  ² Those who don't test him will find him.
  He will reveal himself to those who obey him.
  ³Evil thoughts separate people from God.
      When fools test God, his power exposes them for what they are.
  ⁴Wisdom won't enter an evil person
      or live in anyone involved in sinful behavior.
  ⁵The Holy Spirit is a teacher who has nothing to do with deceit,
      who doesn't take part in foolish thinking,
          and who despises injustice.

⁶Wisdom is a spirit that is kind to humans.
    Yet, wisdom will hold slanderers accountable for what they say.
God is a witness to people's hidden feelings.
    He has keen insight into what they think,
        and he listens to what they say.
⁷The Lord's Spirit fills the world.
The Spirit holds everything together
    and understands everything people say.
⁸So people won't get away with saying anything wicked.
    Justice won't ignore them.
        It will condemn them.
⁹The schemes of people who don't worship the true God
    will be closely examined.
Everything that those people say will be reported to the Lord
    to convict them for their evil conduct.
¹⁰The Lord listens to everything very closely.
    He hears every complaint.
¹¹So stop complaining. It won't do any good.
    Don't say things that destroy other people's reputations,
        because everything said in private will have its consequences.
            Telling lies will destroy a person's life.

¹²Don't make this mistake and bring on your own death.
Don't destroy yourself by what you say.
¹³God didn't create death.
He doesn't enjoy seeing anyone die.
¹⁴He created everything to have life.
Whatever the world produces is beneficial.
It doesn't contain anything destructive.
Death doesn't even have its headquarters on earth.
¹⁵Justice lives forever.

People Who Don't Worship the True God

¹⁶People who don't worship the true God invite death
by what they say and do.
They long for death because they consider death their friend.
They have even made an agreement with death,
because they deserve to die.

2 ¹People who don't worship the true God
are wrong when they think,
"Our lives are short and filled with trouble.
There's no cure for death.
No one has ever been known to come back from the dead.
²We were born by chance.
When our lives are over, it will be as though we had never existed.
Our breath is like a puff of smoke.
Reason is only a spark in our minds.
³When that spark goes out, our bodies will turn to ashes
and our breath will disappear into thin air.
⁴In time, no one will remember anything we have done,
and people will forget our names.
Our lives will disappear like clouds
and evaporate like mist caught by the sun's rays
or exposed to the sun's heat.
⁵Our lives are like passing shadows.
When life ends, no one can get it back.
Death is final. No one has ever come back from the dead.

⁶"Come on! Let's enjoy the good things in life.
Let's get as much out of life as we did when we were young.
⁷ Let's drink as much as we want.
Let's take time to enjoy the spring flowers.
⁸ Let's decorate our hair with roses before they wither.
⁹ Let's do whatever we want.
Let's make sure people know we had a good time.
This is all that life has to offer.

¹⁰ "Let's oppress poor people who worship the true God.
Let's not take care of widows
  or respect older people.
¹¹ Let's take the law into our own hands.
  Weakness gets us nowhere.
¹² Let's set an ambush for the man who worships the true God,
  because he gets in our way.
He opposes everything we do.
He criticizes us for breaking Moses' laws,
  and he accuses us of sinning against everything we were taught.
¹³ He claims that he knows God,
  and he even calls himself the Lord's servant.
¹⁴ He exposes our thoughts.
  It's even difficult for us to look at him.
¹⁵ His lifestyle isn't like other people's.
  Everything he does is different from others.
¹⁶ He thinks we're dishonest.
He avoids everything we do as he would avoid something unclean.ᵃ
He considers those who worship the true God to be blessed
  when their lives end.
He even brags that God is his Father.
¹⁷ Let's see if what he says is true.
Let's test him and see how life turns out for him.
¹⁸ If this man is God's son, God will help him.
  God will rescue him from his enemies.
¹⁹ Let's test him. Let's insult and torture him
  to find out just how gentle he is and how much he can take.
²⁰ Let's condemn him to a shameful death.
  If what he says is true, God will take care of him."

²¹ That's the way people who don't worship the true God think,
  but they're mistaken.
  Their wickedness has blinded them.
²² They don't understand God's mysteries.
They don't believe that there is a reward for being holy.
They don't think that there is a prize for living an innocent life.
²³ God created humans to live forever
  and made them in his own eternal image.
²⁴ But death entered the world because the devil was jealous,
  and those who are under the devil's influence experience death.

ᵃ 2:16 "Unclean" refers to anything that Moses' Teachings say is not presentable to God.

People Who Worship the True God Will Be Treated Kindly

3 ¹People who worship the true God are in God's hands.
Suffering will never affect them.
²To a foolish person, they're dead.
Their deaths were considered tragic.
³Their departure was devastating.
But in reality they're at peace ⌐with God⌐.
⁴To a foolish person, it looks as though they were punished,
but they knew that they would live forever.
⁵Although they were disciplined a little, they will be treated
very kindly.
God has tested them and found that they deserved
to be his own.
⁶He tested them like gold is tested in a smelting furnace.
He accepted them like a burnt offering.
⁷They will shoot up like flames when God judges them.
They will spread like sparks that ignite dry grass.
⁸They will judge nations and rule many people.
The Lord will be their king forever.
⁹Those who trust the Lord will understand what truth is.
Those who are faithful will live in a loving relationship with him,
because he is kind and merciful to the people he has chosen.ᵃ

People Who Don't Worship the True God Will Be Punished

¹⁰People who don't worship the true God
will receive the punishment they deserve for the way they think.
They rebel against the Lord and have no use
for people who worship the true God.
¹¹Those who despise wisdom and instruction are pathetic.
Everything they hope for is worthless.
Their efforts produce no results.
Their achievements have no value.
¹²   Their wives are foolish.
Their children are evil.
Their family is under a curse.

Having Integrity Is Better Than Having Children

¹³Childless women who haven't committed any sexual sins
are blessed.
God will reward them when he judges humanity.

ᵃ 3:9 Some manuscripts add "and he cares for the people who are devoted to him."

¹⁴Eunuchs who haven't broken Moses' laws
    and who haven't made wicked plans against the Lord
        are blessed.
They will be given a special place in the Lord's temple.
    That place will make them very happy
        and will be a reward for their faithfulness.
¹⁵A good reputation is the reward for a job well done,
    and those who understand this will never fail.

¹⁶But children of adulterers won't live long.
    Children born as a result of sexual sins will die.
¹⁷Even if they live a long time, they'll be thought of as nothing.
    No one will honor them, even when they are old.
¹⁸If they die young, they won't have any hope
    or comfort on the day of judgment.
¹⁹The lives of wicked people will come to a terrible end.

4 ¹Having integrity is better than having children.
    God and mortals both recognize integrity,
        and people will remember it forever.
²When integrity is present, people imitate it.
When it's absent, people miss it.
    Integrity marches triumphantly through time.
        It wins an honorable victory in every contest.

³The large crowd of people who don't worship the true God
    won't amount to anything.
None of their illegitimate children will ever become
        well-established
    or have a place in society.
⁴Even if they look like they might succeed for a while,
    they will fail because they have no foundation.
        Their problems will destroy them.
⁵Nothing they attempt will amount to anything.
Everything they do in life will fail.
    None of these things will have any value or benefit.
⁶Children born as a result of sexual sins
    will be used as witnesses against their parents' evil
        when God examines their parents.

A Short, Virtuous Life Is Better Than a Long, Wicked Life
⁷People who worship the true God will rest ⌐with God⌐,
    even if they die young.
⁸Old age is honorable, but not because a person lives a long time.
    Old age isn't measured by the number of years a person lives.

⁹Having insight is like being an older person,
and living a virtuous life is like living a long, full life.

¹⁰Once there was a person who pleased God, and God loved him.
Since he was living among sinners, God took him ⌐to heaven⌐.
¹¹He was taken so that evil wouldn't change the way he thought
or deceive him.
¹²(People who are fascinated by evil can't recognize what is good,
and people who don't have control of their desires
corrupt innocent minds.)
¹³Although this person lived a short time,
he lived a full life.
¹⁴His life was pleasing to the Lord.
So the Lord quickly took him from the evil
that surrounded him.
People saw this, but they didn't understand it.
They couldn't accept this fact:
¹⁵God is kind and merciful to the people he has chosen,
and he cares for the people who are devoted to him.[a]

¹⁶People who worship the true God, even after they have died,
will condemn all living people who don't worship him.
Young people whose lives were cut short
will condemn wicked people who lived a long time.
¹⁷People who don't worship the true God will see a wise person die.
But they won't understand that this was the Lord's plan for him.
They won't understand that the Lord has taken him to
a safe place.
¹⁸When they see this person die, they will think nothing of it.
But the Lord will laugh at them.
¹⁹Later on, when these people die, their corpses will be dishonored.
They will be insulted forever by those who are dead.
God will smash them on the ground. They won't be able to say
a thing.
He will shake them off their foundations.
They will become like a dry, barren land.
They will suffer pain,
and no one will remember them anymore.

Judgment Day
²⁰People who don't worship the true God will come as cowards
⌐to the place⌐ where their sins are counted.
Then the sinful things they have done will convict them.

---

[a] 4:15 Some manuscripts omit verse 15.

5 ¹Then a person who worships the true God will stand confidently.
  He will confront those who have oppressed him
    and made fun of his suffering.
²They will become terrified and upset when they see him.
  They will be shocked because they didn't expect him to be rescued.
³Then they will regret what they did.
  In distress, they will groan and say to each other:
⁴"This is the person we used to insult and treat as a joke.
  We were fools!
  We thought that he was crazy to live the way he did
    and that he died without any honor.
⁵How can he be one of God's children?
  How can he have a place among God's holy people?
⁶We were the ones who wandered from the right way of living.
    We didn't let justice light our way.
    We didn't let the sun guide us with its light.
⁷We explored every path that led to wickedness and disaster.
    We traveled through deserts that had no roads,
      but we never took the road that the Lord wanted us to travel.
⁸What did our arrogance get us?
  What good came from the wealth that we bragged about?
⁹All those things have vanished
    like a shadow,
    like a rumor that no one pays attention to,
¹⁰   like a ship that sails through raging water.
      (When a ship sails by, it leaves no trace.
        Its waves disappear.)
¹¹All those things have vanished
    like a bird flying through the air.
      (When a bird flies through the air, it leaves no trace.
        It passes through the air by flapping its wings.
      But afterward, no one can tell where it flew.)
¹²All those things have vanished
    like an arrow shot at a target.
      (When an arrow is shot at a target, it flies through the air.
        But no one can tell the path that the arrow took.)

¹³"The same is true for us. We're born, and then we fade away.
    We don't have anything worthwhile to show for our lives.
      Rather, we've completely wasted our lives doing
        wicked things."

¹⁴Everything that people who don't worship the true God hope for is
    like dust blown by the wind,

like sleet driven by a violent storm,
like smoke carried in different directions by the wind,
like a person's memory of a guest who stayed only a day.
¹⁵ But people who worship the true God will live forever.
The Lord will reward them.
The Most High will take care of them.
¹⁶ So the Lord will give them a majestic kingdom and
a beautiful crown.
His power will shelter them,
and his strength will defend them.
¹⁷ The Lord will use honor as his armor.
He will use creation as a weapon to take revenge on his enemies.
¹⁸   He will put on justice as his breastplate
and wear impartial judgment as his helmet.
¹⁹   He will take holiness as his invincible shield.
²⁰   Also, he will turn his fierce anger into a sword.
The universe will join him in an all-out war
against those who are crazy enough to oppose him.
²¹ Bolts of lightning will streak from the clouds
like well-aimed arrows that are shot from bows.
Each bolt will hit its target.
²² Hailstones filled with God's fury will be hurled
like rocks from a catapult.
The sea will rage against the Lord's enemies.
Rivers will violently sweep them away.
²³ A strong wind will attack them.
It will blow them away like a violent storm.
Wickedness will ruin the whole world,
and criminal activity will overthrow governments.

Rulers Must Have Wisdom

6 ¹ So listen, you kings, and understand.
Take note, you judges of the earth's farthest regions.
² Pay attention, you rulers who govern large populations
and who brag about the number of nations ⌐you rule⌐.
³   Your right to govern came from the Lord.
Your power to rule came from the Most High.
He will closely examine what you've done
and investigate what you plan to do
⁴   because you, as servants of his kingdom,
didn't make the right decisions.
You didn't uphold the law or live the way God wanted you to.
⁵ The Lord will quickly and fiercely confront you
because he judges people who are in authority more severely.

⁶Unimportant people will be shown mercy,
  but those who are in power will be closely examined.
⁷The Lord, who rules all people, isn't afraid of anyone.
 He doesn't stand in awe of greatness,
  because he made all people—important and unimportant
    alike—
    and he takes care of them in the same way.
⁸But a thorough investigation is in store for those who are in power.
⁹What I say is directed at you rulers
  so that you will learn what wisdom is and won't go astray.
¹⁰Rulers who uphold divine laws
  will be considered divinely appointed rulers.
 The rulers who have been taught these laws
  will discover how to defend themselves ⌞on Judgment Day⌟.
¹¹So eagerly do everything that I've said.
 Concentrate on what I've told you, and you will become educated.

¹²Wisdom shines brightly and never fades away.
  Those who love wisdom easily see it.
  Those who search for wisdom easily find it.
¹³Wisdom comes to those who desire it
  by making itself known to them first.
¹⁴Whoever gets up early in the morning to look for wisdom
  won't grow tired ⌞looking for it⌟,
    because he will find it at his door.
¹⁵To think deeply about wisdom is to show perfect insight.
 Whoever is on the lookout for wisdom
  will soon have no worries,
¹⁶   because wisdom searches for deserving people.
 Wisdom, like a friend, appears to them wherever they are
  and meets them in their every thought.

¹⁷Wisdom begins with a sincere desire to learn.
¹⁸To pay attention to instruction is to love wisdom.
 To love wisdom is to follow its guiding principles.
 To follow its guiding principles
  guarantees that a person will live forever,
¹⁹   and a person who lives forever will be in God's presence.
²⁰The desire for wisdom prepares a person to rule a kingdom.
²¹So, you rulers of nations,
  if you like your thrones and scepters,
    honor wisdom so that you can rule forever.

Solomon's Reason for Talking About Wisdom

²²I'll tell you what wisdom is and how it came into existence.
I won't keep any secrets from you.
I'll trace wisdom's history from the beginning of creation.
I'll make clear everything that can be known about wisdom.
I won't avoid the truth.

²³ I won't keep information to myself out of petty jealousy,
because jealousy doesn't have anything in common
with wisdom.

²⁴The world would be a safer place if there were more wise people
in it.
Kingdoms would be more stable if their kings
had common sense.

²⁵So learn from what I say.
It will be to your advantage.

Solomon's Reasons for Wanting Wisdom

7 ¹I, too, am mortal like everyone else.
I'm a descendant of the first man, who was formed from the earth.
I was conceived from the semen of a man[a]

² during the pleasure of marital relations.
Within a ten-month period, I was formed in my mother's womb.

³When I was born,
I began to breathe the same air that everyone else does.
When I came into the world,
my first sound was a cry, just like everyone else.

⁴I was nursed, wrapped in strips of cloth, and cared for.

⁵No king ever began life in any other way.

⁶People have only one way into life and only one way out.

⁷So I prayed, and I was given insight.
I called to God, and I received spiritual wisdom.

⁸I preferred wisdom to scepters and thrones.
I realized that wealth was nothing compared to wisdom

⁹ and that priceless gems couldn't be compared to wisdom.
All the gold in the world looks like a few grains of sand
by comparison,
and silver looks like mud next to wisdom.

¹⁰I loved wisdom more than health and good looks.
I chose wisdom rather than daylight,
because wisdom's brightness never fades.

---

[a] 7:1 The first part of verse 2 has been placed in verse 1 to express the complex Greek sentence structure more clearly in English.

¹¹ Besides, every good thing came to me along with wisdom.
Wisdom has immeasurable wealth to offer.
¹² I was happy with all these things, because wisdom brought them.
But I didn't realize that wisdom was the source of them all.
¹³ I'm now willing to share what I learned with proper motivation.
I won't keep wisdom's wealth a secret.
¹⁴ Wisdom is a treasure that people can never use up.
Those who acquire wisdom have become God's friends
because of the gifts they received from ˻wisdom's˼ instruction.

¹⁵ May God allow me to speak intelligently.
May he allow me to think in ways that honor
the gifts I've received,
because he leads people to wisdom and directs those
who are wise.
¹⁶ We are under God's control—
our words, our thoughts, and our skills.
¹⁷ He has given me knowledge about everything that exists.
I now know
how the universe was made and how its different parts function,
¹⁸ how eras begin, continue, and end,
how days and seasons change,
¹⁹ how one year changes to the next
and how stars change their positions,
²⁰ how domestic animals live and how wild animals act,
how spiritual forces*ᵃ* work and how people think,
how plants are classified
and how medicine can be taken from their roots.
²¹ I've learned about things that are hidden
and about things that are revealed.
Wisdom, who built everything, was my teacher.

²² Wisdom has a spirit that is intelligent, holy, unique,
diverse, refined,
graceful, clear, pure, distinct, harmless, good, sharp,
²³ irresistible, kind, humane, safe, sure, carefree,
all-powerful, and all-seeing.
Wisdom's spirit spreads throughout everything
that is intelligent, pure, and refined.
²⁴ Wisdom moves faster than any motion.
It spreads throughout and fills everything because it is pure.
²⁵ Wisdom is only a small sign of God's power.
It is a pure stream that comes from the glory of the Almighty.
So nothing impure can find its way into wisdom.

ᵃ 7:20 Or "winds."

²⁶ Wisdom is a reflection of eternal light.
It is a perfect mirror in which God's work is seen.
It is an image of his goodness.
²⁷ Although wisdom acts alone, it can do everything.
Although wisdom always stays the same, it renews everything.
In every generation wisdom enters the souls of devout people
and makes these people God's friends and prophets.
²⁸ God loves, more than anything, the person who lives with wisdom.
²⁹ Wisdom is more beautiful than the sun.
It surpasses the stars in the sky.
Wisdom shines brighter than light itself.
³⁰ Daylight gives way to darkness,
but wisdom is never overpowered by evil.

8 ¹ Wisdom's influence is strongly felt from one end of the earth to the other.
She manages everything well.

Solomon's Love for Wisdom

² I loved Wisdom and looked for her ever since I was young.
I wanted her to be my bride.
I fell in love with her beauty.
³ Wisdom honors her noble birth because she lives with God.
The Lord, who rules everything, loves Wisdom.
⁴ In fact, Wisdom knows God's mysteries firsthand,
and she decides what he will do.
⁵ If wealth is a desired possession in this life,
who has more wealth than Wisdom, since Wisdom
made everything?
⁶ If insight is productive,
who is more productive than Wisdom, since Wisdom
built everything?
⁷ Even if anyone loves justice,
remember that Wisdom, not justice, produces virtues.
In fact, Wisdom teaches self-control, understanding, justice,
and courage.
Nothing in this life is more useful for people than these virtues.
⁸ But if anyone wants to expand their knowledge,
Wisdom knows the past and can predict the future.
She understands subtle twists of logic
and can solve difficult problems.
She knows in advance what miracles and wonderful things
will happen
and how the course of history will turn out.

⁹So I decided to take Wisdom home to live with me.
I knew that she would give me good advice
    and would comfort me when I'm worried and upset.
¹⁰⌐I thought,⌐ "Because of her, I'll be popular among crowds
        of people.
I'll be honored by older leaders, even though I'm young.
¹¹People will find that I make brilliant decisions.
Rulers will admire me.
¹²   When I'm silent, they'll wait for me to speak.
    When I speak, they'll pay attention.
        Even if I talk for a long time,
            they'll be quiet and listen.
¹³Because of Wisdom, I'll live forever.
    I'll always be remembered by those who come after me.
¹⁴I'll govern many people.
    Nations will be under my control.
¹⁵   Even cruel rulers will be afraid when they hear about me.
        People will see that I handle myself well in public
            and am courageous in battle.
¹⁶When I come home, Wisdom will help me unwind.
    Life isn't bitter when living with Wisdom.
        Living with her brings no pain, only joy and happiness."

¹⁷After I thought about these things, this is what I concluded:
    With Wisdom as my companion, I'll live forever.
¹⁸   With Wisdom as my friend, I'll be perfectly happy.
    With Wisdom working for me, I'll have immeasurable wealth.
    With Wisdom as my trainer, I'll have insight.
    With Wisdom as my partner, I'll have a good reputation.
        So I started looking for a way to get Wisdom.
¹⁹I was a naturally gifted child.
I was fortunate to receive a good soul.
²⁰Better yet, since I was good, I was given a pure body.
²¹But I realized that I could never possess Wisdom
    unless God gave her to me.
        (Even to know where the gift of wisdom comes from
            is a sign of insight.)

Solomon's Prayer for Wisdom

So I talked with the Lord and begged him.
I prayed hard about this.

9 ¹⌐I prayed,⌐ "Merciful Lord, God of my ancestors,
    you spoke, and everything was created.

²Through your wisdom you have enabled humans
    to rule everything you created,
³   to manage the world with divine justice,
       and to judge with integrity.
⁴Give me wisdom, your assistant who sits by your throne.
 Don't refuse to give me a place among those who are loyal to you,
⁵   because I'm loyal to you, and so was my mother.
I'm a weak man who won't live long.
I have little knowledge about judgments and laws.
⁶   Even if someone perfect were to exist,
      that person, without the wisdom that comes from you,
       would be thought of as nothing.

⁷"You have chosen me to rule your people
    and to judge them.
⁸You told me to build a temple on your holy mountain
    and to build an altar in the city where you've placed your tent.
      Your tent is a copy of the holy tent,
       which you've set up ⌞in heaven⌟ from the beginning.
⁹Wisdom knows everything you do because it is with you.
    It was present with you when you created the universe.
Wisdom understands what pleases you
    and what agrees with your commands.
¹⁰Send wisdom from heaven, your holy place.
 Send it from your glorious throne
    so that it may help me in my work
    and I may recognize what pleases you.
¹¹Certainly, wisdom knows and understands everything.
    It will give me sound advice in everything I do,
    and its glory will protect me.
¹²Then everything I do will be acceptable.
    I will judge your people fairly
    and show that I deserve my father's throne.

¹³"God, who can figure out what you plan to do?
 Lord, who can know what you want to do?
¹⁴The way we mortals think is worthless,
    and our thoughts are dangerous.
¹⁵(A body that decays weighs down the soul.
    The body, like a tent made of clay, weighs down a mind
      that is already loaded with thoughts.)
¹⁶We can barely explain the things on earth.
    We discover with difficulty the things that are right in front of us.
    So who could ever understand the things in heaven?

¹⁷Lord, no one has ever figured out what you plan to do,
   unless you gave him wisdom
      and sent your Holy Spirit from the highest heaven.
¹⁸So wisdom and the Holy Spirit corrected the way people live
      on earth.
   People were taught what pleases you
      and were saved by wisdom."

Wisdom's Role From Creation to the Exodus

10 ¹Wisdom protected the world's father, the first man formed,
   when he alone had been created.
Wisdom rescued him from his failure
² and gave him strength to rule everything.

³But when a wicked man became angry, he rebelled against wisdom.
   He destroyed himself by killing his brother in a fit of rage.

⁴When the earth was flooded because of that wicked man,
   wisdom saved it again.
Wisdom steered a simple wooden ship
   for a man who worshiped the true God.

⁵When the nations were mixed up in wicked plans,
   wisdom found a man who worshiped the true God
      and helped him remain innocent in God's sight.
Wisdom kept that man's faith strong,
   even while he was grieving for his dear child.

⁶When people who didn't worship the true God were dying,
   wisdom rescued a man who did worship him.
      He escaped from the fire that rained down on the Five Cities.ᵃ
⁷Evidence of their evil still remains.
   Their cities are a smoldering wasteland.
   Plants bear fruits that never ripen,
      and a column of salt still stands there
         as a monument to a woman who wouldn't believe.
⁸Those people ignored wisdom.
   They were hurt for not recognizing what is good,
      and they left behind a reminder of the foolish way they lived.
As a result, no one will ever forget why they were destroyed.

⁹Wisdom rescued those who honored it.
¹⁰When a man who worshiped the true God
   ran away from his brother's anger,
      wisdom guided him in the right direction.

ᵃ 10:6 The Five Cities are Sodom, Gomorrah, Admah, Zeboiim, and Zoar.

It showed him God's kingdom
and gave him knowledge about holy things.
It made his work prosper
and made him successful in everything he did.
¹¹ When greedy people tried to take advantage of him,
wisdom helped him and made him rich.
¹² It protected him from his enemies
and kept him safe from the traps they set for him.
Wisdom gave him victory in his difficult struggle
so that he would realize that a life devoted to God
is more powerful than anything else.

¹³ When a man who worshiped the true God was sold as a slave,
wisdom didn't abandon him.
It rescued him from sinning ⌞with another man's wife⌟.
¹⁴ Wisdom went into prison with him.
It didn't leave him there, but made him ruler of a kingdom
and gave him authority over those who oppressed him.
Wisdom proved that his accusers were wrong,
and it gave him honor that would last forever.

¹⁵ Wisdom rescued a group of holy people, an innocent race,
from a nation that oppressed them.
¹⁶ It entered the soul of one of the Lord's servants
and stood up to cruel kings
by doing amazing things and performing miracles.
¹⁷ Wisdom gave a reward to these holy people for their work.
It guided them on their journey, which was filled with miracles.
It was their shelter during the day and their starlight during
the night.
¹⁸ Wisdom brought them through the Red Sea
and led them through deep water.
¹⁹ But wisdom drowned their enemies.
It washed the bodies up ⌞on the shore⌟ from the bottom of the sea.
²⁰ Then people who worshiped the true God
were able to loot their enemies.
They sang hymns in honor of your holy name, Lord.
Together they praised you for defending them.
²¹ Wisdom enabled those who couldn't talk to speak
and made infants speak clearly.

The Lord Gives Water to Israel but Pollutes Egypt's Water

11 ¹ Through the guidance of a holy prophet,
wisdom made everything that the people
of Israel did successful.

² They traveled through a desert where no one lived
    and pitched their tents in places that had no roads.
³ They stood up to their opponents
    and defended themselves against their enemies.
⁴ When they were thirsty, they prayed to you, Lord,
    and you gave them water that came out of solid rock.
      You gave them something to drink from a hard stone.
⁵ So the same thing that was used to punish their enemies
    was used to show kindness to your people in their time of need.
⁶ The Egyptians issued a decree to kill your people's infants.
    So you punished the Egyptians by mixing their river,
      their everflowing source of water, with blood and filth.
⁷ Later, you let your people go thirsty
    to let them experience how their enemies were punished.
⁸ Then you gave your people plenty of water unexpectedly.ᵃ
⁹ When you tested your people,
    even though you disciplined them mercifully,
      they realized how you became angry, judged,
        and tormented the Egyptians.
¹⁰ You warned your people as a father warns his children.
  But you condemned the Egyptians
    as a ruthless king condemns his people.
¹¹ In addition, all the Egyptians suffered in the same way,
    whether they were near or far away.
¹² Certainly, they suffered twice as much pain,
    and they groaned when they remembered what had happened.
¹³ When they heard that the same thing which was used
      to punish them
    was used to show kindness to your people,
      they realized that you had done this, Lord.
¹⁴ The Egyptians had mocked and refused ⌊to listen to⌋ Moses,
    who had been abandoned as a baby a long time ago and left
      to die.
  But in the end, they admired him for the way things turned out.
    The thirst that the Egyptians had was much worse than
      the thirst that your people had.

The Lord's Patience With the Egyptians
¹⁵ The Egyptians' foolish and wicked thoughts led them astray
    so that they worshiped dumb snakes and animals.
  For that reason, you sent many dumb animals to punish them.

ᵃ 11:8 The sentences in verses 6-8 have been rearranged to express the complex Greek
paragraph structure more clearly in English.

¹⁶ You did this so that the Egyptians would realize
  that those who sin are punished by the very sins they commit.
¹⁷ Your almighty power created the universe
  out of material that had no form.
  You could have sent many bears or ferocious lions to attack them.
¹⁸ You could have created new, vicious animals that no one
    has heard of:
  animals that breathe out fire, blow out smoke,
    or shoot terrifying sparks from their eyes.
¹⁹ These animals wouldn't have had to harm the Egyptians
    to kill them.
  The Egyptians would have been scared to death
    just from looking at these animals.
²⁰ Even without these animals, you could have killed these people
  with one breath when you pursued them with justice.
  You could have blown them away with the slightest show
    of your power.
  But you decided to consider every detail of everything you do.

²¹ You are always able to use your great power.
  Who can stand up to your might?
²² To you, the entire universe is like dust on a scale
  and like a drop of morning dew on the ground.
²³ You show mercy to everyone, even though you can do
    anything you want.
  You overlook the sins that people commit
    so that people can change the way they think and act.
²⁴ You love everything that exists.
  You don't despise anything that you've made.
  If there was something you hated, you wouldn't have made it.
²⁵ How could anything last if you didn't want it to?
  How could anything survive if you didn't allow it?
²⁶ You spare everything, because everything is yours, Lord,
  and you love every living thing.

12 ¹ Your eternal spirit is in everything.
  ² That's why, little by little, you correct people who go astray.
  You remind them about what they have done wrong,
    and you warn them so that they'll free themselves
      from their evil ways and trust you, Lord.

The Lord's Patience With the Canaanites

³ You hated the Canaanites, the people who lived long ago in your
holy land, ⁴ because you hated what they did. They practiced magic, cel-

ebrated unholy ceremonies, ⁵murdered their children without mercy, and ate human flesh and blood at their religious festivals. These people had been initiated into wild cults ⁶in which parents murdered helpless children. You wanted our ancestors to destroy these people ⁷so that the land you like best of all would be a good place for your people to settle. ⁸But you showed mercy even to these Canaanites, since they, too, were human. You sent hornets ahead of your army to destroy them little by little. ⁹You could have allowed your people to destroy in battle those who don't worship you. You also could have destroyed them immediately with terrifying animals or with one harsh command. ¹⁰But you carried out your sentence against them little by little and gave them an opportunity to change the way they think and act. You knew that they were evil from the beginning, that they were wicked from birth, and that they would never change their way of thinking. ¹¹Their whole race was cursed from the beginning.

You offered them forgiveness for the sins they had committed, but not because you were afraid of anyone. ¹²So who can question you about what you've done? Who can challenge your decision? Who can bring a charge against you for destroying nations that you made? Who can come to you and defend wicked people? ¹³No god exists except you. You care for everyone. You don't have to prove that you've made the right decision. ¹⁴No king or ruler can confront you about the way you have punished people. ¹⁵You always do what is right, and you manage everything in the right way. You would never think of using your power to condemn anyone who doesn't deserve to be punished. ¹⁶Your strength is the source of justice. You show mercy to all people because you rule all people. ¹⁷You show your strength when someone doubts that your power is perfect, and you treat with contempt those who show disrespect for your power. ¹⁸Although you are a powerful ruler, you are a lenient judge. You are very merciful to us when you govern us, even though you have the power to do whatever you want.

The Israelites Learn From God's Patience

¹⁹By what you have done, you have taught your people that those who worship you must be kind. Also, you have given your people hope by allowing them to change the way they think and act when they have committed a sin. ²⁰You were very careful and deliberate when you punished your people's enemies. They deserved to die, yet you gave them the time and opportunity to free themselves from their evil ways. ²¹But you were strict when you judged your own people, because you swore oaths to their ancestors and promised them good things. ²²That's why you discipline us, but you punish our enemies ten thousand times more. You do this so

that we will think about your goodness when we judge others and will expect your mercy when we are judged.

People Will Receive the Punishment They Deserve

[23] You tormented those who foolishly lived wicked lives. You tormented them by using the disgusting things they worshiped. [24] They strayed far beyond the paths of error. They treated as gods ugly animals that people despised. They were deceived like thoughtless children. [25] So you mocked them by punishing them as though they were children who couldn't reason. [26] Those who paid no attention to your warning experienced the punishment they deserved. [27] When they suffered, they became angry with those animals that they thought were gods, because these were the same animals by which they were punished. Then they realized that you are the true God, the one whom they had refused to acknowledge in the past. That's why they received this final punishment.

The Foolishness of Worshiping Nature

13 [1] All people who don't know God are foolish by nature. From the good things they see, they aren't able to learn anything about the God who exists. Even while studying the things he has made, they don't recognize the one who made them. [2] Instead, they think that fire, wind, breezes, stars, raging water, and the sun and moon are the gods that rule the world. [3] People are fascinated by the beauty of these things and accept them as gods. But these people need to realize that the Lord is far better than these things. After all, he is the creator of beauty, and he created them. [4] So if people are amazed by the power these things display, they need to understand that the one who made them is much more powerful. [5] People can see the creator in the spectacular beauty of these things.

[6] Maybe we're blaming these people too much. Maybe they really want to find God, but they become deceived while searching for him. [7] They're deeply involved in studying everything that God has made. So they continue to investigate until they are convinced that the things they see are gods, because these things are so beautiful. [8] Yet, even these people have no excuse. [9] If they were able to understand things that were created, why couldn't they quickly discover the creator of these things?

The Hopelessness of Worshiping Idols

[10] People who put their hope in dead things are pathetic. They call things that humans have made gods. But these things are only copies of animals made out of gold and silver by some artist, or else they are useless stones that someone had worked on long ago.

[11] For example, some carpenter cuts down a tree that he can easily handle. He carefully strips off all its bark and skillfully makes an object

that can serve a useful purpose. ¹²Then he burns the scraps of wood left from his work to cook his food and eats until he is full. ¹³But he takes one useless scrap, a crooked piece full of knots, and carefully whittles it in his spare time. With skill he shapes it into something that looks human ¹⁴or into some kind of dumb animal. Then he paints it red, covering every blemish, and puts makeup on its face. ¹⁵Next, he makes a special shelf for it on a wall ⌊in his house⌋, sets it there, and nails it to the shelf. ¹⁶He handles it very carefully so that it won't fall, because he knows that it can't help itself. After all, it's only an idol, and it needs to be helped. ¹⁷Yet, when he prays about his possessions, his marriage, and his children, he's not ashamed to pray to a thing that has no life. For health, he appeals to something that's sick. ¹⁸For life, he prays to something that's dead. For help, he goes to something that can't help anyone. For a safe journey, he turns to something that can't even walk. ¹⁹For employment, money, and success, he looks to something that has absolutely nothing to offer.

14 ¹Here's another example of idolatry. A person who is planning to board a ship that will sail on the stormy seas will pray for help to a piece of wood that's more helpless than the ship he's traveling on. ²Someone who wanted to earn a living designed that ship, but wisdom was the one who built it. ³However, it's your care that steers the ship, Father. You make a highway through the sea and a safe pathway through the waves. ⁴You have shown that you can save people from every danger. So anyone can travel by sea, even a person who doesn't have any sailing skills. ⁵You want everything that your wisdom has made to be put to use. That's why people who trust their lives to the smallest piece of wood can pass through rough water in a boat and reach land safely.

⁶Even in the beginning, when arrogant giants were being destroyed, Noah, the world's only hope for survival, took refuge in a boat. Because your hands steered the boat, Noah provided the world with a family to carry on the human race. ⁷This kind of wood, through which justice comes, is blessed. ⁸But an idol, which someone made, is cursed, and so is the person who made it. The person is cursed because he made it, and the object which decays is cursed because people call it a god. ⁹God hates people who don't worship him the same way he hates the sinful way they live. ¹⁰So the object that was made will be punished together with the person who offers sacrifices to it. ¹¹That's why God will punish the idols of every nation. They have become disgusting things in God's creation. Idols are traps that catch humans, snares that capture foolish people.

The Origin and Consequences of Idol Worship

¹²The idea of making idols is the beginning of sexual sin. When they were invented, life was ruined. ¹³Idols didn't exist in the beginning, and they won't last forever. ¹⁴They came into the world through the imagina-

tion of conceited humans. For that reason, a quick end has been planned for them.

¹⁵Consider the following example. A father was overcome with grief over the unexpected death of his child. So he made a statue of his child and honored a dead human being as a god. He handed down secret rituals and ceremonies to his family. ¹⁶In time, this sinful tradition grew strong and was observed as a custom.

In addition, rulers began to command people to worship carved statues. ¹⁷This is why it happened. People who lived far away from their rulers couldn't honor them in person. So they made a statue of the king whom they honored and pretended that he was present, even though he was far away. By doing this, they would flatter their king by showing him that they were devoted to him, even though he was absent.

¹⁸Eventually, ambitious artists caused this kind of worship to spread, even among people who didn't know the king. ¹⁹An artist, wishing to please his ruler, would skillfully make a statue of him that looked better than the ruler actually looked. ²⁰Then crowds were attracted by his artistic work. So the ruler whom they honored became an object of worship. Earlier, they had honored him only as a human being. ²¹This became a trap in people's lives. People living in slavery, whether because of a disaster or a tyrant, gave to sticks and stones a name that belongs only to the true God.

²²It wasn't enough for them to be wrong about their knowledge of the true God. Their lives were a constant struggle due to ignorance, yet they wrongly thought their wicked lives were peaceful. ²³They offered children as sacrifices, held secret ceremonies, and had wild orgies that involved strange rituals. ²⁴They no longer kept their lives or their marriages free from sexual sins. They murdered each other or caused each other suffering by committing adultery. ²⁵Everything they did was mixed up with bloodshed and murder, fraud, corruption, treachery, disorder, perjury, ²⁶harassment, ingratitude, perversion, homosexuality, irregular marriages, adultery, and promiscuity. ²⁷Clearly, the worship of false gods is the beginning, cause, and end of every evil. Their names should never be mentioned. ²⁸People who worship them are raving lunatics, and they love it. They prophesy lies, live wicked lives, and are quick to commit perjury. ²⁹They lie under oath and expect that nothing bad will happen to them because they trust false gods, which are not alive. ³⁰But justice will punish them on two counts: One, they devoted themselves to false gods because they thought about God in the wrong way. And two, they were wicked and lied under oath because they despised everything that is holy. ³¹The false gods that people swear oaths to have no power. But justice will always punish sinners because of the wicked things they've done.

God's People Reject Idolatry

15 ¹God, you are kind, true, and patient, and you govern everything mercifully. ²Even if we sin, we're still yours because we know your power. But we won't sin, because we know that you consider us to be your people. ³To know you is to know justice, and to know your power is to know the source of immortality. ⁴Certainly, we haven't been deceived by human artists and their evil ideas or by some useless pictures made by painters, who sketch figures and paint them with different colors. ⁵These pictures get foolish people excited so that they desire a lifeless figure of an image. ⁶Some people love these evil pictures. They sacrifice to them, desire them, and worship them. They get what they deserve when they put their confidence in these pictures.

People Should Know Not To Make and Worship Idols

⁷A potter works very hard with soft clay to make different objects. He decides how each object will be used. He uses the same clay and the same technique to make some objects that are honored and some that are not. ⁸So this wicked potter makes a useless god from the same clay that the potter himself originally came from not long ago. After a little while, when his life is demanded back, he will return to the earth from which he was taken. ⁹He doesn't care that he's destined to die or that his life is short. He competes with people who work with gold and silver, and he copies the objects that people who work in copper make. He considers it an honor to make phony gods. ¹⁰His brain is fried, and everything he hopes for is worth less than dirt. His life has less honor than the clay he uses ¹¹because he has never known the one who made him, the one who breathed into him creativity and a living spirit. ¹²So he thinks that human existence is simply a game and that life is a carnival where he can make money. He thinks that people should make money any way they can, even if they know it's wrong. ¹³Clearly, the potter knows better than anyone else that he is sinning when he takes material from the earth and makes statues of gods which will break.

¹⁴The most foolish people of all are the enemies who oppressed your people. They're more helpless than an infant ¹⁵because they thought that all the idols of the nations were really gods. Yet, these idols have eyes that can't see, noses that can't breathe, ears that can't hear, fingers that can't feel, and feet that can't walk. ¹⁶After all, a human being made these idols. Yet, his own spirit is on loan from God. Certainly, no human can make a god that is equal to a human being. ¹⁷Potters are going to die, and everything they make with their evil hands is dead. But they are better than the objects they make ⌐for people⌐ to worship. At least potters are alive, but idols never were and never will be.

Animals Torment Egypt but Serve as Food for Israel

[18]Furthermore, some people worship even the animals that people hate most. When compared to other creatures, these animals are worse because they're dumber. [19]So no one wants these animals because they're ugly. They don't have God's praise or his blessing.

16 [1]The Egyptians received the punishment they deserved through similar creatures, and they were tormented by swarms of them. [2]But instead of punishing your people, you treated them with kindness. You gave them food in an unusual way to satisfy their appetites. You gave them quails to eat. [3]When the Egyptians wanted food, they lost their appetites because the creatures you sent them were so disgusting. By contrast, your people were in need of food for only a short time. Then they ate the food that you gave them. [4]The Egyptians had to experience something that they couldn't avoid, but your people merely had to see how their enemies were being tormented.

Israelites Saved From Snakes; Egyptians Die From Insects

[5]When fierce snakes attacked your people and the bites of these coiled serpents were killing them, you didn't stay angry with your people for very long. [6]Your people were terrified for only a little while. Then you gave them the bronze snake. It was a symbol of how you would save them, and it reminded them of what your laws demand. [7]The people who turned for help to that symbol were saved, not by what they saw, but by you, the savior of all people. [8]Also, by this event, you convinced our enemies that you are the one who rescues people from every evil. [9]Our enemies died from the bites of locusts and flies. No one could find a way to cure them, because they deserved to be punished by such things. [10]By contrast, your people were not defeated even by the bites of poisonous snakes, because, in your mercy, you came to help them and cure them. [11]They were bitten so that they would remember what you had told them. But they were quickly saved so that they wouldn't forget and fail to respond to your kindness. [12]They weren't cured by any medicine or ointment, Lord. Your word healed them. [13]You have power over life and death. You can lead people to the gates of death and back again. [14]An evil person can kill someone, but he can't breathe life into that person again or free that person from death.

Food for Israel; No Food for Egypt

[15]It is impossible to escape from your power. [16]You used your strength to punish people who refused to acknowledge you. They were pursued by rains, hail, and storms that they couldn't avoid, and they were burned up by fire. [17]The most remarkable thing was that the fire burned better

in water, which normally puts fire out. The universe defends people who worship you. [18]At one time, the flames died down so that they wouldn't burn up the creatures sent to attack the people who don't worship you. This happened so that these people could see that God's judgment was pursuing them. [19]At another time, even in the rain, the flames burned more intensely than ever and destroyed the crops in the land where those wicked people lived.

[20]Instead of punishing your people, you gave them the food that angels eat. You didn't get tired when you supplied them with bread from heaven that was ready to eat. The bread that you provided satisfied every person, and it tasted good to everyone. [21]This showed how good you are to your children. You served all those who took the bread by satisfying their sinful desire, because the bread changed itself to taste the way every person wanted. [22]But this bread, which looked like snow and ice, didn't melt in the fire. Then your people realized that the fire, which was accompanied by hail, lightning, and rain, was destroying their enemies' crops. [23]In addition, this fire even held back its own power so that your people could be fed.

[24]Certainly, creation serves you, because you made it. Creation works hard to punish wicked people, but it relaxes to show kindness to those who trust you. [25]So even at that time, creation changed in many ways. It did so to show how you freely and fully served each person the food he needed and wanted. [26]Lord, you did this so that your children, whom you loved, would learn that crops are not what keep people alive. Instead, your word is what keeps those who trust you alive. [27]The food that wasn't destroyed by the fire melted immediately when warmed by one ray of the sun. [28]This happened so that your people would learn to get up before sunrise to give you thanks and pray to you. [29]Whatever an ungrateful person hopes for will melt like frost and will disappear like water down a drain.

Darkness for Egypt; Light for Israel

17 [1]Lord, your judgments are difficult to understand and hard to explain. That's why people who haven't been taught them go astray. [2]The Egyptians, who didn't have your teachings, thought that they had gained control of our holy nation. When this happened, the darkness captured them and imprisoned them in a long night. They lay imprisoned in their own houses because they had run away from your eternal care. [3]They were scattered, frightened, and upset because they were seeing things. They thought their sins would remain secret and unnoticed if they simply forgot about them. [4]They couldn't find protection from their fears, even when they were inside their houses. They heard frightening noises all around them. Gloomy ghosts with grim faces ap-

peared to them. ⁵Not even a blazing fire could give them light, and the bright shining stars weren't able to light up that dreadful night. ⁶Their only light was a fire that flashed here and there and filled them with fear. In their terror, they thought that the fire they saw was worse than the things they could no longer see. ⁷So this made their belief in magic seem foolish. The wisdom that they had bragged about turned out to be completely ridiculous. ⁸These people, who had promised to treat the fears and mental illnesses of sick people, were themselves sick with irrational fears. ⁹Nothing frightening was there to terrify them, but they were scared by prowling wild animals and hissing snakes. ¹⁰They even refused to look around the room, although it couldn't be avoided. So they were very afraid when they died.

¹¹Evil is a cowardly thing and condemns itself. Evil, because of its guilty conscience, always exaggerates its difficulties. ¹²Clearly, fear is nothing but the refusal to accept the help that reason offers. ¹³When people fail to rely on reason because of their fears, they think that it's better to be ignorant than to know what is tormenting them.

¹⁴The Egyptians slept through the night, which really had no power over them. They slept through the night like those who are in the powerless depths of hell. ¹⁵Still, they were haunted by frightening ghosts and were paralyzed because they surrendered themselves to an unexpected fear that suddenly overwhelmed them. ¹⁶So those who fell down were confined to the place where they fell as though they were in a prison without bars. ¹⁷Whether they were farmers, shepherds, or people who worked in the desert, they waited for their inescapable fate, ¹⁸because the chain of darkness had bound all of them. They were paralyzed with fear by the whistling of the wind, the singing of birds in a tree, the roaring of rushing water, ¹⁹the crashing of falling rocks, the rustling of animals that they couldn't see, the howling of wild animals, or a recurring echo from the mountains. ²⁰Yet the whole world had the full light of day and went about its work without any problems. ²¹But this heavy night affected only those people. It was a symbol of the darkness that waited for them. However, they were more of a burden to themselves than the darkness was.

18 ¹Lord, your holy people had all the light they needed. The Egyptians heard your people, but they couldn't see them. They thought that your holy people were fortunate not to have suffered. ²Also, the Egyptians were thankful that your people had not harmed them for the evil things they had done. So they continued to beg your people to do them a favor and leave ⌞their country⌟.

³While you gave the Egyptians darkness, you provided your people with a blazing column of fire to guide them as they traveled through unfamiliar territories. That column was like the sun, but it didn't hurt them

as they made their difficult trip. ⁴The Egyptians certainly deserved to be without light and to be imprisoned in darkness. They had imprisoned your people, the people through whom the eternal light of your teachings would be given to the world.

Egypt's Children Are Killed; God's Children Are Rescued

⁵The Egyptians planned to kill the infants of your holy people. So after one of your children, Moses, had been left outside to die and was rescued, you took away a large number of their children to punish them for their evil plan. You also punished them by drowning their army in deep water. ⁶Our ancestors were told in advance about that night so that they could confidently and joyfully trust your promises and believe that these promises would come true. ⁷So your people expected that they would be rescued and that their enemies would be destroyed. ⁸You used the same power to call us to yourself and to honor us that you used to punish our enemies. ⁹Your holy children had been secretly offering sacrifices to you. They agreed to follow your teachings and to share both blessings and dangers alike. Even at that time they were singing the hymns of praise that their ancestors had sung.

¹⁰But their enemies' sad cries echoed all around, and the pitiful sound of parents crying for their children could be heard everywhere. ¹¹Slaves suffered the same punishment as their masters. Common people suffered the same loss as the king. ¹²There were so many people who died that the bodies couldn't be counted. There weren't enough people left alive to bury them all, because their most precious children had been destroyed instantly. ¹³The Egyptians didn't believe anything you said because they trusted the magic they practiced. Yet, when the first male child born in every family was destroyed, they admitted that Israel was God's son.

¹⁴When everything was peaceful and quiet and midnight had come quickly, ¹⁵your all-powerful word came down to earth from your royal throne in heaven. Like a fierce warrior with a sharp sword,ᵃ your word came into a doomed land ¹⁶and carried out your strict order. Your word stood like a warrior with its feet on the earth and its head in the sky. It filled every place with death. ¹⁷Immediately, nightmares terrified the children who were going to die, and unexpected fears overwhelmed them. ¹⁸Wherever they were dying, these children told others why they were being punished. ¹⁹Their terrifying dreams revealed to them in advance why they were suffering so that they wouldn't die without knowing the reason.

ᵃ 18:15 Part of verse 16 has been placed in verse 15 to express the complex Greek sentence structure more clearly in English.

Prayer Rescues the People of Israel From Death

²⁰ Those who worshiped you also experienced death. A large number of them were slaughtered in the desert. However, your anger didn't last very long. ²¹Aaron, an innocent man, rushed to their defense. He used the armor of his priestly ministry—the prayers and incense offered for forgiveness—to withstand your fury, put an end to the disaster, and show that he was your servant. ²²He didn't overcome your bitter anger with his own strength or with weapons. Instead, his prayers stopped you from punishing them by reminding you of the pledges and promises*a* you made to our ancestors. ²³When dead bodies were piled on top of each other, he interceded, stopped your anger, and prevented it from killing those who were still living. ²⁴The designs on his long robe were symbols of the entire universe. The glorious names of our ancestors were engraved on the four rows of precious stones fastened on his breastplate. Your majestic name was written on the crown that was on his head. ²⁵The angel of death was afraid of these things and backed down. This single experience of your anger was enough ⌞for your people⌟.

The Lord Protects Israel but Punishes Egypt

19 ¹Lord, you showed no mercy to the Egyptians. Your anger toward them never ended. You knew in advance what they were going to do. ²You knew that they would allow your people to go and that they would help your people to leave quickly. But you also knew that they would change their minds and eventually chase after your people. ³So while the Egyptians were still mourning beside the graves of their dead, they foolishly thought that your people were runaway slaves. So even though the Egyptians had just begged and forced them to leave, they chased after them. ⁴You made the Egyptians forget what had happened and led them to do this. As a result, they received their final punishment with its torments. They deserved this fate. ⁵At the Red Sea, they died in an unusual way, but your people experienced a remarkable journey.

⁶ The entire creation obeyed your commands and acted in a way that kept your people from harm. ⁷Your people saw the cloud that overshadowed their camp and dry land appearing where water had once been. They saw a clear way out of the Red Sea through a grassy plain that led out of the pounding waves. ⁸Your people were a nation protected by your power. After they had seen the wonderful things you had done, they passed through those pounding waves. ⁹They were like horses in a pasture and like lambs jumping around, as they praised you, Lord, for rescuing them. ¹⁰They still remembered what had happened in Egypt, the land where

---

a 18:22 Or "covenants."

they had been slaves. They remembered how the land became filled with gnats instead of cattle and how the river swarmed with large numbers of frogs instead of fish. [11]Later, when they wanted more appetizing food and asked for it, they saw a kind of bird that was new to them. [12]Quails came inland from the sea to satisfy their hunger.

[13]Severe thunderstorms served as warnings to the Egyptians that they were about to be punished. Those sinners received a fair punishment for the evil things they had done. They had certainly shown a vicious hatred toward their guests. [14]Other nations had refused to welcome unknown people when they came to them. But these Egyptians made slaves of their own guests, who were their friends. [15]But that's not all. You will punish them in some way because they didn't welcome foreigners with kindness. [16]After the Egyptians had given your people a warm welcome and treated them as equals, they abused them with terrible kinds of work. [17]They were struck with blindness just like the people from Sodom who were at the door of Lot, a man who worshiped you. When they were in complete darkness, each person tried to find the way to his own door.

The Lord Uses Nature To Help His People

[18]Nature changed its arrangement in the same way that the rhythm of notes on a harp changes the beat of a tune, even though each note remains the same. A person can arrive at this conclusion by taking a close look at what happened. [19]People, who live on dry land, went through water like fish, and frogs, which live in water, moved onto the land. [20]Fire burned in water, and water didn't put the fire out. [21]On land, the flames didn't burn up animals, even though the animals walked through them. Flames didn't even melt the heavenly food, which looked like ice, food that would have ordinarily melted.

[22]Lord, you have praised and honored your people in every way. You have never failed to help them at any time or in any place.

Sirach

Foreword

Many great truths have been given to us through Moses' Teachings, the Prophets, and the writers who followed them. We should praise Israel for the instruction and wisdom ⌞its writers have provided⌟. Now, those who read the Scriptures must not keep their knowledge of them to themselves. But, as people who love to learn, they must help others learn ⌞these Scriptures⌟ through the spoken and written word.

Because my grandfather Jesus Ben Sirach had devoted himself to reading Moses' Teachings, the Prophets, and the other books from our ancestors, he became an expert in them. This led him to write about the instruction and wisdom contained in them. By becoming familiar with his book, those who love to learn will be able to make even greater progress in living according to the Lord's Teachings.

I encourage you to be tolerant and open-minded when you read my grandfather's book. I ask you to be forgiving where, despite my best efforts, I may not have translated some phrases very well. Something originally written in Hebrew does not have the same force when translated into another language. This is true of this book, as well as Moses' Teachings, the Prophets, and the rest of the books. Reading a translation of a book is much different from reading it in the original language.

I went to Egypt in the thirty-eighth year of King Euergetes' reign. During my stay there, I found a copy ⌞of my grandfather's book⌟, which offered me a great deal of guidance. I felt the need to translate this book. During that time, I applied my skill day and night to finish translating the book. I published it for those who live in foreign countries and for those who are willing to learn the Lord's Teachings and want to live according to them.

Wisdom's Origin

1 ¹All wisdom comes from the Lord,
　　and it remains with him forever.
　²Who can count the sand on the seashore, the drops of rain,
　　or the days of eternity?

³Who can search the height of the sky, the width of the earth,
  the depth of the ocean, or wisdom?
⁴Wisdom was created before everything,
  and useful knowledge has existed since the beginning.ᵃ
⁶Has the source of wisdom ever been revealed to anyone?
  Who knows its secrets?ᵇ
⁸Only the one who sits on the throne is wise.
  He should be greatly feared.
⁹The Lord is the one who created wisdom.
  He saw it and measured it.
  He applied it to everything he made.
¹⁰ He applied as much of it to every living creature as he wanted.
  He made it available to those who love him.

The Fear of the Lord in Relation to Wisdom

¹¹The fear of the Lord brings honor, praise,
  happiness, and a crown of joy.
¹²The fear of the Lord delights the heart.
  It gives happiness, joy, and long life.
¹³Everything will end well for people who fear the Lord.
  They will be blessed on the day of their death.
¹⁴To fear the Lord is the beginning of wisdom.
  Wisdom forms in faithful people before they are born.
¹⁵ It has made an everlasting home in humans.
  It will be trusted by their descendants.
¹⁶The fear of the Lord fills a person with wisdom.
  Wisdom overwhelms humans with its gifts.
¹⁷ It fills all their homes with treasures
    and their storehouses with its produce.
¹⁸The fear of the Lord is a crown of wisdom.
  It makes peace and good health flourish.
¹⁹ It produces knowledge and the ability to make wise decisions.
  It gives more honor to those who hold on to it tightly.
²⁰To fear the Lord is the root of wisdom,
  and its branches are long life.ᶜ

Anger Versus Patience

²²No one can excuse unjustifiable anger,
  because anger leads to self-destruction.

ᵃ 1:4 Some ancient sources insert another verse.
ᵇ 1:6 Some ancient sources insert another verse.
ᶜ 1:20 Some ancient sources insert another verse.

²³Patient people stay calm until the right moment.
  Then joy returns to them.
²⁴They do not speak until the right moment.
  Then they gain a reputation for their good sense.

Wisdom and Humility

²⁵Examples of knowledge are among wisdom's treasures.
  Being devout is disgusting to a sinner.
²⁶If you want wisdom, then obey the commandments,
  and the Lord will shower you with wisdom.
²⁷The fear of the Lord is wisdom and instruction.
  He is pleased with faithfulness and humility.
²⁸Don't stop fearing the Lord.
  When you approach him, don't say one thing but think another.
²⁹Don't be a hypocrite toward people.
  Instead, watch what you say.
³⁰Don't be arrogant, or else you may fall and disgrace yourself.
  The Lord will reveal your secrets
    and throw you down in front of the whole assembly
      because you didn't fear the Lord
        and your heart was full of deceit.

Serving the Lord Is Difficult at Times

2 ¹My child, if you're going to be the Lord's servant,
  be ready to be tested.
² Make sure your heart is in the right place, and endure
    the tests.
  Don't be hasty when difficult times come.
³ Don't abandon the Lord. Instead, cling to him
    so that you may be honored in your last days.
⁴ Accept whatever happens to you,
    and be patient in times of humiliation.
⁵ Gold is tested in fire,
    and those who are found acceptable
      are tested in a furnace of humiliation.
⁶ Trust the Lord, and he will help you.
  Follow the Lord's straight paths, and have confidence in him.
⁷You people who fear the Lord should wait for his mercy.
  Do not stray, or else you may fall.
⁸You people who fear the Lord should trust him,
  and you won't lose your reward.
⁹You people who fear the Lord should hope for good things,
  for everlasting joy and mercy.

¹⁰Look at previous generations, and consider this:
Has anyone ever trusted the Lord and been disappointed
    by him?
Has anyone ever feared the Lord and been abandoned by him?
Has anyone ever prayed to the Lord and been rejected by him?
¹¹The Lord is compassionate and merciful.
He forgives sins, and he saves people in times of distress.

No Protection for Those Who Give Up

¹²How horrible it will be for cowards, for those who give up,
    and for sinners who lead double lives.
¹³How horrible it will be for those who give up because
    they don't believe.
They won't have any protection.
¹⁴How horrible it will be for you people who have lost hope.
What will you do when the Lord appears?

Follow the Lord No Matter What

¹⁵You people who fear the Lord should obey his words.
You who love him should follow his ways.
¹⁶You people who fear the Lord should do your best to please him.
You who love him should be devoted to his teachings.
¹⁷You people who fear the Lord should get ready
    to humble yourselves in his presence.
¹⁸Let us fall into the Lord's hands,
    but not into human hands,
        because the Lord's mercy is as great as his majesty.

Respect for Parents

3 ¹Children, listen to me because I'm your father.
    Do what I tell you, and you will be safe.
²   The Lord honors a father more than his children.
    He confirms a mother's authority over her children.

³Those who honor their fathers make peace with the Lord
    for their sins,
⁴   and those who respect their mothers
    are like those who store treasures.
⁵Those who honor their fathers will find joy in their own children,
    and when they pray, they will be heard.
⁶Those who respect their fathers will live long lives,
    and those who obey the Lord are a comfort to their mothers.
⁷   They serve their parents in the same way
        that they serve their Lord.

[8] Honor your father by what you say and do
    so that you may have his blessing.
[9] A father's blessing makes the families of his children strong,
    but a mother's curse destroys the ties that bind
       the family together.
[10] Don't make yourself look good by making your father look bad.
    When your father looks bad, you look bad.
[11] Children receive honor when their father is honored.
    Children are disgraced when their mother is not respected.

[12] My child, help your father in his old age.
    Don't make him grieve as long as he lives.
[13]   Be patient with him when his mind fails.
    Since you have all your faculties, you don't have the right to
       despise him.
[14] The kindness you show to your father will not be forgotten.
    It will be taken into account when you sin.
[15]   It will be remembered in your favor when you are in distress.
    Your sins will melt away like frost in the sunshine.
[16] Whoever abandons his father is like someone who curses God.
    Whoever makes his mother angry is cursed by the Lord.

Being Humble

[17] My child, carry out your duties humbly.
    Then you will be loved more than those who give
       expensive gifts.[a]
[18] The more important you are, the more humble you must be.
    Then you will find favor in the Lord's presence.[b]
[20] The Lord's power is great,
    but he accepts honor from humble people.
[21] Don't pry into matters that are too difficult for you.
    Don't investigate things that you are not strong enough to handle.
[22] Reflect on what the Lord has commanded you to do.
    What he has kept hidden is none of your business.
[23] Don't meddle in affairs that are beyond you,
    because you have already been shown more than you
       can understand.
[24] Hasty decisions have led many astray,
    and wrong ideas have clouded people's judgment.[c]
[26] Being stubborn will eventually get you into trouble.
    Whoever loves danger will die as a result of it.

---

[a] 3:17 Or "by those whom God accepts."
[b] 3:18 Some ancient sources insert another verse.
[c] 3:24 Some ancient sources insert another verse.

²⁷Being stubborn will burden you with all sorts of trouble.
    A sinner piles one sin on top of another.
²⁸Arrogance is a disease for which there is no cure
    because evil is too firmly rooted in an arrogant person.
²⁹A sensible person appreciates stories used as illustrations.
    A wise person likes to have an attentive audience.

Giving Gifts to the Poor

³⁰As water extinguishes a raging fire,
    so giving gifts to the poor makes peace with God for sins.
³¹Whoever repays favors keeps the future in mind.
    When that person begins to stumble, he will find support.

4 ¹My child, don't keep poor people from making a living
    or tease needy people.
²Don't make hungry people resentful
    or infuriate those in poverty.
³Don't add to the troubles of people who are desperate
    or wait to give handouts to beggars.
⁴Don't reject the pleas of those in distress
    or turn away from poor people.
⁵Don't look away from beggars
    or give people a reason to curse you.
⁶If someone curses you out of bitterness,
    his Creator will hear his prayer.
⁷Be popular in the community.
 Show respect to important people.
⁸Listen to poor people,
    and be polite and kind when you answer them.
⁹Rescue a victim from someone who is doing wrong.
 Don't hesitate to give a just verdict.
¹⁰Be like a father to orphans,
    and help their mothers as a husband would.
      Then you will be like a child of the Most High,
        and he will love you more than your mother does.

Wisdom Portrayed as a Woman

¹¹Wisdom helps her children rise to greatness
    and helps those who look for her.
¹²Whoever loves her loves life.
    Those who look for her early in the morning are filled with joy.
¹³Whoever holds on to her tightly receives honor.
    The Lord blesses whatever place she enters.
¹⁴Those who serve her serve the Holy One.
    The Lord loves those who love her.

¹⁵ Those who obey her will judge nations,
and all who devote themselves to her will live securely.
¹⁶ If they remain faithful, she will belong to them
and their descendants will continue to hold on to her.
¹⁷ At first she will lead them on winding paths.
She will bring them fear and dread
and will exhaust them with her discipline.
She will test them according to her standards
until she trusts them.
¹⁸ Then she'll come straight back to them and make them happy.
She'll reveal her secrets to them.
¹⁹ If they wander, she will abandon them
and hand them over to be destroyed.

General Advice

²⁰ Take advantage of opportunities, but guard against evil.
Don't be ashamed to be yourself.
²¹ One kind of disgrace leads to sin,
but another kind leads to honor and favor.

²² Don't harm your own reputation by playing favorites.[a]
Don't be intimidated, because that can lead to your downfall.[b]
²³ Don't remain silent when one word could make things right.
Don't hide your wisdom.
²⁴ Wisdom becomes known through speaking,
and knowledge is spread by word of mouth.

²⁵ Never contradict the truth.
Instead, be ashamed of your ignorance.

²⁶ Don't be ashamed to confess your sins.
Don't try to swim against a river's current.
²⁷ Don't become a fool's doormat.
Don't flatter a ruler.

²⁸ If you fight to the death for truth,
then the Lord God will fight for you.

²⁹ Don't be bold when you speak
or lazy and sluggish when you take action.
³⁰ Don't be like a lion in your own home
or suspicious[c] of your servants.

---

a 4:22 English equivalent difficult.
b 4:22 English equivalent difficult.
c 4:30 Greek meaning of this word uncertain.

³¹ Don't hold out your hands when you want something
     and be tight-fisted when you should give something.

Advice About Wealth

5 ¹ Don't rely on your money
     or say, "I have everything I need!"
² Don't count on your mind or strength
     to be able to pursue your desires.
³ Don't say, "No one is my master!"
     The Lord will certainly punish you.
⁴ Don't say, "I have sinned, but nothing has ever happened to me!"
     just because the Lord hasn't done anything to you so far.
⁵ Don't be so overconfident about the Lord's forgiveness
     that you pile one sin on top of another.
⁶ Don't say, "He has so much compassion
     that he will forgive my many sins,"
       since both mercy and anger come from him.
         Sinners will feel the weight of his anger.
⁷ Don't hesitate to return to the Lord.
  Don't postpone your return for another day,
     or else the Lord's anger will suddenly strike you.
       On the day you are punished, you will be destroyed.
⁸ Don't rely on money gained dishonestly,
     because it won't help you in difficult times.

Watch What You Say

⁹ Don't winnow^{*a*} every time the wind blows
     or follow every path you see.
       This is what a two-faced sinner does.
¹⁰ Stand firm on what you know,
     and be consistent in what you say.
¹¹ Be quick to listen
     but slow to answer.
¹² If you know what to say, then answer your neighbor.
  But if you don't, then keep your mouth shut.
¹³   Both honor and disgrace come from talking.
       A big mouth can get a person into trouble.
¹⁴   Don't be accused of being a gossip
     or use words to trap people.
  A thief will suffer shame,
       but a two-faced person will be severely condemned.
¹⁵ Don't say anything that hurts a lot or a little.

---

a 5:9 Winnowing is the process of separating husks from grain.

Don't Let Yourself Get Out of Control

6 ¹Don't be a friend one day and an enemy the next,
because a bad reputation will bring disgrace and insults.
That is what happens to two-faced sinners.
²Don't let your passions get out of control,
or else they will drain you of your strength.*

3   Your leaves will be devoured, your fruit will be destroyed,
and you will be left like a withered tree.
⁴Uncontrollable passions can destroy a person who has them
and make him the laughingstock of his enemies.

Fair-Weather Friends

⁵Pleasant conversation wins many friends,
and kind words win many friendly greetings.
⁶You might be well-liked by a lot of people,
but let only one out of a thousand be your trusted friend.
⁷When you make a friend, begin by testing him.
Don't be too quick to trust him.
⁸Some are friends only when they benefit from you,
but they won't stand by you in times of trouble.
⁹Some friends turn into enemies
and make the details of your quarrel public to embarrass you.
¹⁰Some friends sit at your table,
but they won't stand by you in times of trouble.
¹¹When you are prosperous, they try to be like you
and treat your workers like their own servants.

12   But if you suffer financial losses, they turn against you
and hide from you.
¹³Stay away from your enemies,
and beware of your friends.

A Faithful Friend

¹⁴A faithful friend is a sturdy shelter.
Whoever finds one has found a treasure.
¹⁵A faithful friend is priceless.
Nothing else is as valuable.
¹⁶A faithful friend is a life-saving medicine.
Those who fear the Lord will find one.

17   Those who fear the Lord will make lasting friendships.
They will treat their companions
as well as they treat themselves.

---

a 6:2 Hebrew; Greek "you may be torn apart as by a bull."

The Blessings of Wisdom

[18] My child, if you choose self-discipline from the time you
are young,
then when you have gray hair, you will find wisdom.
[19] Try to be as self-disciplined as a farmer.
He begins by plowing fields and planting seeds
but has to wait for a good harvest.
When you cultivate self-discipline,
you will have to work only a little while
before you eat what your work has produced.
[20] Self-discipline seems very harsh to those who are undisciplined.
Fools find it too demanding.
[21] It's a burden too heavy for them to bear.
They won't hesitate to get rid of it.
[22] Wisdom is like its name.
It is not easy for many people ⌞to use⌟.

[23] Listen, my child, and accept my opinion.
Don't reject my advice:
[24] Put your feet into wisdom's chains
and your neck into its harness.
[25] Put your shoulders under wisdom, carry it,
and don't resent its restrictions.
[26] Go after wisdom wholeheartedly,
and follow its ways with all your strength.
[27] Look for it, track it down, and it will be revealed to you.
When you get it, don't let go of it.
[28] In the end you will find the comfort wisdom gives,
and it will become a ⌞source of⌟ joy for you.
[29] Then its chains will protect you,
and its harness will be like a beautiful, long robe.
[30] Its yoke[a] will be a gold necklace,
and its ropes will be purple threads.
[31] You will wear it like a beautiful robe
and put it on like a splendid crown.

[32] If you are willing, my child, you can gain self-discipline,
and if you apply yourself, you can become clever.
[33] If you love to listen, you can become knowledgeable,
and if you pay attention, you can become wise.
[34] Stay in the company of respected leaders.
If one of them is wise, stick to that person.

---

[a] 6:30 A yoke is a wooden bar placed over the necks of work animals so that they can pull
plows or carts.

³⁵ Be willing to listen to every discussion coming from devout people,
and don't let any wise proverb escape you.
³⁶ If you see a sensible person, then get up early to visit him.
Your feet should wear out his doorstep.
³⁷ Reflect on the Lord's teachings,
and think about his commandments all the time.
He will enlighten you and grant your prayer for wisdom.

Advice About Dealing With the Public

7 ¹ Don't do anything evil, and evil will never overtake you.
² Stay away from dishonesty, and it will turn away from you.
³ Don't plant in the furrows of injustice
or else you will harvest seven times as much injustice.
⁴ Don't seek an important position from the Lord
or the place of honor from a king.
⁵ Don't try to justify your actions in the Lord's presence
or flaunt your wisdom in front of a king.
⁶ Don't try to become a judge.
You may not be strong enough to root out injustice.
You may be swayed by powerful people
and damage your integrity as a result.
⁷ Don't commit any crime against the public.
Don't disgrace yourself among the people.
⁸ Don't commit a sin twice,
because you won't go unpunished for even one sin.
⁹ Don't say, "God will take into account
the large number of offerings I've made.
The Most High God will accept the gifts I offer him."
¹⁰ Don't become impatient when you pray.
Don't forget to be kind to others.
¹¹ Don't ridicule a person who is bitter,
because there is someone who can humble him
or raise him to greatness.
¹² Don't make up any lies about your sibling
or do the same to a friend.
¹³ Refuse to tell lies
because they never result in anything good.
¹⁴ Don't talk too much in an assembly of respected leaders,
and when you pray, don't repeat yourself.
¹⁵ Don't resent hard jobs, including farming,
which were created by the Most High.
¹⁶ Don't sin just because everyone else does.
Remember that God won't delay your punishment.

¹⁷Humble yourself completely
    because fire and worms are the punishment
      in store for people who don't worship God.

Advice About Your Personal Life

¹⁸Don't trade a friend for money
    or a loved one for gold from Ophir.
¹⁹Don't miss the opportunity to marry a woman who is wise
      and good,
    because her charm is worth more than gold.
²⁰Don't abuse slaves who do their work faithfully
    or hired workers who do their best.
²¹   Wholeheartedly love sensible slaves.
    Don't refuse to give them their freedom.
²²Do you have any livestock? Look after them.
    If they are profitable, keep them.
²³Do you have any children? Discipline them,
    and make them obedient from the time they are young.
²⁴Do you have any daughters? Be concerned about their decency.ᵃ
    Don't indulge them.
²⁵When you give a daughter in marriage, you've completed
      a great task.
    But give her to a sensible man.
²⁶Do you have a good wife? Don't divorce her.
    But don't trust a woman you hate.

Honoring Parents

²⁷Honor your father with all your heart,
    and don't forget about the labor pains your mother had.
²⁸   Remember that because of your parents you were born.
      How can you repay them for everything they've done
        for you?

Honoring Priests

²⁹Fear the Lord with all your soul,
    and deeply respect his priests.
³⁰Love your maker with all your strength,
    and don't forget to take care of his ministers.
³¹Fear the Lord, and honor his priests.
    As you have been commanded, give the priests their portion:
      the first produce harvested, the offering for guilt,

ᵃ 7:24 English equivalent difficult.

the shoulders from the sacrificial animals,
the sacrifice that makes people holy,
and the first produce harvested of the holy things.

Showing Compassion

³² Lend a helping hand to poor people
so that your blessing may be complete.
³³ Give generously to everyone alive,
and pay your respects to those who have died.
³⁴ Don't avoid those who are crying.
Instead, mourn with those who mourn.
³⁵ Don't hesitate to visit people who are sick.
After all, you will be loved for doing these things.
³⁶ In everything you do, remember that your life will come to an end.
By remembering this, you will never sin.

General Advice

8 ¹ Don't fight with powerful people,
or else they may gain the advantage over you.
² Don't quarrel with rich people,
or else they may turn others against you.
Gold has ruined many people,
and it has corrupted kings.
³ Don't argue with people who talk too much.
Don't add fuel to their fire.
⁴ Don't make fun of an uneducated person,
or else you may disgrace your own ancestors.
⁵ Don't insult someone who is turning away from sin.
Remember that we all deserve to be punished.
⁶ Don't despise old people,
because all of us are growing old.
⁷ Don't gloat over anyone's death.
Remember that we're all going to die.
⁸ Don't ignore what wise people say.
Instead, reflect on their proverbs,
which will teach you self-discipline
and how to serve influential people.
⁹ Don't miss the opportunity to hear what older people say.
They learned things from their parents.
Now you can learn from them how to give an answer
when you need to.

[10]Don't stir up a sinner's desire to do evil things.
    You may get caught in the backlash.[a]
[11]Don't let arrogant people get you too angry,
    or else they may trap you with your own words.
[12]Don't lend anything to someone who is stronger than you.
    But if you do lend something, consider it a loss.
[13]Don't promise a security deposit beyond your means.
    But if you promise a security deposit, be prepared to pay.
[14]Don't bring a lawsuit against a judge,
    because the verdict will be given in his favor.
[15]Don't travel with reckless people,
    because they will be a burden to you.
        They will do whatever they want,
            and you will die with them because of their stupidity.
[16]Don't pick a fight with a person who has a hot temper,
    and don't go with him into deserted areas.
        Murder means nothing to him,
            and he will attack you when no one is there to help you.
[17]Don't ask a fool for advice,
    because he can't keep your problem a secret.
[18]In front of strangers, don't do anything that should be kept secret,
    because you don't know what they'll reveal.
[19]Don't tell people everything about yourself,
    and don't accept everything they want to give you.

Advice About Women

9 [1]Don't be jealous of your wife, whom you embrace,
    or else you will teach her a bad example that will affect you.
[2]Don't let a woman have control of your life,
    or else she will walk all over you.
[3]Don't have anything to do with a loose woman,
    or else you will fall into her trap.
[4]Don't spend time with a woman who sings,
    or else you will be captivated by her charm.
[5]Don't stare at a virgin,
    or else you may create a scandal
        and end up paying damages for her.
[6]Don't let a prostitute influence you,
    or else you may lose your inheritance.
[7]Don't look around the city streets
    or wander through deserted sections.

---

[a] 8:10 English equivalent difficult.

⁸Don't look at a shapely woman,
> and don't stare at another man's beautiful wife.
>> Many have been seduced by a woman's beauty,
>>> and because of it, passion starts like a fire.

⁹Never go out to eat or drink with a married woman.
> You may become attracted to her
>> and become involved in a bloody confrontation.

Think About the People You Come in Contact With

¹⁰Don't abandon old friends,
> because new ones can't take their place.
>> A new friend is like new wine.
>>> When it has aged, you can drink it with pleasure.

¹¹Don't be jealous of the success sinners have,
> because you don't know how things will turn out for them
>> in the end.

¹²Don't enjoy what unbelievers enjoy.
Remember that they will be considered guilty as long as they live.

¹³Stay away from killers,
> and you won't be haunted with the fear of dying.
>> But if you go near them, watch your step.
>>> They may take your life.
>>>> Be fully aware that you're walking on dangerous ground
>>>>> and that you're an easy target.

¹⁴Get to know your neighbors as well as possible,
> and get advice from the wisest of them.

¹⁵Talk with sensible people,
> and let every discussion be about the teachings
>> of the Most High.

¹⁶   Your dinner companions should be righteous people.
> Your pride and joy should come from your fear of the Lord.

¹⁷A work is praised because of the skill of the artist.
> A leader is praised for his wise words.

¹⁸A person who talks too much is the terror of his city.
> A person who doesn't watch what he says is hated.

The Role of Government Leaders

10

¹A wise ruler will educate his people,
> and a sensible leader will have a well-run government.

²The way a ruler acts is the way his officials will act.
> The way a mayor acts is the way his people will act.

³An undisciplined king will ruin his people,
> but a city grows because of the good sense its rulers have.

⁴All authority on earth is in the Lord's hands.
  He will appoint the right leader for the right time.
⁵A person's success is in the Lord's hands.
  The Lord is the one who allows an official to be honored.

A Warning About Arrogance

⁶Don't get angry with your neighbor for everything he does wrong,
  and don't respond with insults.
⁷Arrogance is hated by the Lord and by people,
  and injustice is offensive to both.
⁸Empires pass from one nation to another
  because of injustice, arrogance, and greed.
⁹What do we have to brag about? We are only dust and ashes.
  Even while we're alive, our bodies are decaying.
¹⁰A long illness frustrates a doctor.
  Today's king will die tomorrow.
¹¹When a person dies,
  creeping things, maggots, and worms take over his body.
¹²Arrogance begins when a person abandons the Lord,
  when a person's heart has pulled away from his maker.
¹³Sin begins with arrogance,
  and the one who clings to sin produces disgusting things.
    For this reason the Lord brings disasters to that person,
      destroys him, and leaves no trace of him.
¹⁴The Lord overthrows kings
  and gives their thrones to humble people.
¹⁵The Lord uproots nations
  and plants humble people in their places.
¹⁶The Lord devastates the lands of the nations,
  and destroys them to the earth's foundations.
¹⁷   He carries off some of them, destroys them,
      and erases every memory of them from the earth.
¹⁸The Creator never intended for humans to be arrogant
  or violently angry.

People Who Deserve Honor

¹⁹What creatures deserve honor?
  Humans.
    Which humans deserve honor?
    Those who fear the Lord.
  What creatures deserve dishonor?
  Humans.
    Which humans deserve dishonor?
    Those who break the commandments.

²⁰ The head of a family deserves honor from that family,
　　but the Lord honors*a* only those who fear him.*b*
²² A convert, a stranger, and a poor person
　　can brag about their fear of the Lord.
²³ Despising a poor person who is sensible isn't right.
　　Honoring a person who is sinful isn't proper.
²⁴ Important people, judges, and rulers are honored,
　　but none of them is greater than the one who fears the Lord.
²⁵ Free people will work for a wise slave,
　　and a sensible person won't complain.
²⁶ Don't flaunt your wisdom when you work,
　　and don't brag when you're in need.
²⁷　　Working and having enough of everything is better
　　　　than bragging everywhere and having nothing to eat.
²⁸ My child, honor yourself by being humble,
　　and give yourself credit for what you've done.
²⁹　　Who will acquit those who condemn themselves?
　　　　Who will honor those who don't respect themselves?
³⁰ A poor person is honored because of his knowledge.
　　A rich person is honored because of his wealth.
³¹ A person who receives honor when he is poor
　　will receive even more honor when he is wealthy.
　　A person who is despised when he is wealthy
　　　　will be even more despised when he is poor.

11 ¹A humble person's wisdom will bring him recognition
　　and seat him with important people.

Appearances May Be Deceiving

²Don't praise individuals for being good-looking
　　or dislike people because of their appearance.
³A bee is small compared to other creatures that fly,
　　but it produces the sweetest of all things.
⁴Don't brag about wearing fine clothes.
　　Don't get carried away when you're honored.
　　The things the Lord has done are amazing.
　　The things he has done have been hidden from mortals.
⁵　　Many kings have been left with nothing
　　　　while the least likely people have worn their crowns.
⁶　　Many rulers have been completely disgraced,
　　　　and many honored leaders
　　　　　　have surrendered to other leaders.

---

a 10:20 English equivalent difficult.
b 10:20 Some ancient sources insert another verse.

Think Before You Speak

⁷Don't blame anyone before you examine the evidence.
   Examine first, and then criticize.
⁸Don't answer before you listen,
   and don't interrupt when someone is speaking.
⁹Don't argue about something that doesn't concern you,
   and don't join sinners when they judge a case.

Trust the Lord To Work Things Out

¹⁰My child, don't get involved in too many things.
   If you increase your activities, you are going to suffer.
   If you pursue them, you won't catch up to them,
      and by running away, you won't escape them.
¹¹Some people work hard, struggle, and are always in a hurry,
   but they still fall behind.
¹²Other people are slow and need help.
   They lack strength and live in poverty,
      but the Lord is looking out for them.
         He pulls them out of their miserable condition.
¹³   He honors them to the amazement of many people
¹⁴Good and bad, life and death,
   and poverty and wealth come from the Lord.ᵃ
¹⁷The Lord's gifts remain with devout people.
   His favor brings lasting success.
¹⁸A person can become rich by being cautious and pinching pennies.
   This is the reward he will receive:
¹⁹   When he says, "I can finally relax and enjoy
         what I've worked for!"
            he doesn't know how long he has
               before he will die and leave his wealth to others.
²⁰Keep your agreements, keep yourself busy with them,
   and grow old while you fulfill them.
²¹Don't be amazed at what sinners do.
   Instead, trust the Lord and keep working.
   The Lord can easily make a poor person instantly rich.
²²The Lord's blessings reward devout people,
   and he makes his blessings develop quickly.
²³Don't say, "I don't need anything,
   and what good can the future bring?"
²⁴Don't say, "I have everything I need,
   and what harm can the future bring?"

ᵃ 11:14 Some ancient sources insert two other verses.

²⁵ Hardships are forgotten during good times.

Good things are not remembered during bad times.

²⁶ When people die,

the Lord can easily reward them based on the way they lived.

²⁷ An hour of misery makes one forget sweet memories.

When life ends, everything a person has done is revealed.

²⁸ Don't consider anyone fortunate before he dies.

A person will be known by the children he leaves.

Think About What Others Can Do to You

²⁹ Be cautious of the people you invite into your home,

because devious people know many tricks.

³⁰ An arrogant person's intellect is like a decoy,

like a spy who looks for your weak point.

³¹   He waits for an opportunity to turn good into evil

and to find fault with anything noble.

³² A spark can start many coals on fire.

A sinner waits in ambush to shed blood.

³³ Beware of criminals because they devise evil schemes

and can ruin your reputation forever.

³⁴ If you allow a stranger into your home, he will cause you trouble.

He will make you a stranger to your own family.

Limitations to Charity

12 ¹ If you do something good, you should know who is benefiting from it.

Then you will be thanked for the good you have done.

² You will be rewarded when you do something good

for a devout person.

If he doesn't reward you, certainly the Most High will.

³ No good ever comes to the person who insists on doing evil

or to the one who doesn't give to needy people.

⁴ Give to a devout person, but do not help a sinner.

⁵   Do something good for a humble person,

but don't give anything to an unbeliever.

Don't even give him any food.

That food might make him stronger than you are.

Then you will receive twice as much evil

for all the good you have done for him.

⁶   The Most High hates sinners

and will punish unbelievers.

⁷ Give to a good person, but don't help a sinner.

Enemies

[8] During good times friends don't prove their worth.
  During bad times you know who your enemies are.
[9] When people do well, their enemies are unhappy,
    but in bad times, even their friends disappear.
[10] Never trust your enemy.
  As copper becomes corroded,
    so you will become corroded with his wickedness.
[11] Even if he humbles himself and walks bent over,
    be careful and be on your guard against him.
      Behave toward him like someone who polishes metal
        so that it doesn't become tarnished.
[12] Don't let him stand next to you,
    or else he may push you aside and take your place.
  Don't let him sit on your right side,
    or else he may try to take your seat.
      Then you will realize that what I said was true
        and be stung by what I have said.
[13] No one has pity on a snake charmer
    or an animal trainer who gets bitten.
[14]   Likewise, no one has pity on a person
      who associates with a sinner
        or becomes involved in another person's sins.
[15] An enemy may remain with you for a while,
    but if you begin to fall, he will not stay.
[16] An enemy may speak sweetly to you,
    but he is planning to throw you into a pit.
  An enemy may have tears in his eyes,
    but given the opportunity, he will kill you.
      Even that won't satisfy him.
[17] If something bad happens to you,
    you will find your enemy waiting for you.
  Pretending to help you, he will trip you up.
[18] Then he will shake his head in disgust, wring his hands,
    whisper insults, and show his true character.

Be Careful When Socializing With Other Classes

13
[1] Whoever touches tar gets dirty,
    and whoever associates with an arrogant person becomes
      like him.
[2] Don't pick up anything that is too heavy for you
    or associate with anyone who is richer or more powerful
      than you.

Why put a clay pot next to an iron kettle?
The clay pot may hit it and shatter.
³ A rich person does wrong and then adds insult to injury.
A poor person is wronged and has to apologize
for being wronged.
⁴ A rich person will exploit you if you can be of use to him,
but he will leave you if you are in need.
⁵   He will live with you as long as you have nice things.
He will take everything you have without any regret.
⁶   When he needs something from you, he will deceive you
by smiling at you and flattering you.
He will compliment you and ask you what you need.
⁷   He will embarrass you at his dinner parties
until he has taken everything you have two
or three times,
and finally, he will mock you.
Later, when he sees you in need, he will leave you
and shake his head in disgust at you.
⁸ Be careful that you are not misled
or humiliated by your own stupidity.
⁹ When a powerful person invites you somewhere, be reluctant.
Then he will encourage you even more to accept his invitation.
¹⁰ Don't be pushy, or else you may be pushed aside.
Don't appear aloof, or else you will be forgotten.
¹¹ Don't try to talk to a powerful person like an equal
or believe anything he says.
He will test you with lengthy conversations.
He will be studying you while he is smiling at you.
¹² The person who doesn't keep your secrets is cruel.
He will not keep you from being harmed or imprisoned.
¹³ Be on your guard. Be very careful
because you are walking into disaster.ᵃ

¹⁵ All creatures love their own kind,
and all people love people who are like themselves.
¹⁶ All animals gather with their own kind,
and people stick close to those like themselves.
¹⁷ Wolves have nothing in common with lambs.
Likewise, sinners have nothing in common with devout people.
¹⁸ Peace can't exist between hyenas and dogs.
Likewise, peace can't exist between rich people and poor people.
¹⁹ Wild donkeys in the wilderness are prey for lions.
Likewise, poor people are prey for rich people.

ᵃ 13:13 Some ancient sources insert another verse.

²⁰Humility is disgusting to arrogant people.

Likewise, poor people are disgusting to rich people.

²¹When a rich person stumbles, his friends will help support him,

but when a humble person falls, his friends will ignore him.

²²When a rich person makes a mistake, many come to his rescue.

Even if he says something outrageous, they praise him for it.

When a humble person makes a mistake, people criticize him.

Even if what he says makes sense, they won't listen to him.

²³When a rich person speaks, people become silent.

They praise what he said to high heaven.

When a poor person speaks, they ask, "Who do you think
you are?"

If he stumbles, they push him down.

²⁴Wealth is good if it is free from sin.

Poverty is considered evil only by unbelievers.

General Statements

²⁵A person's attitude makes the expression on his face change
either for good or bad.

²⁶A cheerful face is a sign of happiness.

Painstaking thought creates proverbs.

People Who Are Blessed

14 ¹Blessed are those who never let careless words slip from
their lips

and never need to feel guilty for such a sin.

²Blessed are those who have clear consciences

and who do not lose hope.

Scrooge

³Riches are worthless to a stingy person.

Wealth is useless to an envious person.

⁴   A stingy person may be depriving himself of things,

but he is collecting them for others.

Others will use his wealth to live lives of luxury.

⁵If a person doesn't allow himself to enjoy his own wealth,

to whom will he be generous?

⁶No one is more stingy than the person who is stingy with himself.

That is what he gets for being wicked.

⁷If he does a good deed, he does it unintentionally.

In the end he reveals his wickedness.

⁸The person who looks at what others have and envies them is evil.

He turns away and ignores their needs.

⁹The greedy person looks around and is never satisfied with what
    he has.
  Greed consumes him.
¹⁰A miser is reluctant to put even a little bit of food on his table.

Live Each Day to Its Fullest

¹¹My child, treat yourself as well as you can afford,
    and give the Lord the kind of offerings he deserves.
¹²Remember that death doesn't wait
    and that you haven't been told the date and time
        when you will go to your grave.
¹³Treat your friends well before you die.
  Reach out to them, and give them as much as you can.
¹⁴Don't deprive yourself of a single day's enjoyment.
  Don't let your share of the good things you want pass you by.
¹⁵Eventually, everything you've worked so hard for
    will be divided up and given to others.
¹⁶Give, take, and pamper yourself,
    because one cannot look for luxury in the grave.
¹⁷All living beings become old and wear out like clothes.
    The ancient decree says that everyone must die.
¹⁸Some leaves fall off a thriving tree, but others will grow
        in their places.
  Each generation is like those leaves.
    One dies, and another is born.
¹⁹The things that people make will all decay and come to an end.
  So will the people who make them.

Good People Seek Wisdom and Its Blessings

²⁰Blessed are those who think about wisdom
    and who use knowledge to consider matters carefully.
²¹   They reflect in their hearts about the way of wisdom
        and ponder its secrets.
²²   They chase wisdom as a hunter chases animals,
        and they ambush it on its path.
²³   They peer through wisdom's windows
        and listen at its doors.
²⁴   They camp near its house
        and fasten their tent pegs to its walls.
²⁵   They pitch their tents near wisdom
            and have an excellent place to camp.
²⁶   They place their children under wisdom's shelter
            and settle under its branches.

27   They are sheltered by it from the heat
      and live in its glory.

15 ¹Whoever fears the Lord will do these things.
      Whoever understands Moses' Teachings will find wisdom.
² Like a mother, wisdom will come to meet him,
      and like a young bride, it will welcome him.
³ It will give him the food of knowledge to eat
      and the water of wisdom to drink.
⁴   He will lean on wisdom and not fall.
      He will rely on it and not be put to shame.
⁵ It will make him more important than his neighbors
      and give him the ability to speak in an assembly.
⁶   He will find happiness and everlasting joy.
      His name will be remembered forever.
⁷ Foolish people will not find wisdom,
      and sinners will not see it.
⁸ It keeps its distance from arrogance,
      and liars will never remember wisdom.
⁹ Praise from a sinner's mouth is inappropriate
      because this kind of praise wasn't inspired by the Lord.
¹⁰ Praise should be an expression of wisdom,
      an expression taught by the Lord.

Don't Blame the Lord for Your Choices

¹¹ The Lord doesn't do what he hates,
      so don't say that he caused you to abandon him.
¹² The Lord has no use for sinners,
      so don't say that he misled you.
¹³ The Lord and those who fear him
      hate everything that is disgusting.
¹⁴ He created humans in the beginning,
      and he allowed them to make their own decisions.
¹⁵ You can obey his commandments
      and faithfully carry out his will, if you choose to do so.
¹⁶ He has placed fire and water in front of you.
      Reach out, and choose between the two.
¹⁷ Each person is offered life or death,
      and he will get whichever one he chooses.
¹⁸ The Lord's wisdom is vast.
      He is powerful and sees everything.
¹⁹ He keeps an eye on those who fear him,
      and he knows everything that people do.
²⁰ He hasn't commanded anyone to be wicked
      or given anyone permission to sin.

Having No Children Is Better Than Having Bad Children

16 ¹Don't wish for a lot of children in case they turn out to be worthless.

Don't be happy about children who don't worship the Lord.
²No matter how many children you may have,
   don't be happy about them unless they fear the Lord.
³Don't count on them living a long time
   or rely on a large number of them to take care of you.
   One child can be better than a thousand children.
   Dying childless would be better
      than having children who don't worship the Lord.

Punishment From God Is Inescapable for Sinners

⁴A city can be filled with people because of one sensible person,
   but it can become deserted because of senseless violence.
⁵I have seen with my own eyes many similar things,
   and I have heard with my own ears more impressive things.
⁶Fire breaks out wherever sinners assemble,
   and punishment is unleashed on disobedient nations.
⁷The Lord did not forgive the ancient giants.
   They had revolted because they were too confident
      of their strength.
⁸He didn't spare the people where Lot lived
   and was disgusted by their arrogance.
⁹He showed no mercy to that doomed nation,
   which was expelled because of its sins.
¹⁰He showed no mercy to the six hundred thousand foot soldiers
   who assembled out of defiance.
¹¹   Even if there had been only one person
      who was impossible to deal with,
         he would not have escaped punishment.
   Mercy and punishment come from the Lord.
   He shows his power in forgiveness and in anger.
¹²He is as merciful as he is strict.
   He will judge people based on what they have done.
¹³A sinner won't escape with loot,
   and a devout person's patience won't be tested forever.
¹⁴The Lord provides opportunities for people to show kindness.
   Each person is rewarded for what he does.ᵃ

The Thoughts of Crazy, Misguided People

¹⁷Don't say,

ᵃ 16:14 Some ancient sources insert two other verses.

"I've hidden from the Lord.
Who up above is going to remember me?
I won't be noticed among so many people.
What am I in comparison to the universe?"
18 Heaven, the highest heaven,
the bottomless pit, and the earth will be shaken when he comes.
19 The earth's mountains and foundations
tremble and quake when he looks at them.
20 But no human mind can comprehend the Lord's ways.
21 Most of what the Lord does is hidden
like wind that no one can see during a storm.
22 Don't say,
"Who will announce that justice has been carried out?
Who can wait for it? He is too slow in carrying out
his promise."
23 These are the kinds of thoughts that a person without insight has.
Only a crazy, misguided person would think like that.

24 Listen to me, my child, and learn.
Pay close attention to what I say.
25   I will show you self-discipline
and give you reliable information.

The Relationship Between Creator and Creation

26 In the beginning the Lord created many different things.
After making them, he set limitations for them.
27   He put them in a specific order for all time,
from beginning to end.
They don't become hungry or tired.
They don't abandon their duties.
28   They don't crowd one another,
and they never disobey him.
29   Then the Lord looked at the earth
and filled it with good things.
30   He covered the earth's surface
with all kinds of living creatures,
but they must return to dust.

17 ¹The Lord created humans out of the earth
and makes them return to dust.
2   He gave them a limited amount of time to live,
but he gave them authority over everything on earth.
3   He gave them strength like his own
and made them in his own image.

⁴ He made all other living creatures afraid of them.
   He gave humans absolute power over animals and birds.^a
⁶ He gave them the ability to reason, a tongue, eyes, ears,
      and he gave them a brain for thinking.
⁷ He filled them with knowledge and understanding
      and showed them good and evil.
⁸ He made them aware of him in their hearts
      and showed them the splendor of what he has done.
⁹ They will praise his holy name
¹⁰ by describing the splendor of what he has done.
¹¹ He gave them knowledge
      and provided them with life-giving teachings.
¹² He made an unbreakable promise to them
      and issued his decrees to them.
¹³ They have seen his glorious majesty with their own eyes
      and have heard his glorious voice
         with their own ears.
¹⁴ He said to them, "Beware of everything that is evil."
   He gave them commandments about their neighbors.
¹⁵ He always knows what people are doing.
   They are never out of his sight.^b
¹⁷ He appointed a leader for every nation,
   but Israel belongs to the Lord.^c
¹⁹ Everything the people of Israel do is as plain as day to him.
   His eyes are always focused on their ways.
²⁰ Their dishonesty is not hidden from the Lord,
      and all their sins are visible to him.^d

²² When a person gives to charity, he has made his name known to
      the Lord.
   The Lord cherishes a person's kindness like the apple of his eye.
²³ Afterwards, he will rise and repay that person.
   Then he will give him what he deserves.
²⁴ However, he gives those who change the way they think and act
      an opportunity to come back to him.
   He encourages those who are losing hope.
²⁵ Return to the Lord, and leave your sins behind.
   Pray to him, and don't be so offensive.
²⁶ Come back to the Most High, and turn away from dishonesty.
   Develop an intense hatred for what he finds disgusting.

---

^a 17:4 Some ancient sources insert another verse.
^b 17:15 Some ancient sources insert another verse.
^c 17:17 Some ancient sources insert another verse.
^d 17:20 Some ancient sources insert another verse.

²⁷ The living can give thanks,
   but the dead can't sing praises to the Most High.
²⁸ Those who are alive and well can sing praises to the Lord.
   Those who are dead and gone can no longer sing praises.
²⁹ The Lord's kindness is great,
   and so is his forgiveness for those who return to him.
³⁰ Not everything is available to humans
   because they are not immortal.
³¹ Nothing is brighter than the sun. Yet, even the sun can be eclipsed.
   Likewise, all the good that humans do can be eclipsed when they
      do evil.
³² He examines the armies of high heaven
   and all humans, who are only dust and ashes.

The Lord Is Greater Than Humans

18 ¹ The Lord, who lives forever, created the whole universe.
   ² Only he is always right.ᵃ
⁴ He hasn't given anyone the ability to understand what he
      has done.
   So who can keep track of his miracles?
⁵   Who can measure his majestic power?
   Who can fully describe his merciful deeds?
⁶   Nothing can be added to them or subtracted from them.
   No one can keep track of the Lord's amazing miracles.
⁷ When humans are finished ⌊with their reports⌋,
   they are really just beginning.
   When they stop, they are still puzzled.
⁸   What are humans, and what purpose do they serve?
   What purpose do their good or evil deeds serve?
⁹ If they live to be a hundred years old, they've lived long lives.
¹⁰   However, compared to eternity,
      their few years are like a drop of water in the ocean
      or a grain of sand on a beach.
¹¹   That is why the Lord is patient with them
   and has compassion for them.
¹²   He sees and recognizes that they are doomed to die.
   That is why he is even more forgiving.
¹³ People have compassion for people they know,
   but the Lord has compassion for everyone.
   The Lord corrects, trains, and teaches people.
   He brings them back as a shepherd brings his flock back.

ᵃ 18:2 Some ancient sources insert another verse.

¹⁴   He has compassion for those who accept his discipline
       and who eagerly accept his decrees.

Genuine Charity

¹⁵ My child, don't criticize someone while you're trying to help him,
      and don't speak harshly while you're giving him a gift.
¹⁶ As rain brings relief from scorching heat,
      so a ⌐kind⌐ word is better than a gift.
¹⁷   Isn't a ⌐kind⌐ word more valuable than a good gift?
       A compassionate person is ready to give both.
¹⁸   A fool is ungrateful and abusive.
    A gift that is reluctantly given won't make a person happy.

Change Before It's Too Late

¹⁹ Know what you're talking about before you speak.
    Take care of your health before you become sick.
²⁰ Examine yourself closely before judgment comes.
       Then when you are examined, you will find forgiveness.
²¹ Humble yourself before you become sick.
    Turn back to the Lord as soon as you have sinned.

Don't Wait To Keep Your Vows

²² Let nothing stop you from keeping your vows; start right away.
       Don't wait until you are dying to set matters straight.
²³ Before you take a vow, make sure you can keep it.
    Don't be like someone who tests the Lord.
²⁴   Think about how angry he may be with you
          when you are about to die.
       Think about the moment the Lord may pass judgment
          and not give you a second chance.
²⁵   When you have plenty to eat, think about famine.
    When you are wealthy, think about poverty and need.
²⁶   From morning to evening, conditions change.
          Everything can change quickly in the Lord's presence.

Don't Let Anything Get Out of Control

²⁷ A wise person is cautious in every situation
       and is on guard against making a mistake when sin
          is widespread.
²⁸ Every intelligent person recognizes wisdom
       and praises those who find it.
²⁹ Those who are skilled in the use of words become wise,
       and they write a lot of meaningful proverbs.

³⁰ Don't let your lust control you.
　　Instead, keep your passion under control.
³¹　　If you give in to your lust,
　　　　you will become a laughingstock to your enemies.
³² Don't pamper yourself with too much luxury,
　　or else its expense may ruin you.
³³ If you have no money in your pocket, don't borrow money
　　　　to throw a party.
　　You will become a beggar.

19 ¹ A drunken worker will never become rich.
　　Whoever despises the small things in life will gradually fail.
² Wine and women lead intelligent men astray.
　　A regular customer of prostitutes becomes more
　　　　and more shameless.
³　　Decay and worms will take possession of him.
　　That shameless person will be destroyed.
⁴ Whoever trusts others too quickly is naive.
　　Sinning hurts the sinner.
⁵ Whoever is happy about wickedness will be condemned.

You Won't Burst If You Don't Gossip

⁶ Evil loses its hold on people who hate gossip.
⁷ You have nothing to lose
　　if you never repeat a conversation.
⁸　　Don't talk about it with a friend or foe.
　　Don't reveal it unless keeping it to yourself would be a sin.
⁹　　Someone may hear or see you gossip,
　　　　and in time that person will hate you.
¹⁰ If you've heard something, let it die with you.
　　Be brave! You won't burst.
¹¹　　After hearing some gossip, a fool will suffer labor pains
　　　　like a woman giving birth to a child.
¹²　　Gossip inside a fool
　　　　is like an arrow stuck in a person's leg.

Find Out the Truth Before You Draw Any Conclusions

¹³ Find out from your friend what he has done; he may have
　　　　done nothing.
　　If he has done something, he won't do it again.
¹⁴ Find out from your neighbor what he has said; he may have
　　　　said nothing.
　　If he has said something, he won't say it again.
¹⁵ Find out from your friend what he has said or done.

Slander is common, so don't believe everything you hear
about him.
16   A person may let something slip unintentionally.
Everyone has said the wrong thing at one time or another.
17 Find out from your neighbor what he has said or done
before you threaten him.
Let the laws of the Most High take their course.*a*

Recognize Good People With the Help of Wisdom

20 To fear the Lord is the essence of wisdom.
Wisdom's goal is to live according to God's laws.*b*
22 To know about wickedness is not wisdom.
No insight is gained from sinners' advice.
23 Cleverness can be disgusting.
A fool may merely lack wisdom.
24 Being a God-fearing person who lacks understanding
is better than being a highly intelligent person who breaks
God's laws.
25 Being sharp-witted can be unfair.
Some people take advantage of a favor to win their case.

26 A scoundrel may be bent over in grief,
but inwardly, he is filled with deceit.
27   He hides his face and pretends to be deaf,
but when no one is looking, he will take advantage of you.
28   Even if he is prevented from sinning because he lacks
the strength,
he will do something evil if he finds the opportunity.

29 You can tell a lot about a person from his appearance.
You can tell that a person is sensible when you first meet.
30 A person's character is revealed by what he wears, how he laughs,
and the way he walks.

When To Speak and When Not To Speak

20 ¹A reprimand can be given at the wrong time.
A person can be wise by remaining silent.
2 Reprimanding someone is better than getting angry.
3 The person who admits his faults won't lose his good reputation.

4 The person who uses force to establish justice
is like a eunuch trying to rape a young girl.

---

a 19:17 Some ancient sources insert two other verses.
b 19:20 Some ancient sources insert another verse.

⁵One person remains silent and is considered wise,
while another person talks too much and is despised.
⁶One person remains silent because he doesn't know what to say,
while another remains silent because he knows when to speak.
⁷A wise person remains silent until the right moment,
but a bragging fool misses the right moment.
⁸Whoever talks all the time is obnoxious,
and whoever seizes control is hated.

Life's Uncertainties

⁹A person may find success in spite of hardships
and losses in spite of good fortune.
¹⁰Sometimes being generous will do you no good,
and sometimes you will get twice as much back.
¹¹Some people have suffered losses in their search for fame,
while others have risen from humble beginnings.
¹²Some find a great bargain
but later pay seven times as much in repairs.

Fools Overestimate the Good They Do

¹³With only a few words, a wise person makes himself popular.
However, polite gestures from fools are wasted.
¹⁴A fool's generosity will do you no good
because it looks bigger to him than to you.
¹⁵   He gives little, but he insults a lot.
He brags about his gift like a town crier.
Today he lends something, and tomorrow he asks for it back.
He is despised by everyone.
¹⁶Then that fool says, "I have no friends,
and no one appreciates what I do."
Those who eat with him say bad things about him
¹⁷   and frequently ridicule him.

Inappropriate Speech and Behavior

¹⁸Slipping on pavement is better than making a slip of the tongue.
Disaster will strike wicked people just as quickly.
¹⁹A rude person is like a vulgar story
that is continually retold by ignorant people.
²⁰A proverb from a fool's lips will be rejected as worthless
because he doesn't say it at the proper time.
²¹Poverty may keep a person from sinning.
When he rests, he feels no regrets.
²²A person may lose his life because of a false sense of shame,

or he may lose his life because of a false sense of honor.
²³ Another person may make promises to a friend
  because of a false sense of shame
    and turn his friend into an enemy for no reason.
²⁴ A lie leaves an ugly scar on a liar.
  The lie is continually retold by ignorant people.
²⁵   Being a thief is better than being a lifelong liar.
    However, both of them will be destroyed in the end.
²⁶ A liar's way leads to disgrace.
  His shame is always with him.

General Statements About Wise People

²⁷ A wise person receives a promotion because he knows
    how to use words.
  A clever person will be able to please important people.
²⁸ Whoever farms the land will harvest the crops.
  Important people will excuse the mistakes made by those
    who please them.
²⁹ Gifts can cloud a wise person's judgment.
  Like a muzzle, they silence criticism.
³⁰ Wisdom is worthless if it is hidden.
  A treasure is worthless if it is buried.
³¹ A person who hides his stupidity is better
  than one who hides his wisdom.

Everything Has a Good or Bad Consequence

21 ¹ My child, have you been sinning? Then stop!
    Ask the Lord to forgive your past sins.
² Run away from sin as if it were a snake
  that will bite you if you go near it.
    It has teeth like lion's teeth,
      and it can destroy human lives.
³ All lawlessness is like a two-edged sword.
  The wound it inflicts will never heal.
⁴ Terror and violence make wealth disappear.
  In the same way, an arrogant person's house will disappear.
⁵ A poor person's prayer leaves his lips
  and enters the Lord's ears.
    The Lord quickly decides how to answer that person's prayer.
⁶ Whoever hates to be corrected will live like a sinner,
  but whoever fears the Lord will turn his life over to him.
⁷ A convincing speaker may be well-known,
  but a sensible person knows

when the speaker makes a slip of the tongue.
⁸Whoever builds his house with other people's money
is like a person who gathers stones for his own tomb.
⁹A gathering of wicked people is like a bundle of straw
that will go up in flames in the end.
¹⁰A sinner's road is smoothly paved,
but it leads to a deep grave.
¹¹A person gains control of his thoughts
by obeying Moses' Teachings.
Wisdom is the goal of fearing the Lord.
¹²A person who isn't clever cannot be taught,
but some clever people inspire jealousy.
¹³A wise person's knowledge will increase like a flood,
and his advice is like a life-giving spring.
¹⁴Like a broken jar that can't hold anything,
a fool's mind can't hold any knowledge.
¹⁵When an educated person hears a wise saying,
he praises it and adds to it.
When a self-indulgent person hears it,
he laughs at it and disregards it.
¹⁶Listening to a fool is like traveling with a heavy suitcase.
However, hearing what a sensible person says is a pleasure.
¹⁷In a meeting, people look to a wise person for advice,
and what he says is taken seriously.
¹⁸To a fool, wisdom is like a house that is run-down.
A fool's knowledge has no value.
¹⁹To a person without any sense,
education is like a chain around his feet
or like handcuffs on his wrists.
²⁰   A fool laughs at the top of his lungs,
but a clever person merely smiles,
if he reacts at all.
²¹To a sensible person,
education is like a gold chain
or like a bracelet on his wrist.
²²A fool walks right into someone's house,
but a more mature person would be ashamed to do that.
²³A fool peeks into a house from the doorway,
but a well-mannered person remains outside.
²⁴An ill-mannered person eavesdrops at a doorway,
but a wise person would be too ashamed to do that.
²⁵Gossips repeat what others have said.
Others carefully consider what wise people say.

²⁶Fools speak before they think,
    but wise people think before they speak.
²⁷When unbelievers curse Satan,
    they are cursing themselves.
²⁸Someone who whispers destroys his own reputation.
    He is hated in his own neighborhood.

Lazy People Are Disgusting

22 ¹A lazy person is like a stone covered with slime.
    Everyone is repulsed by his disgrace.
²A lazy person is like manure
    that someone picks up and shakes off his hand.

Daughters

³Being the father of an undisciplined son is a disgrace.
    Having a daughter is a loss.
⁴A sensible daughter is able to get a husband,
    but a daughter who acts shamefully gives her father grief.
⁵An arrogant daughter disgraces her father and her husband.
    Both of them will despise her.

⁶A comment made at the wrong time
    is like joyful music during a time of mourning.
        However, a spanking and discipline are always appropriate.ᵃ

Fools

⁹Teaching a fool is like gluing pieces of pottery together
    or like waking someone from a deep sleep.
¹⁰Whoever tells a story to a fool
    might as well tell it to a person who is half asleep.
        When it is over, the fool will ask, "What did you say?"
¹¹Cry for a person who has died, because he has left behind the light
        of day.
    Cry for a fool, because he has left behind good sense.
    Don't cry bitterly for a person who died, because he is resting
        in peace.
    However, a fool's life is worse than death.
¹²Mourning for a person who died lasts seven days.
    However, a wicked fool causes a whole lifetime of mourning.
¹³Don't spend a lot of time talking with a fool
    or visiting a person who has no sense.
    Stay away from him, or else you may run into trouble.
    His lifestyle may rub off on you.

ᵃ 22:6 Some ancient sources insert two other verses.

If you avoid him, you will have peace of mind
and never be worn out by his insanity.
¹⁴ What kind of person is more burdensome than lead? A fool!
What else would you call him?
¹⁵ Sand, salt, and a piece of iron
are easier to bear than a person who has no sense.

¹⁶ A wood beam that is properly attached to a building
will not be shaken loose by an earthquake.
Likewise, a clear mind that has carefully thought about an issue
will not be gripped with fear.

¹⁷ A mind that uses good, common sense
is like an inscription on a polished, marble wall.
¹⁸ Pebbles on top of a wall will not stay there
when the wind blows.
Likewise, when a fool's clouded mind is gripped with fear,
it cannot stand up against any more fear.

Friends

¹⁹ If you poke someone's eye, you will make tears flow.
If you hurt someone's feelings, you will see how sensitive the
person is.
²⁰ Whoever throws stones at birds scares them away,
and whoever insults a friend destroys a friendship.
²¹ Even if you pull out a knife against your friend,
don't despair, because you can still correct the situation.
²² If you open your big mouth about your friend,
don't worry, because you can still save your friendship.
However, if you are insulting or arrogant,
if you can't keep secrets,
or if you stab people in the back,
you will make any friend run away.
²³ Gain your neighbor's trust while he is poor
so that you may share in his prosperity.
Stand by him in times of trouble
so that when he receives his inheritance, he will share it
with you.
²⁴ Insults precede bloodshed
as steam and smoke in a furnace precede a fire.
²⁵ I'm not ashamed to give shelter to a friend,
and I won't hide from him.

²⁶   But if I'm harmed because of him,
        everyone who hears what happened to me
           will stay away from him.

A Prayer To Guide My Words and Actions

²⁷I wish I could place a guard at my mouth to watch what I say
    or put an airtight seal over my lips.
        These precautions would prevent my downfall
           and keep my mouth from getting me into trouble.

23 ¹Lord, Father and Master of my life,
    don't leave me at the mercy of my own foolish words.
    Don't let what I say lead to my downfall.
²   I wish you would punish me for all my foolish thoughts
        and put wisdom in control of my mind.
        In this way you wouldn't excuse the mistakes I've made
           or overlook my sins.
³   Otherwise, my mistakes would increase,
        and my sins would multiply.
        Then I would fall in front of my adversaries,
           and my enemies would gloat over me.
⁴Lord, Father and God of my life,
    don't let me be conceited.
⁵   Take evil desires away from me.
⁶   Don't let me become a glutton.
    Don't allow lust to take control of me
        or shameless desires to take over my life.

Watch What You Say

⁷Children, learn how to control what you say.
    Whoever watches what he says will never be trapped
        by his own words.
⁸A sinner is caught because of what he says.
    Even an abusive, arrogant person is tripped up by his
        own words.

Swearing Oaths

⁹Don't become used to swearing oaths
    or continually using the name of the Holy One.
¹⁰   A servant who is always being questioned
        will never be above suspicion.
    Likewise, the person who always swears oaths
        or uses the name of the Holy One
        will never be free from sin.

¹¹Anyone who takes too many oaths is a wicked person.
His house will always be cursed.
If he commits perjury, he is guilty of sin,
and if he ignores his oaths, he is twice as guilty.
If he lies when he takes an oath, he cannot justify his action.
His house will be filled with trouble.

Vulgar Language

¹²The use of vulgar language is comparable to death.
May it never be heard among Jacob's descendants!
Devout people should avoid vulgar language,
and they shouldn't be involved in that kind of sin.
¹³Don't use vulgar, filthy language.
To speak that way is sinful.
¹⁴Remember your father and mother
when you sit with important people.
Otherwise, you may forget yourself when you are with them,
and you may act like a fool because of your bad habits.
Then you will wish that you had never been born.
You will curse the day you were born.
¹⁵Whoever continually uses abusive language
can never become self-disciplined as long as he lives.

Sexual Immorality

¹⁶Two types of people keep sinning more and more,
and a third type brings out God's anger.
Burning desires are like blazing fires.
They can't be extinguished until they burn themselves out.
Whoever commits sexual sins with a family member
won't stop until the fire burns him up.
¹⁷   Whoever commits sexual sins enjoys everything.
He won't become exhausted for as long as he lives.
¹⁸Whoever breaks his marriage vows says to himself,
"Who can see me? Night's darkness surrounds me.
Walls hide me, and no one can see me.
Why should I worry?
The Most High won't remember my sins."
¹⁹An adulterer is afraid only of what human eyes can see.
He doesn't realize that the Lord's eyes
are ten thousand times brighter than the sun.
They look closely at all human activities,
and they see clearly everything done in secret as well.
²⁰The Lord knew everything before the universe was created.
He knew everything after the universe was completed.

²¹ The adulterer will be caught when he least expects it
  and be punished in the streets of the city.
²² The same will happen to the woman who cheats on her husband
  and presents him with a child by another man.
²³ First of all, she has broken the law of the Most High.
Second, she has betrayed her husband.
Third, she is immoral. She has committed adultery
  and conceived children with another man.
²⁴   She will be brought in front of the assembly ˻for judgment˼,
         and her children will suffer the consequences.
²⁵   Her children will never be able to settle anywhere,
         and they will never fit into any community.
²⁶   People will continue to curse her after she has died,
         and her disgrace will never be wiped out.
²⁷   Those who outlive her will realize
         that nothing is more important than fearing the Lord
         and nothing is more valuable
           than obeying the Lord's commandments.

Wisdom Sings Its Own Praises

24 ¹Wisdom sings its own praises.
   Wisdom brags about itself to wise people.
² Wisdom speaks in the assembly of the Most High
  and brags about itself in front of the Lord's armies:
³ "I came out of the mouth of the Most High
  and covered the earth like mist.
⁴ I made my home in the highest heavens,
  and my throne was a column of smoke.
⁵ I have circled the far reaches of the sky by myself
  and have walked the depths of the ocean.
⁶ I have ruled the waves of the sea, the entire earth,
  every group of people, and every nation.
⁷ I looked everywhere for a place to rest,
  but I didn't know where to settle down.

The Creator Speaks to Wisdom

⁸ "Then the Creator of everything gave me an order.
My Creator chose a place for me to live.
He said, 'Make your home with Jacob's descendants,
  and take the land in Israel as your own possession.'
⁹ He created me in the beginning, before the world began.
I will never cease to exist.
¹⁰ I served as a priest in the Lord's holy tent,
  and I became established in Zion.

[11] He chose a place for me to rest in the city he loved most,
and I have authority over Jerusalem.

Wisdom Is Like a Beautiful Plant

[12] "I took my place among an honored group of people.
They are the people who belong to the Creator.
[13] I grew tall like a cedar in Lebanon,
like a cypress on Mount Hermon.
[14] I grew tall like a palm tree in En Gedi,
like a rosebush in Jericho.
I grew tall like a beautiful olive tree in the fields,
like a plane tree.
[15] I give off a fragrance like cinnamon, camel's thorn,
and the finest myrrh.
I give off a fragrance like resins and spices,
like frankincense in the holy tent.
[16] I spread my branches like an oak tree.
My branches are beautiful and graceful.
[17] I am like a grapevine sprouting graceful shoots.
Bunches of grapes replace my beautiful blossoms.[a]

[19] "Come to me, whoever wants me,
and eat your fill of whatever I produce.
[20] Remembering me is sweeter than honey,
and owning me is sweeter than a honeycomb.
[21] Whoever eats what I have will be hungry for more,
and whoever drinks what I have will be thirsty for more.
[22] Whoever obeys me will not be put to shame,
and whoever works with me will not sin."

[23] All these things are in the Most High God's Book of the Promise.
They are the teachings that Moses commanded us to learn.
Jacob's congregations received them as an inheritance.[b]

Wisdom Is Like a River

[25] Moses' Teachings overflow with wisdom
as the Pishon River overflows with water.
They overflow like the Tigris River at the time fruit is first picked.
[26] Moses' Teachings overflow with good sense
as the Euphrates River overflows with water.
They overflow like the Jordan River at harvest time.

---

[a] 24:17 Some ancient sources insert another verse.
[b] 24:23 Some ancient sources insert another verse.

²⁷ They sparkle with knowledge like the Nile River,
　　like the Gihon River at the time grapes are harvested.
²⁸ The first person did not fully grasp wisdom
　　and the last one will not fully understand it.

²⁹ Wisdom's thoughts are deeper than the sea,
　　and its advice is deeper than the deepest ocean.

³⁰ I was like an irrigation ditch leading from a river,
　　like a channel of water leading into a garden.
³¹ I said, "I'll water my garden until it's soaked."
　　My irrigation ditch became a river,
　　　　and my river turned into a sea.
³² I will again make knowledge shine like the sunrise.
　　I will make its light visible from far away.
³³ I will again spread these teachings like prophecies
　　and leave them to future generations.
³⁴ Notice that I haven't worked hard merely for myself
　　but for all who are looking for wisdom.

Love and Hate

25 ¹ I love three things,
　　and they are beautiful in the sight of God and mortals:
　　　brothers and sisters who live in harmony,
　　　　neighbors who are friends,
　　　　　and a husband and wife who love each other.
² I hate three kinds of people,
　　and I am deeply offended by the way they live:
　　　poor people who are arrogant,
　　　rich people who are liars,
　　　　and elderly people who don't have enough sense
　　　　　to stop committing adultery.

Old Age

³ If you didn't gather anything when you were young,
　　how can you expect to find anything when you are old?
⁴ Sound judgments from gray-haired people
　　and good advice from old people
　　　are signs of beauty.
⁵ Wisdom, careful thinking, and good advice from elderly people
　　are signs of beauty.
⁶ Experience is the crowning glory of elderly people.
　　They take pride in being God-fearing people.

Ten Kinds of Exceptional People

⁷I can think of nine kinds of people that I would consider blessed,
> even a tenth kind that I can quickly name:
> a man who enjoys his children,
> a man who lives to see the downfall of his enemies,

⁸ a blessed man who is married to a sensible wife,
> a blessed man who never plows
> > with an ox and donkey harnessed together,^a
> a blessed person who never lets a careless word
> > slip from his tongue,
> a blessed person who has never had to work
> > for an unappreciative boss,

⁹ a blessed person who finds advice,
> a blessed person who describes matters in detail to people
> > who are eager to listen,

¹⁰ and a great person who finds wisdom.
> But no one is greater than the one who fears the Lord.

¹¹ Fearing the Lord is better than anything else.
> > Nothing compares to the power that comes
> > > from fearing the Lord.^b

A Bad Wife

¹³No other injury is as unbearable as a broken heart.
> No other evil is as unbearable as a woman's spitefulness.

¹⁴No other suffering is as unbearable as the suffering caused
> > by hateful people.
> No other punishment is as unbearable as an enemy's revenge.

¹⁵No other venom is worse than a snake's venom,
> and no other anger is worse than a woman's anger.

¹⁶I would rather live with a lion or a serpent
> than with a spiteful woman.

¹⁷Spitefulness changes a woman's appearance.
> It changes her expression so that she looks like a bear.

¹⁸ When her husband eats with the neighbors,
> > he complains bitterly.

¹⁹No other wickedness compares to a woman's wickedness.
> May whatever happens to a sinner happen to her!

²⁰Living with a talkative woman is difficult for a quiet man
> in the same way that climbing a sand dune
> > is difficult for an elderly person.

---

^a 25:8 Syriac; Greek omits these two lines.
^b 25:11 Some ancient sources insert another verse.

²¹Don't be infatuated with a beautiful woman,
    and don't go after a woman because she's rich.*
²²When a wife supports her husband financially,
    he becomes angry, rude, and completely humiliated.
²³An overloaded mind, gloomy face,
    and broken heart come from a spiteful wife.
  Tired arms and weak knees
    come from a wife who doesn't make her husband happy.
²⁴Sin began with a woman,
    and because of that woman, people continue to die.
²⁵You wouldn't let water drip,
    so don't let a spiteful wife spout off.
²⁶If she won't do as you tell her,
    get rid of her.

A Good Wife

26 ¹Blessed is the man who has a good wife.
        She will double the length of his life.
²A devoted wife brings her husband joy,
    and he will live his life in peace.
³A good wife is one of the blessings
    that will be given to a man who fears the Lord.
⁴   He is content whether he is rich or poor.
     He always has a cheerful expression on his face.

More Lessons About a Bad Wife

⁵I am terrified of three things,
    even a fourth thing that I'm really afraid to face,
    and all of these things are worse than death:
        being slandered in public,
        being surrounded by a mob,
        being falsely accused,
⁶   and being around a wife who is jealous of another woman.
        That jealousy brings heartache and misery.
        Everyone will get a tongue-lashing.
⁷A bad wife is like a yoke* that rubs the skin raw.
    Taking hold of her is like grabbing a scorpion.
⁸A wife who is always drunk stirs up a lot of anger.
    She cannot completely hide her disgrace.

ᵃ 25:21 Syriac; Greek omits "because she's rich."
ᵇ 26:7 A yoke is a wooden bar placed over the necks of work animals so that they can pull plows or carts.

⁹A flirting look reveals an adulterous wife.
Batting her eyelashes gives her away.

A Rebellious Daughter

¹⁰Watch a rebellious daughter closely
so that she doesn't take advantage of any chance she gets.
¹¹Keep her seductive glances in check,
and don't be surprised if she turns against you.
¹²Like a thirsty traveler who drinks any water he sees,
a rebellious daughter makes herself available to any man she sees.

More Lessons About a Good Wife

¹³A charming wife brings her husband joy,
and she knows how to put meat on his bones.
¹⁴A quiet wife is a gift from the Lord,
and nothing is as valuable as her self-discipline.
¹⁵A modest wife is the most charming woman,
and nothing can measure the value of her self-control.
¹⁶A good wife in a well-kept house
is as beautiful as a sunrise over the Lord's mountains.
¹⁷A beautiful face on a beautiful figure
is like a bright light on the holy lamp stand.
¹⁸Shapely legs with beautiful feet
are like golden pillars with silver bases.ᵃ

²⁸Two things break my heart,
and a third matter makes me furious:
a veteran who lives in poverty,
a sensible person who is treated with contempt,
and a person who turns from right to wrong.
The Lord is ready to destroy that sinner!

Business Ethics

²⁹A salesperson can rarely keep from doing something wrong,
and a dealer is rarely free from sin.

27 ¹Many people have sinned while making a profit.
Those who want to become rich will have to learn to look
the other way.
² Someone can put a wedge between two bricks
in the same way that sin can put a wedge between buyer
and seller.

ᵃ 26:18 Some ancient sources insert nine other verses.

³If a person stops fearing the Lord,
    his home will be quickly destroyed.

Words Reveal a Person's True Character

⁴When a sieve is shaken, the rubbish surfaces.
    When a person speaks, his faults surface.
⁵A kiln tests clay that a person has molded
    in the same way that a conversation tests a person.
⁶Fruit says a lot about the tree it comes from.
    Likewise, words say a lot about the person who speaks them.
⁷   Don't praise someone before he speaks.
      After all, a person can be tested only by what he says.

⁸If you pursue justice,
    you will find it and wear it like expensive clothes.
⁹Birds of a feather flock together.
    The truth is natural for truthful people.

¹⁰A lion waits in ambush to catch prey.
    Likewise, sin waits in ambush to catch wicked people.

The Offensive Language of Fools

¹¹Statements made by devout people are always wise,
    but stories told by fools change like the phases of the moon.
¹²Don't waste your time with stupid people,
    but spend plenty of time with intelligent people.
¹³Statements made by fools are offensive.
    Fools laugh about the worst kinds of immorality.
¹⁴   The way they curse and swear makes a person's hair stand
      on end.
    The way they fight makes other people plug their ears.
¹⁵   Fights among arrogant people lead to bloodshed.
      Their foul language is unbearable.

Don't Reveal Secrets

¹⁶You betray a confidence when you reveal a secret,
    and you will never find a close friend again.
¹⁷Love your friend as though he were family, and remain loyal
    to him.
    However, if you reveal his secrets, you might as well stay away
      from him.
¹⁸   You'll kill that friendship
      in the same way that a person kills an enemy.
¹⁹   You'll lose your friend

in the same way that a bird escapes from your hands.
    You won't be able to catch him again.
20   You might as well stay away from him
            because he's gone.
                He'll escape like a gazelle from a trap.
21   A wound can be bandaged,
        and an insult can be forgiven,
            but someone who has revealed a friend's secret
            has no hope of restoring the friendship.

Deceitful People Are Hated

22 Whoever winks his eye is plotting something evil.
    So whoever knows him will stay away from him.
23   He flatters you as long as he is with you,
        and he admires your way with words.
            Later, he will say the opposite,
                and he will use your own words to trap you.
24 I've hated many things,
    but I've hated nothing as much as that kind of person.
    The Lord hates him too.

Evil Brings Punishment

25 Whoever throws a rock straight up in the air
    is throwing it on top of his own head.
    Whoever throws a punch is only hurting himself.*
26 Whoever digs a pit will fall into it,
    and whoever sets a trap will be caught in it.
27 If a person does something evil, then something evil will happen
        to him,
    and he won't know where it is coming from.
28 Ridicule and insults come from arrogant people,
    but vengeance ambushes them like a lion.
29 Those who celebrate when devout people fall will be caught
        in a trap.
    Pain will fill their lives until they die.
30 Anger that knows no bounds is disgusting,
    but a sinner is controlled by it.

General Statements

28 ¹Whoever takes revenge will face the Lord's vengeance.
    The Lord is keeping a detailed record of that person's sins.

---

a 27:25 English equivalent difficult.

² Forgive your neighbor,
  and then, when you pray, you will be forgiven.
³ No one can hold a grudge against another person
  and expect to be healed by the Lord.
⁴ If a person doesn't show any mercy toward others,
  he can't be forgiven for his own sins.
⁵ If a mortal holds a grudge,
  he can't make peace with the Lord for his sins.
⁶ If you remember that your life will end,
  then you will stop hating people.
 If you remember that you will die and decay,
  then you will be faithful to the commandments.
⁷ If you remember the commandments,
  then you won't be angry with your neighbor.
 If you remember the promise from the Most High,
  then you will overlook people's mistakes.
⁸ If you avoid conflict, then you will sin less often.
  People with hot tempers start fights.
⁹ A sinner causes trouble between friends,
  and he plants false accusations in the minds of peaceful people.
¹⁰ A forest fire will burn as long as trees fuel the fire.
 Conflict will spread as long as stubbornness fuels the conflict.
  A person's anger will be as fierce as he is strong.
  A person will be as furious as he can afford to be.
¹¹ An unexpected quarrel starts a fire.
 An unexpected conflict leads to bloodshed.
¹² If you blow on a spark, it will begin to burn.
  If you spit on it, it will go out.
   Both blowing and spitting come from your mouth.

Slander and Rumors

¹³ Slanderers and two-faced people will be cursed
  because they harm a lot of peaceful people.
¹⁴ Rumors have ruined a lot of people's lives
  and forced these people from one country to another.
 Rumors have leveled strong cities
  and have brought an end to important families.
¹⁵ Rumors have forced decent women from their homes
  and deprived them of everything they've worked so hard for.
¹⁶ Those who pay attention to rumors will never get any rest.
  They will never experience peace and quiet.
¹⁷ A lash from a whip leaves a welt,
  but a lash from a tongue shatters lives.

¹⁸ Many people have been killed by swords,
  but more people have been killed by rumors.
¹⁹ Blessed is the person
  who has been shielded from rumors,
  who has not had to suffer from their consequences,
  who has not had to bear up under their weight,
    and who has not been imprisoned by their chains.
²⁰ Rumors are as oppressive as iron bars
  or strong, bronze chains.
²¹   The death that rumors cause is a horrible death.
    Even hell would be better!
²²   Rumors have no impact on devout people,
    and devout people will not be burned by the flames
      from those tongues.
²³   Anyone who deserts the Lord will fall victim to rumors.
    They will burn that person, and they will not be extinguished.
    They will be sent to attack him like a lion.
    They will maul him like a leopard.
²⁴ For the same reason you would put a fence around your property,
  you should put a door over your mouth and lock it.
²⁵ For the same reason you weigh your silver and gold,
  make sure you weigh your words carefully.
²⁶ Be careful that you don't make a slip of the tongue,
  or else you may fall victim to someone
    who is waiting for you to say the wrong thing.

Loans

29 ¹Whoever is compassionate will lend his neighbors what
    they need.
  Whoever lends a helping hand obeys Moses' Teachings.
²Lend money to your neighbor when he's in need,
  and pay him back on time.
³Keep your promise, and give him a reason to trust you.
  Then you will always find what you need.
⁴Many people think of a loan as a gift,
  and they give those who helped them nothing but trouble.
⁵A person kisses another's feet until he gets a loan
  and speaks respectfully about his neighbor's money.
  However, when the time comes to repay the loan, he stalls
    for more time.
  He repays the lender with empty promises
    and blames the delay on insufficient time.
⁶   If he can pay, he will barely pay back half of the loan
    because he considers it a gift.

If he cannot pay, he has robbed the lender of his money.
The borrower has made him an enemy for no reason
and repays him with curses and insults,
with contempt instead of honor.
⁷Many generous people refuse to lend money
because they are afraid of being cheated.

Be Generous

⁸Nevertheless, be patient with poor people.
Don't make them wait for you to show kindness.
⁹Moses' Teachings instruct you to help poor people.
Don't send them away empty-handed when they are in need.
¹⁰Use your money to help a relative or friend.
Money helps no one when it isn't being used.
¹¹Use your treasures as the Most High has commanded,
and they will be more valuable to you than gold.
¹²Store acts of kindness in your treasury,
and they will rescue you from disaster.
¹³   They will fight for you against your enemy
better than a sturdy shield and an unbreakable spear.

Guaranteeing Loans

¹⁴A good person puts up collateral for his neighbor's loan.
Only a person who has no sense of honor will desert him.
¹⁵Don't forget the kindness of the person guaranteeing your loan,
because he has put his life on the line for you.
¹⁶A sinner ruins the property of the person guaranteeing his loan.
¹⁷   That ungrateful sinner deserts the person who rescued him.
¹⁸Guaranteeing a loan has ruined many prosperous people
by tossing them around like waves on the sea.
Guaranteeing loans has forced influential people into exile
and made them wander through foreign nations.
¹⁹When a sinner guarantees a loan in the hope of making a profit,
he will find himself involved in lawsuits.
²⁰Help your neighbor as much as you can,
but be careful that you don't get yourself into trouble.

Advice About Homes and Hospitality

²¹The necessities in life are food, water, clothing,
and a home for the sake of privacy.
²²A poor person is better off living under his own leaky roof
than eating expensive foods in other people's homes.
²³Be content with what you have, whether you have a lot or a little.
Then you won't hear the insults about your conduct as a guest.

²⁴Life is miserable when you have to beg from house to house.
Don't complain when you are a guest.
²⁵ Someday you may have to serve as the host.
You will have to serve drinks without being thanked
and hear degrading comments like these:
²⁶ "Hey, you! Come here, and get this table ready.
Give me something to eat.
²⁷ Get out of here! I've got an important guest.
My brother has come for a visit, and I need your room."

Summary
²⁸ Two things are difficult for a sensitive person to bear:
to be criticized for being a guest
and to be insulted by a moneylender.

When a Father Takes Responsibility for Raising His Son

30 ¹A father who loves his son will frequently spank him
and later be happy with the way his son turns out.
²A father who disciplines his son will be able to take pride in him
and later brag about him to acquaintances.
³A father will make his enemies envious because he teaches his son.
Then he will enjoy talking about his son with his friends.
⁴ After this kind of father dies, he will seem alive,
because he has left behind a copy of himself.
⁵ While he was alive, his son brought him joy,
and on his deathbed, he had no regrets.
⁶ The son he has left behind will punish his enemies
and repay his friends with kindness.

When a Father Spoils His Son
⁷A father who spoils his son will bandage his son's wounds.
That father's heart will stop every time he hears a cry.
⁸A wild son remains reckless
in the same way that an untamed horse remains uncontrollable.

The Need for Disciplining Children
⁹If you pamper a child, he will terrorize you.
If you indulge him, he will cause you pain.
¹⁰Don't laugh with him, or else you will cry with him.
In the end he will leave you gritting your teeth.
¹¹Don't give him unlimited freedom when he is young,
and don't overlook his mistakes.
¹²Don't let him become wild when he is young.

Spank him while he's young enough,
>   or else he will become stubborn and disobedient.
>   Then he will cause you nothing but grief.
> [13]Discipline your son and make him work
>   so that you won't be disgusted by the disgraceful way he lives.

Being Healthy

> [14]Being poor, healthy, and fit
>   is better than being rich and unhealthy.
> [15]Being healthy and physically fit is better than any amount of gold.
>   A strong body is better than countless possessions.
> [16]No treasure is better than a healthy body.
>   No happiness is better than genuine cheerfulness.
> [17]Death is better than a life of misery.
>   Eternal rest is better than a chronic illness.

Things That Are Useless

> [18]Trying to feed someone a delicacy
>   when his mouth is shut is useless.
>   Likewise, placing a gift of food on a dead person's grave
>   is useless.
> [19]Offerings can't benefit an idol,
>   since it can't eat or smell.
>   Likewise, the person who has been punished by the Lord
>   can't eat or smell.
> [20]   He sees the food and groans
>   as a eunuch groans when hugging a young woman.

Stay Happy

> [21]Don't give in to despair,
>   and don't create problems for yourself.
> [22]A heart filled with joy keeps a person alive.
>   Joy prolongs his life.
> [23]Turn your attention toward something good,
>   and give yourself some encouragement.
>   Distance yourself from despair
>   because despair has destroyed many people.
>   Nothing good has ever come from it.
> [24]Jealousy and anger shorten a person's life.
>   Anxiety leads to premature aging.
> [25]A Cheerful person, someone who has a good outlook on life,
>   will enjoy his meals.

Money Problems

31 ¹Worrying about money makes a person lose sleep.
Losing sleep over money makes a person lose weight.

² Like a serious illness, worrying keeps a person
from falling asleep.

³A rich person works hard to acquire a fortune,
and when he relaxes, he enjoys the luxuries that go with it.

⁴A poor person works hard to earn a meager living,
but when he relaxes, he still is needy.

The Love of Gold

⁵Whoever loves gold is unable to do what is right.
Whoever goes after valuable things will be misled by them.

⁶Many people have been ruined because of their love of gold,
even though they knew it would lead to their downfall.

⁷Gold makes those who are obsessed with it stumble.
Every fool will fall into its trap.

⁸Blessed is the rich person who doesn't go after gold
and is found blameless.

⁹ Who is he so that we can congratulate him?
He has done something amazing among his people.

¹⁰Who has ever been tempted by gold but never gave in?
That person has a reason to brag.
Who has ever had an opportunity to sin but didn't?

¹¹ His wealth will be secure,
and community leaders will praise his acts of charity.

Table Manners

¹²If you're sitting at a table with important people,
don't say, "Look at all this food!"
and then eat everything in sight.

¹³ Remember that looking with envy at something is wrong.
Of everything that has been created,
only the human eye envies what it sees.
That is why human eyes frequently shed tears.

¹⁴When you're sitting at a table with important people,
Don't help yourself to everything you see,
and don't elbow another person to get to the food.

¹⁵ Think about what the other guests would like
by thinking about what you would like,
and be considerate in every way.

¹⁶ Eat whatever is set in front of you,
but don't gulp it down, or else people will find you disgusting.

¹⁷ Out of politeness, be the first to stop eating,
     and don't be a glutton, or else you will become offensive.
¹⁸ If you're sitting with a lot of people,
     don't help yourself to the food before they do.

More About Food and Good Manners

¹⁹ A little bit of food is enough for a well-mannered person.
     When he goes to bed, he doesn't have a hard time breathing.
²⁰ If you don't overeat, you'll have a good night's sleep.
     When you get up early, you'll feel refreshed.
   Gluttons suffer from sleeplessness, nausea, and stomachaches.
²¹ If you've overeaten,
     leave the table and make yourself vomit, and you'll feel better.
²² Listen to me, my child, and don't ignore me.
     In the end you'll appreciate what I've said.
   If you don't go to extremes in whatever you do,
     you won't be faced with illness.
²³ People bless anyone who is generous with food,
     because the proof of his generosity is believable.
²⁴ Everyone in town complains about someone who is stingy
       with food,
     because the proof of his stinginess is painfully clear.

Wine

²⁵ Don't try to prove you're a man by getting drunk,
     because drinking too much has destroyed many lives.
²⁶ The true character of arrogant people shows
     when they drink too much wine and get into fights
       as the quality of iron shows
         when the iron is heated and dipped in water.
²⁷ Wine can be invigorating if you drink it in moderation.
   What's life without wine?
     Wine was created to make people happy.
²⁸   It can make you lighthearted and cheerful
     if you drink at the proper time and in moderation.
²⁹ Drinking too much wine
     leads to bitterness, resentment, and conflict.
³⁰ Being drunk makes a fool lose his temper.
     This is to his disadvantage
       because he becomes weaker and gets injured more often.
³¹ Don't argue with another person when you both
     have been drinking,
   and don't ridicule him when he's enjoying himself.

Don't insult him,
>   and don't put pressure on him by demanding anything
>   from him.

Good Manners at a Banquet

32 ¹If you're asked to be in charge of a banquet, don't
>   become conceited.
>   Act like one of the guests.
>   Take care of them first, and then sit down.
²   After you've carried out all your duties, take your seat.
>   Then you can enjoy yourself
>   because you know they're having a good time
>   and you'll receive an award
>   for your outstanding leadership.
³Elderly guests are entitled to speak because of their age,
>   but they need to be brief and not interrupt the music.
⁴   Don't continue to talk during the entertainment.
>   That's not the time to show everyone how wise you are.
⁵A concert during a banquet where wine is served
>   is like a ruby in a gold setting.
⁶Good music with good wine
>   is like an emerald in a gold setting.
⁷Young people should speak only if necessary.
>   They should speak no more than twice and only if asked
>   a question.
⁸   Be brief, but say a lot in a few words.
>   Show people that you are knowledgeable
>   but that you know when to be quiet.
⁹When you're with important people,
>   don't act as though you're one of them.
>   When someone else is speaking, don't interrupt.
¹⁰   A modest person's good reputation precedes him
>   in the same way that lightning precedes the sound
>   of thunder.
¹¹   When the banquet is over, don't be the last to leave.
>   Go home quickly, and don't linger.
¹²   While you're at the banquet,
>   enjoy yourself to your heart's content,
>   but don't sin by talking arrogantly.
¹³Above all, praise your Creator,
>   who showers you with good gifts.

The Lord's Teachings Will Guide You on the Road of Life

¹⁴Whoever fears the Lord will accept discipline from him.
   Those who pray first thing in the morning will gain his approval.
¹⁵If a person studies the Lord's teachings,
   those teachings will affect every aspect of his life.
      However, they will be offensive to a hypocrite.
¹⁶Those who fear the Lord will make wise judgments.
   and the wrong things they have set right will shine like light.
¹⁷A sinner will avoid having his errors exposed
   and will say anything to justify his actions.
¹⁸A sensible person won't overlook another person's idea.
   An arrogant person won't be stopped by fear.
¹⁹Never do anything without thinking first.
   Then you won't regret what you've done.
²⁰Don't travel on a dangerous road.
   You'll stumble over rocks.
²¹Don't be overconfident on a safe road.
²²   Instead, always watch where you're going.*
²³Be on guard in everything you do*
   because this is in keeping with the commandments.
²⁴Whoever trusts the Lord's teachings
   pays attention to the commandments.
   Whoever trusts the Lord will never suffer any losses.

33 ¹No harm will come to a person who fears the Lord.
   No matter how often a person is tested, he will be rescued.
²A wise person doesn't hate the Lord's teachings.
   However, a hypocrite who pretends to love the Lord's teachings
      is going to be tossed around like a boat in a storm.
³A sensible person trusts the Lord's teachings.
   They are as trustworthy for him as a direct response
      from the Lord.

General Statements

⁴If you want to be heard, prepare what you want to say.
   Use your training to help prepare your responses.
⁵A fool's emotions are like a wagon wheel,
   and his thoughts are like a spinning axle.
⁶A sarcastic friend is like a stallion
   that neighs no matter who the rider is.

ᵃ 32:22 Hebrew; Greek "watch your children."
ᵇ 32:23 Hebrew; Greek "trust yourself in every deed."

Some Distinctions Are More Important Than Others

⁷ Why is one day more important than another
   when every day of the year gets its light from the sun?
⁸ Through wisdom, the Lord made distinctions.
   He made the different seasons and festivals.
⁹ He made some days important and holy,
   and he made other days ordinary.
¹⁰ All humans come from the ground.
   Adam was created out of the earth.
¹¹ Out of vast wisdom, the Lord made distinctions.
   He made humans go their different ways.
¹² He blessed some of them by making them important.
   He made some of them holy by making them his friends.
   However, he cursed and humiliated some of them
     by removing them from their positions.
¹³ As a potter molds clay
   in whichever way he pleases,
   the Creator shapes human lives
   in whichever way he decides.

¹⁴ Good is the opposite of evil,
   life is the opposite of death,
     and a sinner is the opposite of a devout person.
¹⁵ Look at all the things the Most High has created.
   They come in pairs; one thing is the opposite of another.

A Personal Reflection

¹⁶ I was always the last one to be alert.
   I was like a person who picks up the remaining grapes
     after the grape harvest.
¹⁷ Thanks to the Lord, I now am the first to arrive on the scene,
   and like a grape picker, I fill my winepress.
¹⁸ I want you to understand that I haven't been working hard
     only for myself
   but for everyone who is looking for wisdom.

Remain Independent

¹⁹ Listen to me, you important people.
   Pay attention, you leaders.
²⁰ Never let your child, spouse, sibling, or friend
   have control of your legal affairs.
   Don't hand your property over to anyone
   in the event you change your mind.
     Then you would have to ask for it back.

²¹Don't let anyone take away your responsibilities
    as long as you are alive and well.
²²Having your children ask you for help
    is better than looking to them for help.
²³Be in control of everything you do.
    Don't let your reputation be tarnished.
²⁴Wait until the last day of your life,
    until your final hour,
        to give away your inheritance.

Slaves

²⁵Give a donkey something to eat, a beating when necessary,
    and a load to carry.
Give a slave food, discipline, and work.
²⁶If you put your slave to work, you will have peace of mind.
If you leave him with nothing to do, he will look for his freedom.
²⁷A harness and reins will keep a donkey under control.
A rack and other forms of torture will keep a wicked slave
        under control.
²⁸Keep him hard at work so that he isn't standing around.
²⁹   An idle mind is busy inventing trouble.
³⁰Give him work to do. That's what a slave is for.
If he doesn't obey, make his chains heavier.
    However, don't be too hard on him,
        and don't treat him unfairly.
³¹If you have a slave, treat him the way you would like to be treated.
After all, you paid a high price for him.
If you have a slave, treat him like a brother,
    because you will need him as much as you need yourself.
³²If you mistreat him and he runs away,
³³   where will you start to look for him?

Dreams

34 ¹A fool holds on to a worthless and false hope,
    and dreams give a fool high expectations.
²Anyone who believes in dreams
    is like a person who tries to catch a shadow or chase the wind.
³What you see in a dream is only a reflection,
    a face looking at itself in a mirror.
⁴   How can something clean come from something dirty?
    How can something true come from something false?
⁵Fortunetelling, omens, and dreams are worthless.
    People can't stop fantasizing about these things

any more than a woman can stop herself from going
  into labor.
⁶Unless the Most High sends dreams to help you,
  don't pay any attention to them.
⁷Dreams have misled many people.
  Those who base their hope on dreams will be disappointed.
⁸The Lord's teachings are complete without those lies.
  Wisdom is complete when faithful people talk
    ⌐about his teachings⌐.

Traveling Brings Experience

⁹A person who has traveled a lot knows many things.
  A person with a lot of experience knows what he's talking about.
¹⁰An inexperienced person has limited knowledge,
¹¹ but the person who travels a lot becomes more clever.
¹²I have seen many things in my travels,
  and I understand more than I can put into words.
¹³I have been in danger of being killed many times,
  but because of my past experiences, I have escaped.

The Lord Is the Basis of Hope

¹⁴Those who fear the Lord will live
¹⁵ because their hope rests on him, their savior.
¹⁶Those who fear the Lord will never be afraid of anything,
  because he is the basis of their hope.
¹⁷Blessed are those who fear the Lord
¹⁸ because they hold on to the Lord and the Lord supports them.
¹⁹The Lord takes care of those who love him.
  He is a mighty shield and strong support,
    a shelter from scorching wind and a shade
      from the noonday sun,
    a guard against stumbling and a help against falling.
²⁰ He lifts people's spirits and puts a gleam in their eyes.
  He gives health, life, and blessings.

Disgusting Sacrifices

²¹The Most High is disgusted by anyone
  who sacrifices anything that's obtained dishonestly.
²²Gifts from wicked people are not acceptable to the Most High.
²³The Most High is not pleased with offerings from hypocrites.
  A large number of sacrifices won't influence him to forgive sins.
²⁴Someone who would offer a poor person's property as a sacrifice
  is like someone who would kill a son in front of his father.

25   A poor diet sustains the lives of poor people.
        Whoever deprives them of their food is a killer.
26   Whoever takes away another's livelihood is a murderer.
27   Whoever deprives an employee of his wages is bloodthirsty.
28 When one person builds something up and another person tears
        it down,
     what do they gain but a lot of hard work?
29 When one prays and another curses,
     to whom will the Lord listen?
30 If a person washes after touching a corpse but touches it again,
     what has been gained by washing himself?
31 If someone fasts because of his sins but then commits the same
        sins again,
     who will listen to his prayer?
     What has he gained by humbling himself?

Acceptable Ways To Worship the Lord

35 ¹Following Moses' Teachings is like offering many sacrifices.
     ²Obeying the commandments is like bringing a thank offering.
   ³Repaying a favor is like bringing a grain offering.
   ⁴Giving to charity is like bringing a sacrifice of praise.
   ⁵The way to please the Lord is to stay away from evil.
   The way to make peace with him is to stay away from dishonesty.
7   All these things have been commanded,
6   so don't appear in the Lord's presence empty-handed.
   ⁸An offering brought by someone who has God's approval
        adds to the beauty of the altar.
        The offering's fragrance rises in the presence
             of the Most High.
   ⁹A sacrifice brought by someone who has God's approval
        is acceptable,
     and it will never be forgotten.
10 Be generous with your offerings when you worship the Lord.
   Don't be stingy when you offer the first produce from your crops.
11   Give every gift cheerfully,
        and joyfully dedicate a tenth of your income.
12   Give to the Most High as he has given to you.
        Be as generous as you can
13   because the Lord is the one who rewards generous people.
             He will reward you seven times over.
14 However, don't offer him a bribe, because he won't take it.
15 Don't rely on a sacrifice obtained dishonestly,
        because the Lord is a judge
             who doesn't favor one person over another.

¹⁶He won't grant special favors to a poor person,
    but he will listen to prayers from anyone who has been wronged.
¹⁷He won't ignore humble prayers from an orphan
    or from a widow when she pours out her troubles.
¹⁸   (Don't tears run down a widow's cheek
¹⁹   as she accuses the person who makes her cry?)
²⁰Whoever gladly serves the Lord will be accepted,
    and his prayers will reach the clouds.
²¹Prayers from a humble person will go through the clouds,
    and he will not stop praying until his prayers are answered.
    He will not give up until the Most High responds
²²   by seeing that justice is served
        and guilty people are punished.
    The Lord will respond quickly.
    He won't be slow in dealing with the guilty,
      merciless people.
    He will break their backs
²³   and take revenge on their nations.
    He will destroy the large number of arrogant people
      and take away the power of dishonest rulers.
²⁴   He will repay people for what they have done
      and for everything they intended to do.
²⁵   He will give his people justice
      and fill them with joy because of his mercy.
²⁶His mercy in times of trouble is as welcome
    as rain clouds during a drought.

A Prayer for Israel

36¹Lord God of the universe, have mercy on us,
² and make every nation fear you.
³Take action against foreign nations,
    and let them see your power.
⁴   You have used us to show your holiness to them,
      so use them to show your glory to us.
⁵   Then they will know, as we've always known,
      that there is no other God except you, Lord.
⁶Show us miraculous signs again, and perform
    other amazing miracles.
⁷Display your glorious power.
⁸Get angry! Unleash your fury!
⁹Destroy your opponents. Wipe out your enemies.
¹⁰Remember the appointment you made
    for your people to tell about the miracles you've performed.
    Make that appointed time come quickly.

¹¹ Don't let your enemies escape your burning anger.
  Destroy those who mistreat your people.
¹² Crush the heads of hostile rulers
  who say that they're the only people who matter.
¹³ Gather all of Jacob's tribes,ᵃ
¹⁶   and give them back the land you gave them long ago.
¹⁷ Lord, have mercy on those who are known as your people.
  Have mercy on Israel, whom you treated as your firstborn.
¹⁸   Have compassion on your holy city, Jerusalem, the place
      where you live.
¹⁹   Fill Zion with praise for everything you've done,
      and fill your temple with your glory.
²⁰   Prove to those whom you created in the beginning
      that the prophecies spoken in your name will come true.
²¹   Reward those who patiently wait for you,
      and let your prophets be considered trustworthy.
²² Lord, because of your good will toward your people,
      listen to the prayers of those who serve you.
      Everyone on earth will come to know
          that you are the Lord, the everlasting God.

A Few Proverbs

²³ A stomach can handle all kinds of food,
      but some foods are better than others.
²⁴ A tongue can detect different kinds of meat.
      Likewise, a sharp mind can detect when a person is lying.
²⁵ A warped mind causes problems,
      but an experienced person will know how to deal
          with those problems.

The Need for a Wife

²⁶ A woman will accept any man as a husband,
      but a man may like one woman better than another.
²⁷ To a man, nothing is more desirable than a beautiful woman.
      Her beauty can put a smile on his face.
²⁸ If she speaks with tenderness and humility,
      her husband is the most fortunate man alive.
²⁹ A man who has found a wife has gotten off to a good start.
      She can help him and be a pillar of strength for him.
³⁰ If a yard doesn't have a fence, valuable things can be stolen easily.
  If a man doesn't have a wife, he will become a pathetic drifter.

ᵃ 36:13 Some ancient sources insert two other verses.

³¹ No one would trust a thief
   who strikes one city after another.
Likewise, no one would trust a man who has no home
   and spends the night wherever he happens to be.

Friends

37 ¹Every friend says, "Of course, I'm your friend."
   However, some friends are friends in name only.
²When a colleague or friend becomes an enemy,
   the loss feels like a death.
³   What an evil urge we have! Where did it come from?
      It covers the earth with deceit.
⁴Some people share in a friend's happiness,
   but they stay far away from him when he is in trouble.
⁵Some people help a friend only to get something in return,
   and yet they may come to his defense in a battle.
⁶Don't forget a real friend.
Don't neglect him if you become rich.

Advisers

⁷Every adviser gives advice,
   but some give advice that is to their own advantage.
⁸Be on your guard against someone who gives advice.
Determine right away what his interest in the matter is
   because he will consider what is best for him first.
      He may decide not to help you
⁹   but he will tell you, "You've made an excellent decision."
         Then he will stand by to see what happens to you.
¹⁰Don't seek advice from people who are suspicious of you.
   Hide your plans from those who are jealous of you.
¹¹Don't seek advice from
   a woman about her rival,
   a coward about war,
   a salesperson about a bargain,
   a buyer about a sale,
   an envious person about gratitude,
   a cruel person about kindness,
   a lazy person about working,
   a temporary worker about finishing a job,
      or a slow worker about a big project.
Don't pay any attention to the advice they give you.
¹²Instead, remain in constant contact with devout people.
   To the best of your knowledge,
      they should be people who follow the commandments.

They should think the way you do
　　and sympathize with you if you make a mistake.
[13] Also, follow your own intuition
　　because nothing is more reliable.
[14]　　Sometimes our own minds keep us better informed
　　　　than seven guards sitting in a high watchtower.
[15] Above all else, pray to the Most High
　　that he will lead you to the truth.

Wise and Unwise Choices

[16] A discussion should take place at the beginning of every project.
　　A planning session should take place before every undertaking.
[17] The mind is the source for all choices.
[18]　　It can go in four directions:
　　　　good, evil, life, or death.
　　However, what a person says always determines the direction
　　　　he will go.
[19] One person may be clever enough to teach a lot of people
　　and yet be useless to himself.
[20] Another person may be able to trap people with his subtle use
　　of words,
　　but he will end up starving because people hate him.
[21]　　The Lord didn't give him any tact.
　　　　That person didn't use any wisdom.
[22] If a person applies wisdom to his own life,
　　people will talk about the benefits of his good sense.
[23] If a wise person teaches his own people,
　　the benefits of his good sense will be lasting.
[24] A wise person's life will be filled with blessings,
　　and everyone who sees him will praise him.
[25] An individual's life lasts a limited number of days,
　　but Israel's days are countless.
[26] Someone who deals with people wisely
　　will earn their trust.
　　His name will always be remembered.

Do Things in Moderation

[27] My child, constantly evaluate your life.
　　Determine all the things that are bad for you, and don't give in
　　　　to them.
[28]　　Everything isn't good for everyone,
　　　　and everyone doesn't necessarily enjoy everything.
[29]　　Don't eat every delicacy in sight.
　　　　Don't overeat.

30   Overeating leads to all sorts of serious illnesses,
   particularly stomach problems.
31   Many have died from overeating,
   but a person who is careful can prolong his life.

The Lord and Medical Doctors

38 ¹Give doctors the respect they deserve for their work.
  The Lord created them.
2   Their gift of healing comes from the Most High,
   and they are rewarded by kings.
3   A doctor's skills make him a respected person,
   someone who is admired by important people.
⁴The Lord created medicine from things on the earth,
  and no sensible person will despise medicine.
5   For example, water was sweetened with a piece of wood
   so that people would come to know the Lord's power.
⁶The Lord gave skills to humans
  so that he would be honored for his amazing miracles.
7   With those skills, pharmacists make drugs
   that doctors use to heal people and relieve pain.
⁸The Lord's creative work is never finished.
  It restores health to people all over the world.

⁹My child, when you have an illness, don't ignore it.
  Instead, pray to the Lord, and he will heal you.
10   Confess your sins, do what is right,
   and don't let your heart be controlled by sin.
11   Offer a sweet-smelling sacrifice and a grain offering.
   Pour on your offering as much olive oil as you can afford.
12   Then let the doctor take over because the Lord created him.
  You need him, so don't send him away.
13   A time may come when your recovery lies in the doctor's hands.
14   Doctors, too, must pray to the Lord
   that he will grant them success in relieving pain
   and healing patients.
¹⁵Whoever sins against his Creator
  deserves to fall into the hands of a quack.

Wisdom About Mourning

¹⁶My child, let the tears run down your face for a person who died.
  Sing a funeral song to show your terrible loss.
  Prepare the body in the usual way,
   and don't forget to attend the burial.

¹⁷   Cry bitterly. Sob loudly.
     In public, display your grief in a way
          that honors the dead person's memory—
               at least for a day or two to avoid criticism.
     Then allow yourself to be comforted.
¹⁸   Depression can drain your strength,
          and grief can result in your own death.
¹⁹ After you bury your loved one, the loss remains.
     However, a life of misery is hard to take.
²⁰   Don't allow yourself to become depressed.
     Get rid of depression
          because you don't want to remain depressed the rest
               of your life.
²¹   Remember that you won't get a second chance.
          You can't help the dead person, but you can harm yourself.
²²   Remember his fate because it will be your fate as well.
     Yesterday he died, and tomorrow you will die.
²³ When he has breathed his last breath,
     allow yourself to be comforted.
     When the dead person has been laid to rest,
          allow yourself to go on living.

Laborers Make Up the Very Fabric of This World

²⁴ An educated person needs a lot of time to study in order
          to become wise.
     Only a person who has few demands on his time can
               become wise.
²⁵ No one can become wise when he holds on to a plow all day.
     His ambition in life is to use a cattle prod,
     he's preoccupied with taking care of cattle,
          and all he talks about is cows.
²⁶   He puts his whole heart into plowing furrows,
          and he always feeds the heifers right on time.
²⁷ The same is true for all the artists and craftsmen who labor night
          and day.
     They engrave inscriptions
          and are determined to make a large variety.
     Each puts his whole heart into painting lifelike images
          and works nonstop until he finishes.
²⁸ The same is true for blacksmiths
     who sit by anvils and concentrate on their work.
          The heat from the fire burns their skin.
               They struggle to withstand the heat from the furnace.
     The noise from their hammers makes them grow deaf.

Their eyes are focused on the shape of the metal.
Each puts his whole heart into finishing his projects
and works nonstop to complete every detail.
²⁹The same is true for potters who sit at the wheel
and turn it with their feet.
They are always careful about everything they make
and that they make enough of every kind.
³⁰   They mold clay with their hands
and make it pliable with their feet.
Each puts his whole heart into finishing the glazing process
and is careful how he gets the kiln ready.
³¹All of these people rely on the use of their hands,
and each of them becomes skilled in his own profession.
³²   No one could begin a new colony without them.
No one would settle or live in a city without them.
Yet, no one asks them to be on the city council.
³³   They don't become prominent among the city's leading citizens.
They don't become judges
or even understand the decisions handed down by a court.
They don't teach or make decisions,
and they don't quote philosophers.
³⁴However, they do make up the very fabric of this world,
and all they ask is to be left alone so that they can do their jobs.

Scholars, Too, Are Part of the Very Fabric of the World

The person who devotes himself to studying the teachings
of the Most High
is different from other people.

39 ¹He searches for all the ancient wisdom there is
and spends his time thinking about what the prophets said.
²He treasures the sayings of famous people
and studies the complicated statements of philosophers.
³He searches for hidden meanings in proverbs
and comprehends the obscure points made by philosophers.
⁴He associates with important people
and appears in the presence of rulers.
He travels to foreign countries
and experiences both the good and bad in humanity.
⁵He puts his whole heart into praying to the Lord, his Creator.
First thing in the morning, he prays to the Most High.
He begins his prayer by asking to be forgiven for his sins.
⁶If the Almighty Lord is willing,
that person will be filled with good sense.

Then that person will speak his own words of wisdom
and praise the Lord in his prayers.
⁷The Lord will guide him in giving advice and sharing knowledge.
The Lord will guide him as he studies the mysterious ways
of the Lord.
⁸   That person will display the wisdom that he has gained
and brag about the Lord's teachings and the Lord's promise.
⁹Many people will praise his good sense.
It will never be wiped out.
His good reputation will never be forgotten,
and his good name will be remembered for generations to come.
¹⁰Nations will talk about his wisdom,
and when people are gathered together, they will praise him.
¹¹While he is alive,
he will have the best reputation in the city.
When he is laid to rest,
he will be content.

Praise the Lord for Creation

¹²I have a lot on my mind that I want to talk about.
I am as full as a full moon.
¹³Listen to me, my devout children,
and blossom like roses growing by a stream.
¹⁴   Give off a fragrance like incense, and bloom like lilies.
Spread your fragrance by singing a hymn of praise.
Praise the Lord for everything he has done.
¹⁵Honor his name with the majesty it deserves.
Thank and praise him by singing and playing the harp.
This is what you should say when you thank him:
¹⁶"Everything the Lord has done is very good.
Everything he commands will take place at the right time.
¹⁷   No one should ask, 'What is this?' or 'Why is that?'
Those questions will be answered at the right time.
When he spoke, the waters piled up.
When the words came from his mouth, the reservoirs took shape.
¹⁸When he gives a command, his will is carried out.
No one can stop his saving power.
¹⁹He sees everything humans do.
Nothing can be hidden from him.
²⁰He has seen everything from the beginning to the end of time.
Nothing amazes him.
²¹   No one should ask, 'What is this?' or 'Why is that?'
Everything has been created for a purpose.

²² "His blessings cover dry land like a river
   and soak it like a flood.

²³   As surely as he turned fresh water into salt water,
       he will spread his anger throughout the nations.

²⁴ To devout people, the Lord's roads are smooth,
   but to wicked people, the roads are full of obstacles.

²⁵ Good things were created for good people from the beginning,
   but bad things were created for sinners.

²⁶ The basic necessities for human life are
   water, fire, iron, salt, flour, milk, honey,
       wine, olive oil, and clothing.

²⁷   These are good things for devout people,
       but they turn into evil things for sinners.

²⁸ "He has created some winds to bring punishment,
   and he will use them as whips when he is angry.
   They will unleash their power on the last day,
   but they will cool their Creator's anger.

²⁹ He has created fire, hail, famine, and disease
   to bring punishment.

³⁰ Meat-eating animals, scorpions, vipers,
   and swords that punish wicked people with destruction

³¹   enjoy carrying out his command.
       They are always ready on earth whenever he needs them.
       They never refuse to carry out his orders
       at the appropriate times."

Everything the Lord Has Done Is Good

³² I have been convinced of this from the beginning.
   I intended to put this in writing:

³³   "Everything the Lord has done is good.
       He supplies whatever is needed at the right time.

³⁴   No one should say, 'This is worse than that.'
       Everything proves its value at the right time.

³⁵   So sing hymns with all your heart,
       and praise the Lord's name."

Hard Work and Suffering

40 ¹Hard work was created for everyone,
   and a heavy yoke[a] has been placed on Adam's descendants.
   From the day they come from their mothers' wombs

---

[a] 40:1 A yoke is a wooden bar placed over the necks of work animals so that they can pull
plows or carts.

until the day they return to the earth
(the mother of all living things),
they will have to work hard.
2 They are uncertain and fearful.
They are worried as they think about the day they will die.
3   Those who sit on glorious thrones,
those who grovel in dust and ashes,
4   those who wear expensive clothes and crowns,
and those who are dressed in sackcloth
5   all experience anger, jealousy, trouble, unrest,
guilt, conflict, and fear of death.
Even when people go to bed at night,
dreams give them new things to worry about.
6   They get little or no rest.
They struggle in their sleep
as much as they do when they are awake.
They are frightened by nightmares.
They dream about running from an enemy,
7   and as they are about to reach safety, they wake up.
They are surprised when they realize
that they had nothing to fear.
9 Death, bloodshed, conflict, weapons,
disaster, famine, misery, and plagues
8   affect all creatures, but they affect sinners seven times worse.
10   All of these catastrophes were created for wicked people.
The flood came because of them.
11 Everything that is from the earth returns to the earth.
Everything that is from the water returns to the sea.

Things That Last and Things That Don't Last

12 Bribery and injustice will be wiped out,
but honesty will last forever.
13 Money gained dishonestly will dry up like a river.
It will fade away like a loud clap of thunder during a storm.
14 A generous person has a reason to be happy.
Sinners will fail to reach their goals.
15 The descendants of unbelievers sprout only a few branches.
These people are like unhealthy roots planted on a rocky cliff.
16 The reeds along any body of water, especially along any riverbank,
are pulled out before grass is.
17   Kindness is like a garden of blessings,
and acts of kindness last forever.

The Better Things in Life

¹⁸Life is sweet for those who are wealthy and for those who work,
>   but a person who finds a treasure is better off than either group.
¹⁹Having children and building a city can establish
>   a person's reputation,
>   but having a well-respected wife is better.
²⁰Wine and music make a person cheerful,
>   but the love of wisdom is better than either of those things.
²¹A flute and a harp sound good together,
>   but a beautiful voice is better than either instrument.
²²People long to see grace and beauty
>   but not as much as they long to see crops sprouting.
²³A friend or an acquaintance is always welcome,
>   but a wife makes a better companion.
²⁴Relatives and allies are good to have in times of trouble,
>   but acts of kindness protect a person better than people can.
²⁵Gold and silver strengthen a person's status,
>   but good advice carries more influence.
²⁶Wealth and strength build a person's confidence,
>   but fear of the Lord is better.
>   When you fear the Lord, nothing is lacking,
>   and you don't need to look for any other help.
²⁷   Fear of the Lord is like a garden of blessings,
>   and it covers a person better than the highest praise.

Don't Become a Beggar

²⁸My child, don't live like a beggar.
>   Being dead is better than being a beggar.
²⁹If you're always looking for other people to give you something
>   to eat,
>   then your way of life cannot be considered a life at all.
>   You lose your self-respect
>   when you depend on someone else for food.
>   However, a sensible person who is brought up well will guard
>   against that.
³⁰Begging tastes sweet to a shameless fool,
>   but it burns like fire in his stomach.

About Death

41 ¹Death, you are so bitter for a person
>   who is living peacefully with his possessions,
>   who doesn't worry about anything and is successful
>   in everything,
>   and who is still strong enough to enjoy food.

² Death, you are welcomed by a person
    who is poor and whose health is failing,
    who is worn down by old age and upset by everything,
      and who is spiteful and impatient.
³ Don't be afraid of death.
    Remember those who went before you
      and those who will come after you.
⁴ The Lord has given a death sentence to every living thing.
    Why would you reject what the Most High wants?
    No one who has died cares if you live to be 10, 100, or 1,000.

The Children of Sinners

⁵ The children of sinners are disgusting.
    They frequently visit places where wicked people like to go.
⁶ The children of sinners will inherit nothing.
    Their descendants will inherit unending disgrace.
⁷   Children will blame their wicked father.
      They suffer disgrace because of him.
⁸ How horrible it will be for you wicked people!
    You have rejected the teachings of God Most High.
⁹   You were born under a curse.
    You will divide that curse among your descendants
      when you die.
¹⁰ Whatever comes from the earth returns to the earth.
    Wicked people live and die under a curse.
¹¹ People grieve over a body that decays.
    However, a sinner's notoriety will not be remembered for long.
¹² Be concerned about your reputation because it will outlast you.
    It will last longer than a thousand vaults filled with gold.
¹³ A good life has a limited number of days,
    but a good reputation lasts forever.

When To Feel Ashamed

¹⁴ My children, follow my instructions, and be at peace.
    Hidden wisdom, like buried treasure, is useless.
¹⁵   Hiding stupidity is better than hiding wisdom.
¹⁶ Therefore, pay attention to what I'm saying.
    You shouldn't be ashamed of some things,
      but other things are not considered appropriate by everyone.
¹⁷ You should be ashamed of the following things:
    being caught having premarital sex by your father or mother,
    being caught in a lie by a leader or an official,
¹⁸   being caught committing a crime by a judge or police officer,
    being caught breaking God's laws by a congregation,

being caught in a dishonest business deal by your partner
    or friend,
19 being caught stealing by your neighbors,
    breaking an oath or an agreement,[a]
    leaning on your elbows at the table,
    being rude when you give or receive something,
20 ignoring people who greet you,
    staring at a prostitute,
21 refusing to help a relative,
    depriving someone of what is rightfully his,
    looking at another man's wife,
22 flirting with another man's female servant (don't go near
    her bed!),
    insulting friends (don't follow up a gift with insults!),
1 repeating something you've heard,
    and betraying secrets.
When you know what you should be ashamed of,
    you will find favor with everyone.

42

So never commit a sin in order to be accepted by other people.
You should not be ashamed of the following things:
2 believing in the teachings of the Most High and his promise,
    giving a fair verdict of not guilty to a wicked person,
3 settling expenses with a partner or a traveling companion,
    dividing an inheritance with other heirs,
4 using accurate measurements and weights,
    acquiring a small or large amount of money,
5 making a profit from dealing with merchants,
    disciplining children frequently,
    and whipping a wicked slave until he starts to bleed.

Guidelines for Handling Certain Situations

6If your wife is unfaithful, lock the door.
  If a lot of people are around, lock things up.
7When you make a deposit, make sure it is counted
    and double-checked.
  Keep records of everything you give or receive.
8Don't be afraid of correcting a foolish or ignorant person.
  Don't be afraid of correcting an old person who is guilty
    of sexual immorality.

---

[a] 41:19 Hebrew; Greek "before the truth and God's promise."

When you show how well you've been brought up,
   you'll be accepted by everyone.

Daughters

⁹A daughter is unaware that she keeps her father awake at night.
   He is robbed of his sleep because he worries about her.
   He worries
      when she is young that she won't get married,
      when she is married that her husband may stop liking her,
¹⁰   when she is a virgin that she may lose her virginity
        and become pregnant while she's living in his house,
      when she has a husband that she may be unfaithful,
        and when she gets married
          that she may not be able to have children.
¹¹Watch a rebellious daughter closely,
   or else she may make you the laughingstock of your enemies.
   She will become the talk of the town, the subject of gossip,
      and you will be publicly humiliated.
¹²Don't let her flirt with any man.
Don't let her talk with other women.ᵃ
¹³ A woman can destroy another woman
   in the same way that a moth can destroy clothes.
¹⁴ A man's wickedness is better than a woman's goodness.
   Women are the ones who bring shame and disgrace.

Seeing the Glory of the Lord in His Creation

¹⁵I want to remind you of what the Lord has done.
   I will talk about what I have seen.
      Through the Lord's words everything was made.
      All of his creatures do what he wants.
¹⁶The sun shines on everything with its light.
   The Lord's glory fills everything that he has made.
¹⁷The Lord hasn't even given his holy ones the ability
   to understand all his amazing miracles.
      The Lord Almighty has established these miracles
        so that the universe may stand firm in his glory.
¹⁸He searches the depths of the ocean and the human heart.
   He understands their innermost secrets.
   The Most High knows everything that there is to know.
   He sees the signs of the times.
¹⁹ He uncovers what has been and what will be.
   He reveals clues about hidden things.

ᵃ 42:12 Hebrew; Greek meaning uncertain.

20   Not a single thought escapes him.
     He doesn't miss a single word.
21   He has set in place the magnificent things his wisdom
         has achieved.
     He has been and always will be the same.
         Nothing can be added to him or taken away from him.
     He doesn't need anyone to be his adviser.
22 Everything he made is so lovely that it sparkles.
23   Everything is active and enduring.
     Everything does what he intended it to do.
24   Everything comes in pairs, one thing matching the other.
     Nothing he has made has been left unfinished.
25   Every single thing adds to the good qualities
         of the other things.
     Who could ever grow tired of looking at his glory?

The Sky

43 ¹The sky is a clear dome that is the pride of the heavens
     and a glorious sight to see.

The Sun

²When the sun rises, it announces
     throughout its journey across the sky
         what an amazing creation it is—
             something only the Most High could have made.
3   At noon it dries up the land.
     No one can endure its burning heat.
4   A person who works near a blast furnace experiences
         burning heat.
     However, the sun, which scorches the mountains,
         is three times hotter.
             Fiery rays flare from it.
             Its bright rays blind a person.
⁵The Lord, who made the sun, is great!
     His words make it travel quickly along its path.

The Moon

⁶The moon indicates the passage of time.
     It announces the seasons and serves as a constant guide.
⁷The moon indicates the time for a festival.
     Then its light grows dimmer until the end of that phase.
⁸The new moon, as its name suggests, renews itself.
     The way the moon changes its size is amazing.

It is a beacon to the armies high above.
It shines in the sky.

The Stars

⁹The shining stars make the sky beautiful.
They are like glittering ornaments in the Lord's heavens.
¹⁰   They stay in the places assigned to them by the Holy One.
They are always alert as they stand guard.

The Rainbow

¹¹Look at the rainbow, and praise its Creator.
Its brilliant colors are so beautiful.
¹²   That shining arch reaches across the sky.
The hands of the Most High have shaped it.

The Wonders of Creation

¹³His command sends the driving snow,
and his judgment makes the lightning travel quickly.
¹⁴   That is why the storehouses are opened
and the clouds fly out of them like birds.
¹⁵His great power gives the storms their power,
and he carves the ice into hailstones.
¹⁶At the sight of him, the mountains shake.
He makes the south wind begin to blow.
¹⁷Thunder, squalls, and windstorms make the earth shake.
He sprinkles snowflakes, and they look like birds flying downward.
The snowflakes come down like locusts.
¹⁸   People are dazzled by the beauty of the snow's whiteness
and amazed at how it falls.
¹⁹He pours frost over the earth like salt,
and when it freezes, it forms icicles.
²⁰The cold north wind blows,
and ice freezes on top of the water.
It settles on every pool
and covers the water like a breastplate.
²¹He dries up the mountains and scorches the wilderness.
Like fire, he makes tender grass shrivel.
²²   Rain quickly heals everything.
Dew brings relief from the heat.
²³He calmed the oceans
and placed islands in them according to his plan.
²⁴   When sailors tell about the dangers they faced at sea,
we are amazed by what we hear.

²⁵ Strange and amazing creatures, all kinds of living things,
and huge sea monsters live in the sea.
²⁶ Because of the Lord, his messenger succeeds.
Everything is held together by the Lord's word.
²⁷ We could say more, but we could never say enough.
We can conclude by saying, "He is everything."
²⁸ Where can we find enough strength to praise him?
He is greater than everything that he has created.
²⁹ The Lord is awe-inspiring and very great.
His power is amazing.
³⁰ Praise the Lord!
Honor him as much as you can.
Even then, he still deserves more praise than you can give him.
Honor him with all your strength.
You cannot praise him enough,
so don't let yourself become exhausted from trying.
³¹ No one has seen him, so no one can describe him.
No one can praise him as much as he deserves.
³² I have seen only a few of the things he has done.
Mysteries greater than these still lie hidden.
³³ The Lord created everything.
He has given wisdom to devout people.

A Hymn About Our Ancestors: Introduction

44 ¹ Let's praise devout men, our ancestors,
in chronological order.
² The Lord brought them a lot of glory.
His greatness has been seen in them since the beginning of time.
³ Some ruled as kings
and were famous for their courage.
Some served as advisers because they had good sense.
Some were prophets.
⁴ Some guided people with their advice
and their knowledge of history.
Some created wise sayings when they taught.
⁵ Some composed music,
while others wrote poetry.
⁶ Some were rich and powerful
and lived peacefully in their homes.
⁷ Each of these men was honored by his own generation
and was a legend in his own time.
⁸ Some of them have left behind good reputations,
so people still praise them.

⁹Some of them left behind no records of themselves.
They have disappeared as though they had never existed,
as though they and their children had never been born.
¹⁰Here is a list of faithful men.
The good things they did will never be forgotten.
¹¹ Their virtues are passed on as an inheritance
to their descendants,
who passed these virtues on to the next generation.
¹² Because of those men,
their descendants and their descendants' children
are committed
to keeping the terms of the Lord's promises.
¹³ Their family lines will continue for a long time.
The glory of those ancestors will never be wiped out.
¹⁴ Their bodies were laid to rest,
but their good reputations will endure throughout
every generation.
¹⁵ Nations will talk about the wisdom
they received from those faithful ancestors.
Congregations will sing the praises of those men.

Enoch

¹⁶Enoch pleased the Lord, so the Lord took him.
His example has led people in every generation
to change the way they think and act.

Noah

¹⁷Noah had the Lord's complete approval.
He kept the human race alive during that time of anger.
Because of him, a faithful few were left on the earth
after the flood.
¹⁸The Lord made Noah everlasting promises
that never again would all life be wiped out by a flood.

Abraham

¹⁹Abraham was the father of many nations.
No one equaled him in glory.
²⁰ He followed the teachings of the Most High
and entered into an agreement with him.
Circumcision became the sign of this agreement.
When he was tested, he proved to be faithful.
²¹That is why the Lord assured him with a sworn oath:

The nations would be blessed through his descendant.
The Lord would make Abraham's descendants
   as numerous as the specks of dust on the earth.
He would lift them up like stars.
He would give them land from sea to sea,
   from the Euphrates River to the ends of the earth.

Isaac

²²The Lord gave Isaac the same assurance
   that all people would be blessed for the sake
     of his father, Abraham.

Jacob

²³The Lord passed the promise on to Jacob
   and acknowledged him ⌞as the firstborn son⌟
     by giving him blessings and land.
He divided the land into twelve parts
   and distributed one part to each of the twelve tribes.

Moses

45 ¹The Lord brought a devout man from Jacob's descendants into the world.
This man found favor with everyone.
   He was loved by God and people.
     To remember Moses is a blessing itself.
²The Lord made him as glorious as the holy angels.
  God made him so great that his enemies were terrified of him.
³   With words Moses performed miraculous signs.
The Lord honored him in the presence of kings
and gave him the commandments for his people.
The Lord revealed his glory to Moses.
⁴   Since Moses was faithful and humble, the Lord made him holy.
The Lord chose him over everyone else.
⁵   The Lord allowed Moses to hear his voice,
   led him into the dark cloud,
     and gave him the commandments face to face.
The Lord gave Moses the teachings about life and knowledge
   so that he would teach Jacob's descendants the promise
     and teach Israel the Lord's decisions.

Aaron

⁶The Lord honored Aaron, who was holy like Moses.
   Aaron and his brother, Moses, were from the tribe of Levi.

⁷The Lord made an everlasting promise to Aaron.
The Lord turned the priesthood over to him.
The Lord blessed him with ornate vestments,
    put a glorious robe on him,
⁸   and clothed him in perfect splendor.
The Lord strengthened Aaron's position by giving him symbols
    of authority:
    the linen undergarments, the long robe, and the ephod.*
⁹   He put pomegranates and a lot of gold bells all around
      Aaron's robe.
He put the bells all around the robe
    so that their ringing would be heard in the temple
      whenever Aaron walked.
        This would serve as a reminder to his people.
¹⁰ He put on Aaron this holy garment,
    which was made of gold, violet, purple,
      and embroidered designs.
He put on Aaron the breastplate with the Urim and Thummim,ᵇ
    which determined the Lord's decisions on various matters.
¹¹   This breastplate, which was attached by a craftsman
      using bright red yarn, also had precious stones.
    The stones were engraved and set in gold by a jeweler.
    These engraved stones were reminders
      of Israel's twelve tribes.
¹²   The Lord put a gold crown on Aaron's turban.
    A seal on the crown was inscribed with the word holy.
      The crown was a symbol of distinction—a work of art.
      It was so beautiful to look at.
¹³These beautiful works of art did not exist before Aaron became
    a priest.
No outsider has ever worn them.
    Only his sons and his descendants can wear them.
¹⁴Aaron had to sacrifice burnt offerings twice each day
    on a daily basis.
¹⁵Moses ordained him and anointed him with holy oil.
    This was an everlasting agreement made with him
      and his descendants as long as heaven endures.
    Aaron had to serve the Lord as his priest
      and bless the people in the Lord's name.

---

a 45:8 *Ephod* is a technical term for a part of the priest's clothes. Its exact usage and shape are unknown.
b 45:10 The Urim and Thummim were used by the chief priest to determine God's answer to questions.

[16] The Lord chose Aaron out of all people to offer sacrifices to him.
Aaron had to offer incense as a reminder.
It was a soothing aroma that made peace with the Lord for
the people.

[17] On the basis of the Lord's commandments, Aaron
was given authority
to make legal decisions,
to teach Jacob's descendants the Lord's decrees,
and to enlighten Israel with the Lord's teachings.

[18] Jealous outsiders conspired against Aaron in the desert.
Dathan, Abiram, their men,
and Korah's followers were infuriated with him.

[19] The Lord saw what they were doing and was not pleased.
He was so infuriated with them that he killed them.
The way he destroyed them in a raging fire was amazing.

[20] Then the Lord gave Aaron a special honor.
He gave Aaron and the priests the right
to the first and best produce harvested
and made sure they had plenty to eat.

[21]   The Lord has given the priests the right
to eat the Lord's sacrifices,
which he gave to Aaron and his descendants.

[22] Nevertheless, Aaron received no land in Israel.
Unlike the rest of the people of Israel, he received no land
because serving the Lord took the place of owning land.

Phinehas

[23] Phinehas, Eleazar's son, ranks third in honor
because he was so devoted to defending the Lord's honor.
He stood firm, even though the people turned away.
He was a good, courageous individual.
He made peace with the Lord when Israel rebelled.

[24] That is why the Lord made a promise of peace to Phinehas.
He wanted Phinehas to be the leader of the holy place and
of his people.
He wanted Aaron and his descendants
to have the honor of being priests forever.

[25] The Lord made a promise to David,
son of Jesse, from the tribe of Judah.
The Lord promised that the kingship
would be passed on only from one son to the next son,
but he promised that the priesthood
would be passed on to all of Aaron's descendants.

²⁶ May the Lord grant you the wisdom necessary
to judge his people with justice
so that their virtues will not disappear
and that their glory will be passed on to all
their descendants.

Joshua

46 ¹Joshua, son of Nun, was an unstoppable soldier in battle.
He took Moses' place and assumed the duties of a prophet.
Joshua [The LORD Saves] became, as his name denotes,
a great savior of the Lord's chosen people.
He took revenge on Israel's enemies
so that he could give the Lord's people the land
promised to them.
²How glorious he was when he lifted his hands up high
and used his sword against the people in the cities!
³   No one could stand in his way,
since he was fighting battles for the Lord.
⁴Because of Joshua, the sun stood still,
and one day became as long as two.
⁵When enemies were putting pressure on him from every side,
he called on the Most High, the Almighty Lord.
The great Lord answered him by sending
powerful hailstones to destroy his enemies.
⁶   He crushed that nation in battle,
and on the slope of Beth Horon, he destroyed his opponents.
In this way the other nations learned about his source
of strength.
They also learned that he was fighting battles for the Lord.
Joshua was a devoted follower of the Almighty Lord.

Caleb

⁷During Moses' lifetime, Caleb had proven his devotion to the Lord.
Joshua and Caleb, son of Jephunneh, opposed the congregation.
They kept the people from sinning
and made them stop their wicked complaining.
⁸Only these two men were spared
out of six hundred thousand infantrymen.
They led the people to the land promised to them,
the land flowing with milk and honey.
⁹The Lord gave Caleb strength.
Caleb was so strong that even when he was old,
he was able to capture the mountain region
and give it to his children as an inheritance.

10   All the Israelites could see
            that following the Lord is good.

The Judges

11 Israel has a long list of famous judges.
    They never worshiped other gods.
    They never turned away from the Lord.
    May they be a blessing to everyone who remembers them.
12 May their bones send out new life from their graves.
    May their honored names inspire their descendants to follow
        the Lord.

Samuel

13 Samuel was loved by his Lord.
    He was one of the Lord's prophets.
    He established the kingdom of Israel
        and anointed the rulers of his people.
14   He made decisions for the people
            and based those decisions on the Lord's teachings.
        The Lord took care of Jacob's descendants.
15 Samuel was recognized as a prophet because of his faithfulness.
    He became known as a reliable seer[a] because of what he said.
16 When his enemies put pressure on him from every side,
    he prayed to the Almighty Lord
        and offered a lamb as a sacrifice.
17 Then the Lord's voice thundered from heaven.
    He made his voice heard clearly
18   and destroyed the leaders of Tyre
            and all the rulers of the Philistines.
19 Before Samuel fell into his eternal sleep,
    he testified in front of the Lord and his anointed king:
        "I haven't taken anyone's property,
            not even a pair of shoes."
                And no one accused him of taking anything.
20 Even after he had been laid to rest,
    he prophesied that the king was going to die.
        His voice rose from the ground to prophesy,
            to wipe out the people's wickedness.

---

[a] 46:15 A seer is a prophet.

Nathan

47 ¹During David's lifetime, after Samuel's death, Nathan began to prophesy.

David

²As fat is set apart from a sacrifice,
  David was set apart from the Israelites.
³   He played with lions as though they were young goats
      and with bears as though they were lambs.
⁴When he was young, he killed Goliath.
  When he hurled a stone in a sling
    and stopped the arrogant giant,
      he removed his people's disgrace.
⁵He prayed to the Lord, the Most High.
  The Lord strengthened David's right arm
    so that he could eliminate that fierce warrior
      and display the power of his own people.
⁶The people honored him for defeating tens of thousands.
  When he was crowned king,
    they congratulated him for the blessings he received
      from the Lord.
⁷   He had wiped out his enemies on every side
      and annihilated his opponents, the Philistines.
        Even at the present time, they are no threat.
⁸With words of praise, he thanked the Holy One, the Most High,
  in everything he did.
    He put his whole heart into singing hymns of praise
      to show his love for his Creator.
⁹   He placed a choir in front of the altar
      to sing along to beautiful harp music.
¹⁰   He turned the festivals into dignified celebrations.
    He established the yearly cycle of festivals.
      This cycle determines
        when people should praise the Lord's holy name
          and when music should fill the holy place.
      (The music should begin early in the morning.)
¹¹The Lord forgave David's sins and gave him great
    and enduring power.
  The Lord promised him a royal dynasty and a glorious throne
    in Israel.

Solomon

¹² After David's death, his wise son succeeded him.
 Solomon had security because of what David had achieved.
¹³　Solomon ruled in an age of peace.
 God gave him peace along every border
 so that he could build a house for God's name
 and provide a holy place that would last forever.
¹⁴ Solomon, you were so wise when you were young.
 You overflowed with understanding
 in the same way that a river overflows with water.
¹⁵ You influenced the whole world,
 and you filled it with thought-provoking stories.
¹⁶ Your reputation has reached distant islands,
 and people loved you because you brought peace.
¹⁷ Your songs, proverbs, stories,
 and answers amazed the world.
¹⁸ In the name of the Lord God, who is called the God of Israel,
 you collected gold as though it were tin
 and gathered silver as though it were lead.

¹⁹ However, you slept with many women.
 You became a slave to your body's desires.
²⁰　You tarnished your honor and corrupted your family.
 You made the Lord angry at your children,
 and they suffered because of your stupidity.
²¹　　The kingdom split in two.
 Ephraim became a rival kingdom.
²² In spite of Solomon's sins, the Lord will never stop being merciful
 or break any of his promises.
 The Lord will never wipe out the descendants
 of his chosen one
 or destroy the family of the one who loved him.
 So he let Jacob have a few remaining descendants.
 Also, the Lord left David a root from his own family.

Rehoboam and Jeroboam

²³ Solomon rested in peace with his ancestors
 and left one of his sons as his successor.
 Rehoboam was the most stupid person in the nation.
 He lacked good sense.
 His policies forced the people to revolt.
 Then Jeroboam, Nebat's son, led Israel to commit sins.
 He led Ephraim on its sinful journey.

24 The people of Ephraim sinned so much
that they were exiled from their land.
25 They went out of their way to do every kind of evil
until their punishment caught up with them.

Elijah

48 ¹Then came Elijah. He was a fiery prophet.
His words burned like torches.
2 He brought a famine to the people of Israel.
He killed a lot of them because of his devotion to the Lord.
3 Using the Lord's words, he stopped the rain from falling.
In the same way, he made fire
come down from heaven three times.
⁴Elijah, you were glorious when you performed
your amazing miracles.
No one else could perform miracles like those.
5 Using the words of the Most High,
you brought a corpse that was in the grave back to life.
6 You dragged kings to destruction
and famous men from their sickbeds.
7 At Sinai you heard the Lord question you,
and at Horeb you heard decisions made about punishment.
8 You anointed kings to inflict punishment
and prophets to succeed you.
9 You were taken to heaven in a fiery windstorm,
in a chariot with fiery horses.
¹⁰Scripture says that at the designated time you will
calm God's anger before it erupts,
change parents' attitudes toward their children,
and reestablish the tribes of Jacob.
¹¹Blessed are those who will see you
and have fallen asleep in love.
We will certainly live!

Elisha

¹²When Elijah disappeared in the windstorm,
Elisha was filled with his spirit.
No ruler could ever make Elisha tremble.
No one could control him.
13 Nothing was too hard for him!
Even when he was dead, his body still prophesied.
¹⁴While Elisha was alive, he performed miracles,
and while he was dead, he did amazing things.

¹⁵In spite of all these things,
  people didn't change the way they thought or acted.
  They didn't abandon their sinful ways
    until they were carried away from their own land like loot
    and were scattered all over the earth.
 Only a few people were left,
  but they did have a ruler from David's descendants.
¹⁶Some of them did what pleased the Lord,
  but others continued to sin.

Hezekiah and Isaiah

¹⁷Hezekiah fortified his city.
  He made water accessible to the city
    by tunneling through rock with iron tools.
  He built cisterns to hold the water.
¹⁸During Hezekiah's lifetime, King Sennacherib attacked him.
  Sennacherib sent his commander-in-chief,
    who shook his fist at Zion and bragged.
¹⁹ Then the people lost courage, and they became afraid.
  They were in as much pain as a woman in labor.
²⁰ They prayed to the merciful Lord
    and stretched out their hands to him in prayer.
 The Holy One from heaven quickly responded to them.
  He used Isaiah to save them.
²¹The Lord struck the soldiers in the Assyrian camp,
  and his angel wiped them out.
²²Hezekiah did what was pleasing to the Lord.
  He closely followed the ways of his ancestor David
    as the prophet Isaiah had commanded him to do.
 Isaiah was a great prophet whose visions were reliable.
²³He made the sun move backwards.
  As a result, he prolonged the king's life.
²⁴ Under the influence of the Spirit, he saw the last days.
  So he was able to comfort those who were mourning in Zion.
²⁵ He revealed hidden things before they happened,
    things that were going to happen in the future.

Josiah

49¹Memories of Josiah are like blended incense
    that is prepared with the skill of a perfumer.
 Memories of Josiah are as sweet as honey
    and like music at a banquet where wine is served.
²He corrected a misguided nation
    and took away their disgusting idols.

³He kept his mind focused on the Lord
    and encouraged the worship of the true God in a lawless age.

Jeremiah

⁴Except for David, Hezekiah, and Josiah,
    all the kings committed one sin after another.
  They abandoned the teachings of the Most High,
    and as a result, the kings of Judah lost their kingdom.
⁵They gave their power to other people
    and their glory to a foreign nation.
⁶The chosen city, the city of the holy place, was burned down.
  Its streets were deserted
⁷   as Jeremiah had predicted.
  They had mistreated Jeremiah.
    He had been set apart in his mother's womb to serve as
      a prophet.
    He was called to uproot, ruin, and destroy,
      but he was also called to build and plant.

Ezekiel and Job

⁸Ezekiel saw the vision of glory
    that God showed him above the chariot of the angels.ᵃ
⁹   God reminded him about Job,
      who always followed the right path.

The Twelve Minor Prophets

¹⁰May the bones of the twelve prophets
    send out new life from their graves.
    These prophets had a confident hope
      that comforted and saved Jacob's people.

Zerubbabel and the Chief Priest Joshua

¹¹How can we ever praise Zerubbabel enough for being so great?
    He was like a signet ring on the right hand,
¹²   and so was Joshua, the son of Jehozadak.
  They rebuilt the Lord's house
    and erected a holy temple to the Lord.
      This was begun and completed in their lifetime.
      The temple was destined for everlasting glory.

ᵃ 49:8 Or "cherubim."

Nehemiah

[13] Memories of Nehemiah are just as great.
He reconstructed our fallen walls,
reinstalled the gates with their bars,
and rebuilt our homes.

Some Other Faithful Men

[14] No one created on earth was ever like Enoch.
He was taken from earth.
[15] No one born was ever like Joseph.
He was the leader of his brothers and the supporter
of his people.
Even his bones were carefully guarded.
[16] People honor Shem and Seth,
but they honor Adam above every other creature.

The Chief Priest—Simon II[a]

50 [1] Simon, son of Onias, was the chief priest.
He repaired the Lord's house.
He fortified the temple.
Both tasks were begun and completed in his lifetime.
[2] He laid the foundations for high double walls,
the high retaining walls for the temple courtyard.
[3] He dug a cistern to hold water.
This cistern was a reservoir that was as large as the sea.
[4] He was concerned about protecting his people from an attack,
so he fortified the city in the event of a siege.
[5] He looked glorious when he was surrounded by the people.
As he came from behind the curtain in the temple, he was
[6] like the morning star shining through the clouds,
like the full moon on a festival day,
[7] like the sun shining on the temple of the Most High,
like a rainbow appearing with beautiful clouds,
[8] like roses in the spring,
like lilies by a stream,
like a green shoot on a frankincense tree in the summer,
[9] like fire and incense in the incense burner,
like a cup made out of gold
and decorated with all kinds of precious stones,
[10] like an olive tree weighed down with olives,

---

[a] 50:1 Simon II was the son of Onias III and lived around 220–195 B.C. Simon was a contemporary of Ben Sirach.

and like a cypress tree towering in the clouds.

¹¹ After he put on his glorious robe
and clothed himself in splendor,
he went up the steps to the holy altar
and filled the courtyard of the holy place with glory.

¹² As Simon took the offerings from the priests,
he stood by the altar for burnt offerings.
The other priests stood in a circle around him like a crown.
He was like one of Mount Lebanon's young cedars
surrounded by palm trees.

¹³   All of Aaron's descendants stood there in their splendor.
In front of the whole congregation of Israel,
they held the offerings for the Lord.

¹⁴   They finished the ritual at the altars
and prepared the offering for the Most High, the Almighty.

¹⁵ Next, Simon held out his hand to take the offering cup
and poured a wine offering made from grapes.
He poured it out at the base of the altar.
The aroma was soothing to the Most High, the king of all.

¹⁶   Then Aaron's descendants shouted.
They blew their silver trumpets.
They sounded a loud fanfare
as a reminder to the Most High.

¹⁷   Immediately, all the people bowed
with their faces touching the ground
to worship their Lord, the Almighty, God Most High.

¹⁸   Then the choir praised the Lord.
The beautiful music was heard everywhere.

¹⁹   Meanwhile, the people of the merciful Lord Most High
continued to offer their prayers
until the Lord's order of worship came to an end
and they finished all the rituals
for worshiping the Lord.

²⁰ Then Simon came down from the altar
and raised his hands over the whole congregation of Israel
to speak the Lord's blessing.
Using the Lord's name in this blessing was an honor.

²¹   The people bowed down in worship a second time
to receive the blessing from the Most High.

A Blessing

²² Praise the God of all creation.
He has done great things everywhere.
He has cared for us since birth

and has treated us mercifully.
²³ May he make us happy.
May he make Israel as peaceful now
as it was long ago.
²⁴ May he continue to sh ow us his mercy,
and may he save us in our own lifetime.[a]

Three Disgusting Groups of People

²⁵ Two groups of people disgust me,
and a third one is a religious sect:
²⁶   the Edomites, the Philistines, and those foolish Samaritans.

Conclusion by Ben Sirach

²⁷ I am Jesus Ben Sirach Eleazar of Jerusalem.
I have written this book
about the discipline of good sense and knowledge
because wisdom flowed from my mind.
²⁸ Blessed is the person who dwells on these things.
Anyone who takes these things to heart will become wise.
²⁹   Whoever puts them into practice will be able to handle anything
because the Lord's light will guide him on the right path.

My Prayer of Thanks

51 ¹ I thank you, Lord and King,
and praise you, God, my savior.
I give thanks to your name
²   because you have protected me and helped me.
You have rescued me
from harm,
from the traps laid by people who slandered me,
from lies that someone made up,
and from those who oppose me.
³ Because of the richness of your mercy and of your name,
you have rescued me
from teeth that were about to devour me,
from hands that wanted to take my life,
from the many troubles I have endured,
⁴   from stifling heat all around me,
from the midst of a fire that I didn't start,
⁵   from the deep belly of the grave,
from half truths and outright lies,
⁶   and from vicious slander reported to the king.

---

[a] 50:24 Greek meaning of this verse uncertain.

I was close to dying.
My life was about to end.
⁷I was surrounded on all sides,
and no one was there to help me.
I looked for someone to help me,
but no one was there.

⁸ Then, Lord, I remembered your mercy
and the things you did long ago.
You rescued those who trusted you.
You saved them from the power of their enemies.

⁹ So, from here on earth, I sent up my prayer
and begged you to rescue me from death.

¹⁰ I cried out, "Lord, you are my Father!
Don't abandon me in times of trouble.
Don't abandon me
when no one else can help me
against arrogant people.

¹¹ I will always praise your name.
I will sing hymns of thanksgiving to you."
My prayer was heard.

¹² You saved me from harm
and rescued me in a time of trouble.
For this reason I will thank you, praise you,
and bless your name.

My Search for Wisdom

¹³While I was still young, before I started traveling,
I explicitly asked for wisdom when I prayed.

¹⁴ I even begged for it in front of the temple,
and I will continue to search for it until the day I die.

¹⁵My heart has found joy in wisdom
from the first time it began to bloom in my life
until it began to ripen.
My feet have walked on wisdom's straight path.
I have been following it ever since I was young.

¹⁶I listened a little, and wisdom entered my ears
and provided me with a wealth of knowledge.

¹⁷I continued to make progress in becoming wiser.
I will honor the Lord, who gives me wisdom.

¹⁸I was determined to put it into practice.
I was enthusiastic about what was good,
and I will never regret it.

¹⁹I struggled with wisdom,

and I strictly followed its teachings.
I stretched out my hands to heaven,
   and I was sorry that I knew so little about wisdom.
²⁰I focused my attention on finding wisdom,
   and by keeping myself pure, I found it.
I gained understanding through it from the very beginning.
   That is why it will never abandon me.
²¹I was determined to find it.
   That is why I have gained such a wonderful prize.
²² As a reward, the Lord gave me the skill to communicate,
   and I will praise him with it.
²³Anyone who needs instruction
   can always study in my school.
²⁴So you have no reason to complain about not having any
     of these things
   and being so thirsty for them.
²⁵I said,
   "You can acquire wisdom for yourselves,
     and doing so won't cost you any money.
²⁶ Put your necks under wisdom's yoke,ᵃ
     and let your souls receive instruction.
     Wisdom is available to you."
²⁷Look at how little I have worked
   and yet, I've found so much peace of mind.
²⁸Your instruction may cost you a lot of silver,
   but you will gain a lot of gold from it.
²⁹May you find joy in the Lord's mercy,
   and may you never be ashamed of praising him.
³⁰If you do your work at the right time,
   then the Lord will give you your reward at the right time.

ᵃ 51:26 A yoke is a wooden bar placed over the necks of work animals so that they can pull plows or carts.

Baruch

Baruch Meets With the Jews Living in Babylon

1 ¹This book was written by Baruch, who was the son of Neriah, the grandson of Mahseiah, and a descendant of Zedekiah, Hasadiah, and Hilkiah. It was written in Babylon ²on the seventh day of the month in the fifth year after the Babylonians captured Jerusalem and burned it down. ³Baruch read this book aloud to Judah's King Jeconiah, who was the son of Jehoiakim, and to everyone who lived in Babylon by the Sud River. These are all the people who came to hear it read: ⁴the nobles, the king's children, the leaders, and all the people, from the most important to the least important.ᵃ

Baruch Returns to Jerusalem

⁵After the book was read, they cried, fasted, and prayed to the Lord. ⁶Then they collected money. Each person gave as much as he could. ⁷They sent the money to Jerusalem to the priest Jehoiakim, son of Hilkiah and grandson of Shallum, to the other priests, and to all the people who were with him in Jerusalem.

⁸At the same time, on the tenth day of Sivan, Baruch took the utensils that belonged to the Lord's house, the utensils that were removed from the temple, and he returned them to Judah. These were the silver utensils that Judah's King Zedekiah, son of Josiah, had made ⁹after King Nebuchadnezzar of Babylon had captured Jeconiah, the princes, the craftsmen,ᵇ the nobles, and the common people in Jerusalem and brought them to Babylon.

A Message to the Jews in Jerusalem

¹⁰The Jews living in Babylon also sent ⌐with Baruch⌐ the following message: We are sending you money to buy ⌐animals⌐ for burnt offerings and offerings for sin. Also, use some of the money to buy incense and to provide grain offerings. Offer them on the altar of the Lord our God.

ᵃ 1:4 The last part of verse 4 has been placed in verse 3 to express the complex Greek sentence structure more clearly in English.

ᵇ 1:9 Jeremiah 24:1; 29:2; Greek "prisoners."

[11]Pray for King Nebuchadnezzar of Babylon and for his son Belshazzar that they may live on earth as long as heaven lasts. [12]Then the Lord will give us strength and a newfound hope. We will live under the protection of King Nebuchadnezzar of Babylon and his son Belshazzar. We will serve them for a long time, and they will be pleased with us. [13]Also, pray to the Lord our God for us, because we have sinned against him and he is still very angry with us. [14]Finally, you must read aloud this scroll that we are sending you and confess your sins in the Lord's house on the first day of festivals and on the other days when you assemble for worship.

Confess Your Sins

[15]You must say, "The Lord our God has done what is right. Those of us here today have shamefully done what is wrong. We, the people of Judah and the inhabitants of Jerusalem, [16]our kings, our rulers, our priests, our prophets, and our ancestors, [17]are ashamed because we have sinned against the Lord. [18]We have disobeyed him and have not listened to the Lord our God. We have not lived by the commands that the Lord gave us. [19]From the time the Lord brought our ancestors out of Egypt until now, we have disobeyed the Lord our God. All too often we have ignored him. [20]When the Lord brought our ancestors out of Egypt to give us a land flowing with milk and honey, he threatened to bring disasters and curses on us through his servant Moses. These disasters and curses are still with us today. [21]We did not listen to the Lord our God when he spoke to us through the prophets he sent us. [22]Instead, all of us followed the desires of our own wicked hearts. We served other gods and did what the Lord our God considered evil.

2 [1]"So the Lord carried out his threat against us and against our judges, our kings, our rulers, and the people of Israel and Judah. [2]Nowhere else in the world has the Lord done what he did to Jerusalem. These things were predicted in Moses' Teachings. [3]We even ate the flesh of our own sons and daughters. [4]So the Lord put us under the control of all the kingdoms around us. Then we were disgraced and rejected by all the people living in those nations where the Lord had scattered us. [5]We were humiliated, not honored, because our nation had sinned against the Lord our God by refusing to obey him.

[6]"The Lord our God has done what is right. Our ancestors and those of us here today have shamefully done what is wrong. [7]All the disasters that the Lord threatened us with have happened to us. [8]Yet, we have not asked the Lord to help each of us remove the thoughts that come from our wicked hearts. [9]The Lord watched for the right moment to bring these disasters on us. The Lord is right about everything that he has commanded us to do. [10]But we didn't obey him or live by the laws he gave us.

Pray to the Lord for Help

¹¹ "Lord God of Israel, you used your mighty hand to bring your people out of Egypt. You used miraculous signs, amazing things, spectacular miracles, and your powerful arm. You made a name for yourself that is still famous today. ¹²Lord our God, we have sinned, we have been ungodly, and we have disobeyed all your commands. ¹³Don't be angry with us anymore. There are only a few of us left among the nations where you have scattered us. ¹⁴Lord, listen to our prayer and our plea for help. For your own sake rescue us, and make those who have captured us be kind to us. ¹⁵Then the whole earth will know that you are the Lord our God and that the people of Israel and their descendants are called by your name.

¹⁶ "Lord, look down from your holy dwelling place, and keep us in mind. Open your ears, Lord, and listen ˻to our prayers˼. ¹⁷Open your eyes, Lord, and see ˻our misery˼. The dead, who are in the grave and whose spirits have been taken from their bodies, cannot give you glory or do what you command. ¹⁸People who are overwhelmed with grief, who walk bent over and are weak, or who have failing eyesight and are hungry will give you glory and do what you command, Lord.

¹⁹ "Lord our God, we're begging you for mercy, but not because our ancestors or our kings did what you considered right. ²⁰You warned us through your servants the prophets that you would show us how very angry you were with us. You said, ²¹"This is what the Lord says: Surrender to the king of Babylon, and serve him. Then you may remain in the land that I gave to your ancestors. ²²But if you will not obey the Lord and serve the king of Babylon, ²³I will banish the sounds of joy and happiness and the sounds of brides and grooms from the towns of Judah and from the region around Jerusalem. The whole land will become deserted.'

²⁴ "But we did not obey you and serve the king of Babylon. So you carried out the threat that you spoke through your servants the prophets: The bones of our kings and our ancestors were taken out of their graves. ²⁵In fact, their bones were thrown out and exposed to the heat of day and the cold of night. These men died painful deaths from famines, wars, and plagues. ²⁶You have made this house, which is called by your name, what it is today because of the wickedness of the people of Israel and Judah.

²⁷ "And yet, Lord our God, you have been kind to us and have shown us your rich mercy. ²⁸This is what you promised through your servant Moses on the day you commanded him to write down your teachings in the presence of the people of Israel. You said, ²⁹"If you will not obey me, even though you are a very large and noisy crowd, you will certainly be reduced to a small number of people among the nations where I will scatter you. ³⁰I know you won't obey me. You people are impossible to

deal with. But in the land where you are captives, you will come to your senses [31]and realize that I am the Lord your God. I will give you hearts that obey and ears that hear. [32]You will praise me in the land where you are captives, and you will remember my name. [33]You will no longer be impossible to deal with, and you will no longer do evil things. Instead, you will remember how your ancestors sinned against the Lord. [34]Then I will bring you back to the land that I swore to give to your ancestors Abraham, Isaac, and Jacob, and you will take possession of it. I will increase your population; it will never decrease. [35]I will make an eternal promise to[a] you: I will be your God, you will be my people, and I will never again remove you, my people Israel, from the land that I have given you.'

3 [1]"Almighty Lord, God of Israel, we are depressed and in distress. So we cry out to you. [2]Listen to us, Lord, and have mercy on us, because we have sinned against you. [3]You are enthroned forever, but we are lost forever. [4]Almighty Lord, God of Israel, listen now to the prayer of the people of Israel. We are the descendants of those who sinned against you. Our ancestors did not obey you, the Lord their God. So we have suffered one disaster after another. [5]Do not remember the evil things our ancestors did. Instead, remember your power and your name. [6]You are the Lord our God, and we will praise you, Lord. [7]You put the fear of God in our hearts so that we would call on your name. We will praise you in the land where we are in exile, because we have turned away from all the evil things done by our ancestors, who sinned against you. [8]Today we are living as exiles in the land where you have scattered us. We are being insulted, cursed, and punished for all the evil things done by our ancestors, who deserted you, the Lord our God."

Desire Wisdom

[9]Israel, listen to the commands that bring life.
    Pay attention, and gain insight.
[10]Israel, why is it that you are in the land of your enemies?
    Why are you growing old in a foreign country?
[11] Why are you unclean[b] like dead bodies?
    Why are you compared to those who are in the grave?
[12]You have deserted the fountain of wisdom.
[13] If you had followed God's directions,
      you would have lived in peace forever.
[14]Learn where to find insight, where to find strength,
    and where to find understanding.

---

[a] 2:35 Or "covenant with."

[b] 3:11 "Unclean" refers to anything that Moses' Teachings say is not presentable to God.

Then you will know where to find a long and full life.
You will also know where to find peace and light to see ⌞clearly⌟.

¹⁵ Who has found where wisdom is located?
Who has entered its storehouses?
¹⁶ Where are the rulers of the nations?
Where are those who tamed wild animals
¹⁷   and hunted birds for sport?
Where are those who hoarded silver and gold?
    (Those people trusted silver and gold,
       and they always wanted more and more.)
¹⁸ Where are those silversmiths who worked so carefully
    but left no trace of their work?
¹⁹ They have vanished and gone to their graves,
    and others have replaced them.
²⁰ People from recent generations have seen the light of day
    and have lived on earth.
But they have not learned the way of knowledge,
²¹   understood its paths, or even had any grasp of it.
Their descendants have strayed far from its paths.
²² Knowledge has never been heard of in Canaan or seen in Teman.
²³ Hagar's descendants look for understanding on earth.
    The merchants from Merran and Teman,
       the storytellers, and the philosophers
       have not learned the way of wisdom
         or remembered where its paths are.

²⁴ Israel, God's universe is so great!
The territory that he possesses is so vast!
²⁵   It is wide and endless.
It is high and immeasurable.
²⁶ The giants, who were famous long ago, were born there.
    They were very tall and were experienced soldiers.
²⁷ Yet, God did not choose them or show them the way
       of knowledge.
²⁸   They died because of their lack of insight.
They died because of their stupidity.

²⁹ Who has gone up to heaven to get wisdom
    and brought it down from the clouds?
³⁰ Who has crossed the sea to find wisdom
    and bought it with pure gold?
³¹ No one knows the way to ⌞find⌟ it
    or thinks about ⌞finding⌟ the path to it.

³²But the one who knows everything knows wisdom.
He found it by using his understanding.
He is the one who built the earth to last forever
and filled it with four-footed animals.
³³ He is the one who tells the light to go, and it goes.
He calls it ˻back˼, and it respectfully obeys him.
³⁴The stars shine where he has put them, and they are happy.
³⁵ He calls for them, and they say, "Here we are!"
They are happy to shine for their maker.
³⁶This is our God. No one can compare to him.
³⁷ He found every way ˻that leads˼ to knowledge,
and he gave wisdom to his servant Jacob,
to Israel, whom he loved.
³⁸Later, wisdom appeared on earth and lived among humans.

4 ¹Wisdom is the book of God's commands
and the law that lasts forever.
All who hold on to wisdom will live,
but those who reject it will die.
²Descendants of Jacob, go back and take hold of wisdom.
Walk toward its shining light.
³Don't give your glory to anyone else
or your privileges to any other nation.
⁴People of Israel, we are blessed.
We know what pleases God.

The People of Israel Are Reassured

⁵Cheer up, my people! You keep Israel's name alive.
⁶ You were sold to the nations ˻by God˼, but not to be destroyed.
You were handed over to your enemies
because you made God angry.
⁷ You provoked the one who made you
by sacrificing to demons, not to God.
⁸ You forgot the eternal God, who nourished you.
You upset Jerusalem, who raised you like a mother.
⁹When Jerusalem saw that God unleashed his anger against you,
she said:
"Listen, you neighbors of Zion.
God has brought me so much misery.
¹⁰ I've seen my sons and daughters taken captive.
The eternal God brought this on them.
¹¹ It was a joy for me to raise them.
But I cried and mourned when I saw them taken away.
¹² No one should be happy now that I'm a widow
and have been abandoned by so many ˻loved ones˼.

I'm a deserted city because of the sins my children committed.
> They turned away from God's teachings.
13   They didn't want to know his laws.
> They wouldn't follow the directions in God's commandments
> or live in the right ways that he taught them.

14 "Come here, you neighbors of Zion.
> Remember that my sons and daughters were taken captive.
> The eternal God brought this on them.
15   He brought people from a nation far away to attack them.
> They were shameless people who spoke a foreign language.
> They had no respect for the elderly
> and no pity for young people.
16   They led away my dear sons and daughters,
> and I was left a widow, completely alone.
17 But how can I help you, ⌐my children⌐?
18 Only the one who brought this disaster on you
> can rescue you from your enemies.
19 Go, my children. Go.
> I have been left as a deserted city.
20   I have taken off the robe ⌐I wore when there was⌐ peace
> and have put on sackcloth to make my plea for help.
> I will cry out to the eternal God as long as I live.

21   "Cheer up, my children! Cry out to God for help.
> He will rescue you
> from the power and oppression of your enemies.
22   I trust the eternal God to save you.
> The Holy One, your eternal savior, has made me joyful
> because of the mercy he will soon show to you.
23   I cried and mourned when I saw you taken away.
> But I will rejoice and be glad forever
> when God brings you back to me.
24   The neighbors of Zion watched as you were taken captive.
> Soon they will see you rescued by God.
> This rescue will happen to you with great glory
> and with the splendor of the eternal God.

25   "My children, patiently endure the anger
> that God has unleashed against you.
> Your enemies have hunted you down,
> but you will soon see their destruction
> and put your feet on their necks.
26   My pampered children, you have traveled rough roads.
> You were taken away like a flock captured in an enemy raid.

²⁷   Cheer up, my children, and cry out to God for help.
        The one who did this to you will not forget you.
²⁸   Your minds were once set on wandering away from God.
        But now go back and look for him
            with ten times the determination.
²⁹   The one who brought this disaster on you
            will bring you everlasting joy when he rescues you."

Jerusalem Is Reassured

³⁰Cheer up, Jerusalem!
        The one who gave you your name will comfort you.
³¹Those who mistreated you and rejoiced when you fell will be sorry.
³²The cities where your children were slaves will be sorry.
        The city that took your sons ˹and daughters˼ will be sorry.
³³Just as that city rejoiced when you fell
        and was glad when you were destroyed,
            so it will grieve when it, too, becomes a deserted city.
³⁴I will remove the large population that made that city so happy,
        and I will turn its arrogance into mourning.
³⁵Fire from the eternal God will rain down on it for many days.
        For a long time to come, it will be inhabited by demons.

³⁶Look to the east, Jerusalem.
        See the joy that is coming to you from God.
³⁷   Look! Your children that were taken away are coming ˹home˼.
        They are coming from the east and the west.
        They were gathered at the command of the Holy One
            and are rejoicing in the glory of God.

5 ¹Jerusalem, take off the clothes you wore
        when you were in mourning and distress.
            Put on the beauty of God's glory and wear it forever.
²   Wrap the robe of his justice around you.
        Put on the turban of eternal glory.
³   God will show your splendor to every nation under heaven.
⁴   God will always call you
            Peace through Justice and Glory through Godliness.

⁵Arise, Jerusalem! Stand in a high place.
    Look toward the east, and see your children.
        They are coming from the east and the west
            at the command of the Holy One.
        They are rejoicing because God has remembered them.
⁶They left you on foot.
        They were led away by their enemies.

But God will bring your children back to you.
    They will be carried in glory, like a king on a throne.
⁷God has given the following order:
    Every high mountain and everlasting hill will be lowered,
        and the valleys will be filled to make the ground level.
            Then the people of Israel will walk safely in God's glory.
⁸At God's command the woods and every fragrant tree
    will give shade to the people of Israel.
⁹God will lead the joyful people of Israel with the light of his glory
    and guide them with his mercy and justice.

The Letter of Jeremiah[a]

Introduction

This is a copy of a letter that Jeremiah sent to the prisoners who were about to be taken to Babylon by the king of the Babylonians. This letter contains the message that God had commanded Jeremiah to give them.

The People Will Be Prisoners in Babylon for Many Years

[1] Because of the sins that you have committed against God, you will be taken as prisoners to Babylon by King Nebuchadnezzar. [2] Once you arrive in Babylon, you will stay there for many years, for a long time, for up to seven generations. After that, God[b] will bring you back home safely.

[3] In Babylon you will see gods made of gold, silver, and wood. They will be carried around on people's shoulders, and they will impress the people from other nations. [4] You must be careful that you never become like those foreigners. Don't let those gods impress you [5] when you see them paraded around and worshiped by crowds of people. Instead, say to yourselves, "Lord, you're the only one who should be worshiped." [6] The angel of the Lord[c] will be with you. He will take care of you.

Idols Are Helpless

[7] These gods are ⌊only statues⌋ covered with gold and silver. Their tongues are delicately carved by carpenters. But they're not real gods, and they can't speak. [8] People make gold crowns for their gods to wear, as if their gods were girls who love jewelry. [9] Sometimes the priests steal gold and silver from their gods and spend it on themselves.[d] [10] The priests even give some of the gold and silver to the prostitutes on the temple terrace. These gods are made of gold, silver, and wood, yet they are dressed in clothes like humans. [11] They can't even protect themselves against corro-

---

[a] The Letter of Jeremiah appears as the sixth chapter of Baruch in some translations.
[b] 2 Greek "I."
[c] 6 Syriac; Greek "My angel."
[d] 9 The first part of verse 9 has been placed in verse 8 to express the complex Greek sentence structure more clearly in English.

sion and decay. [12]Even though they are dressed in purple, their faces have to be wiped because of the thick dust that settles on them in the temple. [13]One of these gods holds a scepter like a local judge, but that god is unable to execute anyone who sins against it. [14]Another god[a] has a dagger and an ax in its right hand, but that god can't save itself from war and robbers. All of these things prove that they're not gods. So don't be afraid of them.

[15]These gods, who are placed in their temples, are as useless as a broken dish. [16]Their eyes are filled with dust that is kicked up by people who enter ⌊the temples⌋. [17]A king's courtyard is locked when someone who has committed a crime against the king is about to be executed. In the same way, the priests secure the gods' temples with doors, locks, and bars so that robbers can't get in. [18]The priests light more lamps for their gods than they light for themselves. Yet, their gods can't see a thing. [19]These gods are like one of the beams in the temple. As people admit, the insides of the gods are eaten away by crawling creatures that devour the gods and their clothes. Yet, these gods aren't even aware of what's happening. [20]Their faces are black from the smoke in the temple. [21]Bats, swallows, and other birds fly all around them. Even cats sit on them. [22]All of these things prove that they're not gods. So don't be afraid of them.

[23]These gods wear gold that makes them look beautiful. But the gold[b] doesn't shine unless someone polishes it. When they were being poured into molds, they didn't even feel it. [24]No matter how expensive they are, they still can't breathe. [25]Since they have no feet, they have to be carried around on people's shoulders. That shows people how worthless these gods really are. Even those who serve these gods feel ashamed. If one of these gods falls on the ground, it can't get up by itself. [26]Even if someone stands it back up again, it can't move by itself. And if it's leaning to one side, it can't straighten itself. Offering gifts to these gods is like offering gifts to the dead. [27]The priests sell the sacrifices that the gods have been offered and use the money for themselves. The priests' wives are no better. They take some of the meat from the sacrifices and preserve it with salt. But they give none of it to the poor or needy. [28]Women who are having their monthly periods or have recently given birth are even allowed to touch sacrifices to these gods. All of these things prove that these gods are not gods. So don't be afraid of them.

[29]How can they be called gods? These gods made of gold, silver, and wood have their meals served by women. [30]In the temples the priests of these gods sit with their clothes torn, their heads and beards shaved, and their heads uncovered. [31]They shout and howl in front of their gods as

---

[a] 13 Or "It."
[b] 23 Latin, Syriac; Greek "they."

some people do at funerals. ³²The priests take the clothes off their gods and give it to their wives and children to wear. ³³It makes no difference whether a person helps or harms these gods. They can't do anything about it. They can't appoint a king or overthrow one. ³⁴They can't make anyone wealthy or give him money. If anyone makes a vow to them and doesn't keep it, these gods can't do anything about it. ³⁵They can't save anyone from death or rescue weak people from those who are strong. ³⁶They can't make blind people see again. They can't rescue anyone who's in trouble. ³⁷They have no pity for widows and can't do anything good for orphans. ³⁸These things that are made out of wood and covered with gold and silver are no better than stones ⌐quarried⌐ from mountains. People who serve them should be ashamed. ³⁹How can anyone think that they are gods or call them gods?

Everyone Who Worships Idols Is Foolish

⁴⁰Besides, even the Babylonians themselves dishonor these gods. When they see someone who is unable to speak, they bring him to Bel's temple and pray that Bel will make him able to speak, as if Bel could understand. ⁴¹Yet, these people themselves don't understand. So they never abandon their gods. They have no sense. ⁴²Women wrap cords around their waists, sit in the streets, and burn bran for incense. ⁴³After a man passing by has stopped and picked a woman to have sex, that woman goes back and ridicules the woman who was sitting next to her, because the other woman wasn't pretty enough to be chosen. ⁴⁴Everything to do with these gods is a lie. How can anyone think that they are gods or call them gods?

⁴⁵These gods are made by carpenters and goldsmiths. They can never be anything more than what their craftsmen wanted them to be. ⁴⁶Even those who make them don't live very long. ⁴⁷How can things that are made by craftsmen be gods? These men have left only disgraceful lies for generations to come. ⁴⁸When wars or other disasters affect these gods, the priests hold meetings to decide where they and their gods can hide. ⁴⁹Why can't anyone understand that these are not gods? They can't save themselves from wars or any other disasters. ⁵⁰Since these gods are ⌐nothing but⌐ wood covered with gold and silver, someday people will realize that they are false gods. These gods are not gods. They are only objects made by humans and have no divine power. This fact will become obvious to every nation and king. ⁵¹Then everyone will realize that these gods are not gods.

⁵²These gods can't appoint anyone as king of a country, and they can't give anyone rain. ⁵³They can't make any decisions for themselves or hand down justice to anyone who has been wronged. ⁵⁴They're as helpless as

clouds[a] between heaven and earth. When a fire breaks out in a temple, the priests run away to save themselves, but the wooden gods covered with gold and silver stay inside the temple and burn up like beams of wood. [55]These gods can't fight against kings or enemies. [56]How can anyone think or say that they are gods?

Gods made of wood and covered with gold and silver can't save themselves from thieves or robbers. [57]Strong people can strip these gods of their gold and silver and of the clothes they're wearing and walk away with everything. These gods can't do anything about it. [58]A king who shows his courage is better than these false gods. A household pot that is still useful to its owner is better than these false gods. A door that protects the contents of a house is better than these false gods. Even a wooden pillar in the palace is better than these false gods.

[59] The sun, moon, and stars shine brightly. This is the job they've been given to do, and they do it. [60]Likewise, lightning, when it flashes, is easily seen. The same is true of wind. It, too, has been given a job to do. So it blows in every land. [61]When God commands the clouds to travel all over the world, they obey his command. [62]When fire is sent from above to consume mountains and woods, it does what it's ordered to do. But these gods can't be compared to these things. They don't look like these things or have their power. [63]So no one should think that they are gods or call them gods. They're not able to punish or reward anyone. [64]All of these things prove that they're not gods. So don't be afraid of them.

[65] These gods can't curse or bless kings. [66]These gods can't display any miraculous signs in the sky for the nations ⌊to see⌋. They can't shine like the sun or give off light like the moon. [67]Wild animals are better off than these gods. Animals at least can run from danger and take cover. [68]We have absolutely no evidence that these gods are gods. So don't be afraid of them.

[69] These Babylonian gods, which are made of wood and covered with gold and silver, are about as effective as a scarecrow in a cucumber garden. They protect no one. [70]In the same way, these gods, which are made of wood and covered with gold and silver, are about as useful as a thornbush in a garden. Instead of keeping birds away, birds sit on them. These gods are like a dead body thrown outside into the darkness. [71]The purple and linen material rotting away on them proves that they are not gods. In the end these gods will be eaten up by insects, much to everyone's disgrace. [72]So it is better for a person to have God's approval than to have idols. This person will never be disgraced.

---

[a] 54 Greek "crows." Greek meaning of this sentence uncertain.

The Prayer of Azariah and the Song of the Three Young Men[a]

Azariah Prays in the Furnace

[1] The three young men, Hananiah, Mishael, and Azariah,[b] were walking around in the flames, singing hymns to God, and praising the Lord. [2] Then Azariah stood still, and in the fire, he prayed aloud:

[3] "We praise and worship you, Lord God of our ancestors.
   We will honor your name forever.
[4] Everything you do is right and fair, every choice you make is good,
   and every decision you make is fair.
[5] You made the right decision when you brought disaster on us
   and on Jerusalem, the holy city of our ancestors.
   We deserved this destruction because of our sins.
[6]   We sinned; we broke your laws by rebelling against you.
   We committed every kind of sin.
[7]   We didn't obey your commands.
   We didn't follow them or do what you told us to do.
      If we had obeyed, things would have gone better for us.
[8] So every disaster you brought on us—
   everything you decided to do to us—was fair.
[9] You handed us over to our enemies, who were lawless
      and hateful rebels,
   and to an evil king, the most wicked king in the entire world.
[10] Now we are too ashamed to speak.
   We, your servants who worship you,
      are publicly humiliated and disgraced.

---

[a] The Prayer of Azariah and the Song of the Three Young Men in English Bibles is Daniel 3:24-90 in the Greek Bible. This is a Greek addition inserted between Daniel 3:23 and 3:24 in the Hebrew Bible.

[b] 1 In Babylon Hananiah, Mishael, and Azariah were called Shadrach, Meshach, and Abednego. See Daniel 1:7.

¹¹ "For the sake of your name, never abandon us,
and never break your promise^a to us.
¹² Always be merciful to us.
Do this for the sake of your friend Abraham,
for the sake of your servant Isaac,
and for the sake of your holy one Israel.
¹³ You promised to make their descendants
as numerous as the stars in the sky
and the grains of sand on the seashore.
¹⁴ Yet, Lord, we have decreased in number more than
any other nation.
Because of our sins, we are humiliated all over the world.
¹⁵ We have no ruler, prophet, or leader now.
There are no more burnt offerings,
sacrifices, grain offerings, or incense.
There's no place where we can bring these gifts
into your presence
and find mercy.
¹⁶ So please accept our sorrowful hearts and broken spirits.
¹⁷   Accept them as you would accept burnt offerings of rams, bulls,
or thousands of fat lambs.
Then we will be at peace with you.^b
No one who trusts you will ever be put to shame.
¹⁸ Now we are following you wholeheartedly.
We fear you, and we are looking for you.
¹⁹   Never let us be put to shame.
Be kind to us, and show us your rich mercy.
²⁰ Rescue us by using your amazing miracles.
Bring honor to your name, Lord.
²¹ Humiliate all those who harm us.
Strip them of all their power.
Drain their strength.
²²   Let them know that you alone are the Lord God
and that you are honored throughout the whole world."

²³ The king's servants who had thrown the three men into the furnace continued to fuel the fire with oil, tar, flax, and brushwood. ²⁴ The flames shot up 75 feet above the furnace. ²⁵ They spread out and burned up the Babylonians who were standing near the furnace. ²⁶ But the angel of the Lord came down into the furnace to be with Azariah and his companions.

---

^a 11 Or "covenant."
^b 17 Some Greek manuscripts; other Greek manuscripts "We will wholeheartedly follow you."

The angel forced the flames out of the furnace [27]so that it felt as if a cool breeze were blowing in the middle of the furnace. The fire never touched the men. It never hurt or affected them in any way.

The Three Men Sing Hymns To Praise God

[28]Then the three men in the furnace started praising and honoring God by singing the following hymn:

[29]"We praise and worship you, Lord God of our ancestors.
>   We always want to give you the highest honor.
[30]We praise your glorious and holy name.
>   We always want to give your name the highest praise and honor.
[31]We praise you in your glorious and holy temple.
>   We always want to give you the highest praise and glory.
[32]We praise you; you are enthroned over the angels.[a]
>   We praise you; you can look into the bottomless pit.
>   We want to sing your praise and always give you
>   the highest honor.
[33]We praise you; you are seated on your royal throne.
>   We always want to give you the highest praise and honor.
[34]We praise you in the highest heavens.
>   We always want to give you praise and honor.

[35]"Praise the Lord, all creation.
>   Sing songs to praise him, and always give him the highest honor.
[36]Praise the Lord, you heavens.
>   Sing songs to praise him, and always give him the highest honor.
[37]Praise the Lord, angels of the Lord.
>   Sing songs to praise him, and always give him the highest honor.
[38]Praise the Lord, water above the sky.
>   Sing songs to praise him, and always give him the highest honor.
[39]Praise the Lord, all you ⌞heavenly⌟ powers.
>   Sing songs to praise him, and always give him the highest honor.
[40]Praise the Lord, sun and moon.
>   Sing songs to praise him, and always give him the highest honor.
[41]Praise the Lord, stars of heaven.
>   Sing songs to praise him, and always give him the highest honor.

[42]"Praise the Lord, all rain and dew.
>   Sing songs to praise him, and always give him the highest honor.
[43]Praise the Lord, all you winds.
>   Sing songs to praise him, and always give him the highest honor.

---

[a] 32 Or "cherubim."

⁴⁴Praise the Lord, fire and heat.
Sing songs to praise him, and always give him the highest honor.
⁴⁵Praise the Lord, bitter cold and scorching heat.
Sing songs to praise him, and always give him the highest honor.
⁴⁶Praise the Lord, sleet and snowflakes.
Sing songs to praise him, and always give him the highest honor.
⁴⁷Praise the Lord, you nights and days.
Sing songs to praise him, and always give him the highest honor.
⁴⁸Praise the Lord, light and darkness.
Sing songs to praise him, and always give him the highest honor.
⁴⁹Praise the Lord, ice and cold.
Sing songs to praise him, and always give him the highest honor.
⁵⁰Praise the Lord, frost and snow.
Sing songs to praise him, and always give him the highest honor.
⁵¹Praise the Lord, lightning and clouds.
Sing songs to praise him, and always give him the highest honor.

⁵²"Let the earth praise the Lord.
Sing songs to praise him, and always give him the highest honor.
⁵³Praise the Lord, mountains and hills.
Sing songs to praise him, and always give him the highest honor.
⁵⁴Praise the Lord, everything that grows on the ground.
Sing songs to praise him, and always give him the highest honor.
⁵⁵Praise the Lord, seas and rivers.
Sing songs to praise him, and always give him the highest honor.
⁵⁶Praise the Lord, you springs.
Sing songs to praise him, and always give him the highest honor.
⁵⁷Praise the Lord, you whales and all you swimming creatures.
Sing songs to praise him, and always give him the highest honor.
⁵⁸Praise the Lord, all you birds.
Sing songs to praise him, and always give him the highest honor.
⁵⁹Praise the Lord, all you domestic and wild animals.
Sing songs to praise him, and always give him the highest honor.

⁶⁰"Praise the Lord, all you people on earth.
Sing songs to praise him, and always give him the highest honor.
⁶¹Praise the Lord, Israel.
Sing songs to praise him, and always give him the highest honor.
⁶²Praise the Lord, you priests of the Lord.
Sing songs to praise him, and always give him the highest honor.
⁶³Praise the Lord, you servants of the Lord.
Sing songs to praise him, and always give him the highest honor.
⁶⁴Praise the Lord, you spirits and souls of righteous people.
Sing songs to praise him, and always give him the highest honor.

⁶⁵Praise the Lord, you people who are holy and humble at heart.
  Sing songs to praise him, and always give him the highest honor.

⁶⁶"Hananiah, Azariah, and Mishael, praise the Lord.
  Sing songs to praise him, and always give him the highest honor.
    He has rescued us from a fiery tomb
      and saved us from the power of death.
        He has rescued us from the flames in the blazing furnace
          and saved us from the fire.
⁶⁷Give thanks to the Lord because he is good,
  because his mercy endures forever.
⁶⁸Praise the Lord, the God of gods, all those who worship him.
  Sing songs to praise him, and give thanks to him,
    because his mercy endures forever."

Susanna[a]

Two Jewish Leaders Become Obsessed With Susanna

[1]A man named Joakim lived in Babylon. [2]He married a woman named Susanna, who was the daughter of Hilkiah. Susanna was very beautiful, and she feared the Lord. [3]Her parents were devout people, and they had brought up their daughter to live according to Moses' Teachings. [4]Joakim was very rich and had a beautiful garden next to his house. The Jews who lived in Babylon used to come to his house because he was the most respected of them all.

[5]That year two leaders from the Jewish community were appointed as judges. (The Lord said this about the judges: "The judges, who are leaders and are supposed to guide my people, are doing wicked things in Babylon.") [6]These two men spent a lot of time at Joakim's house. So everyone who had a case to be tried would go there.

[7]At noon, when the people would leave, Susanna would go for a walk in her husband's garden. [8]Every day the two leaders would watch her go to the garden for her walk. Soon they began to lust for her. [9]They stopped thinking clearly. They no longer looked to the Lord ⌐for guidance⌐, and they forgot about their responsibilities as judges. [10]Both were obsessed with her, but they didn't tell each other how deep their feelings were for her. [11]They were embarrassed to admit that they wanted to have sex with her. [12]Day after day they watched eagerly to catch a glimpse of her.

[13]One day they said to each other, "Let's go home. It's time for lunch." So they went off in different directions. [14]But then both of them came back and ⌐accidentally⌐ ran into each other. When they asked each other why they were there, they finally admitted that they lusted for Susanna. So they agreed to look for a time when they could find her alone.

The Two Leaders Try To Seduce Susanna

[15]One day, while they were waiting for the right moment, Susanna went into the garden as usual. Only two of her female slaves accompanied her. Since it was hot that day, she decided to take a bath in the garden. [16]No

---

[a] The book of Susanna is Daniel chapter 13 in some translations.

one else was there except the two leaders, who had hidden themselves and were watching her closely. ¹⁷Susanna said to her slaves, "Bring me some bath oil and body lotion. Then lock the garden doors so that I can take my bath ⌐undisturbed⌐." ¹⁸They did as they were told: They locked the main doors of the garden and left through the side doors to get what Susanna had asked for. The slaves didn't see the leaders, because the leaders were hiding.

¹⁹As soon as the slaves left, the two leaders got up and ran to Susanna. ²⁰They said, "Look, the doors are locked, and no one can see us. We want you. So give us what we want, and have sex with us. ²¹If you refuse, we'll testify against you in court. We'll say that a young man was here with you and that's the reason you sent your slaves away."

²²Susanna groaned and said, "I'm trapped! If I do this, I'll get the death penalty. If I don't do this, I'll be at your mercy. ²³I've made my choice: I won't do what you've asked. I'd rather suffer the consequences of your threat than sin against the Lord."

²⁴Then Susanna screamed as loud as she could. But the two leaders began shouting accusations against her, ²⁵and one of them ran to open the doors. ²⁶The people in the house heard all the shouting that was coming from the garden. So they rushed into the garden through one of the side doors to see what had happened to Susanna. ²⁷When the leaders told their story, the servants were shocked. Nothing like this had ever been said about Susanna.

The Two Leaders Testify Against Susanna

²⁸The next day, the Jewish community gathered at Joakim's house. (Joakim was Susanna's husband.) The two leaders came determined to carry out their wicked plot to have Susanna put to death. ²⁹In front of everyone, they said, "Send for Susanna, daughter of Hilkiah and wife of Joakim." So the people sent for her, ³⁰and she came with her parents, her children, and all her relatives.

³¹Now, Susanna was very delicate and beautiful. ³²She was fully clothed, but the two evil leaders ordered that her clothes be taken off so that they could get a full view of her beauty. ³³Her family and everyone else who saw her began to cry.

³⁴Then the two leaders stood up in front of the people and placed their hands on Susanna's head. ³⁵Through her tears she looked up to heaven, because she wholeheartedly trusted the Lord. ³⁶The leaders said, "While we were walking in the garden alone, this woman came in with two female servants. She locked the ⌐main⌐ doors to the garden and dismissed the servants. ³⁷Then a young man, who had been hiding there, came up to her and had sexual intercourse with her. ³⁸We were in a corner of the garden, and when we saw this wicked thing going on, we ran over to

them. [39]We caught them in the act, but we couldn't hang on to the man. He was too strong for us. He opened the doors and got away. [40]However, we were able to seize this woman. When we asked her who the man was, [41]she wouldn't tell us. This is our testimony."

Because the two men were leaders and judges in the Jewish community, the assembly believed them and sentenced Susanna to death.

Daniel Saves Susanna

[42]Then Susanna shouted, "Eternal God, you know every secret, and you know everything before it happens. [43]You know that these men have lied in their testimony about me. I'm about to die, even though I'm completely innocent of the charges these wicked men have brought against me."

[44]The Lord heard Susanna's prayer. [45]As she was being led away to be executed, God stirred up the Holy Spirit in a young man named Daniel. [46]So Daniel shouted, "I won't be responsible for killing this woman!"

[47]Everyone turned around to look at him and asked, "What are you talking about?"

[48]Daniel stood in front of them and said, "How foolish can you Israelites be? Are you going to condemn an Israelite woman without a proper investigation and without finding out the truth? [49]Reopen the case. These men have lied in their testimony about this woman."

[50]So all the people hurried back ⌞to where the trial had taken place⌟. The rest of the leaders said to Daniel, "Please sit with us, and give us your opinion. God seems to have made you a leader like us."

[51]Daniel said to them, "Separate the two men. I will question them ⌞one at a time⌟."

[52]After the two men had been separated, Daniel called one of them and said to him, "You wicked old man, your past sins have caught up with you. [53]You've been unfair in the cases you've been judging. You've been condemning innocent people and pardoning guilty people. Yet, the Lord has said, 'Don't kill innocent or honest people.' [54]Now, if you really did catch this woman in the act, tell me: Under what kind of tree did you see her having intercourse?"

He answered, "Under a small gum tree."

[55]Daniel said, "This lie has cost you your life. God's angel has already been told to carry out your sentence: You will be cut in two."[a]

[56]Then Daniel had the first leader removed and the second one brought to him.

Daniel said to him, "You act like a Canaanite, not a Jew! Beauty has deceived you, and lust has corrupted you. [57]So this is how the two of you

---

[a] 55 There is a play on words here between Greek *schinon* (small gum tree) and *schisei* (cut in two).

have been treating Israelite women! You've intimidated them into having intercourse with you. But this woman of Judah wouldn't put up with your wickedness. ⁵⁸Now then, tell me: Under what kind of tree did you catch this woman having intercourse?"

He answered, "Under an oak tree."

⁵⁹Daniel said to him, "This lie has cost you your life also. God's angel is waiting with his sword to chop you in two.ᵃ He will destroy you both."

⁶⁰Then all the people shouted and praised God, who saves those who put their hope in him. ⁶¹They turned against the two leaders, because Daniel had used the testimony of these two leaders to convict them of perjury. The people punished the leaders the same way these leaders had wickedly planned to punish one of their own people. ⁶²The people followed the instructions in Moses' Teachings: They put the two leaders to death. So an innocent life was saved that day.

⁶³Hilkiah and his wife praised God for their daughter Susanna, and so did Susanna's husband Joakim and all her relatives, because she was cleared of the shameful charges. ⁶⁴From that day on, Daniel was highly respected by his people.

ᵃ 59 There is a play on words here between Greek *prinon* (oak tree) and *prisai* (chop in two).

Bel and the Snake[a]

Daniel Proves Bel Is a False God

[1] When King Astyages joined his ancestors in death, Cyrus of Persia succeeded him as king. [2] Daniel was one of King Cyrus' closest companions and was the most respected of all the king's friends.

[3] The Babylonians had an idol called Bel. Every day they provided Bel with 12 bushels of flour, 40 sheep, and 60 gallons of wine. [4] King Cyrus believed that Bel was a god and would go to Bel's temple every day to worship him. But Daniel worshiped his own God. So the king asked him, "Why don't you worship Bel?"

[5] Daniel answered, "I don't worship idols, which are made by humans. I worship the living God, who made heaven and earth and is the Lord of all people."

[6] The king asked, "Don't you think that Bel is a living god? Don't you see how much he eats and drinks every day?"

[7] Daniel laughed and said, "Don't be fooled, Your Majesty. This god of yours is only clay on the inside and bronze on the outside. It has never eaten or drunk anything."

[8] This made the king angry. So he called for the priests of Bel. (There were 70 priests of Bel, not including their wives and children.)[b] The king said to the priests, "Unless you tell me who's eating all the food given to Bel, you will all be put to death. [9] But if you can prove that Bel is eating the food, Daniel will be put to death because he insulted Bel."

Daniel said to the king, "I agree to everything you've said."

[10] The king went with Daniel to Bel's temple. When they were inside, [11] the priests said, "Your Majesty, we're leaving now. Set out the food yourself, and pour the wine. Then shut the door, and seal it with your own signet ring. [12] When you return in the morning, if you find that Bel hasn't eaten everything, you can put us to death. But if he has eaten everything, Daniel must be put to death because he lied about us." [13] (The priests weren't worried at all, because they had made a secret entrance to

---

[a] The book of Bel and the Snake is Daniel chapter 14 in some translations.

[b] 8 The first part of verse 10 has been placed in verse 8 to express the complex Greek paragraph structure more clearly in English.

the temple underneath the table. They used this secret entrance regularly to go in and eat the food given to Bel.)

¹⁴When the priests were gone, the king set out the food for Bel. Then Daniel ordered his servants to bring some ashes and scatter them all over the temple floor. No one except the king saw them do this. Then they went outside the temple, shut the door, sealed it with the king's signet ring, and left.

¹⁵That night, as usual, the priests, their wives, and their children entered the temple, and they ate and drank everything.

¹⁶Early the next morning, the king went with Daniel to the temple. ¹⁷The king asked, "Has the seal on the doors been broken, Daniel?"

Daniel answered, "The doors are still sealed shut, Your Majesty."

¹⁸As soon as the doors were opened, the king looked at the table and shouted, "You are great, Bel! You really are a god!"

¹⁹But Daniel laughed and stopped the king from entering the temple. Daniel said, "Look at the floor, and tell me whose footprints these are."

²⁰The king said, "I see the footprints of men, women, and children."

²¹The king was furious. He immediately had the priests, their wives, and their children arrested. They showed him the secret doors that they had used in order to enter the temple and eat what was on the table. ²²Then the king had all of them put to death, and he handed Bel over to Daniel, who destroyed both the idol and its temple.

Daniel Proves the Snake Is a False God

²³The Babylonians also worshiped a huge snake. ²⁴The king said to Daniel, "You can't tell me that this isn't a living god. So worship it."

²⁵Daniel said, "I worship the Lord my God. He's the ⌐only⌐ living God. ²⁶Give me permission, Your Majesty, and I will kill the snake without using a sword or a club."

The king said, "You have my permission."

²⁷So Daniel took some tar, fat, and hair and boiled them together. He made some cakes from this mixture and fed them to the snake. The snake ate them and burst open. Then Daniel said, "See what you've been worshiping!"

²⁸When the Babylonians heard about what had happened, they became very angry and staged a demonstration against the king. They said, "The king has become a Jew. He has destroyed Bel, killed the snake, and slaughtered the priests." ²⁹The Babylonians went to the king and demanded that he hand Daniel over to them. They threatened to have him and his whole family put to death if he refused to meet their demands. ³⁰When the king realized that they posed a serious threat to him, he was forced to hand Daniel over to them.

³¹ They threw Daniel into a lions' den, and he stayed there for six days. ³²Seven lions were in the den, and every day they were fed two humans*a* and two sheep. But during the six days that Daniel was in the den, the lions were given nothing to eat so that they would surely devour Daniel.

³³ At that time the prophet Habakkuk was in Judea. He had made some stew and had broken some bread into it. As he was taking the stew to some people who were harvesting in the fields, ³⁴an angel of the Lord said to him, "Take the food that you have to Babylon. It's for Daniel, who's in the lions' den."

³⁵Habakkuk said, "Sir, I've never been to Babylon, and I don't know where the lions' den is."

³⁶ Then the angel of the Lord grabbed Habakkuk by his hair and, with a gust of wind, carried him to Babylon. The angel set him down in Babylon at the edge of the den. ³⁷Habakkuk shouted, "Daniel, Daniel! Take this food that God has sent you."

³⁸ Daniel said, "You have remembered me, God. You have never abandoned those who love you." ³⁹Daniel got up and ate, and the angel of God immediately took Habakkuk home.

⁴⁰ On the seventh day the king went to mourn for Daniel. But when he came to the den and looked inside, he saw Daniel sitting there. ⁴¹The king shouted, "Lord, the God of Daniel, you are great! There's no other God except you!" ⁴²Then the king pulled Daniel out of the lion's den and had those who had plotted Daniel's destruction thrown into it. Immediately, they were devoured as the king watched.

---

a 32 Or "two slaves."

1 Maccabees

Alexander and His Kingdom

1 ¹The events in this book began after Philip's son, Alexander from Macedonia, marched from Greece and defeated Darius, king of Persia and Media. Alexander succeeded Darius as king and became the first king of the Greek Empire. ²Alexander fought many battles, took control of fortifications, and killed any king who got in his way. ³As he continued his campaign to conquer the whole world, he looted many nations. When the world was at peace, he became conceited and arrogant. ⁴With a very powerful army, which he had recruited, he ruled territories, nations, and local rulers and made them pay taxes to him.

⁵Eventually, Alexander became sick and realized that he was about to die. ⁶So he summoned his generals. They were well-known men who had grown up with him. He divided his kingdom among them while he was still alive. ⁷Alexander had been king for 12 years at the time of his death. ⁸After Alexander died, each general began to rule his own region. ⁹All of the generals, as well as their descendants, ruled for many years and caused a lot of trouble in the world.

The Rule of Antiochus IV—*2 Maccabees 4:7-17*

¹⁰One of the descendants of these generals was a wicked man named Antiochus IV, who was also called Epiphanes. He was the son of King Antiochus III of Syria and had been held hostage in Rome until he became king of the Syrian part of the Greek Empire in the year 175 B.C.

¹¹At that time, there were some Israelites who didn't follow Moses' Teachings. They misled many people by saying, "Let's make a treaty with the surrounding nations. Ever since we've separated ourselves from them, we've had nothing but trouble." ¹²The people liked what they heard. ¹³Some of them were so enthusiastic that they went to see King Antiochus, who gave them permission to live like non-Jewish people. ¹⁴So they built a gymnasium in Jerusalem like those that were found in other nations, ¹⁵and they had operations to hide the fact that they were circumcised.

They disregarded the terms of God's holy promise,*a* married people from other nations, and became devoted to doing wicked things.

[16] When Antiochus had firm control of his kingdom in Syria, he was determined to make himself king of Egypt as well. He wanted to rule both kingdoms. [17] So he invaded Egypt with a large army made up of chariots, elephants, and cavalry. In addition, he was assisted by a large fleet. [18] He fought a battle with Egypt's King Ptolemy VI, and Ptolemy fled from him. Many of Ptolemy's soldiers were killed. [19] Then Antiochus and his army captured Egypt's fortified cities and looted the country.

[20] Antiochus defeated Egypt in the year 169 B.C. As he returned to Syria, he attacked Israel by entering Jerusalem with his large army. [21] He arrogantly entered the holy place and took the gold altar and the lamp stand with its utensils. [22] He also took the table for the bread of the presence, the cups for wine offerings, the bowls, the gold incense burners, and the curtain. He also stripped the gold molding and the gold decorations from the front of the temple [23] and took the silver, the gold, the precious utensils, and all the treasures he found deposited there. [24] Then Antiochus returned to his own country with all these things. He had murdered a lot of people and had bragged about everything he had done. [25] Wherever the people of Israel lived, they mourned.

[26] Their rulers and leaders groaned.
   Their young men and women became weak.
   Their women no longer wore beautiful clothes.
[27] Every groom sang a funeral song.
   Every bride sat in her room and cried.
[28] The earth and those who lived on it trembled.
   All of Jacob's descendants felt ashamed.

Antiochus Sends a Tax Collector to Judea

[29] Two years later, King Antiochus sent a tax collector to the cities in Judea. This official came to Jerusalem with a large army. [30] He gained the people's trust because he spoke to them in a friendly way, but he was really trying to deceive them. Then he suddenly attacked the city and killed many Israelites. The defeat was overwhelming. [31] He looted the city, set it on fire, and tore down its houses and surrounding walls. [32] He and his army took women and children as prisoners and seized the livestock. [33] Then he had his soldiers build a fortress in David's city. It had large walls and towers. [34] In the fortress he stationed a group of men who didn't follow Moses' Teachings. These men strengthened their position in the fortress. [35] They stored weapons and food there along with the loot

---

a 1:15 Or "covenant."

they had collected from Jerusalem. These men became a real danger to the people in the city.

³⁶ The fortress was a threat to the holy place
and a constant source of evil to Israel.
³⁷ Men from the fortress murdered innocent people around
the holy place.
So the holy place was dishonored.
³⁸ People who lived in Jerusalem fled.
Jerusalem became a colony of foreign soldiers.
It became a foreign city to those who were born there.
Its citizens left.
³⁹   Its holy place was abandoned like a desert.
Its festivals were turned into times of grief.
Its days of worship were turned into times of disgrace.
Its honor was turned into insults.
⁴⁰   Its dishonor became as great as its former glory.
Its pride was turned into grief.

⁴¹ King Antiochus wrote to all the nations in his kingdom. He wrote that everyone should be united ⁴²and that each nation should give up its traditions. ⁴³Every nation accepted what King Antiochus wrote. Many people from Israel approved of his religion, sacrificed to false gods, and did things on the day of worship that the Jewish religion didn't allow.

⁴⁴ The king sent messengers with a written order to Jerusalem and the cities in Judea. He ordered the people to follow foreign traditions. ⁴⁵He ordered them not to sacrifice burnt offerings, grain offerings, or wine offerings in the holy place. He also ordered them to do things that the Jewish religion didn't allow on the days of worship and on festival days. ⁴⁶He ordered them to dishonor the holy place and the priests, ⁴⁷to build altars, illegal worship sites, and temples to false gods, and to sacrifice pigs and other unclean^a animals. ⁴⁸He forbid them to circumcise their sons and ordered them to do disgusting things that would make them unclean. ⁴⁹He wanted them to do things that the Jewish religion didn't allow so that they would forget Moses' Teachings and change their religious practices. ⁵⁰Whoever disobeyed the king would be put to death.

⁵¹ King Antiochus sent all these orders to his entire kingdom, appointed officials to watch everyone, and ordered every city in Judea to offer sacrifices to false gods. ⁵²Many of the people (that is, everyone who had abandoned Moses' Teachings), joined the officials. They did so many terrible things in their own country ⁵³that they forced their own people to find a safe place to hide.

---

^a 1:47 "Unclean" refers to anything that Moses' Teachings say is not presentable to God.

⁵⁴On the fifteenth day of the month of Chislev in the year 167 B.C., King Antiochus built a disgusting thing on top of the temple altar for burnt offerings. People built altars in the surrounding cities of Judea ⁵⁵and offered sacrifices at the entrances to their houses and in the streets. ⁵⁶Wherever the officials found a copy of the Book of Moses' Teachings, they tore it up and burned it. ⁵⁷The king decreed that whenever people were found with the Book of the Promise in their possession or were found practicing what Moses taught, they must be put to death. ⁵⁸Month after month the officials intimidated the Israelites whom they found in the cities. ⁵⁹On the twenty-fifth day of the month, the officials offered sacrifices on the pagan altar that was on top of the temple altar for burnt offerings. ⁶⁰In keeping with the king's order, women who had their children circumcised were put to death. ⁶¹Infants were hung from their mothers' necks. The women's families were also put to death along with those who had circumcised the infants.

⁶²Many people in Israel were absolutely determined not to eat unclean food. ⁶³They chose to die rather than to dishonor themselves by eating unclean food or by breaking the terms of God's holy promise. So they died. ⁶⁴God unleashed his furious anger on Israel.

Mattathias and His Five Sons

2 ¹At that time a priest named Mattathias, who was a descendant of Jorib, moved from Jerusalem to the city of Modein. Mattathias was the son of John and the grandson of Simeon. ²He had five sons: John (who was nicknamed Gaddi), ³Simon (who was called Thassi), ⁴Judas (who was called Maccabeus), ⁵Eleazar (who was called Avaran), and Jonathan (who was called Apphus). ⁶When Mattathias saw all the disgusting things that were happening in Judea and Jerusalem, ⁷he said,

> "What a tragedy this is!
> Why was I born to see the ruin of my people
>   and the ruin of the holy city?
> Why was I born to live in Jerusalem
>   when it was taken over by enemies
>   and the holy place was taken over by foreigners?
> ⁸Jerusalem's temple has become like a person who has
>   been dishonored.
> ⁹   Its splendid utensils have been carried off as loot.
> Its infants have been killed in the streets.
> Its young people have been killed in battle.
> ¹⁰Every nation in the world has occupied Jerusalem's palaces
>   or taken its loot.
> ¹¹All its beautiful decorations have been taken away.
> Jerusalem is no longer free. It has become a slave.

[12]Look around! Our beautiful holy place, which we honor,
    has been destroyed.
Nations have treated our holy place
    in ways that our Jewish religion doesn't allow.
[13]We have nothing left to live for!"

[14]Then Mattathias and his sons tore their clothes in grief and put on sackcloth, because they were overwhelmed with sorrow.

Mattathias Refuses To Sacrifice to False Gods

[15]The king's officials, who were trying to force the Israelites to abandon their religion, came to the city of Modein to make the people offer sacrifices to false gods. [16]Many Israelites went willingly to talk with the officials, but the officials had to send for Mattathias and his sons. [17]The king's officials said to Mattathias, "You're a highly respected leader in this city, and you have the support of your sons and relatives. [18]Be the first to come forward and do what the king has ordered. Be like all the people in the other nations, like the people in Judea, and like the people who are left in Jerusalem. Then you and your sons will receive the title 'Friend of the King.' You will be honored with silver, gold, and many other gifts."

[19]Mattathias shouted, "All the nations in the king's empire may have obeyed him. They may have chosen to follow his orders by abandoning the religion of their ancestors. [20]But even if they have, my sons, my relatives, and I will keep the terms of the promise[a] God made to our ancestors. [21]It's unthinkable for us to desert our teachings and religious practices. [22]We won't obey the king's orders, and we won't worship in any other way."

[23]When Mattathias had finished speaking, a Jewish man came forward in front of everyone to offer a sacrifice on the altar in Modein as the king had ordered. [24]Because Mattathias was so devoted to his religion, he was shocked to see this. He lost his temper, ran up to the man, and killed him on the altar. [25]He also killed the king's official, who was forcing the people to sacrifice, and he tore down the altar. [26]He showed his devotion to Moses' Teachings just as Phinehas had done when he killed Zimri, who was Salu's son.

[27]Mattathias went throughout the city and shouted, "Everyone who is devoted to Moses' Teachings and is willing to stand up for God's promise, follow me!" [28]Then he and his sons fled to the mountains and left everything they owned in the city.

[29]At that time, many people were looking for God to punish the foreigners justly. Because these people were suffering severe persecutions,

---

[a] 2:20 Or "covenant."

they went into the desert to live.[a] [30]They took their children, wives, and livestock with them. [31]A report about them reached the king's officials and the troops in Jerusalem, David's city. The officials were told that some Jewish people had rejected the king's order and had gone to hide in the caves in the desert. [32]Many troops quickly pursued them and caught up with them. The troops set up their camp facing the people and prepared for a battle that would take place on the day of worship. [33]The troops said to the people, "Come out right now! Do what the king has ordered, and we'll let you live!"

[34]But the people replied, "We won't come out. We refuse to do things that our religion doesn't allow on the day of worship. We won't obey the king's order." [35]So the troops quickly attacked them. [36]But the people didn't fight back. They didn't even throw a stone at the troops or block the entrances to the caves where they were hiding. [37]They simply said, "Let's all die with clear consciences. Heaven and earth will be our witnesses that you are killing us unjustly." [38]So the troops attacked them on the day of worship. The men died along with their wives, children, and livestock. About 1,000 people were killed.

Mattathias Organizes an Army

[39]When Mattathias and his friends found out about this, they were overwhelmed with sorrow. [40]They said to each other, "If all of us do what they did and refuse to fight these foreigners to save ourselves and our religious practices, these foreigners will quickly destroy us." [41]So that day they decided that if anyone attacked them on a day of worship, they would fight back. They decided that they would never die hiding in caves as the others had.

[42]At that time, Mattathias and his friends were joined by a group of Jewish people called the Hasidim. The Hasidim were the strongest people in Israel. All of them volunteered for the sake of Moses' Teachings. [43]Everyone who had fled because of the persecutions also joined Mattathias and his friends. This made their forces stronger. [44]They organized an army, and in their fury they killed people who sinned by not following Moses' Teachings. The people who survived their attacks fled to the foreigners for safety. [45]Mattathias and his friends also went around the countryside tearing down the altars dedicated to false gods. [46]They forced every uncircumcised boy that they found in Israel to be circumcised. [47]They were also successful in hunting down arrogant foreign officials. [48]They didn't allow foreigners and kings to do away with Moses' Teachings. They didn't allow sinners to gain any power.

---

[a] 2:29 The last part of verse 30 has been placed in verse 29 to express the complex Greek sentence structure more clearly in English.

Mattathias Instructs His Sons Before He Dies

⁴⁹The time came for Mattathias to die. So he said to his sons, "We're living in disastrous and violent times because arrogant foreigners are treating us with contempt. ⁵⁰My children, now is the time for you to show your devotion to Moses' Teachings. Offer your lives for the sake of the promise God made to our ancestors.

⁵¹"Remember what our ancestors did when they were alive. If you do what they did, you will always be highly honored and famous. ⁵²Didn't Abraham prove that he was faithful when he was tested? Didn't Abraham's faith receive God's approval? ⁵³When Joseph was in a difficult situation, he obeyed God's command and eventually became ruler of Egypt. ⁵⁴Our ancestor Phinehas received the promise of a permanent priesthood because he was very devoted to God. ⁵⁵Joshua became a judge in Israel because he did everything Moses had told him to do. ⁵⁶Caleb received a part of the land as his inheritance because of his report to the community of Israel. ⁵⁷David inherited the throne of an eternal kingdom because he was merciful. ⁵⁸Elijah was taken to heaven because of his devotion to Moses' Teachings. ⁵⁹Hananiah, Azariah, and Mishael believed and were saved from the fire. ⁶⁰Daniel was rescued from the lion's mouth because he was innocent.

⁶¹"So keep in mind that in every generation those who trust God will have the strength they need. ⁶²Don't be afraid of a sinful king who threatens you. His honor will come to an end when he dies and his body is covered with manure and worms. ⁶³Today he may be honored, but tomorrow no one will be able to find him because he will have returned to dust, and his plans will be ruined. ⁶⁴My children, be strong and courageous while defending Moses' Teachings because you will receive honor.

⁶⁵"I know that your brother Simon is wise. Listen to him as long as you live. He will serve as your father. ⁶⁶Judas Maccabeus has been very strong ever since he was young. He will be the commander of your army and will fight against the foreigners. ⁶⁷Recruit everyone who follows Moses' Teachings, and punish the enemies of your people. ⁶⁸Take revenge on the foreigners, and do everything that Moses' Teachings require.

⁶⁹Then Mattathias blessed his sons and joined his ancestors in death. ⁷⁰He died in the year 166 B.C. and was placed in his ancestors' tomb at Modein. All the people in Israel held a solemn ceremony to mourn his death.

Judas Maccabeus Takes Mattathias' Place—*2 Maccabees 8:1-7*

3 ¹Then Mattathias' son Judas (who was called Maccabeus) took his father's place. ²All of Judas' brothers and all who had faithfully supported his father helped Judas. They were happy to fight for Israel.

³ Judas brought his people widespread honor.
   He wore his breastplate like a hero.
   He put on his weapons, fought battles,
      and used his sword to protect his camp.
⁴ He was like a lion in everything he did,
      like a young lion when it roars at its prey.
⁵ He hunted down those who didn't follow Moses' Teachings.
   He set fire to the cities of those who caused trouble for his people.
⁶   Those who didn't follow Moses' Teachings retreated in fear.
   Everyone who rejected Moses' Teachings became confused.
   He used his own power to successfully rescue his people.
⁷ He made life bitter for many kings,
      but he made Jacob's descendants happy with everything he did.
   He will be remembered and praised forever.
⁸ He went through the cities of Judea
      and destroyed Jews who had betrayed their religion.
   He turned God's anger away from Israel.
⁹ His name became known throughout the world.
   He united those who were about to be destroyed.

Judas Defeats Apollonius

¹⁰ Then Apollonius recruited some foreigners (including a large army from Samaria) to fight Israel. ¹¹ When Judas found out about this, he attacked Apollonius. He defeated Apollonius and killed him. Many of Apollonius' soldiers were killed, and the rest of them fled. ¹² Judas and his men looted the enemy. Judas took Apollonius' sword and used it in battle for the rest of his life.

Judas Defeats Seron

¹³ Seron, the commander of the Syrian army, heard that Judas had gathered a group of followers. This group was made up of men who were loyal to God and who were ready to help Judas fight. ¹⁴ Seron thought to himself, "I can become famous and honored in the kingdom. I'll fight Judas and his men, since they have no respect for the king's orders." ¹⁵ A powerful army of Jews who had betrayed their religion went with Seron to help him punish the people of Israel.

¹⁶ When Seron reached the pass at Beth Horon, Judas went to attack him with the few men that he had. ¹⁷ But when Judas' men saw Seron's army coming to attack them, they said to Judas, "We don't have enough men. How can we fight such a large and powerful army? Besides, we're weak because we haven't eaten anything today."

[18] Judas replied, "A few men can easily surround and overpower many. The Lord[a] doesn't care if the rescue is made by many men or by a few. [19] Victory doesn't depend on the size of the armies that are fighting but on the strength that comes from the Lord. [20] Seron and his army are coming to attack us. They'll do anything to kill us, our wives, and our children. They want to take everything we have. [21] We're fighting for our lives and our religious traditions. [22] The Lord will defeat Seron and his army right in front of our eyes, so don't be afraid of them."

[23] When Judas finished speaking, he and his men suddenly attacked Seron and his army. Seron and his army were defeated right in front of them. [24] Judas and his men chased them down the pass at Beth Horon and into the plain. About 800 of Seron's soldiers were killed. The rest of them fled into Philistine territory. [25] Then the nations around them became afraid. They were terrified of Judas and his brothers. [26] Even King Antiochus heard about Judas' reputation, and people in foreign countries talked about the battles that Judas had fought.

King Antiochus Plans To Destroy Judea

[27] When King Antiochus heard the reports about Judas, he became furious. So he ordered all the armies in his kingdom to assemble into one large, powerful army. [28] He took money from his treasury, gave a year's pay to his soldiers, and ordered them to be ready for duty. [29] Afterward, he realized that his treasury was out of money because tax revenues from his territory had decreased. This decrease was due to the disorder and disaster he had caused by doing away with the religious traditions that people had been following for a long time. [30] He was afraid that he wouldn't have sufficient funds. This had happened once or twice before when he needed the funds for his expenses and for the gifts that he gave. (He used to give people more generous gifts than previous kings.) [31] Antiochus didn't know what to do. Eventually, he decided to raise a lot of money by going to the country of Persia to collect taxes from the territories there.

[32] Antiochus appointed Lysias as his chief of state. Lysias was responsible for an area that extended from the Euphrates River to the borders of Egypt. He was a respected man who held the title "Relative of the King." [33] Lysias was also responsible for taking care of the king's son, Antiochus V, until the king returned. [34] King Antiochus gave his elephants and half of his army to Lysias. He told Lysias everything he wanted done, especially to the people who lived in Judea and Jerusalem. [35] He ordered Lysias to send an army to wipe out Israel's soldiers and the people left in Jerusalem. He also ordered Lysias to make sure that no one would remember that

---

[a] 3:18 Greek "Heaven." The author of 1 Maccabees uses the word *Heaven* in place of God's name, the Lord.

the Israelites ever lived there. ³⁶He told Lysias to make foreigners settle throughout Israelite territory and to redistribute the land. ³⁷Then, in the year 165 B.C., King Antiochus took the other half of his army and left Antioch, his capital city. He crossed the Euphrates River and marched through the inland territories.

Lysias Sends Troops to Judea—*2 Maccabees 8:8-29, 34-36*

³⁸Lysias chose Nicanor, Gorgias, and Ptolemy (who was the son of Dorymenes) to command his army. They were influential men who held the title "Friend of the King." ³⁹Lysias sent them with 40,000 infantrymen and 7,000 cavalrymen into Judea to destroy it as the king had ordered. ⁴⁰So these men left with their entire army and eventually camped in the plain near the city of Emmaus. ⁴¹An army from Syria and Philistia joined them there. The slave traders in the region heard about this impressive army. So they took a lot of money and chains and went to the camp. They wanted to buy Israelites to sell as slaves.

⁴²Judas and his brothers saw that they were in a lot of trouble because of the armies that were camped in their territory. In addition, they found out that the king had ordered Lysias to destroy the Jewish people. ⁴³So they said to each other, "Let's get back everything that our nation has lost. Let's fight for our nation and our holy place." ⁴⁴Then the Jewish community gathered to prepare for battle and to pray for God's mercy and compassion.

⁴⁵Jerusalem was as difficult to live in as a desert.
   None of its citizens entered or left the city.
   People were trampling its holy place.
   Foreigners controlled the fortress
      and made it a place for other foreigners to stay.
   Jacob's descendants were no longer happy.
   No one played flutes and harps anymore.

⁴⁶Then Judas, his brothers, and the Jewish community went to Mizpah because Mizpah was a place where the Israelites went to pray in the past. From Mizpah they could see Jerusalem.ᵃ ⁴⁷All day long they fasted, wore sackcloth, sprinkled ashes on their heads, and tore their clothes in grief. ⁴⁸They opened the Book of Moses' Teachings and searched for answers. (People in other nations search for answers from the statues of their false gods.)ᵇ ⁴⁹Israelites brought the clothes that the priests wear, the first produce harvested, and one-tenth of their income. They even encouraged the Nazirites who had completed their vows to go to Mizpah.

ᵃ 3:46 Or "Mizpah faces Jerusalem."
ᵇ 3:48 Greek meaning of this sentence uncertain.

⁵⁰Everyone there prayed loudly to the LORD, "What should we do with all these things that we've brought? Where should we take them? ⁵¹Your holy place has been trampled and dishonored. Your priests are in mourning and are humiliated. ⁵²Look around at the nations! They have assembled to destroy us. You know what they plan to do to us. ⁵³How can we stand up to them if you don't help us?" ⁵⁴Then they blew trumpets and shouted.

⁵⁵ After this, Judas divided his men into groups of 10, 50, 100, and 1,000 and appointed a leader for each group. ⁵⁶He sent home those who were building houses, those who were engaged to be married, those who were planting a vineyard, and those who were scared. This is what Moses' Teachings required. ⁵⁷Then Judas' army left Mizpah and camped south of the city of Emmaus.

⁵⁸ Judas said, "Prepare to fight with all your might! Be ready early in the morning to fight these foreigners who have assembled to destroy us and our holy place. ⁵⁹Dying in battle is better than standing by and watching the terrible things that will be done to our nation and our holy place. ⁶⁰But the LORD will do whatever he wants."

Judas Defeats Gorgias

4 ¹During the night, Gorgias left his camp with a division of 5,000 infantrymen and 1,000 of his best cavalrymen. ²He wanted to take the Jewish camp by surprise, so he had some men from the fortress in Jerusalem as his guides. ³When Judas heard about this, he and his soldiers left the camp. Judas wanted to attack the king's army at Emmaus ⁴while Gorgias' troops were still separated from the rest of the army. ⁵Gorgias entered Judas' camp during the night, but he didn't find anyone there. So he began looking for Judas and his soldiers in the mountains because he thought that they were running away.

⁶ At dawn Judas appeared in the plain with 3,000 soldiers. The soldiers didn't have as many weapons as they would have liked. ⁷They saw that the foreigners' camp was strongly fortified and had cavalry surrounding it. They knew that these foreign soldiers were well trained. ⁸But Judas said to his men, "Don't be afraid of how many men they have or get scared when they attack. ⁹Remember how our ancestors were rescued at the Red Sea when Pharaoh was chasing them with his army. ¹⁰Let's pray loudly to the LORDᵃ now. If it pleases him, he will remember us and the promiseᵇ he made to our ancestors and will defeat the army we're going to face today. ¹¹Then every nation will know that Israel has someone to rescue it and set it free."

ᵃ 4:10 Greek "to Heaven." The author of 1 Maccabees uses the word *Heaven* in place of God's name, the LORD.

ᵇ 4:10 Or "covenant."

[12] When the foreign soldiers[a] saw Judas and his army coming to attack them, [13] they marched out of their camp to fight. Then Judas' soldiers blew their trumpets, [14] and the battle began. The foreign soldiers were defeated. They ran into the plain, [15] and all who trailed behind were killed. Judas and his army chased the rest of them as far as the city of Gezer, the plains of Idumea, and the cities of Azotus and Jamnia. About 3,000 foreign soldiers were killed. [16] When Judas and his army returned from chasing them, [17] he said to his army, "Forget about taking loot right now. There's still more fighting ahead of us. [18] Gorgias and his army are in the mountains nearby. So for now, we have to stand up to our enemies and fight them. After that, take all the loot you want."

[19] As soon as Judas had finished saying this, a division of foreign soldiers appeared. They were surveying the situation from the mountains. [20] When they saw smoke coming from their camp, they realized that their army had been defeated and that Judas' soldiers were burning the camp. [21] So they became really scared. When they also saw Judas' army ready to fight them in the plain, [22] all of them fled into Philistine territory. [23] Then Judas returned to loot their camp. He and his men took a lot of silver and gold, blue and purple cloth, and other riches. [24] As they returned to their own camp, they sang this hymn of praise to the LORD: "The LORD is good, because his mercy endures forever." [25] That day Israel was rescued in a wonderful way.

Judas Defeats Lysias—2 Maccabees 11:1-12

[26] The foreign soldiers who survived reported to Lysias. When he heard everything that had happened, [27] he became upset and discouraged. Things in Israel had not turned out the way he had intended or as the king had ordered.

[28] During the following year, Lysias organized 60,000 of his best infantrymen and 5,000 cavalrymen to fight Judas' army. [29] They advanced into Idumea and set up camp near the city of Beth Zur, where Judas met them with 10,000 soldiers.

[30] Judas saw that Lysias had a powerful army, so he prayed, "Savior of Israel, we praise you! You used your servant David to defeat the mighty warrior Goliath, and you handed over the Philistine camp to Saul's son Jonathan and to the man who carried his weapons. [31] Do the same for us! Let your people Israel surround this army, and let the foreigners' army and cavalry be put to shame. [32] Scare them and make them powerless. Let them suffer a crushing defeat. [33] Use the weapons of those who love you to destroy them. Let everyone who knows your name sing hymns of praise to you."

---

[a] 4:12 Greek "the Philistines."

³⁴Then both sides attacked. About 5,000 of Lysias' men were killed in the front lines. ³⁵Lysias saw that his troops were being defeated and that Judas' troops had courage and were ready to live or die honorably. So he retreated to the city of Antioch and began hiring an even larger number of foreign soldiers so that he could invade Judea again.

The Holy Place Is Cleansed and the New Altar Is Dedicated—
2 Maccabees 10:1-8

³⁶Then Judas and his brothers said, "Our enemies have been defeated. Let's go to Jerusalem to cleanse and rededicate the holy place." ³⁷So all the soldiers in Judas' army assembled and went to Mount Zion. ³⁸They saw that the holy place was deserted, that the altar had been dishonored, and that the gates had been burned down. Weeds were growing all over the courtyards like in a forest or on a mountainside, and the priests' rooms were in ruins. ³⁹Judas and his soldiers tore their clothes in grief, mourned, sprinkled ashes on themselves, ⁴⁰and bowed with their faces touching the ground. When the signal was given with trumpets, the people prayed loudly to the LORD.

⁴¹Judas ordered some of his soldiers to fight the enemy troops who were in the fortress while he cleansed the holy place. ⁴²Judas chose some priests who led holy lives and were devoted to Moses' Teachings. ⁴³These priests cleansed the holy place. They removed the stones that had been dishonored and put them in an unclean*a* place. ⁴⁴Then they discussed what they should do with the altar used for burnt offerings since it had been dishonored. ⁴⁵They came up with a good plan. They decided to tear down the altar so that they wouldn't be disgraced by the way the nations had dishonored it. So they tore down the altar. ⁴⁶They stored its stones in a suitable place on the temple mountain and left them there until a prophet would come to tell them what to do with them. ⁴⁷They took uncut stones, as Moses' Teachings required, and built a new altar like the original one. ⁴⁸They also rebuilt the holy place and cleansed the interior of the temple and its courtyards. ⁴⁹They made new utensils that were holy, and they brought the lamp stand, the altar for incense, and the table for the bread of the presence into the temple. ⁵⁰Then they burned incense on the altar and lit the lamps on the lamp stand to light up the temple. ⁵¹They put bread on the table, hung the curtains, and finished all their work.

⁵²On the twenty-fifth day of the ninth month (the month of Chislev) in the year 164 B.C., ⁵³the people got up early in the morning. As Moses' Teachings required, they offered a sacrifice on the new altar that they had built. ⁵⁴While the altar was being dedicated, people sang and played

---

a 4:43 "Unclean" refers to anything that Moses' Teachings say is not presentable to God.

music on harps, lyres, and cymbals. The dedication took place on the anniversary of the day that the foreigners had dishonored the original altar. [55]All the people bowed with their faces touching the ground. They worshiped and praised the LORD for the success he had given them.

[56]The people celebrated the dedication of the altar for eight days. They joyfully offered burnt offerings, fellowship offerings, and thank offerings. [57]They redecorated the front of the temple with gold molding and decorations. They even rededicated the gates and the priests' rooms and installed new doors. [58]The people were extremely happy because they had removed the disgrace brought on them by the foreigners.

[59]Then Judas, his brothers, and the entire assembly of Israel established these days as holidays for the Jews to celebrate the altar's dedication. At the same time every year, eight days were celebrated with joy and happiness. The celebration was to begin on the twenty-fifth day of the month of Chislev.

[60]At that time they also rebuilt the high walls and fortified towers that surrounded Mount Zion. Never again did they want foreigners to trample the holy place. [61]Judas assigned a special army to guard Mount Zion. He also fortified the city of Beth Zur so that the people would have a fortress that faced Idumea.

Wars With the Surrounding Nations—*2 Maccabees 10:14-33; 12:10-45*

5 [1]When the surrounding nations heard that the Jews had built a new altar and had rededicated the holy place, they became very angry. [2]They decided to destroy Jacob's descendants who lived among them. So they began to murder people to get rid of them.

[3]Judas went to war with Esau's descendants in the region called Akrabattene in Idumea. He did this because they were trying to set up a blockade around Israel. He overwhelmingly defeated them and then humiliated them by taking all their weapons. [4]After that, Judas remembered how badly the descendants of Baean had treated the Israelites. The descendants of Baean caused serious problems for the Israelites because they ambushed them on the highways. [5]So Judas surrounded them and forced them into their fortified towers. He set up camp by the towers so that they couldn't get out. He vowed to destroy them completely and did so by burning up their fortified towers and everyone who was in them.

[6]Next, Judas went to attack the Ammonites. He found out that they had a very large, powerful army and that Timothy was their leader. [7]Judas fought many battles with them and eventually defeated them. [8]He took possession of the city of Jazer and the villages around it. Then he returned to Judea.

[9]The foreigners in Gilead joined forces to attack the Israelites who lived in their territory. They wanted to get rid of them. But the Israelites

fled to the fortification in the city of Dathema. [10]From there they sent the following message to Judas and his brothers: "The foreigners who live around us have joined forces. They want to get rid of us. [11]They are preparing to take possession of the fortification where we have fled for protection. Timothy is the leader of their army. [12]Come immediately and rescue us because they have already killed many of our people. [13]All our relatives who were soldiers for Tobias have been killed. The foreigners have taken their wives and children as prisoners and have also taken their property and destroyed a division of about 1,000 soldiers here."

[14]While Judas and his brothers were reading the letter, other messengers arrived from Galilee with their clothes torn in grief. These messengers reported [15]that the people from Ptolemais, Tyre, Sidon, and all the foreigners[a] in Galilee had also joined forces to wipe them out. [16]When Judas and his army heard these messages, they held a meeting that everyone attended. They wanted to decide what to do to help the Jewish people who were in trouble because of enemy attacks. [17]Then Judas said to his brother Simon, "Choose some soldiers, and go to rescue the people in Galilee. Jonathan and I will go to Gilead." [18]Judas left the rest of his soldiers in Judea to defend it and placed Azariah and Joseph (who was Zechariah's son) in charge of them. [19]Judas gave Azariah and Joseph this order: "You are in charge of these soldiers. Don't fight any battles with the foreigners until we return." [20]Then a division of 3,000 soldiers went with Simon to Galilee, and a division of 8,000 soldiers went with Judas to Gilead.

[21]Simon went to Galilee and fought a number of battles against the foreigners and defeated them. [22]He chased them to the city gate of Ptolemais. About 3,000 foreign soldiers were killed, and Simon took their weapons. [23]Then he led the men, women, and children out of Galilee and the Arbatta region. Simon took them and all their possessions back to Judea. Everyone was very happy.

[24]Meanwhile, Judas Maccabeus and his brother Jonathan crossed the Jordan River and marched for three days into the desert. [25]They met the Nabateans and exchanged friendly greetings with them. The Nabateans told them everything that had happened to the Jewish people in Gilead. [26]They told Judas and Jonathan that many Jewish people were trapped in the fortified cities of Bozrah, Bosor (in Alema), Chaspho, Maked, and Karnaim. [27]In addition, the Nabateans said that some Jewish people were trapped in other cities in Gilead, that the enemy was going to attack these fortifications the next day, and that the enemy intended to capture and get rid of all these Jewish people in a single day.

[28]Then Judas and his army quickly changed direction and took a desert road that led to the city of Bozrah. He captured Bozrah, killed all the

---

[a] 5:15 Greek "the Philistines."

men there, took all their weapons, and burned down the city. ²⁹During the night, Judas and his army left Bozrah and marched to the fortress at the city of Dathema. ³⁰Early in the morning, they saw an army so large that they couldn't even count the soldiers. The soldiers were carrying ladders to climb over the walls of the city. They were also carrying large weapons to capture the fortification. These soldiers were just starting to fight the people inside the fortification. ³¹When Judas heard battle cries, loud shouting, and the sound of trumpets coming from the city, he knew that the battle had begun.

³²So Judas said to the soldiers in his army, "Fight for your people today!" ³³Then Judas marched with three companies of soldiers to attack the enemy from the rear. They blew their trumpets and prayed loudly for help. ³⁴When Timothy's soldiers saw Judas Maccabeus, they fled and were overwhelmingly defeated. About 8,000 of Timothy's troops were killed that day.

³⁵Next, Judas marched to the city of Maapha. He fought against Maapha, captured it, and killed every man there. Then he looted and burned down the city. ³⁶He left Maapha and took possession of the cities of Chaspho, Maked, Bosor, and the other cities in Gilead.

³⁷After this, Timothy recruited another army and set up camp on the other side of a river facing the city of Raphon. ³⁸Judas sent men to spy on Timothy's camp. The spies reported to Judas that all the foreigners in the surrounding territories had formed a very large army under Timothy's command. ³⁹They also reported that Timothy had hired Arab soldiers to help him and that Timothy and his army had set up camp across the river and were ready to attack. So Judas went to attack them.

⁴⁰As Judas and his army approached the river, Timothy said to the commanders of his army, "If Judas crosses the river before we do, we won't be able to stand up to him, and he'll overpower us. ⁴¹But if he's scared and stops on the other side, we'll cross the river and overpower him."

⁴²When Judas arrived at the river, he placed officers there and ordered them not to let the soldiers stop but to make all of them cross the river and fight. ⁴³Judas was the first to cross the river to attack the foreigners, and his whole army followed him. He and his men defeated the entire foreign army. The foreigners threw down their weapons and fled to the city of Karnaim, where they went into a temple dedicated to false gods. ⁴⁴Judas captured the city and burned down the temple with everyone in it. After the defeat at Karnaim, the foreigners could no longer stand up to Judas.

⁴⁵Then Judas gathered all the Israelites living in Gilead to take them back with him to Judea. This very large group consisted of rich and poor men with their wives, children, and personal belongings. ⁴⁶They went as

far as Ephron, a large and heavily fortified city. Since the city was built on the road, they couldn't go around it. They had to go through it. ⁴⁷But the citizens of Ephron wouldn't let them enter their city, and they blocked the city gates with stones. ⁴⁸Judas sent the citizens of Ephron this message: "We come in peace. Let us pass through your territory to get to our own. No one will harm you. All we want to do is to walk through." But the citizens of Ephron wouldn't allow Judas to enter their city. ⁴⁹Then Judas ordered the entire army to camp right where they were. ⁵⁰So the army set up camp there. Judas fought against the city all day and all night until he captured it. ⁵¹He had all the men in the city killed. Then he looted and leveled the city and marched through it over the dead bodies.

⁵²Judas and the people crossed the Jordan River into the large plain that faced the city of Beth Shan. ⁵³Along the way Judas kept the stragglers together and encouraged the people until they arrived in Judea. ⁵⁴They went joyfully and happily to Mount Zion. There they sacrificed burnt offerings because they had returned safely without suffering any casualties.

⁵⁵While Judas and Jonathan were in Gilead and their brother Simon was in Galilee near the city of Ptolemais, ⁵⁶Joseph (who was Zechariah's son) and Azariah were in charge of the army left in Judea. Joseph and Azariah heard about the brave things that Judas, Jonathan, and Simon had done and about the wars they had fought. ⁵⁷So Joseph and Azariah said, "We can become famous too. Let's fight the foreigners who live around us." ⁵⁸They ordered the part of the army that they were in charge of to attack the city of Jamnia. ⁵⁹Gorgias and his soldiers marched out of Jamnia to meet them in battle. ⁶⁰Gorgias defeated Joseph and Azariah and chased them to the borders of Judea. About 2,000 men from Israel's army died that day. ⁶¹So part of Israel's army was decisively defeated because Joseph and Azariah thought they, too, could be heroes and didn't obey Judas and his brothers. ⁶²Besides, Joseph and Azariah were not part of the family through whom Israel was to be rescued.

⁶³Judas and his brothers were highly honored wherever their reputation spread. Throughout Israel and the nations, ⁶⁴people crowded around them and praised them.

⁶⁵Then Judas and his brothers went south to fight Esau's descendants. Judas defeated the city of Hebron and the villages around it. He also tore down its fortifications and burned up the towers that surrounded it. ⁶⁶Then he left that foreign territory and marched through the city of Marisa. ⁶⁷That day some priests recklessly went into battle and died, because they, too, wanted to become heroes. ⁶⁸Next, Judas marched to the Philistine city of Azotus. He tore down its altars, burned up the carved

statues of its gods, and looted other Philistine cities. Then he returned
to Judea.

The Death of Antiochus IV—*2 Maccabees 1:11-17; 9:1-29; 10:9-11*

6 ¹As King Antiochus was marching through the inland territories, he
heard about a city famous for its large amounts of silver and gold.
The city was located in the territory of Elymais in Persia. ²He also heard
that the temple in Elymais was very rich. In the temple were gold helmets, breastplates, and weapons left by Macedonia's King Alexander,
Philip's son. Alexander was the first king to rule the Greek Empire. ³So
Antiochus went to Elymais and tried to capture and loot the city. But
he was unable to do this because the people in the city found out about
his plan. ⁴They resisted him in battle. So he fled from there to return to
Babylon. He was very depressed.

⁵While Antiochus was in Persia, a messenger came to him and reported
that the armies which had marched to Judea had been defeated. ⁶The
messenger reported that Lysias led a powerful army into battle against
the Israelites and had suffered a humiliating defeat. So the Israelites were
even more powerful now because of the weapons, supplies, and the large
amount of loot they had taken from the armies they had destroyed. ⁷The
Israelites had torn down the disgusting thing that Antiochus had built on
the altar in Jerusalem. They had built high walls around the holy place
as in the past, and they had even built walls around Beth Zur, his city.ᵃ

⁸The king was stunned and very upset when he heard this report. He
was so depressed about things not turning out the way he had planned
that he became sick and went to bed. ⁹He couldn't get over his depression, and he realized that he was about to die. So he stayed in bed for
many days. ¹⁰He summoned all those who held the title "Friend of the
King" and said to them, "I'm very worried, and I can't sleep. ¹¹I thought
to myself, 'How did I ever get into the kind of trouble I'm in now? After
all, I've always been kind, and people loved the way I ruled.' ¹²But then I
remembered all the terrible things I did to Jerusalem. I took all its silver
and gold utensils. Without any good reason, I sent armies to destroy the
people who live in Judea. ¹³Now I know that all these things are happening to me because of the terrible things I've done. I'm being destroyed
by depression in a foreign land."

¹⁴Then Antiochus summoned Philip, who held the title "Friend of the
King," and put him in charge of his entire kingdom. ¹⁵Antiochus wanted
Philip to raise his son Antiochus V and to train him to be the next king.
So he gave his crown, robe, and signet ring to Philip. ¹⁶King Antiochus
died in Persia in the year 163 B.C.

ᵃ 6:7 Some manuscripts read "their city."

[17] When Lysias learned that the king was dead, he appointed the king's son Antiochus V to be king. Lysias had raised the king's son from childhood and named him Eupator.

Judas Maccabeus Attacks the Fortress in Jerusalem—
2 Maccabees 11:22-26; 13:1-26

[18] Meanwhile, the men from the fortress surrounded the people of Israel in the holy place. They wanted to harm the people in every way possible and to give support to the foreigners. [19] Judas decided to get rid of these men. So he assembled his entire army to set up a blockade against them. [20] The army set up the blockade around the fortress in the year 162 B.C. Judas had catapults and other large weapons built.

[21] Even though the fortress was surrounded, some of the men escaped, and some Israelites who had betrayed their religion joined them. [22] They went to King Antiochus V and asked him, "How long are you going to wait before you take revenge for what has been done to the people of our country? [23] We willingly served your father, obeyed everything he said, and followed his official orders. [24] As a result, our own people have set up a blockade around the fortress and have become our enemies. In addition, they have killed as many of us as they could find and have looted our possessions. [25] We're not the only ones they've attacked. They've also attacked the people who live on their borders. [26] Just look at what they've done! Today they've attacked the fortress in Jerusalem and are planning to capture it. They've fortified the holy place and the city of Beth Zur. [27] Unless you stop them immediately, they'll do things that are even worse, and you'll never be able to stop them."

King Antiochus V Defeats Judas

[28] When King Antiochus V heard this, he became angry. He assembled all the commanders of his troops and cavalry, the commanders who held the title "Friend of the King." [29] He also hired troops from other kingdoms and from the Greek islands. [30] He had 100,000 infantrymen, 20,000 cavalrymen, and 32 elephants that were trained for war. [31] They marched through Idumea, set up camp at the city of Beth Zur, made large weapons, and fought against the city for a long time. But the Jews marched out of the city, burned the weapons, and fought bravely.

[32] Then Judas left the fortress and moved to a position that blocked the king's army near the city of Beth Zechariah. [33] Early in the morning the king left his camp and quickly positioned his troops along the road that led to Beth Zechariah. His troops prepared for battle and blew their trumpets. [34] They used grape and mulberry wine to arouse the elephants for battle. [35] They positioned the elephants throughout the battle lines. Stationed with each elephant were 1,000 well-equipped soldiers wearing

brass helmets and 500 of the best cavalrymen. ³⁶These soldiers always went wherever the elephants went. They never left them. ³⁷A wooden shield was fastened by special straps on the back of each elephant. Each elephant carried an elephant driver and four soldiers, who fought from behind the shield. ³⁸Lysias stationed the rest of the cavalry on each end of the battle line. The cavalry would harass the enemy and protect the battle lines. ³⁹When sunlight reflected off the soldiers' polished bronze shields, the hillside sparkled like flaming torches.

⁴⁰One division of the king's army marched in formation on the hillsides. The other division marched in formation in the valley. Their orderly movement showed that they were well-organized. ⁴¹All the soldiers in Judas' army were afraid when they heard the king's soldiers shouting, marching, and clashing their weapons. The king's army was very large and powerful.

⁴²Judas and his army advanced into battle and killed 600 of the king's soldiers. ⁴³Eleazar Avaran saw that one of the elephants was covered with royal armor and that it was taller than all the other elephants. So he thought that the king was riding on it. ⁴⁴Eleazar risked his life to save his people and make himself famous forever. ⁴⁵He boldly ran into the middle of the battle line and cut a path to the elephant by killing soldiers on his right and left. ⁴⁶When he got to the elephant, he stabbed and killed it. But the elephant fell to the ground on top of Eleazar and killed him. ⁴⁷Judas and his soldiers retreated because they saw how powerful the king's troops were and how fiercely they were fighting.

King Antiochus V Makes a Peace Treaty With the Jews

⁴⁸The king and his army went to Jerusalem to fight the Jews. The king set up military camps in Judea and at Mount Zion. ⁴⁹He made a peace treaty with the citizens of Beth Zur. After this, the citizens of Beth Zur left the city because they didn't have enough food to withstand a blockade. The land had not been cultivated that year because that year was a festival year for the land. ⁵⁰The king captured Beth Zur and stationed soldiers there to guard it. ⁵¹Then he camped near the holy place for a long time. He set up many kinds of catapults and other large weapons to throw flaming objects, stones, and arrows. ⁵²The Jews made large weapons to match the king's and fought the king and his army for a long time. ⁵³But they had no food in storage, because that year was a festival year for the land. Those who had been rescued from the foreigners and brought back to Judea had eaten the last of the food supply. ⁵⁴Only a few men were left in the holy place. The rest scattered to their homes because the food shortage was so severe.

⁵⁵While King Antiochus IV was still alive, he had appointed Philip to train his son Antiochus V to be the next king. Now Lysias heard that

Philip had returned from Persia and Media with the king's army[a] 56and was trying to take over the government. 57So he quickly ordered his soldiers to withdraw. He said to the king, the army commanders, and the soldiers, "We are growing weaker every day. We're running short of supplies, and the place that we're fighting is strong. We have more important matters to take care of in the kingdom. 58So let's make a peace treaty with the Jews and their entire nation. 59Let's make an agreement that will allow them to live by their own religious traditions as they did before. They became angry and did all these things because we abolished their traditions."

60The king and his commanders liked what Lysias said. So the king sent the terms for a peace treaty to the Jews, and the Jews accepted them. 61After the king and his commanders had promised with an oath to abide by the peace treaty, the Jews came out of the fortress. 62But when the king was on Mount Zion and saw how the Jews had fortified the place, he broke his promise and ordered his soldiers to tear down the wall that surrounded it. 63Then he quickly left and returned to the city of Antioch, where he found Philip in control of the city. The king and his army fought Philip and captured the city by force.

Demetrius I Becomes King—*2 Maccabees 14:1-36; 15:1-36*

7 1In the year 161 B.C., Demetrius I (who was the son of Seleucus) left Rome and sailed with a few men to Tripolis, a city on the coast, where he began to rule as king. 2As Demetrius was marching into Antioch, the capital city of his ancestors, his soldiers arrested Antiochus and Lysias and intended to bring them to him. 3But when Demetrius found out about this, he told his soldiers, "I don't want to see them!" 4So the soldiers killed Antiochus and Lysias, and Demetrius took control of the kingdom.

5Then all the Israelites who betrayed their religion by not following Moses' Teachings went to Demetrius. Alcimus, who wanted to be chief priest, was their leader. 6They brought accusations to the king against their own people. They said, "Judas and his brothers have killed all your friends, and they have forced us to leave our country. 7Send someone you trust to inspect all the destruction that Judas has caused to our property and to your territory, Your Majesty. Let him punish Judas, Judas' brothers, and everyone who supports them."

Demetrius Sends Bacchides and Alcimus To Punish Judea

8So King Demetrius chose Bacchides. Bacchides was one of the people who held the title "Friend of the King" and was governor of the territory

---

[a] 6:55 The first part of verse 56 has been placed in verse 55 to express the complex Greek sentence structure more clearly in English.

west of the Euphrates River. He was an important man in the kingdom and was loyal to the king. ⁹Demetrius sent Bacchides and Alcimus
to punish the people of Israel. (Demetrius had appointed Alcimus as
chief priest even though Alcimus had betrayed the Jewish religion.) ¹⁰So
Bacchides and Alcimus left Antioch with a large army and marched
into Judea. Bacchides sent messengers to Judas and his brothers with
a friendly greeting, but he was really trying to deceive them. ¹¹Judas
and his brothers didn't pay any attention to what the messengers said
because they saw that Bacchides and Alcimus had come with a large
army.

¹²Then a group of scribes went to Alcimus and Bacchides and asked
for a fair agreement. ¹³These scribes, who belonged to a group of Jewish
people called the Hasidim, were the first Israelites to seek a peace treaty
with Alcimus and Bacchides. ¹⁴They thought, "Alcimus is with the army.
He is a priest and a descendant of Aaron. He won't harm us."

¹⁵Alcimus spoke in a friendly way to the scribes. He promised with an
oath not to harm them or their friends. ¹⁶So the Hasidim trusted him.
But Alcimus had 60 of them arrested and killed on the same day. The
passage that Alcimus himself wrote came true,

¹⁷"They poured out the blood of your Hasidim
    and left their dead bodies lying around Jerusalem.
There is no one to bury your people."

¹⁸After this, all the Israelites were terrified. They said, "These men
don't know anything about truth or justice. They broke our agreement.
They didn't keep their promise."

¹⁹Bacchides left Jerusalem and set up camp near the city of Beth
Zaith. He seized many of the Jews who had deserted to his side and
some other Jewish people. He had them slaughtered and thrown into
a large cistern. ²⁰He put Alcimus in charge of the country and left an
army with him to give him support. Then Bacchides returned to the
king.

²¹Alcimus continually struggled to remain chief priest. ²²All the troublemakers in the country joined him. They overwhelmingly defeated
Israel and took control of Judea. ²³Judas saw all the terrible things that
Alcimus and his men had done to the people of Israel. He realized that
these things were much worse than anything the foreigners were doing.
²⁴So Judas went throughout the entire territory of Judea and punished
those who had deserted, and he prevented people from leaving the city
to go into the countryside. ²⁵Alcimus saw that Judas and his men had
become powerful. He realized that he couldn't stand up to Judas and his
men anymore, so he returned to the king and brought criminal charges
against them.

King Demetrius Sends Nicanor To Get Rid of the Israelites

²⁶ Then King Demetrius sent Nicanor, who was one of his most respected commanders, to Judea. Nicanor had a bitter hatred for the people of Israel. The king ordered Nicanor to get rid of the Israelites. ²⁷So Nicanor went to Jerusalem with a large army. He sent messengers to Judas and his brothers with a friendly greeting, but he was really trying to deceive them. He said, ²⁸"Let's not fight. I'll come with a few men to meet with you peacefully."

²⁹ When Nicanor went to meet Judas, both men greeted each other peacefully. But Judas' enemies were ready to take him by force. ³⁰Judas found out that Nicanor had deceived him. So Judas was afraid of him and refused to meet with him again. ³¹When Nicanor found out that Judas knew about his plan, he attacked Judas near the city of Caphar Salama. ³²About 500 of Nicanor's soldiers were killed. The rest of his soldiers fled into David's city.

Nicanor Threatens To Burn Down the Temple

³³ After this, Nicanor went to Mount Zion. Some of the priests from the holy place and some of the leaders of the Jewish people went to greet him peacefully. They wanted to show him the burnt offering that was being sacrificed for the king. ³⁴But Nicanor mocked the priests, laughed at them, and made them unclean*ᵃ* ⌊by spitting on them⌋. He spoke arrogantly, ³⁵and he angrily swore this oath: "Unless Judas and his army are handed over to me right now, I'll burn down this temple when I come back from my victory." He was extremely angry when he left.

³⁶ The priests went back to the holy place and stood in front of the altar and the temple. They cried and prayed,

³⁷ "LORD, you chose this temple and placed your name here.
You chose it to be a house of prayer,
    a house where your people can pray to you.
³⁸ Punish Nicanor and his army.
Let them die in battle.
Remember the slanderous things they said,
    and don't let any of them survive."

Nicanor Is Killed in Battle

³⁹ Nicanor marched from Jerusalem and set up camp near the city of Beth Horon. The Syrian army joined him there. ⁴⁰Judas had 3,000 soldiers with him and set up camp near the city of Adasa. Then Judas prayed, ⁴¹"LORD, when King Sennacherib's messengers said disgusting things, your

---

ᵃ 7:34 "Unclean" refers to anything that Moses' Teachings say is not presentable to God.

angel killed 185,000 of his soldiers. ⁴²In the same way, defeat the army we're going to face today. Let everyone know that Nicanor said terrible things about your holy place. Judge him for the terrible things he has done."

⁴³The armies fought on the thirteenth day of the month of Adar. Nicanor's army was defeated, and he was the first one killed in battle. ⁴⁴When the soldiers in Nicanor's army saw that he had been killed, they threw down their weapons and fled. ⁴⁵Judas and his soldiers chased them all day long from the city of Adasa to the city of Gezer. They kept sounding the battle call on their trumpets as they chased Nicanor's soldiers. ⁴⁶People came from all the surrounding Judean villages, outflanked Nicanor's soldiers, and forced them to turn back toward those who where chasing them. As a result, all of Nicanor's soldiers were killed in battle. Not even one of them survived. ⁴⁷Then the people stripped them of their valuables and looted their camp. They cut off Nicanor's head and his right hand, which he had raised so arrogantly ⌐when he threatened to burn down the temple⌐. The people brought his head and hand to a place near Jerusalem and put them on display. ⁴⁸The people were very happy. They set that day apart as a special day for joyful celebration. ⁴⁹They established the thirteenth day of the month of Adar to celebrate as an annual holiday. ⁵⁰So Judea had peace for a short time.

Judas Learns About the Romans

8 ¹Judas heard about the reputation of the Romans. He heard that they were very powerful, that they welcomed anyone who wanted to become their allies, and that they had established friendly relations with everyone who approached them. ²People had told Judas about the wars the Romans had fought, about the brave things that they had done in their war against the Gauls, and about how they had conquered the Gauls and forced them to pay taxes. ³People had also told Judas what the Romans had done in Spain to take control of the silver and gold mines there. ⁴By using careful planning and patience, the Romans had taken over that whole region, even though it was far away from Rome. The Romans had fought kings who had come from distant places to attack them. They fought these kings until they had overwhelmingly defeated and conquered them. The survivors still pay taxes to them every year.

⁵The Romans had also fought and conquered Philip, Macedonia's King Perseus, and everyone else who had opposed them. ⁶They had defeated Syria's King Antiochus the Great,ᵃ even though he had a very large army consisting of cavalry, chariots, and 120 elephants. ⁷They took Antiochus alive and forced him and the kings who ruled after him to pay high taxes,

---

ᵃ 8:6 Antiochus the Great is another name for Antiochus III.

to give them hostages, and to turn over to them [8]India, Media, and Lydia, which were some of the best provinces. The Romans took these provinces from Antiochus and gave them to King Eumenes.

[9]The Greeks had planned to destroy the Romans, [10]but the Romans found out about their plan and sent a general to fight them. The Romans wounded and killed many Greeks, took their wives and children as prisoners, looted their property, took possession of their land, tore down their fortresses, and made them slaves, as they are today. [11]The Romans had also destroyed all the other kingdoms and Greek islands that opposed them, and they made the people in these places slaves. [12]But the Romans maintained friendly relations with those who were on good terms with them and who relied on them. They conquered kings from far and near, and everyone who heard about their reputation was afraid of them. [13]Whoever the Romans wanted to become king was made king, and whoever they didn't want to be king was removed from office and killed.

So the Romans had become very powerful. [14]Yet, no Roman ever put on a crown or wore royal robes to show off his power. [15]The Romans had formed a senate. Every day 320 senators met to discuss issues that affected the Roman people in order to govern their people well. [16]Each year the Romans relied on one man to rule them and to control all their land. Everyone obeyed that man, and no one was envious or jealous of him.

Judas Makes an Alliance With Rome

[17]Judas chose Eupolemus (who was John's son and Accos' grandson) and Jason (who was Eleazar's son) and sent them to Rome. He wanted to establish friendly relations with the Romans and make an alliance that would [18]free the Jewish people from oppression. The Romans knew that the Greeks were making slaves out of the people of Israel. [19]That's why Eupolemus and Jason made the long trip to Rome. They entered the senate and addressed it as follows: [20]"Judas Maccabeus, his brothers, and the Jewish people have sent us to make an alliance and a peace treaty with you. We want to be included in your list of friends and allies."

[21]The Romans were pleased with the Jews' proposal. [22]The following letter is a copy of the reply that the Romans wrote on bronze plaques. They sent these plaques to Jerusalem to remain there as a record of the peace treaty and the alliance. The letter read:

> [23]"May everything always go well on land and sea between the Romans and the Jewish nation. May we never become enemies and go to war against each other.
>
> [24]"If war breaks out against Rome or against Rome's allies, wherever they may be, [25]the Jewish nation, as Rome's ally, must

lend complete support to Rome as the situation requires. ²⁶As both parties agreed in Rome, the Jewish nation must not supply food, weapons, money, or ships to Rome's enemy and must keep its commitments to Rome without expecting anything in return. ²⁷In the same way, if war breaks out against the Jewish nation, Rome, as its ally, must lend full support to the Jewish nation as the situation requires. ²⁸As both parties agreed in Rome, the Romans must not give food, weapons, money, or ships to an enemy of the Jewish nation and must keep their commitments to the Jewish nation in good faith.

²⁹ "These are the terms of the treaty that the Romans made with the Jewish people. ³⁰If both parties agree to add or delete anything from this treaty after these terms are in effect, they may do so as they chose. Any addition or deletion that they make will be valid.

³¹ "We have written the following to King Demetrius about the way he is treating you: 'Why have you oppressed the Jewish people? They are our friends and allies. ³²If they complain about you one more time, we will defend them. We will go to war against you on land and sea.'"

Judas Maccabeus Dies in Battle

9 ¹Demetrius heard that Nicanor and his army had been defeated in battle. So Demetrius sent Bacchides, Alcimus, and the right flank of his army to Judea again. ²They marched on the road that leads to Gilgal and set up camp near Mesaloth in the vicinity of the city of Arbela. They took possession of Mesaloth and killed many people there. ³In the first month of the year 160 B.C., they set up camp near Jerusalem. ⁴Later, they left Jerusalem and went to the city of Berea with 20,000 infantrymen and 2,000 cavalrymen.

⁵Judas set up camp near the city of Elasa. He had 3,000 of his best soldiers with him. ⁶When Judas' soldiers saw how many enemy troops there were, they became terrified. Many soldiers sneaked out of Judas' camp until only 800 soldiers were left.

⁷Judas realized that many of his soldiers had sneaked away and that he was going to be forced into battle. So he became worried because he didn't have enough time to regroup. ⁸Although he was discouraged, he said to the soldiers who were left, "Quick! Let's attack our enemies. Maybe we still have enough men to fight them."

⁹His men tried to change his mind. They said to him, "We don't have enough men. Let's save our own lives and come back to fight them when the other men are with us. We just don't have enough men right now."

¹⁰But Judas replied, "That's unthinkable! We can't run away. If it's time for us to die, then let's die bravely for our people. Let's not give anyone a reason to question our honor."

¹¹Bacchides' army left its camp and got ready to attack Judas and his men. Bacchides' cavalry was divided into two divisions. The soldiers who had slings for weapons, the archers, and all the best soldiers marched in the front lines. ¹²Two infantry divisions formed the battle line, and Bacchides was on the right flank. Soldiers in both armies blew trumpets as they advanced. ¹³The ground shook from all the noise that these armies made. The battle lasted from morning until evening.

¹⁴Judas saw that Bacchides and the strongest part of his army were on the right. So all of Judas' bravest men went with him. ¹⁵They defeated the soldiers in the right flank, and chased them as far as Mount Azotus. ¹⁶When the soldiers on the left flank saw that the right flank was defeated, they turned around, chased Judas and his men, and attacked them from behind. ¹⁷The battle became fierce, and many soldiers on both sides were killed. ¹⁸Eventually, Judas was killed, and the rest of his soldiers fled.

¹⁹Jonathan and Simon took their brother Judas and placed him in their ancestors' tomb in the city of Modein. ²⁰His brothers cried for him, and all the people in Israel held a solemn ceremony for many days to mourn his death. They said,

²¹"How can this be?
Our hero Judas, the savior of Israel, is dead."

²²Many other things about Judas—the wars he fought, the brave things he did, and the important things he accomplished—have not been recorded. There are just too many of them to write down.

Jonathan Takes Judas' Place

²³After Judas died, the people who didn't follow Moses' Teachings came out of hiding throughout Israel, and all the wicked people reappeared. ²⁴At that time there was a severe famine, and the whole country deserted Judas' brothers and sided with these wicked people. ²⁵Bacchides chose Jews who had betrayed their religion and appointed them to be in charge of the country. ²⁶These men investigated Judas' friends, searched for them, and brought them to Bacchides, who punished and tortured them. ²⁷So the people of Israel were in serious trouble. This trouble was worse than any they had experienced since the last time prophets appeared to them.

²⁸Then all of Judas' friends went to Jonathan and said, ²⁹"Since your brother Judas died, we have no one like him to fight our enemies, enemies like Bacchides and our own people who hate us. ³⁰Today we have chosen you to be our commander and leader. We want you to take Judas' place

and fight for us." ³¹So Jonathan became their leader that day and took the place of his brother Judas.

³²When Bacchides found out about this, he wanted to kill Jonathan. ³³But Jonathan, his brother Simon, and everyone who was with them found out what Bacchides wanted to do. So they fled into the desert of Tekoa and camped by the pond of Asphar. ³⁴Bacchides learned about this on the day of worship, and he and his entire army marched across the Jordan River.

³⁵Jonathan sent his brother John, who was in charge of the common people, to his friends the Nabateans. He wanted John to ask the Nabateans if they would store all the personal belongings that the people were carrying with them. ³⁶But the Jambrites, who were from the city of Medeba, captured John and took everything he had.

³⁷Later, some people told Jonathan and his brother Simon that the Jambrites were about to celebrate an important marriage. The bride was a daughter from one of the most important families in Canaan. She was to be escorted by a large procession from the city of Nadabath. ³⁸Jonathan and Simon remembered that the Jambrites had murdered their brother. They went up a mountain and hid. ³⁹As they watched, they saw a noisy procession carrying a lot of personal belongings. The groom came to meet the procession with his friends and his brothers. There were also musicians playing drums and many other musical instruments. ⁴⁰Jonathan and his men ambushed the people in the procession and began to kill them. Many people were killed, and those who survived fled into the mountains. Then Jonathan and his men took all their possessions. ⁴¹So the wedding turned into a funeral, and the wedding songs turned into funeral songs. ⁴²After Jonathan and Simon had taken revenge on the Jambrites for the murder of their brother, they returned to the marshes along the Jordan River.

⁴³When Bacchides heard about this, he went with a large army to the banks of the Jordan River on the day of worship. ⁴⁴Jonathan said to his men, "Quick! Let's fight for our lives! We've never been in a situation like this before. ⁴⁵Look around! Enemy soldiers are in front of us, the Jordan River is behind us, and marshes and thickets are on both sides of us. There's no way out! ⁴⁶So pray to the LORDᵃ for help. Pray that he will rescue us from our enemies."

⁴⁷The battle began. Jonathan tried to kill Bacchides, but Bacchides got away from him by escaping to the back of his army. ⁴⁸Then Jonathan and his men jumped into the Jordan River and swam to the other side. The

---

ᵃ 9:46 Greek "to Heaven." The author of 1 Maccabees uses the word *Heaven* in place of God's name, the LORD.

enemy didn't cross the river to attack them. ⁴⁹About 1,000 of Bacchides' soldiers were killed that day. ⁵⁰Bacchides returned to Jerusalem. He began to fortify some Judean cities with high walls, gates, and iron bars. These cities were: Jericho, Emmaus, Beth Horon, Bethel, Timnath, Pharathon, and Tephon. ⁵¹Bacchides placed soldiers in these cities to harass the people of Israel. ⁵²He also fortified the cities of Beth Zur and Gezer and strengthened the fortress in Jerusalem. He placed troops and food supplies in these locations. ⁵³Then he took the sons of the country's leaders as hostages and imprisoned them in the fortress in Jerusalem.

⁵⁴In the second month of the year 159 B.C., Alcimus ordered that the wall in the inner courtyard of the holy place be torn down. But as soon as Alcimus began to tear down what the prophets had built, ⁵⁵he had a stroke, and the work was stopped. He was paralyzed and couldn't talk anymore. He couldn't say a word or even tell his family what to write in his will. ⁵⁶Then Alcimus died in severe pain. ⁵⁷When Bacchides saw that Alcimus was dead, he returned to the king. So Judea had peace for two years.

Jonathan Defeats Bacchides

⁵⁸Then all the Jewish people who didn't follow Moses' Teachings came up with a plan. They said, "Look! Jonathan and his men are confident. They are living in peace. If we bring Bacchides back here, he could capture all of them in one night." ⁵⁹They went to tell Bacchides their plan. ⁶⁰Bacchides left the city of Antioch with a large army and marched to Judea. He secretly sent letters to all his allies in Judea and ordered them to capture Jonathan and his men. But his allies were unable to capture them because Jonathan found out about their plan. ⁶¹Jonathan and his men captured and killed about 50 Jewish men who had organized this wicked plan.

⁶²Then Jonathan, Simon, and their men withdrew to the desert city of Beth Basi. They rebuilt the city's ruins and strengthened its fortifications. ⁶³When Bacchides found out about this, he gathered his entire army and asked his allies in Judea for help. ⁶⁴He marched to Beth Basi, set up camp there, and built large weapons. He attacked the city for many days.

⁶⁵Then Jonathan left his brother Simon in charge of the city and went into the countryside with only a few men. ⁶⁶He arrived at the place where Odomera, Odomera's relatives, and the descendants of Phasiron had set up camp. He ordered them to start harassing and attacking Bacchides' troops.^a ⁶⁷Meanwhile, Simon and his men left the city to set fire to Bacchides' large weapons. ⁶⁸They fought Bacchides and defeated him. They

---

^a 9:66 Some manuscripts read "He killed them."

put so much pressure on Bacchides that his planned invasion failed. [69]Bacchides became furious with the Jewish people who didn't follow Moses' Teachings, because they had advised him to come to their country. So he killed many of them.

Afterward, Bacchides decided to return to his own country. [70]When Jonathan realized that Bacchides was going home, he sent ambassadors to make a peace treaty with him and arrange for the release of Jewish prisoners. [71]Bacchides agreed to make a peace treaty and release the prisoners. In addition, he promised with an oath that he would never again harm Jonathan. [72]Bacchides released the prisoners he had taken from Judea. Then he returned to his own country and never entered Jewish territory again. [73]So the war in Israel ended. Jonathan settled in the city of Michmash. He began to serve as the judge, getting rid of all the Israelites who had betrayed their religion.

Alexander Epiphanes Appoints Jonathan Chief Priest

10 [1]In the year 152 B.C., Alexander Epiphanes (who was the son of Antiochus IV) sailed to the city of Ptolemais and captured it. The people of Ptolemais welcomed him, and he began to rule there as king. [2]When King Demetrius heard about this, he recruited a very large army and went to attack Alexander Epiphanes. [3]Demetrius sent Jonathan a friendly letter in which he praised him highly. [4]Demetrius thought, "I want to make a peace treaty with Jonathan before he makes a peace treaty with Alexander. [5]I'm sure he remembers all the terrible things that I did to him, his brothers, and his nation." [6]So Demetrius made Jonathan his ally and gave him the right to recruit troops and make weapons. Also, Demetrius ordered all hostages in the fortress to be released to Jonathan.

[7]Jonathan went to Jerusalem and read the letter to all the people, even to the soldiers in the fortress. [8]The soldiers in the fortress became terrified when they heard that the king had given Jonathan the right to recruit troops. [9]So they released the hostages to Jonathan, and he returned them to their families.

[10]Jonathan stayed in Jerusalem. He began to rebuild and restore the city. [11]He told the workers to use square stones to reinforce the walls around the city and Mount Zion. So that's what the workers did.

[12]The foreigners who lived in the fortifications that Bacchides had built fled. [13]Each person deserted his post and went back to his own country. [14]Some of the Jews who had abandoned Moses' Teachings and commands remained behind but only in Beth Zur, because Beth Zur served as a city of refuge.

[15]King Alexander heard about all the promises that Demetrius had made to Jonathan. He also heard about the battles that Jonathan and

his brothers had fought, the brave things they had done, and the hard times that they had gone through. [16]King Alexander said, "I'll never find another man like Jonathan. I should make him my friend and ally right away." [17]So King Alexander wrote the following letter and sent it to Jonathan:

[18]"From King Alexander.
To my dear friend Jonathan.
Greetings!

[19]"I've heard all about you. I've heard that you are known for your strength and that you deserve to be one of my friends. [20]So today I have appointed you chief priest of your nation and have given you the title 'Friend of the King.' I want you to support my policies and maintain our friendship."

King Alexander also sent Jonathan royal robes and a gold crown.

[21]So in the seventh month of the year 152 B.C., at the Festival of Booths, Jonathan, as the chief priest, put on his holy clothes. He also recruited troops and provided many weapons for them.

King Demetrius I Sends a Letter to Jonathan

[22]When Demetrius heard what Alexander had done, he became worried and thought, [23]"What have I done? I let Alexander gain an advantage over me. He made a peace treaty with the Jews before I did. [24]I, too, am going to write to the Jews and encourage them. I'll promise them positions of honor and other gifts so that they'll continue to give me their support." [25]So Demetrius sent the following letter to them:

"From Demetrius.
To the Jewish people.
Greetings!

[26]"I am very happy to hear that you have kept your treaty with my nation, that you have maintained friendly relations with us, and that you haven't supported our enemies. [27]Stay loyal to us now, and we will reward you generously for everything you do for us. [28]We will no longer require you to pay a lot of taxes, and we will give you other gifts.

[29]"Starting today, I will no longer require all Jewish people to pay national taxes, salt tax, and the taxes I personally impose. [30]In addition, I will no longer require you to pay the 33 percent tax on the grain you harvest and the 50 percent tax on the fruit you grow, even though I have the right to receive these taxes. From now on I won't collect these taxes from Judea, Samaria,

Galilee, or the three districts annexed to Judea. ³¹I will no longer require Jerusalem and the areas around it to pay me one-tenth of all their income. Jerusalem, the areas around it, and one-tenth of all their income will be set apart as holy. ³²I will also give up my authority over the fortress in Jerusalem and give the chief priest the right to choose his own men to guard it. ³³Also, I will free all Jewish people who are imprisoned throughout my kingdom. ⌐When they return to Judea,⌐ I will not require them to pay taxes, even on their livestock.

³⁴"All Jewish people who live in my kingdom will no longer be required to pay taxes on all festival days, days of worship, New Moon Festivals, and special holy days. In addition, no taxes will be collected from them three days before or after these holy days. ³⁵No one will have the right to collect taxes from them or bother them in any way.

³⁶"Up to 30,000 Jewish men may enlist in my army. They will be paid the same amount as all the other soldiers in my army. ³⁷Some will be stationed in my most important fortifications, and others will be appointed to serve throughout the kingdom in military positions that require security clearance. These Jewish soldiers will have Jewish officers and leaders. I will allow them to follow their own traditions, as I have allowed the people in Judea.

³⁸"The three districts that Judea has annexed from the territory of Samaria will be placed under the control of one ruler, the chief priest. All the people in these districts must obey only him. ³⁹I will give the city of Ptolemais and the land around it to the holy place in Jerusalem to cover its expenses. ⁴⁰I will even include an annual grant of 15,000 silver coins from my royal treasury. ⁴¹I will give you all the extra money that my government has not paid in recent years for work on the temple.

⁴²"In addition to this, I will no longer require the 5,000 silver coins that I have received yearly from the treasury of the holy place. This money belongs to the priests who perform their duties in the holy place. ⁴³All those who owe anything to the government and have taken refuge in the temple complex in Jerusalem will be released from their debts. Everything in my kingdom that was taken from them will be given back.

⁴⁴"Government funds will be used to rebuild the holy place ⁴⁵and Jerusalem's walls. They will also be used to fortify the area around the city and rebuild the walls around other cities in Judea."

⁴⁶When Jonathan and the Jewish people heard the promises that King Demetrius made, they didn't believe them or accept them. They remembered the terrible things that Demetrius had done to them and how severely he had oppressed them. ⁴⁷But they liked Alexander, because he was friendly to them before Demetrius was. So they remained his allies as long as he lived.

King Demetrius I Is Killed in Battle

⁴⁸King Alexander recruited a large army and set up camp facing Demetrius' army. ⁴⁹The two kings fought, and Demetrius'ᵃ army fled. Alexander pursued Demetriusᵇ and his army and defeated them. ⁵⁰Alexander fought a fierce battle until sunset, and Demetrius was killed that day.

⁵¹Then Alexander sent ambassadors to King Ptolemy VI of Egypt with the following message: ⁵²"I have returned to my kingdom, taken my place on my ancestors' throne, and begun to rule. I have defeated Demetrius and have taken control of my country. ⁵³I fought him, defeated his army, and have taken control of his kingdom. ⁵⁴We need to establish friendly relations now. Let me marry your daughter and become your son-in-law. I will give to both of you the kind of gifts you deserve."

⁵⁵King Ptolemy replied, "The day you returned to your ancestors' country and took control of their kingdom was a great day. ⁵⁶I'll do what you wrote in your message. Let's meet in the city of Ptolemais so that we can get acquainted first. Then I'll become your father-in-law as you have suggested."

⁵⁷So Ptolemy and his daughter Cleopatra left Egypt and arrived in Ptolemais in the year 150 B.C. ⁵⁸King Alexander met Ptolemy, and Ptolemy let Alexander marry his daughter Cleopatra in Ptolemais. Like other kings, Ptolemy held a magnificent wedding reception for his daughter.

⁵⁹Afterward, King Alexander wrote to Jonathan and mentioned that he would like to meet with him. ⁶⁰So Jonathan traveled in style to the city of Ptolemais. There he met the two kings, Ptolemy and Alexander. He gave them and their friends silver, gold, and many other gifts and made a good impression on them. ⁶¹Meanwhile, some Israelite troublemakers who didn't follow Moses' Teachings came and brought charges against Jonathan. But King Alexander didn't pay any attention to them. ⁶²Instead, the king ordered his servants to take off Jonathan's clothes and to put royal robes on him. The servants did what the king had ordered. ⁶³The king also had Jonathan sit next to him. The king told his officials, "Take Jonathan to the center of the city. Tell everyone there that no one is to bring charges against him for any reason and that no one is to bother

---

ᵃ 10:49 Some manuscripts read "Alexander's."

ᵇ 10:49 Some manuscripts read "Demetrius pursued Alexander."

him in any way." ⁶⁴When Jonathan's accusers saw how the king honored him in public and that Jonathan was wearing royal robes, all of them fled. ⁶⁵The king also honored him by including him among those who held the title "Most Important Friend of the King." He appointed Jonathan to be general and governor of the province of Judea. ⁶⁶Then Jonathan returned joyfully and safely to Jerusalem.

Jonathan Defeats Apollonius

⁶⁷In the year 147 B.C., Demetrius II (who was the son of King Demetrius I) went from the island of Crete to his ancestors' country. ⁶⁸When King Alexander heard about this, he was very worried and returned to the city of Antioch. ⁶⁹Demetrius reappointed Apollonius as the governor of Coelesyria. Apollonius recruited a large army and set up camp near the city of Jamnia. Then he sent the following message to the chief priest Jonathan: ⁷⁰"You are the only one who rebels against me. I've been ridiculed and disgraced because of you. In the mountains where you live, you're using your authority against me! Why are you doing that? ⁷¹If you have any confidence in your army, come down and fight me in the plain. Let's see who has the stronger army. I have the backing of the cities on my side. ⁷²Ask around! People will tell you about the kind of fighter I am and about the others who are helping me. They'll tell you that you have no way of defeating us. Remember, your ancestors were defeated twice in their own country. ⁷³Likewise, you won't be able to defeat my cavalry and my powerful army in the plain. In the plain you won't find so much as a stone, pebble, or place to hide behind."

⁷⁴Jonathan was upset when he heard Apollonius' message. He chose 10,000 soldiers and marched out of Jerusalem. His brother Simon joined him with reinforcements. ⁷⁵Jonathan and his soldiers set up camp near the city of Joppa, but the citizens of Joppa wouldn't let them enter, because Apollonius had stationed soldiers there. ⁷⁶So Jonathan and his army fought against Apollonius' soldiers. The citizens of Joppa opened the city gates because they were afraid, and Jonathan took control of the city.

⁷⁷When Apollonius heard about this, he left camp with 3,000 cavalrymen and a large army. He went to the city of Azotus and pretended that he was going to march through the city. Instead, he advanced into the plain because he had confidence in his large cavalry. ⁷⁸Jonathan chased Apollonius to Azotus, where they fought. ⁷⁹Apollonius had secretly left 1,000 cavalrymen behind Jonathan and his army. ⁸⁰Soon Jonathan realized that he was caught in an ambush. The enemy surrounded his army and shot arrows at his men from early morning until late afternoon. ⁸¹But Jonathan's soldiers held their ground, as he had ordered, and the enemy's cavalry grew tired.

⁸²When the enemy's cavalry was exhausted, Simon's soldiers attacked. They fought the enemy soldiers and defeated them. The enemy soldiers fled, ⁸³and their cavalry was scattered all over the plain. Many enemy soldiers fled into the city of Azotus and ran for safety into the temple of their god Dagon. ⁸⁴But Jonathan burned the temple of Dagon along with the enemy soldiers who ran there for safety. Then Jonathan set fire to the city of Azotus and the surrounding towns and looted them. ⁸⁵About 8,000 people were either killed in battle or burned to death.

⁸⁶After that, Jonathan left there and set up camp near the city of Ashkelon. The people formed a parade and marched out of the city to welcome him.

⁸⁷Jonathan and his men returned to Jerusalem with a lot of loot. ⁸⁸When King Alexander heard about this, he gave Jonathan even more honors ⁸⁹and sent him a gold shoulder clasp. This kind of clasp was given only to people who hold the title "Relative of the King." The king also gave Jonathan the city of Ekron and all the area around it.

The Deaths of Alexander Epiphanes and Ptolemy VI

11 ¹Then King Ptolemy VI of Egypt assembled an army with troops as numerous as the grains of sand on the seashore. He also gathered a large fleet of ships. He wanted to take over Alexander's kingdom and secretly annex it to his own. ²So he left for Syria as though he were on a peace mission. The people opened their cities to him and welcomed him, because King Alexander told them to. After all, Ptolemy was Alexander's father-in-law. ³But when Ptolemy entered the cities, he stationed his own soldiers in each of them.

⁴When King Ptolemy arrived in the city of Azotus, the people showed him Dagon's temple (which had been burned down) and all the destruction in Azotus and the villages around it. The bodies of the people Jonathan had burned to death in the war were lying everywhere. The people had piled the bodies in heaps on the road that the king was taking. ⁵They told the king about everything Jonathan had done, and they blamed Jonathan for everything that had happened. But the king said nothing. ⁶Later, Jonathan met the king in the city of Joppa, and the king was impressed with him. They greeted each other and stayed there that night. ⁷Jonathan traveled with the king until they reached the Eleutherus River. Then he returned to Jerusalem.

⁸King Ptolemy kept plotting against Alexander. He took control of the cities along the coast as far as the city of Seleucia. ⁹He sent ambassadors to King Demetrius with this message: "Let's get together and come to an agreement. I'll let you marry my daughter, who is now Alexander's wife, and let you rule your father's kingdom. ¹⁰I'm really sorry that I ever let my daughter marry Alexander, because he has tried to kill me."

¹¹Ptolemy accused Alexander of this only because he wanted Alexander's kingdom. ¹²So Ptolemy took his daughter away from Alexander and let Demetrius marry her. Ptolemy ended his friendship with Alexander, and their hatred for each other became well-known.

¹³After that, Ptolemy entered the city of Antioch and made himself king. So now he was the ruler of two kingdoms, the kingdom of Egypt and the kingdom of Syria.

¹⁴Meanwhile, King Alexander was in Cilicia because the people in that region were rebelling against him. ¹⁵When Alexander heard what Ptolemy had done, he went to attack him. Ptolemy had a powerful army. He marched from Antioch, fought Alexander, and defeated him. ¹⁶So Alexander fled to Arabia for safety while King Ptolemy enjoyed his victory. ¹⁷An Arab named Zabdiel cut off Alexander's head and sent it to Ptolemy. ¹⁸Three days later King Ptolemy died, and the local soldiers who lived in the fortifications killed the soldiers that Ptolemy had stationed in them. ¹⁹As a result, Demetrius II became king in the year 145 B.C.

Jonathan Meets With King Demetrius II

²⁰At that time Jonathan recruited soldiers from Judea to attack the fortress in Jerusalem. He built many large weapons to use in the attack. ²¹But some Jewish men who hated their own nation and didn't follow Moses' Teachings went to the king and told him that Jonathan had set up a blockade around the fortress. ²²When the king heard this, he became angry and immediately left for the city of Ptolemais. He wrote to Jonathan and ordered him to call off the blockade and to meet with him for a conference in Ptolemais as quickly as possible.

²³When Demetrius' letter was read to Jonathan, he ordered his soldiers to continue the blockade. Then he did something very dangerous: He went to Ptolemais to meet with the king. He chose some of Israel's leaders and priests ²⁴and took some silver, gold, clothes, and a lot of other gifts with him. Jonathan made a good impression on the king. ²⁵Even though some Israelites who didn't follow Moses' Teachings had brought charges against Jonathan, ²⁶the king treated Jonathan well. Like the earlier kings, Demetrius honored Jonathan in front of everyone who held the title "Friend of the King." ²⁷The king reappointed Jonathan as chief priest and restored all the other honors Jonathan previously had. The king also included him among those who held the title "Most Important Friend of the King."

²⁸Jonathan asked the king not to force Judea, the three districts, and Samaria to pay taxes.ᵃ He promised the king 22,500 pounds of silver if

---

ᵃ 11:28 Some manuscripts read "Jonathan asked the king not to force Judea and the three districts of Samaria to pay taxes."

the king would do as he asked. ²⁹The king agreed and wrote the following letter to Jonathan to document all of these things.

³⁰ " 'From King Demetrius.
To my dear friend Jonathan and to the Jewish people.
Greetings!

³¹ "For your information, I am sending you a copy of the letter that I sent to Lasthenes, who holds the title 'Relative of the King.'

³² "'From King Demetrius.
To Lasthenes, a gentleman I highly respect.
Greetings!

³³ " 'I have decided to reward the Jewish people for the loyalty they have shown us. They are our friends because they have kept their agreement with us. ³⁴So I have assured them that the territory of Judea as well as the three districts of Aphairema, Lydda, and Rathamin belong to them. These three districts, along with the areas that border them, were annexed to Judea from Samaria. This was done for the benefit of all those who offer sacrifices in Jerusalem to make up for the annual taxes they paid to the government from their crops and orchards. ³⁵From now on they will not have to pay the ten percent tax on their income, the toll tax, the salt tax, and all the other taxes I personally impose. I will allow the Jewish people all of these tax exemptions. ³⁶None of these tax exemptions may ever be canceled. ³⁷Be sure to make a copy of this agreement. Give the copy to Jonathan to post in Jerusalem on the holy mountain where everyone can see it.' "

Jonathan Sends Soldiers To Help King Demetrius II

³⁸King Demetrius saw that the land was at peace under his rule. Since he had no further opposition, he discharged all his soldiers and sent them home, except the foreign soldiers he had hired from the Greek islands. As a result, all the soldiers who had served the previous rulers hated him. ³⁹A man named Trypho, who had been one of Alexander's supporters, noticed that all of Demetrius' soldiers were complaining about what Demetrius had done to them. So Trypho went to see a man named Imalkue, an Arab who was raising Alexander's young son Antiochus VI. ⁴⁰Trypho stayed with Imalkue for many days. He kept telling Imalkue to hand over Antiochus. Trypho wanted Antiochus to take his father's place

as king. He explained to Imalkue what Demetrius had done and how Demetrius' soldiers hated him.

⁴¹Meanwhile, Jonathan asked King Demetrius to remove his soldiers from the fortress in Jerusalem and from the fortifications in Judea, because these soldiers were constantly fighting the people of Israel. ⁴²Demetrius sent this reply to Jonathan: "Not only will I do this for you and your nation, but I'll also honor you and your nation when I find an opportunity. ⁴³Do me a special favor. Send some soldiers to help me right away, because all my soldiers have revolted." ⁴⁴So Jonathan sent 3,000 of his best soldiers to Demetrius in the city of Antioch. The king was happy when they arrived.

⁴⁵Then 120,000 citizens who wanted to kill the king gathered in the center of Antioch. ⁴⁶The king fled into his palace, but the citizens took control of the main streets of Antioch and began to revolt. ⁴⁷So the king called the Jewish soldiers for help. All of them rallied around the king. They went throughout the city and killed about 100,000 people that day. ⁴⁸They burned down the city, took a lot of loot, and saved the king's life. ⁴⁹When the citizens of Antioch saw that the Jewish soldiers had easily gained control of their city, they lost their courage and made this appeal to the king: ⁵⁰"Let's call a truce! Order the Jewish soldiers to stop attacking us and our city." ⁵¹Then the people laid down their weapons and made a peace treaty. Now the king and all the people in his kingdom had high respect for the Jewish soldiers. The soldiers returned to Jerusalem with a lot of loot.

⁵²So King Demetrius regained control of his kingdom, and the land was at peace under his rule. ⁵³But Demetrius lied about everything he had said and became hostile to Jonathan. He didn't repay Jonathan for his loyalty. Instead, he caused him a lot of trouble.

Jonathan Attacks King Demetrius II

⁵⁴Later, Trypho returned to Antioch with Antiochus VI, who was a very young boy. Even though Antiochus was young, he took over the kingdom and began to rule as king. ⁵⁵All the troops that Demetrius had discharged rallied around young Antiochus and fought against Demetrius. Demetrius fled and was defeated. ⁵⁶Trypho captured Demetrius' elephants and took control of Antioch. ⁵⁷Then young Antiochus wrote Jonathan a letter, which read, "I'm reappointing you as chief priest. In addition, I'm putting you in charge of the four districts and giving you the title 'Friend of the King.'" ⁵⁸Antiochus also sent Jonathan gold table settings and gave him the right to drink from gold cups and to wear royal robes with a gold shoulder clasp. ⁵⁹He appointed Jonathan's brother Simon as governor of the territory extending from the mountainous coast of Tyre to the Egyptian border.

⁶⁰Then Jonathan marched through the cities west of the Euphrates River. The entire Syrian army joined him as allies. When he arrived in the

city of Ashkelon, the citizens gave him a royal welcome. [61]From Ashkelon he went to the city of Gaza. The citizens of Gaza wouldn't let him enter their city. So Jonathan set up a blockade, looted the villages around Gaza, and burned them. [62]Eventually, the citizens of Gaza begged Jonathan to call a truce. Jonathan called a truce, but he took their rulers' sons as hostages and sent them to Jerusalem. He continued to march through the country as far as the city of Damascus.

[63] Jonathan heard that Demetrius' generals were in the city of Kadesh in Galilee. They had a large army and intended to stop him from what he was doing. [64]Jonathan left his brother Simon in Judea and went to attack Demetrius. [65]Simon set up camp near the city of Beth Zur. He attacked Beth Zur for many days and set up a blockade around it. [66]Eventually, the citizens of Beth Zur begged Simon to call a truce, so he did. However, he forced the people out of the city, took control of the city, and stationed soldiers there.

[67] Jonathan and his army camped by Lake Gennesaret. Early in the morning they marched into the plain near the city of Hazor. [68]In the plain of Hazor the army of foreigners[a] attacked Jonathan. However, the foreigners had left soldiers in the mountains in order to ambush him. The main part of the army met Jonathan head-on. [69]Then the soldiers came out of their ambush and attacked. [70]All of Jonathan's soldiers fled. Mattathias (who was Absalom's son) and Judas (who was Chalphi's son) were the only soldiers who stayed with Jonathan. These two men were commanders in Jonathan's army. [71]Jonathan tore his clothes in grief, put dirt on his head, and prayed. [72]Then he returned to the battle and defeated the foreign soldiers, and they fled. [73]When Jonathan's soldiers (who were running away) saw this, they returned and chased the enemy as far as the enemy's campsite, which was near the city of Kadesh. Then Jonathan and his army set up camp there. [74]About 3,000 foreign soldiers were killed that day. After that, Jonathan returned to Jerusalem.

Jonathan Sends Ambassadors to Rome and Sparta

12 [1]When Jonathan saw that the time was right, he chose ambassadors and sent them to Rome. He wanted these ambassadors to renew friendly relations with the Romans. [2]He sent letters to Sparta and to some other places to renew friendly relations with them too. [3]So the ambassadors made the trip to Rome. They entered the senate and addressed it as follows: "The chief priest Jonathan and the Jewish nation have sent us to renew our previous friendship and alliance with you." [4]Then the Romans gave the ambassadors letters to present to the leaders in every country

---

[a] 11:68 Greek "Philistines."

they would travel through. The letters asked these leaders to support the ambassadors on their trip so that they could return safely to Judea.

⁵ This is a copy of the letter that Jonathan wrote to the Spartans:

> ⁶ "From the chief priest Jonathan, the Jewish council, and the
> rest of the Jewish people.
> To our dear friends in Sparta.
> Greetings!

> ⁷ "Some time ago your king Arius sent our chief priest Onias a letter. In this letter Arius stated that you are related to us. (See the enclosed copy.) ⁸Onias gave your ambassador a royal welcome and accepted your letter, which outlined the terms for a friendship and an alliance. ⁹We don't need alliances and friendships with other nations, because we have our holy books to encourage us. ¹⁰Nevertheless, we have sent our ambassadors to you in an attempt to renew our relationship with you. A lot of time has passed since you sent your letter to us, and we don't want to lose those ties of friendship with you. ¹¹We remember you every time we celebrate our festivals and other holy days and when we offer sacrifices or pray. It is only right to remember relatives. ¹²We are happy that you have a good reputation.

> ¹³ "However, we have had many difficult times and have had to fight many wars because neighboring kings have been constantly attacking us. ¹⁴We didn't want to involve you, our other allies, or our friends when we were fighting these wars. ¹⁵The LORD*ᵃ* sent us the help we needed and rescued us from our enemies. So our enemies have been humiliated. ¹⁶We have chosen Numenius (who is Antiochus' son) and Antipater (who is Jason's son) and have sent them to Rome to renew our previous friendship and alliance with the Romans. ¹⁷Also, we have ordered them to visit you, greet you, and deliver our letter about renewing our relationship with you. ¹⁸Please send us a reply."

¹⁹ This is a copy of the letter that the Spartans sent to Onias:

> ²⁰ "From King Arius of Sparta.
> To the chief priest Onias.
> Greetings!

> ²¹ "I have discovered a document which states that the Spartans and the Jews are related. We are all descendants of Abraham. ²²Now that I have found out about this, please write me and tell

---

ᵃ 12:15 Greek "Heaven." The author of 1 Maccabees uses the word *Heaven* in place of God's name, the LORD.

me how you are doing. [23]As far as I'm concerned, we can share our livestock and property. So I've ordered my ambassadors to work out the details with you."

The Activities of Jonathan and Simon

[24]Jonathan heard that Demetrius' commanders had returned to attack him with an army that was larger than before. [25]Because Jonathan didn't want to give them an opportunity to invade his own country, he left Jerusalem and met them in the region of Hamath. [26]Jonathan sent spies into their camp, and the spies reported to him that the enemy was planning to attack that night. [27]So when the sun had set, Jonathan ordered his troops to stay awake all night and be ready to fight. He stationed troops at a distance outside the camp to prevent a surprise attack. [28]When the enemy soldiers heard that Jonathan and his troops were ready to fight, they were panic-stricken. They lit fires in their camp and then left. [29]Jonathan and his troops saw the fires burning and didn't realize until morning that the enemy soldiers had left. [30]Jonathan pursued them, but he couldn't catch up with them because they had already crossed the Eleutherus River. [31]So Jonathan changed direction and attacked a group of Arabs called the Zabadeans. He defeated them in battle and looted them. [32]Then he left there and marched through that region on his way toward the city of Damascus.

[33]Meanwhile, Simon marched through the country as far as the city of Ashkelon and its nearby fortifications. Then he changed direction, attacked the city of Joppa, and took it by surprise. [34]He had heard that the citizens wanted to turn over the fortification to the soldiers Demetrius had sent. Simon stationed soldiers at Joppa to guard the city.

[35]When Jonathan returned to Jerusalem, he called the leaders of the people together. He made plans with them to build fortifications in Judea, [36]increase the height of Jerusalem's walls, and build a high wall between the fortress and the city. He wanted to separate the fortress from the city and isolate it so that he could stop the soldiers in the fortress from buying or selling in the city. [37]The people came together to begin the building projects. They repaired a section of the wall that had collapsed in the eastern valley. That section of the wall was called the Chaphenatha. [38]In addition, Simon rebuilt the city of Adida, which was located in the foothills. He fortified the city and put up gates that could be secured with iron bars.

Trypho Captures Jonathan

[39]Then Trypho wanted to assassinate King Antiochus VI, take over his kingdom, and become the next king of Syria. [40]But Trypho was afraid because he thought that Jonathan would fight him and prevent him from

doing this. So Trypho looked for a way to arrest Jonathan and kill him. He marched to the city of Beth Shan, [41]and Jonathan marched there with 40,000 of his best soldiers to fight Trypho. [42]When Trypho saw that Jonathan had arrived with a large army, he was afraid to assassinate him. [43]So Trypho gave Jonathan a royal welcome, introduced him to all his friends, and gave him gifts. Trypho also ordered his friends and troops to obey Jonathan the same way they would obey him. [44]Then he said to Jonathan, "Why have you forced your whole army to march so hard when we're not even at war? [45]Choose a few soldiers to stay with you, and send the rest of your soldiers home. Then let's go to the city of Ptolemais. I came here so that I could give you the city, its other fortresses, soldiers, and officials. After that, I'll go home."

[46]Jonathan believed Trypho and did what Trypho suggested. He kept 3,000 soldiers and sent the rest of his soldiers back to Judea.[a] [47]He left 2,000 soldiers in Galilee and took 1,000 with him to Ptolemais. [48]When Jonathan entered Ptolemais, the citizens closed the gates, arrested him, and killed all the soldiers who were with him.

[49]Trypho sent infantrymen and cavalrymen into Galilee and into the valley of Zezreel to kill the rest of Jonathan's soldiers. [50]But Jonathan's soldiers assumed that Jonathan and all the soldiers who were with him had been captured and killed. So they encouraged each other and marched in battle formation, ready to fight. [51]When the enemy troops were approaching, they saw that Jonathan's soldiers were ready to fight for their lives, so they turned back. [52]Then Jonathan's soldiers returned safely to Judea. The soldiers and all the people of Israel mourned for Jonathan and the soldiers who had been with him. They were terrified because [53]all the surrounding nations wanted to destroy the people of Israel. These nations said, "The people of Israel don't have a leader to help them. Let's attack them now. Let's make sure that no one will remember that they ever existed."

Simon Takes Jonathan's Place

13 [1]Simon heard that Trypho had recruited a large army to invade and destroy Judea, [2]and he saw that the people were trembling and afraid. So he went to Jerusalem, gathered the people together, [3]and encouraged them. He told them, "You know about all the things that my father's family, my brothers, and I have done. We did those things for the sake of Moses' Teachings and the holy place. You also know about the wars and difficult times that my brothers and I have been through. [4]All my brothers have died for Israel, and I'm the only one left. [5]It would be

---

[a] 12:46 The first part of verse 47 has been placed in verse 46 to express the complex Greek sentence structure more clearly in English.

unthinkable for me not to risk my own life in a time of trouble. I'm not any better than my brothers. ⁶Since all the nations have gathered together to destroy us because they hate us, I will get revenge for my nation, the holy place, and your wives and children."

⁷When the people heard what Simon said, they regained their courage. ⁸They responded by shouting, "You're our leader! Take over for Judas and your brother Jonathan. ⁹Fight for us! We'll do whatever you tell us." ¹⁰So Simon recruited all the soldiers he could find. He quickly finished repairing Jerusalem's walls and fortifying the city. ¹¹He sent Jonathan (who was Absalom's son) to the city of Joppa with an army large enough to force out the people who lived there and to occupy the city.

Trypho Kills Jonathan

¹²Then Trypho left the city of Ptolemais with a large army to invade Judea. He took Jonathan with him as a prisoner. ¹³Simon set up camp near Adida, a city that overlooked the plain. ¹⁴Trypho found out that Simon had taken his brother Jonathan's place and that Simon was ready to attack him. So he sent ambassadors to Simon. The ambassadors said, ¹⁵"We have your brother Jonathan under arrest because of the money he owes to the government for the offices he held. ¹⁶We'll release him if you send us 7,500 pounds of silver and two of his sons as hostages. If we hold his sons hostage, he won't revolt against us when we release him."

¹⁷Even though Simon knew that they were trying to deceive him, he sent for the silver and the children. ¹⁸He was afraid that if Jonathan was killed, the Jewish people would despise him for not paying the ransom. ¹⁹So he sent the children and the 7,500 pounds of silver. But Trypho lied and didn't release Jonathan.

²⁰After this, Trypho set out to invade Judea and destroy it. He and his army marched around the country on a road that led to the city of Adora. But everywhere that Trypho and his army went, Simon and his army were there to confront them. ²¹Meanwhile, the soldiers in the fortress in Jerusalem kept sending messengers to Trypho. They wanted him to come to them quickly through the desert and bring them supplies. ²²Trypho got his entire cavalry ready to go. But a big snowstorm during the night prevented him from going. So he left there and marched into Gilead. ²³When Trypho came near the city of Baskama, he killed Jonathan and buried him there. ²⁴Then he returned to his own country.

²⁵Simon had some men bring back the body of his brother Jonathan to Modein, the city of his ancestors. There they buried Jonathan. ²⁶All the people in Israel held a solemn ceremony for many days to mourn his death. ²⁷Simon built a monument over the tomb of his father and his brothers. The monument was so large that people could see it from far away. Simon covered the front and the back of the monument with polished stones.

[28]He also had seven pyramids built for his father, mother, and four brothers. The pyramids faced each other. [29]He created an elaborate layout by setting up large columns around the pyramids. He placed suits of armor on the columns to honor the memory of his family forever. Next to the suits of armor he had ships carved so that everyone who sailed by could see them. [30]This tomb that he built in Modein still exists today.

[31]Trypho pretended to support young King Antiochus VI, but he eventually killed him. [32]Then he took his place as king, ruled the kingdom of Syria, and caused a lot of trouble.

King Demetrius II Makes a Treaty With Simon

[33]Simon built fortifications in Judea. He surrounded them with high walls and towers, put up gates with iron bars, and stored food in them. [34]Simon chose some ambassadors and sent them to King Demetrius. He didn't want the king to collect taxes from the people in Judea anymore, because Trypho was robbing them by overtaxing them. [35]King Demetrius wrote the following letter and sent it to Simon.

> [36]"From King Demetrius.
> To Simon, chief priest and friend of kings, to the Jewish leaders, and to the Jewish people.
> Greetings!

> [37]"I received the gold crown and the palm branch that you sent. I'm ready to make a peace treaty with you and order my officials to stop collecting taxes from you. [38]Every agreement that I have made with you in the past is still valid. You may keep every fortification that you have built. [39]I will pardon you for all the things you have done wrong, intentionally or unintentionally, up to the present. I will also cancel any taxes that you still owe me. I will no longer require you to pay the other taxes I have collected from Jerusalem in the past. [40]Any of your friends who would like to work in my government may apply for positions. Let's have peace."

[41]In the year 142 B.C., the people of Israel had relief from foreign oppression. [42]They began to date their documents and contracts as follows: "In the first year of Simon, the highly respected chief priest, commander, and leader of the Jewish people."

Simon Captures the City of Gezer

[43]At that time Simon set up camp near the city of Gezer and surrounded the city with his troops. He made a large moveable ramp, brought it up to the city wall, and used it to attack and capture one of

the city's fortified towers. ⁴⁴The soldiers jumped off the moveable ramp into the city. Panic swept throughout the city. ⁴⁵The men in the city, their wives, and their children tore their clothes in grief and climbed on top of the wall. They shouted to Simon and begged him to call a truce. ⁴⁶They said, "Be merciful. Don't punish us for the terrible things we've done to you." ⁴⁷So Simon reached a settlement with them and stopped the fighting. He made the citizens leave the city and cleansed the houses where there were false gods. After that, he and his troops entered the city singing hymns of praise. ⁴⁸He took everything that was unclean*ᵃ* out of the city and allowed only those who followed Moses' Teachings to live there. He also strengthened the city's fortifications and built a house there for himself.

Simon Takes Over the Fortress in Jerusalem

⁴⁹Those who lived in the fortress in Jerusalem were not allowed to go in or out of the fortress to buy or sell in the countryside. So they became very hungry, and many of them starved to death. ⁵⁰They shouted to Simon from the fortress. They wanted him to call a truce, so Simon did. But he made the people leave the fortress, and he had it cleansed. ⁵¹On the twenty-third day of the second month in the year 141 B.C., Simon and his soldiers entered the fortress as they sang songs of praise and held palm branches in their hands. They sang hymns and songs and played harps, cymbals, and stringed instruments because a terrible enemy had been defeated and removed from Israel. ⁵²Simon established the twenty-third day of the second month as a holiday for the Jews to celebrate every year. He strengthened the fortifications on the temple mountain next to the fortress, and he and his soldiers lived there. ⁵³His son John was now a grown man, so he made him the commander of all the soldiers. Then John began to live in the city of Gezer.

Demetrius II Is Captured and Put in Prison

14 ¹In the year 140 B.C., King Demetrius II recruited some soldiers and marched into Media. He wanted to get some additional help for his war against Trypho. ²When King Arsaces of Persia and Media heard that Demetrius had entered his territory, he sent one of his commanders to capture Demetrius and bring him back alive. ³The commander defeated Demetrius' army, captured Demetrius, and brought him back to Arsaces, who put him in prison.

ᵃ 13:48 "Unclean" refers to anything that Moses' Teachings say is not presentable to God.

A Poem About Simon

⁴Judea had peace throughout Simon's lifetime.
Simon wanted only good things for his nation.
His rule and reputation pleased the people throughout
his lifetime.
⁵Simon was highly honored for capturing the city of Joppa.
He made its harbor a gateway to the Greek islands.
⁶He took control of his country
and extended his nation's borders.
⁷He brought back a lot of Jewish people who had been
taken prisoner.
He took control of Gezer, Beth Zur, and the fortress in Jerusalem.
He removed from the fortress everything that was unclean,ᵃ
and no one opposed him.
⁸The Jewish people farmed their land in peace.
The ground produced crops,
and the trees in the valleys produced fruit.
⁹Old men sat in the city's parks,
and all of them talked about their blessings.
Young men proudly wore their military uniforms.
¹⁰Simon supplied the cities with food
and provided the people with weapons to defend themselves.
His fame spread to the ends of the earth.
¹¹Simon brought peace to his country,
and the people of Israel were extremely happy.
¹²People sat under their grapevines and fig trees,
and no one made them afraid.
¹³No one was left in the land to fight them.
The enemy kings had been defeated at that time.
¹⁴Simon supported all the poor people in his nation.
He studied Moses' Teachings
and got rid of every evil person who didn't follow them.
¹⁵Simon made the holy place a place of splendor
and added more furnishings.

The Spartans Renew Their Alliance With Simon

¹⁶When the people in Rome and as far away as Sparta heard that Jonathan had died, they were very worried. ¹⁷The Spartans heard that Simon had taken his brother's place as chief priest and that he was ruling the country and its cities. ¹⁸So the Spartans wrote a letter on bronze plaques and sent it to Simon. They wanted to renew the friendship and the al-

---

ᵃ 14:7 "Unclean" refers to anything that Moses' Teachings say is not presentable to God.

liance that they had made with his brothers Judas and Jonathan. [19] The plaques were read in front of the assembly in Jerusalem.

[20] This is a copy of the letter that the Spartans sent:

"From the city of Sparta and its rulers.

To the chief priest Simon, to the Jewish leaders and priests, and to the rest of the Jewish people, who are our relatives. Greetings!

[21] "The ambassadors you sent to our people arrived and told us about your honorable reputation. We are happy that they came. [22] Based on everything the ambassadors said, we have written down the following entry in our official records: 'The Jewish ambassadors, Numenius (who is Antiochus' son) and Antipater (who is Jason's son) have visited us in an effort to renew their friendly relations with us. [23] The Spartan people were pleased to give these ambassadors a royal welcome. Our people were also pleased to place a copy of everything the ambassadors said in our public archives so that the citizens of Sparta have these things on record. In addition, we have made copies for the chief priest Simon.'"

[24] After this, Simon sent Numenius to Rome to confirm the alliance with the Romans. Numenius brought along a large gold shield as a gift. The shield weighed 1,250 pounds.

The Jewish People Pass a Resolution About Simon's Position

[25] When the Jewish people heard these things, they asked, "How can we ever thank Simon and his sons enough? [26] Simon, his brothers, and his father's family have supported us. They have fought off our enemies and set Israel free." So they recorded the following resolution on bronze plaques and mounted the plaques on columns on Mount Zion. [27] This is a copy of the resolution:

On the eighteenth day of the month of Elul, in the year 140 B.C., the third year that Simon was the highly respected chief priest and prince of God's people, [28] at a large assembly of priests, citizens, national rulers, and our country's leaders, the following resolution was made:

[29] Whereas, Whenever wars broke out in our country, Simon, who is Mattathias' son and a priest from the family of Joarib, and his brothers risked their lives to defend us. They stood up to our nation's enemies to ensure that the holy place and Moses' Teachings would last forever.

They have brought honor to our nation because of their reputations. [30]Jonathan brought our nation together and became our chief priest. Then he joined his ancestors in death. [31]Our enemies decided to invade our country and destroy our holy place. [32]But Simon stood up to our enemies and fought for his nation. He spent a lot of his own money to provide weapons for his soldiers and to pay their wages. [33]He fortified the cities in Judea, even the city of Beth Zur, which is on the border of Judea. Simon stationed Jewish soldiers there. (Previously, our enemies stored their weapons in Beth Zur.) [34]Simon also fortified the cities of Joppa, which is on the coast, and Gezer, which borders the city of Azotus. (Previously, our enemies lived in Gezer.) Simon had Jewish people settle in these cities, and he gave the people whatever was needed to restore them.

[35]Whereas, The people saw Simon's loyalty and that he wanted to bring honor to his nation, so they appointed him to be their leader and chief priest. They did this because of everything he had done and because of the decency and loyalty he had shown to his nation. Simon wanted to bring honor to his people in every way. He has been successful his whole life. [36]He removed foreigners from the country and those who had built the fortress in Jerusalem, David's city. The people who used to live in the fortress would leave it and go throughout the holy place. They would dishonor the holy place and do terrible things to make it unclean. [37]So Simon had Jewish soldiers live in the fortress. He fortified it to make the country and the city safe. He also built Jerusalem's walls higher.

[38]Whereas, Based on all of Simon's accomplishments, King Demetrius appointed Simon to be chief priest, [39]gave him the title "Friend of the King," and highly honored him. [40]Demetrius did this because he heard that the Romans had called the Jews their friends, allies, and relatives and that the Romans had given Simon's ambassadors a royal welcome. Therefore, be it

[41]*Resolved,* That we, the Jewish people and priests, appoint Simon to be our permanent leader and chief priest until a true prophet appears. Be it further

[42]*Resolved,* That we appoint Simon to be our commander so that he can take charge of the holy place and appoint people to work in it, to govern the country, to

make weapons, and to supervise the fortifications. Be it finally

⁴³*Resolved*, That everyone is to obey Simon, that all contracts in the country are to be drawn up in his name, and that he has the right to wear royal robes and a gold medallion.

⁴⁴Neither the people nor the priests will have the right to cancel any part of this resolution, oppose any of Simon's orders, have meetings in the country without his permission, or wear royal robes with a gold shoulder clasp. ⁴⁵Whoever disobeys this resolution or cancels any part of it will be given the death penalty.

⁴⁶All the people agreed to give Simon the right to carry out this resolution. ⁴⁷Simon agreed to be the chief priest, commander, and ruler of the Jewish people and priests. He also agreed to protect everyone. ⁴⁸The people inscribed this resolution on bronze plaques and hung the plaques on the wall that surrounds the holy place so that everyone could see them. ⁴⁹They also placed copies of the resolution in the treasury so that Simon and his sons could have access to it.

King Antiochus VII Sends a Letter to Simon

15 ¹While Antiochus VII (who was the son of King Demetrius I) was in the Greek islands, he sent a letter to Simon, the priest and ruler of the Jewish people, and to the entire Jewish nation. ²This is a copy of the letter:

"From King Antiochus.
To Simon, the chief priest and ruler, and to the Jewish people.
Greetings!

³"Some dangerous men have taken control of my ancestors' kingdom. I intend to regain control of the kingdom so that I can restore it to what it once was. So I hired a large number of soldiers and prepared warships for battle. ⁴I plan to invade the country so that I can attack those who have ruined my country and have destroyed many cities in my kingdom.

⁵"Therefore, I have decided to give you the same tax exemptions that the other kings have given you. ⁶I will also give you permission to mint your own coins as money for your country. ⁷I will free Jerusalem and the holy place from foreign control. In addition, all the weapons that you have made and the fortifications that you have built and control will remain yours. ⁸Finally, as of today, all your debts to the government, both now and in

the future, will be canceled. [9]As soon as I regain control of my kingdom, I will make you, your nation, and the temple highly honored everywhere in the world."

[10]In the year 138 B.C., Antiochus marched into his ancestors' country. All the soldiers in the country joined Antiochus, so Trypho had only a few soldiers. [11]Antiochus chased Trypho, and Trypho fled to the city of Dor, which is on the coast. [12]Trypho knew that he was in danger because his soldiers had deserted him. [13]Antiochus attacked the city of Dor with 120,000 infantrymen and 8,000 cavalrymen. [14]He surrounded the city, and his ships joined the attack from the sea. He used his army and navy to blockade the city and wouldn't allow anyone to enter or leave.

The Jewish Ambassadors Return From Rome

[15]Then Numenius and those who were with him arrived in Judea from Rome with letters to various kings and countries. One of the letters read as follows:

[16]"From Lucius, the Roman consul.
To King Ptolemy.
Greetings!

[17]"The Jewish ambassadors, who are our friends and allies, have visited us to renew the friendship and the alliance that we made in the past. The chief priest Simon and the Jewish people sent them to us. [18]They brought a gold shield that weighs 1,250 pounds. [19]We have decided to write to you as well as to various kings and countries to warn you not to harm the Jews. You must not attack them, their cities, or their country or make alliances with those who attack them. [20]We have also decided to accept the shield from them. [21]If any dangerous men have fled to you from their country, turn them over to the chief priest Simon so that he can punish them according to the laws of the Jewish people."

[22]The consul Lucius wrote the same letter to the following kings: Demetrius, Attalus, Ariarathes, and Arsaces. [23]He also sent the same letter to each of the following places: Sampsames, Sparta, Delos, Myndos, Sicyon, Caria, Samos, Pamphylia, Lycia, Halicarnassus, Rhodes, Phaselis, Cos, Side, Aradus, Gortyna, Cnidus, Cyprus, and Cyrene. [24]He also had a copy of the letter sent to the chief priest Simon.

King Antiochus VII Becomes Hostile to Simon

[25]On the second day of his attack on Dor, King Antiochus sent one unit of soldiers after another against the city. He also used large weapons, which he had made. As a result, Trypho was trapped in the city and

couldn't escape. [26]Simon sent 2,000 of his best soldiers to help Antiochus. He also sent him silver, gold, and a lot of weapons. [27]But Antiochus refused to accept any of these things. In fact, he broke all his previous agreements with Simon and became hostile to him. [28]He sent Athenobius, who held the title "Friend of the King," to deliver the following message to Simon: "You control Joppa, Gezer, and the fortress in Jerusalem. These places belong to my kingdom. [29]You destroyed these territories, caused a lot of trouble in Judea, and took control of many places in my kingdom. [30]Give back the cities you took and the taxes you collected from the places you conquered outside Judea, [31]or pay me 37,500 pounds of silver for the destruction you caused and another 37,500 pounds of silver for the taxes you took from those cities. Otherwise, I will come and attack you."

Cendebeus Invades Judea

[32]Athenobius, the king's friend, went to Jerusalem. He was shocked to see Simon's luxurious lifestyle, his gold and silver table settings, and all the servants Simon had. After Athenobius delivered the king's message, [33]Simon replied, "We haven't stolen land from any foreign countries. All we've done is take back the land that our enemies had unjustly taken from our ancestors at one time or another. [34]Now that we have the opportunity, we're going to hold on to our ancestors' land. [35]You're demanding that we give you Joppa and Gezer, the cities that caused our people and country a lot of trouble. We will give you 7,500 pounds of silver for them." Athenobius didn't say a word to Simon. [36]He was very angry. He returned to the king and told him everything Simon had said. He also told him about Simon's luxurious lifestyle and everything else he had seen. When the king heard all this, he became furious.

[37]Meanwhile, Trypho got on a ship and escaped to the city of Orthosia. [38]King Antiochus appointed Cendebeus commander of the territory along the coast and gave him infantrymen and cavalrymen. [39]The king ordered Cendebeus to set up camps throughout Judea, rebuild the city of Kedron, and fortify the city gates so that Cendebeus could attack the Jewish people. Then the king pursued Trypho.

[40]Cendebeus arrived in the city of Jamnia and began to harass the Jewish people. He invaded Judea, took prisoners, and murdered them. [41]He rebuilt Kedron and stationed cavalrymen and infantrymen there so that they could use the Judean roads for the attacks the king had ordered.

Simon Defeats Cendebeus

16 [1]John left the city of Gezer and went to Jerusalem. He told his father Simon everything Cendebeus had done. [2]So Simon said to his two oldest sons, Judas and John, "My father's family, my brothers, and I have been fighting for Israel ever since we were young. We have been successful many times in our attempts to rescue Israel. [3]I'm old now, but you, because of our merciful God, are old enough to assume responsibility. So take my place and my brother's place. Fight for our nation. May the LORD[a] help you and be with you."

[4]Then Simon chose 20,000 of the nation's infantrymen and cavalrymen and went to fight Cendebeus. They spent the night in the city of Modein. [5]Early in the morning, they marched into the plain. They saw a large number of enemy infantrymen and cavalrymen coming to attack them. A river separated the two armies. [6]Simon and his army stopped at the river. Simon saw that his soldiers were too scared to cross, so he went across first. When his soldiers saw him do this, they followed him. [7]Then Simon divided the army into cavalry and infantry units, since the enemy had a large cavalry.[b] [8]Simon's soldiers blew their trumpets. Cendebeus and his army were defeated. Many enemy soldiers were killed, and the rest fled into the fortification at Kedron. [9]Even though Judas (who was John's brother) was wounded in the battle, John chased Cendebeus and his soldiers until they reached Kedron, the city that Cendebeus had rebuilt. [10]John burned down the city. Some of the enemy soldiers ran inside the towers located in the fields around the city of Azotus. About 2,000 enemy soldiers were killed. Then John returned safely to Judea.

Simon and His Sons Are Killed

[11]Ptolemy (who was the son of Abubus) was the governor of the Plain of Jericho. He was a wealthy man who owned a lot of silver and gold [12]because he was the chief priest's son-in-law. [13]But he became arrogant and wanted to gain control of the country. So he secretly plotted to kill Simon and his sons. [14]Simon was visiting the cities throughout the country. He was inspecting the cities and taking note of what each city needed. In the eleventh month (the month of Shebat) in the year 134 B.C., Simon went to the city of Jericho. His sons Mattathias and Judas went with him. [15]Ptolemy (who was the son of Abubus) made Simon and his sons think they were welcome. He invited them into the Dok, which was a small fortification that he had built, and he threw a big party for them. However, he had assassins hidden in the fortification. [16]When Simon and his sons were drunk, Ptolemy and his armed assassins rushed into the party and killed Simon, his two sons, and some of his servants. [17]Ptolemy committed a terrible act of treason by doing something wicked to Simon, even though Simon had been good to him.

---

[a] 16:3 Greek "May Heaven." The author of 1 Maccabees uses the word *Heaven* in place of God's name, the LORD.

[b] 16:7 Greek meaning of this verse uncertain.

¹⁸ Then Ptolemy sent a letter to King Antiochus VII and told him what had happened. He asked the king to send some soldiers to help him so that he could turn over the cities and the country to the king. ¹⁹He also sent letters to Jewish military leaders. He asked them to meet with him. He wanted them to join him, so he planned to bribe them with silver, gold, and other gifts. Ptolemy sent some soldiers to Gezer to kill John. ²⁰He also sent some soldiers to take possession of Jerusalem and the temple mountain. ²¹But someone ran to Gezer ahead of Ptolemy's soldiers and told John that his father and brothers had been killed and that Ptolemy had sent men to kill him too. ²²When John heard this, he was stunned. Because he knew that Ptolemy's men were intending to kill him, he arrested them and killed them when they arrived.

²³ Many other things about John—the wars he fought, the brave things he did, the walls he rebuilt, and all the other things he accomplished from the time he succeeded his father as chief priest—²⁴are written in the official records of his priesthood.

2 Maccabees

The First Letter to the Jewish People in Egypt

1 ¹"From the Jewish people in Jerusalem and Judea.
To the Jewish people in Egypt.
Greetings!

²"May God make you successful. May he remember the promise*a* that he made to his faithful servants Abraham, Isaac, and Jacob. ³May he fill all of you with the desire to worship him and with the courage to do everything he wants you to do. ⁴May he make you willing to follow his teachings and commands, and may he give you peace. ⁵May he hear your prayers, restore your relationship with him, and never abandon you in times of trouble. ⁶We are praying for you here in Jerusalem. ⁷"In the year 143 B.C., when Demetrius II was king ⌐of Syria⌐, we, the Jewish people ⌐in Jerusalem and Judea⌐, wrote the following message to you: 'After Jason and his followers rebelled against the holy land and the kingdom ⁸and after he and his followers set fire to the temple gateway and murdered innocent people, we experienced a lot of suffering and distress. So we prayed to the Lord, and the Lord heard us. Then we offered sacrifices and grain offerings, lit the lights on the lamp stand, and set out the bread of the presence.' ⁹So we want you to celebrate the Days of Dedication in the month of Chislev as you would celebrate the Festival of Booths."

¹⁰This letter was written in the year 124 B.C.

The Second Letter to the Jewish People in Egypt

"From the Jewish people in Jerusalem and Judea, the Jewish council, and Judas.
To Aristobulus, a descendant of the anointed priests and teacher of King Ptolemy, and to the Jewish people in Egypt.
Greetings and good health!

---

a 1:2 Or "covenant."

[11] "We are very thankful to God because he saved us from many dangerous situations when he fought for us in our battle against King Antiochus IV. [12]God threw out of Jerusalem the people who fought against it. [13]Their leader Antiochus arrived in Persia with an army that looked as though it couldn't be stopped. Yet, he and some of his soldiers were cut to pieces in the temple of the goddess Nanea by her priests, who had deceived them. [14]Antiochus had gone with his friends to the temple of the goddess. He acted as though he wanted to marry her so that he could get from her temple treasury a large amount of money as a wedding gift. [15]When Nanea's priests set out the money, Antiochus and a few of his soldiers went into her temple complex. As soon as Antiochus entered the temple, the priests closed the temple doors. [16]Then they removed a secret panel in the ceiling and threw stones, which struck Antiochus and his soldiers like bolts of lightning. After Antiochus and his soldiers were dead, the priests cut up the bodies and threw the heads to the people outside. [17]Praise God for everything, especially for punishing those evil people.

How the Altar Fire Was Brought Back to Jerusalem

[18] "We're going to celebrate the cleansing of the temple on the twenty-fifth day of the month of Chislev. We want to make this very clear to you. Then you, too, can celebrate the Days of Dedication (that is, the Days of the Fire) as you would celebrate the Festival of Booths. You should celebrate these days at the same time that Nehemiah, who rebuilt the temple and the altar, offered sacrifices.

[19] "When our ancestors were taken as prisoners to Persia, some devout priests secretly took with them some fire from the altar. They hid the fire in a dry cistern. Then they covered up the cistern so that no one else could ever find it. [20]Many years later, when God decided the time was right, the Persian king authorized Nehemiah to go back to Jerusalem. Nehemiah sent descendants of those priests to get the fire and bring it back to Jerusalem. When they returned, the priests told Nehemiah that they didn't find any fire but only a thick liquid. So Nehemiah ordered them to get the liquid out of the cistern and bring it back to Jerusalem. [21]When the priests offered a sacrifice, Nehemiah ordered them to sprinkle the liquid on the wood and on the sacrifice. [22]So the priests did that. Later, the sun, which had been hidden behind the clouds, came out, and the sacrifice burst into flames. Everyone was amazed. [23]While the fire was burning

up the sacrifice, the priests and everyone else prayed. Jonathan led the prayer, and Nehemiah repeated it with everyone else.
²⁴"The prayer went like this:

'Lord, Lord, you are God. You created everything. You are awesome, strong, merciful, and just. You are the only king, and you are kind. ²⁵You alone provide for everyone. You are the only one who is almighty, eternal, and just. You rescue Israel from all its troubles. You chose our ancestors and set them apart as holy. ²⁶Accept this sacrifice, which we offer on behalf of all your people Israel. Watch closely over us, the people who belong to you, and make us holy. ²⁷Gather together our people, who have been scattered everywhere. Free those who are slaves in foreign countries. Care for those who are despised and detested. Make foreign people realize that you are our God. ²⁸Torture those who are arrogant and those who violently oppress us. ²⁹Bring your people to your holy place, as Moses said you would.'

³⁰"Then the priests sang hymns. ³¹After the sacrifice was burned, Nehemiah ordered the priests to pour the rest of the liquid on some large stones. ³²As soon as the priests did this, a flame shot up. But the flame went out because the fire on the altar overpowered it. ³³People found out about this and told the Persian king that a liquid had been found in the place where the exiled priests had hidden the fire. They said that Nehemiah and his followers had used the liquid to burn the sacrifice. ³⁴After the king had verified the report, he made the place into a shrine and put a fence around it. ³⁵The king made a lot of money from this shrine, and he shared the money with Nehemiah and his followers. ³⁶Nehemiah and his followers called this liquid *nephthar*. Nephthar means 'cleansing.' But most people called it *naphtha*.

How Jeremiah Prepared the People for Exile

2 ¹"We have learned from our records that the prophet Jeremiah ordered the priests who were being led into exile to take the fire from the altar along with them. We have already told you about this. ²We have also learned from our records that Jeremiah gave the captives a copy of Moses' Teachings and told them not to forget the Lord's commands. He also told them not to let the false gods that they would see lead them astray, gods which were gold and silver statues with decorations. ³Jeremiah said many other things like this, and he urged the captives to continue to follow Moses' Teachings.

[4] "We have also learned from our records that Jeremiah, after receiving a message from God, ordered that the tent of meeting and the ark of the promise should be given to him. Then he took them to the mountain where Moses saw the land God had promised our ancestors. [5]On the mountain Jeremiah found a cave. He put the tent, the ark, and the incense altar inside the cave. Then he sealed the entrance. [6]Later, some of his followers tried to go back and mark the way, but they couldn't find it. [7]When Jeremiah found out what they had done, he reprimanded them and said, 'No one will find the cave until God gathers his people together again and shows them his mercy. [8]At that time, the Lord will reveal where these things are. The Lord's glory and the cloud will appear again as they did in the time of Moses and as they did when Solomon asked God to make the temple a very holy place.'

How Solomon Celebrated the Dedication of the Temple

[9] "We have also learned from our records that Solomon, who was a wise man, offered a sacrifice of dedication after the temple was completed. [10]Just as Moses prayed to the Lord and fire came from the sky and burned up the sacrifices, so Solomon prayed and fire came and completely burned his offerings. [11](Moses had said, 'Because the offering for sin had not been eaten, it was consumed by fire.') [12]Solomon celebrated the dedication for eight days.[a]

How Nehemiah Established a Library

[13] "Nehemiah's records and memoirs report the same things. They also report how Nehemiah established a library and collected books about the kings, books written by the prophets, and David's writings. He also collected letters from kings about the gifts they had dedicated to the temple. [14]Similarly, Judas collected all the books that had been lost because of the war we just fought. We have these books with us now. [15]So if you ever need any of them, you can send someone to get them.

An Invitation to Celebrate the Cleansing of the Temple

[16] "Since we are about to celebrate the cleansing of the temple, we are writing to urge you, too, to celebrate this holiday. [17]God

---

[a] 2:12 Meaning of verses 11 and 12 uncertain.

has saved all of his people. He has given us back our land, kingdom, priesthood, and holy way of life [18]as he promised us in Moses' Teachings. He has rescued us from many disasters and has cleansed the temple. So we can be confident that God will show us his mercy soon and that he will gather us to his holy place from everywhere in the world."

The Writer's Goal: A Summary of the Work of Jason of Cyrene

[19]Jason of Cyrene wrote five books, which contain stories about Judas Maccabeus and his brothers, the cleansing of the world's greatest temple, and the dedication of that temple's altar. [20]In addition, Jason's five books contain stories about the wars against Antiochus Epiphanes and his son Eupator [21]and about the miraculous things that appeared in the sky to those who fought bravely and enthusiastically for the Jewish religion. Even though the Jewish forces didn't have many soldiers, they regained control of their entire country and chased out the foreigners. [22]They also regained control of the temple that is famous throughout the world, freed the city of Jerusalem, and reestablished Moses' Teachings, which were about to be abolished. They accomplished all these things because the Lord was merciful and kind to them. [23]So I will attempt to summarize in one book everything that Jason of Cyrene wrote in his five books.

[24]I have noticed how many statistics there are and the difficulties that exist because of the large amounts of material available to those who want to read about these historical events. [25]So I've taken into consideration those who read for pleasure and those who want something easy to memorize as they pursue wisdom. I've tried to write in a way that will benefit everyone who reads this book. [26]Summarizing Jason's five books is stressful. It's a project that demands hard work and sleepless nights. [27]Summarizing his work is like holding a banquet and trying to please everyone. It's not an easy job. Nevertheless, I will gladly put up with the stress to hear the public say, "Thank you." [28]I will leave the exact details to the original author and try to provide an organized summary of the events. [29]I'm not like a builder of a new house. He must consider every single detail of the structure that he's building. But I compare myself to a painter. He is only concerned with painting and decorating the house. [30]Every author who writes a history book must know his entire subject and investigate every detail. [31]But the person who summarizes the text should be excused if he leaves out details and doesn't investigate the facts. [32]Therefore, I'll begin my story at this point since I've already said enough. There is no sense in making the introduction long while trying to summarize the history itself.

The Story of Heliodorus

3 ¹Because the chief priest Onias was a devout man who hated evil, people lived in the holy city of Jerusalem in perfect peace and followed Moses' Teachings faithfully. ²Even foreign kings honored the temple and added to its beauty by donating their best gifts to it. ³In fact, King Seleucus of Syria paid all the expenses for the sacrifices from the revenues he collected.

⁴But a man named Simon, who was from Bilgah's family, had been appointed chief administrator of the temple. Simon had an argument with the chief priest Onias over who should run the city market. ⁵When he realized he wasn't going to win his argument with Onias, he went to see Apollonius, who was Thraseus' son. Apollonius was the governor of Coelesyria and Phoenicia at that time. ⁶Simon informed Apollonius that Jerusalem's treasury was so full of money that no one knew how much there was because the money couldn't be counted. He told Apollonius that the money wasn't designated for sacrifices and that it could be placed under the king's control.

⁷After that, Apollonius met with the king. He told the king the secret information that Simon had given him. The king ordered Heliodorus, his chief of state, to get the money. ⁸Heliodorus immediately left for Jerusalem. He gave the impression that he was touring the cities of Coelesyria and Phoenicia to inspect them. But he was really doing what the king ordered him to do.

⁹When Heliodorus arrived in Jerusalem, he was given a friendly welcome by the chief priest and the citizens. Heliodorus told them about the information he had received from Simon and about the real reason he had come to Jerusalem. Then he asked them if this information was true. ¹⁰The chief priest explained that some of the money belonged to widows and orphans ¹¹and that some belonged to Hyrcanus, who was Tobias' son and was a very important man. The chief priest told Heliodorus that, contrary to what the evil Simon had said, the total amount of money in the treasury was only 30,000 pounds of silver and 15,000 pounds of gold. ¹²The chief priest said that it would be unthinkable to treat unfairly the people who trusted this holy place. After all, these people believed that the temple, which is honored throughout the world, is the safest place to keep their money.

¹³Because of the orders that he had from the king, Heliodorus said that he had no choice. He had to take the money for the king's treasury. ¹⁴So he set aside a day when he could enter the temple to supervise the counting of the money.

All the people in the city were very distressed. ¹⁵The priests wore their robes and bowed on the ground in front of the altar. They prayed

to the LORD[a], who had made the laws about deposits, and asked him to
guard the money that the people had deposited in the temple. [16]Everyone
who saw the chief priest became very upset. The expression on the chief
priest's face showed just how distressed he was. [17]His body trembled
with fear, and everyone could see how much he was suffering. [18]People
ran out of their houses and joined together in prayer because the temple
was about to be dishonored. [19]Women, wearing only skirts made out of
sackcloth, gathered in the streets. Unmarried girls, who were not allowed
to leave their homes, ran to their front doors, went to their balconies,
or watched from their windows. [20]All of them stretched out their hands
toward heaven as they prayed. [21]It was pitiful to see all these people on
their knees with their faces touching the ground and to see the chief
priest so distressed.

[22]As the people prayed to the Almighty Lord and asked him to protect
the money that had been deposited in the temple, [23]Heliodorus began to
carry out the king's plan. [24]But the Lord (the ruler who controls the spirits
and every power) made a miracle happen in the temple treasury when
Heliodorus arrived with his bodyguards. Everyone who was brave enough
to go with Heliodorus was terrified by God's power when they saw this
awesome miracle. In fact, they became timid and cowardly [25]because they
saw a horse and a rider. The horse had on a beautiful harness, and the
rider was frightening. The horse reared up and attacked Heliodorus with
its front hoofs. The rider's armor looked as though it was made of gold.
[26]Then two young men appeared to Heliodorus. These men were very
strong, extremely handsome, and well-dressed. They stood on opposite
sides of Heliodorus and whipped him repeatedly. [27]Suddenly, Heliodorus fainted and fell to the ground. His men picked him up, put him on
a stretcher, [28]and carried him out. This man, who had just entered the
treasury with many assistants and all his bodyguards, was now totally
helpless. All of them realized that God's power caused these things to
happen.

[29]Heliodorus lay there. He couldn't talk, and he didn't have any hope
of recovering from what God had done to him. [30]But the Jews praised
the Lord because he had taken care of his temple in a miraculous way.
Because the Almighty Lord had appeared, the temple courtyard, which
only a short time earlier had been filled with fear and confusion, was
now filled with happiness and celebration.

[31]Some of Heliodorus' friends went quickly to Onias. They asked
Onias to beg the Most High to spare the life of Heliodorus, who was
about to die. [32]The chief priest was afraid that the king might think the

---

[a] 3:15 Greek "Heaven." The author of 2 Maccabees uses the word *Heaven* in place of
God's name, the LORD.

Jewish people had done this terrible thing to Heliodorus. So he offered a sacrifice for Heliodorus' recovery. ³³While the chief priest was offering the sacrifice to make peace with God for Heliodorus' sins, the two young men appeared to Heliodorus again. Wearing the same clothes as before, they stood next to him and said, "Thank the chief priest Onias. Because of him, the Lord has allowed you to live. ³⁴You were whipped by the LORD, so tell everyone about his magnificent power." After the two young men said this, they disappeared.

³⁵ Then Heliodorus offered a sacrifice and made some impressive vows to the Lord, who had saved his life. He said goodbye to Onias and returned with his army to the king. ³⁶He told everyone about the things he had seen the Almighty God do.

³⁷ Then the king asked Heliodorus, "Who would be the best person to send on the next mission to Jerusalem?"

Heliodorus replied, ³⁸"Send someone who is your enemy or someone who is plotting against your government. He'll come back to you, if he's lucky enough to survive a whipping. There's some kind of divine power there ³⁹because the God of heaven watches over that place and helps it. He beats to death everyone who tries to harm it."

⁴⁰This is the end of the story about Heliodorus and about how the temple treasury was protected.

Onias Goes to the King for Help

4 ¹Simon continued to spread lies about Onias. (As mentioned earlier, Simon was the one who informed Apollonius about the money and betrayed his own country.) Simon claimed that Onias was the one who assaulted Heliodorus and caused these terrible things to happen to him. ²Onias had helped Jerusalem, protected his own people, and was devoted to Moses' Teachings. Yet, Simon had the nerve to accuse him of plotting against the government. ³Simon's hatred became so vicious that he even had one of his followers murder people.

⁴Onias realized that his rivalry with Simon had become dangerous. He also realized that Apollonius, who was Menestheus' son and the governor of Coelesyria and Phoenicia, was encouraging Simon to become more hostile. ⁵So Onias went to see the king. He didn't intend to accuse any of his own people but to work for the public and private welfare of everyone. ⁶He knew that without the king's intervention the government would be unable to maintain peace and that Simon would continue his senseless behavior.

Jason Becomes Chief Priest

⁷Later, Seleucus died, and Antiochus IV, who was also called Epiphanes, succeeded him as king. At that time Jason, Onias' brother, became chief

priest in an underhanded way. [8]He met with the king and promised him 27,000 pounds of silver as well as an additional 6,000 pounds from other public revenue. [9]Jason also promised the king another 11,250 pounds if the king would allow him to build a gymnasium with a center for training young men. He asked the king for permission to record the names of people in Jerusalem who wanted to become citizens of Antioch. [10]The king approved Jason's request.

When Jason gained control, he immediately forced the Jewish people to live the way the Greeks lived. [11]Jason took away the special privileges that John, Eupolemus' father, had secured for the Jews from earlier kings. (Eupolemus was the man who led a group of ambassadors to Rome to establish friendly relations with the Romans and to make an alliance with them.) In addition, Jason put an end to Jewish traditions and introduced new traditions that were contrary to Moses' Teachings. [12]He gladly built a gymnasium next to the fortress in Jerusalem and educated the finest young men by making them exercise in the nude. [13]Jason was an extremely wicked man who wasn't fit to be chief priest. So because Jason introduced foreign traditions, the desire for the Greek way of life reached an all-time high. [14]Priests were no longer eager to serve at the altar. They despised the temple and didn't care about the sacrifices. But when they heard the gym bell, they would rush to enjoy the wrestling matches, which were contrary to Moses' Teachings. [15]They thought that everything their ancestors honored was worthless and that being Greek was the best thing in the world. [16]That's why they eventually found themselves in serious trouble. The Greeks, whom they wanted to be like and whose way of life they envied, became their enemies and oppressed them. [17]Those who violate God's laws will be severely punished, as we will see from the following events.

[18]When the king was present in the city of Tyre for the athletic competition that was held every four years, [19]Jason sent some ambassadors there. Jason, who was a disgusting man, chose from Jerusalem men who claimed to be citizens of Antioch. These men brought 300 silver coins to pay for the sacrifice offered to Hercules. But they thought it was wrong to use the money to pay for this kind of a sacrifice. So they chose to spend the money on something else. [20]Instead of using Jason's money on the sacrifice to Hercules, the men spent the money on the construction of battleships.

[21]When Apollonius, Menestheus' son, was sent to Egypt for a special meeting called by King Philometor, Antiochus IV was informed that Philometor had become an enemy of his government. So because Antiochus was concerned about his own safety, he didn't stop when he arrived in the city of Joppa. He continued to Jerusalem. [22]Jason and the citizens of Jerusalem gave Antiochus a royal welcome. They escorted Antiochus

into the city with torches and loud cheering. Later, when Antiochus and his army left for Phoenicia, the citizens escorted him out of Jerusalem in the same way.

Menelaus Replaces Jason as Chief Priest

²³Three years later, Jason sent Menelaus to bring money to the king. (Menelaus was the brother of Simon, who was mentioned earlier.) He was also sent to complete negotiations with the king on important business matters. ²⁴But when Menelaus was introduced to the king, he made himself look like a person who had authority. Then, outbidding Jason by 22,500 pounds of silver, he purchased the position of chief priest for himself. ²⁵After the king appointed him chief priest, Menelaus returned to Jerusalem. He had no qualifications to be the chief priest. But he did have the temper of a cruel tyrant and was as ferocious as a wild animal. ²⁶So Jason, who had taken his own brother's position in an underhanded way, was replaced in an underhanded way by someone else. Jason was forced to flee to the country of Ammon. ²⁷Menelaus held on to the position of chief priest, but he never made any of the regular payments that he had promised the king. ²⁸Sostratus, the commander of the fortress in Jerusalem, kept demanding Menelaus to make the payments, since Sostratus was in charge of collecting the money. So eventually the king summoned both of them because neither of them made the payments. ²⁹While they were gone, Menelaus appointed his brother Lysimachus as chief priest, and Sostratus appointed Crates, the commander of the Cyprian army, to be in charge of the fortress in Jerusalem.

Menelaus Has Onias Murdered

³⁰Meanwhile, the citizens of Tarsus and Mallus revolted against the king because their cities had been given as a gift to Antiochis, the king's concubine.ᵃ ³¹So the king quickly went to settle the problem. He left Andronicus, a high-ranking official, in charge. ³²But Menelaus, thinking that the time was right, stole gold utensils from the temple and gave some of them as a present to Andronicus. Menelaus sold the rest of the utensils to people in Tyre and other nearby cities. ³³When Onias found out about this, he left Jerusalem and went to hide in a safe place at Daphne near the city of Antioch. At Daphne he began to make the public aware of what Menelaus had done. ³⁴Because of this, Menelaus secretly met with Andronicus and urged him to kill Onias. So Andronicus went to visit Onias. He deceived Onias by shaking his hand and promising not to hurt him, and he persuaded Onias to come out of hiding, even though

---

ᵃ 4:30 A concubine is considered a wife except she has fewer rights under the law.

Onias was very suspicious. Then, with no respect for justice, Andronicus immediately killed Onias.

[35] As a result, not only Jews but also many people from other nations were horrified and angry that Onias had been murdered unjustly. [36] When the king returned to Antioch from Cilicia, the Jews in the city and the Greeks who also detested the senseless murder made an appeal to him. [37] Antiochus became very sad. He was so sorrowful that he began to cry, because Onias was a sensible man who had lived a very good life. [38] Antiochus became so furious that he immediately stripped Andronicus of his royal position, tore off his clothes, and led him naked through the entire city to the exact spot where he had done this evil thing to Onias. There Antiochus killed that bloodthirsty murderer. So the Lord gave Andronicus the punishment he deserved.

Lysimachus Is Killed

[39] Lysimachus had taken many gold utensils from the temple in Jerusalem with Menelaus' knowledge. When the news about this spread outside Jerusalem, a mob gathered to confront Lysimachus because many gold utensils had already been sold outside the country. [40] Eventually, the crowds became enraged, so Lysimachus sent about 3,000 fully armed soldiers to attack them brutally. A very old and stupid man named Auranus led the soldiers. [41] But when the crowds realized that the soldiers attacking them were sent by Lysimachus, they picked up stones, blocks of wood, or ashes that were lying around. Then they wildly threw them at Lysimachus' men. [42] They killed some soldiers, wounded many others, and forced the rest to flee. They even killed Lysimachus, the temple robber, next to the temple treasury.

Menelaus Is Acquitted

[43] Menelaus was brought to trial because of what had happened. [44] When the king arrived in the city of Tyre, the Jewish council sent three men to present its case in his court. [45] Menelaus knew that he wasn't going to win his case. So he bribed Ptolemy, Dorymenes' son, with a lot of money to have the king rule in his favor. [46] Ptolemy took the king outside the courtroom and into a hallway, as if they were taking a break, and got the king to change his mind. [47] The king acquitted Menelaus, who had caused all the trouble, and sentenced the three men to death. Even the uncivilized Scythians would have acquitted these three poor men because the men were innocent. [48] So the three men, who had spoken in defense of their city, its villages, and the holy utensils, were quickly killed, even though they were innocent. [49] As a result, even the citizens of Tyre showed how much they detested the execution of these men by generously paying for their funeral. [50] Menelaus remained chief priest because of the greedy

people who were in power. He grew more wicked than ever and became the number one enemy of his own people.

Antiochus IV Makes a Second Attack on Egypt

5 ¹Around this time, Antiochus IV began to make his second attack on Egypt. ²For nearly 40 days everyone in Jerusalem could see cavalrymen galloping across the sky. The cavalrymen had uniforms and weapons made with gold. They rode in companies, were fully armed, and had their swords drawn. ³The cavalry troops formed battle lines, and they attacked and counterattacked each other. Shields were waving, spears were sailing, and arrows were flying through the sky. The troops' equipment glistened, and they had every kind of weapon imaginable. ⁴So everyone in Jerusalem prayed that this miraculous sight would prove to be a good sign.

Jason Attacks Jerusalem

⁵When a false report spread that Antiochus had died, Jason took more than 1,000 soldiers and suddenly attacked the city of Jerusalem. Jason and his soldiers forced the troops who were stationed on the city wall to retreat, and he eventually captured the city. Menelaus escaped into the fortress for protection. ⁶But Jason showed no mercy and kept killing his own people. He didn't realize that gaining a victory over one's own people is really self-defeating. He thought he was winning a victory over his enemies, not his own people. ⁷But Jason didn't gain control of the government. He was forced to flee again into Ammonite territory. In the end, his scheme brought him nothing but disgrace.

⁸Eventually, his life came to a miserable end. Someone brought criminal charges against him to an Arab ruler named Aretas. So Jason fled from city to city. Everyone tried to hunt him down. People hated him because he rebelled against Moses' Teachings. They despised him because he had publicly executed people from his own country. So he was forced to go to Egypt. ⁹Later, he took a ship to Sparta. He hoped to find a safe place to live among the Spartans, who were related to him. Finally, this man, who had forced many people to go into exile, died in exile in Sparta. ¹⁰This man, who had left many people without a burial, had no one to mourn for him. He didn't even have a funeral, and he wasn't placed in his ancestors' tomb.

Antiochus Attacks Jerusalem—1 Maccabees 1:20-63

¹¹When King Antiochus heard what had happened, he thought that all the people in Judea had revolted. This made the king as angry as a wild animal. So he left Egypt, attacked Jerusalem, and captured it. ¹²He ordered his soldiers to show no mercy to anyone, kill everyone they met, and slaughter those who retreated into their houses. ¹³So the soldiers put

to death young and old people alike. They killed women and children, and they slaughtered young girls and infants. [14]In three days 80,000 people were lost: Half were killed in combat, and the rest were sold as slaves.

[15]Even after the city had been captured and many citizens were killed, Antiochus still was not satisfied. So he had the nerve to enter the holiest temple in the world. Menelaus, who had betrayed Moses' Teachings and his own country, was his guide. [16]With his bloodstained and unholy hands, Antiochus took away the holy utensils and the gifts that other kings had given to add to the beauty and honor of the temple.

[17]Antiochus was so arrogant that he didn't realize the Lord was allowing the temple to be dishonored. At this time the Lord was angry because the people of Jerusalem had sinned. [18]But if the people hadn't sinned so much, Antiochus would have been immediately whipped and carried out of the temple. He would have been punished because of his arrogance just like Heliodorus, whom King Seleucus had sent to inspect the treasury. [19]Certainly, the Lord didn't choose his people for the sake of his holy place. He chose his holy place for the sake of his people. [20]That's why the holy place shared in the people's bad times and later took part in their good times. The holy place, which had been abandoned when the Almighty was angry, was restored again in all its glory when the great Lord restored his people's relationship with him.

[21]So Antiochus carried away 135,000 pounds ⌐of precious metals⌐ from the temple and hurried back to the city of Antioch. He was so arrogant and his imagination was so wild that he thought he could sail on land and walk on water. [22]He left the following administrators in Judea to harass the people. In Jerusalem he left Philip, who was a Phrygian by birth and was more vicious than Antiochus. [23]At Mount Gerizim he left Andronicus. In addition to these men, he also left Menelaus in Jerusalem. Menelaus was worse than the other men because he arrogantly used his authority against his own people.

Antiochus Sends Apollonius to Attack Jerusalem

Antiochus grew to hate the Jewish people more and more. [24]So he sent Apollonius, the commander of the Mysians, with an army of 22,000 soldiers to attack the Jewish people. He ordered Apollonius to slaughter all the men and to sell the women and children as slaves. [25]When Apollonius arrived in Jerusalem, he acted as though he were on a peace mission. But on a holy day of worship, a day when the Jews must not work, he ordered an inspection of his troops. [26]When the Jewish people came out of the city to watch, he killed all of them. After that, he ran into the city with his soldiers and killed so many people that dead bodies were scattered all over.

[27]But Judas Maccabeus and a group of about nine men had already left the city and gone into the mountains where no one could find them. They survived like animals by eating plants so that they wouldn't become unclean.[a]

Antiochus IV Tries to Destroy Jewish Traditions

6 [1]A short time later King Antiochus IV sent Geron, an Athenian, to force the Jews to abandon their ancestors' traditions and stop following God's Teachings. [2]In addition, Antiochus ordered Geron to dishonor the temple in Jerusalem and the temple on Mount Gerizim. Geron renamed the temple in Jerusalem after Zeus, the god of Mount Olympus, and renamed the temple on Mount Gerizim after Zeus, the Friend of Strangers. This was something the people of that region wanted anyway.

[3]The terrible things that happened were intensely cruel and disgusting. [4]In the temple courtyard foreigners did immoral things and held wild parties. Men spent their free time with prostitutes and had sex with women inside the holy areas of the temple. They brought forbidden things into the temple courtyard [5]and even placed on the altar many offerings that Moses' Teachings didn't allow. [6]People weren't able to observe the day of worship, celebrate traditional festivals, or even admit that they were Jews.

[7]Every month, when the king's birthday was celebrated, the Jews were cruelly forced to celebrate too. They were forced to eat meat that was sacrificed to false gods. Also, when the festival of the god Dionysus was celebrated, the Jews were forced to wear ivy wreaths on their heads and march in the parade.

[8]Based on a suggestion that was made by the citizens of Ptolemais, a decree was published in the neighboring Greek cities. The decree required all the Greeks to force the Jews to eat meat that was sacrificed to false gods [9]and to kill all the Jews who refused to adopt the Greek way of life. So the Jews were experiencing difficult times. [10]For example, two Jewish women were arrested because they had their children circumcised. Then, after the women were paraded around the city with their babies hanging from their necks, they were thrown off the city wall. [11]Some Jewish people gathered together secretly in nearby caves to observe a day of worship. But someone told Philip about them, and Philip burned them to death. These Jewish people were so devoted to honoring that most holy day that they didn't try to defend themselves.

[12]I want to encourage the people who read this book not to get depressed by the terrible things that happened. You need to realize that these punishments from God were not intended to destroy our people,

---

[a] 5:27 "Unclean" refers to anything that Moses' Teachings say is not presentable to God.

but to teach them. [13]In fact, when God punishes evil people immediately, instead of waiting a long time, it's a sign of God's rich kindness. [14]The Lord waits patiently to punish other nations. He doesn't punish them until their sins have gotten out of control. But that's not the way he deals with us. [15]The Lord punishes us before our sins get out of control. [16]He never stops showing us his mercy. Although he teaches us with disasters, he never abandons us, his people. [17]Let everything I've just said serve as a reminder to you. Now let's continue our story.

The Story of Eleazar

[18]There was a high-ranking scribe named Eleazar who was a very handsome old man. He was being forced to open his mouth and eat some pork. [19]But he preferred to die an honorable death rather than live an unclean[a] life. [20]He chose to be tortured to death. So he spit out the pork. Let this be an example for everyone. He endured this torture because he was willing to give up his life rather than eat something that shouldn't even be tasted.

[21]Some men who had known Eleazar for a long time were in charge of a sacrifice that was contrary to Moses' Teachings. These men took Eleazar aside, and in private they urged him to bring his own meat, meat that was proper for him to eat. They wanted Eleazar to pretend that he was eating the pork as the king had ordered. [22]Because Eleazar was an old friend of theirs, the men told him that if he did this, they would do a favor for him and not put him to death.

[23]But Eleazar made a wise decision. His decision was based on his maturity, dignity, experience, and the fact that he had lived an honorable life ever since he was young. But most importantly, Eleazar's decision was based on the holy teachings that God had given. He immediately refused their plan and said, "Send me to my grave! [24]It's not right for an old man like me to deceive anyone. I don't want a lot of young people to think that I've taken up a foreign religion when I'm 90 years old. [25]If I pretend to eat pork, just to live a few more years, I'll lead many young people astray and become morally unclean for the rest of my life. [26]I may escape the punishment you've planned for me. But whether I live or die, I won't be able to escape the punishment of the Almighty God. [27]So if I die bravely now, I'll show that I deserved to live as long as I have. [28]Also, I'll leave the young people an honorable example of how to give their lives willingly and nobly for the sake of our honored and holy teachings."

After Eleazar said this, he immediately went to be tortured. [29]The same men who had been kind to him earlier were now unkind to him because they thought that everything he just said was foolish. [30]When Eleazar

---

[a] 6:19 "Unclean" refers to anything that Moses' Teachings say is not presentable to God.

had been beaten and was about to die, he groaned and said, "The Lord in his holy knowledge obviously knows that I could have avoided dying. Even though my body has been beaten and I'm in terrible pain, I gladly suffer because I fear him."

³¹ So this is the way that Eleazar died. His death served as an example of honor and virtue. Eleazar's death will be remembered not only by young people, but also by most of the people in his nation.

The Story of a Mother and Her Seven Sons

7 ¹After the incident with Eleazar, the king had a Jewish mother and her seven sons arrested. He tried to force them to eat pork by whipping and torturing them. (Eating pork is contrary to Moses' Teachings.) ²Then one of the sons spoke for all of them. He asked the king, "What do you want from us? You know that we'd rather die than disobey what our ancestors taught us."

³ The king became furious. He ordered his soldiers to heat up frying pans and kettles until they were red hot. ⁴His soldiers did this immediately. Then the king ordered his soldiers to cut out the tongue of the son who had spoken, to scalp him, and to cut off his hands and feet. The son's mother and the rest of his brothers were forced to watch. ⁵Next, the king ordered his soldiers to take the helpless son, put him in one of the pans, and fry him alive. As clouds of smoke drifted from the pan toward his mother and brothers, they encouraged each other to die bravely. They said, ⁶"The Lord God is watching over us. He truly has compassion on us. Moses made this clear when he wrote a song that testified against his people. Moses said, 'The Lord will have compassion on his servants.' "

⁷ After the first brother died in the way just described, the king's soldiers brought the second brother forward. They began to mock and torture him in the same way. They grabbed his hair and tore off his scalp. Then they said to him, "Eat some pork, or we will tear your body apart!"

⁸He replied in his native language, "Never!" So he was tortured just like the first brother. ⁹Just before he died, he said to the king, "You're cruel and vicious! You may be able to kill us now, but the king of the universe will bring us back to life. Then we'll live forever because we died for the sake of his teachings."

¹⁰After him, the third brother was mocked and tortured. When the king's soldiers demanded that he stick out his tongue, he quickly did. He courageously held out his hands ¹¹and said bravely, "The Lord*ᵃ* gave me my tongue and my hands, but compared to his teachings, they mean nothing to me. Besides, I'm confident that he will give them back to me

---

ᵃ 7:11 Greek "Heaven." The author of 2 Maccabees uses the word *Heaven* in place of God's name, the Lord.

again." [12]The king and his soldiers were surprised at the young man's courage, because the young man didn't care how much he suffered.

[13] After this brother died, the king's soldiers began to torture the fourth brother in the same cruel way. [14]When he was about to die, he said to the king, "I've chosen to let you kill me and to believe that God will bring me back to life again. You, too, will be brought back to life—a life of shame and disgrace!"[a]

[15] Next, the king's soldiers brought forward the fifth brother and treated him cruelly. [16]But he looked directly at the king and said, "You have authority to do whatever you want, even though you're mortal. But don't think that God has abandoned the people of Israel. [17]Wait! You'll see! God will use his awesome power to torture you and your descendants."

[18] After him, the king's soldiers brought the sixth brother forward. When he was about to die, he said to the king, "Don't be fooled! It's our own fault that we're suffering like this. We've sinned against our God. That's why these shocking things are happening to us. [19]But don't think that you'll go unpunished for trying to fight against God."

[20] The mother was a remarkable woman and deserves special mention. She saw her seven sons die in a single day. Yet, she held up courageously because she trusted the Lord. [21]She encouraged each of her sons in their native language. She was so courageous that she expressed herself very bravely by saying to them, [22]"I don't know how you came to life in my womb. I didn't give any of you your breath or life or make you what you are. [23]The Creator of the universe did these things. He formed humans in the beginning and designed everything that exists. He will mercifully give your life and your breath back to you because you consider his teachings to be more important than your own lives."

[24]King Antiochus felt that the mother was being disrespectful to him. He thought what she said was insulting. Since the youngest brother was still alive, Antiochus kept making him offers. He even promised with an oath that he would make him rich and that people would envy him. The king also promised to give the young man the title "Friend of the King" and entrust him with public duties if the young man would abandon his ancestors' traditions. [25]But the young man didn't pay any attention to the king. So the king summoned the mother and urged her to advise her son to save himself. [26]After much urging by the king, she agreed to persuade her son. [27]However, she leaned over, whispered in her son's ear, and mocked the cruel tyrant. She said to her son in their native language, "Son, have mercy on me. I carried you in my womb for nine months and nursed you for three years. I raised you and took care of you. [28]My child, I want you to take a good look at the earth, the sky, and everything that's in them. I

---

[a] 7:14 Or "But you will never be brought back to life!"

want you to realize that God made those things and people out of nothing. [29]So don't be afraid of the king, that public executioner. Prove that you're like your brothers. Die willingly so that God will mercifully give you back to me along with your brothers."

[30]While she was still speaking, the young man said, "What are all of you waiting for? I won't obey the king's order. I'll only obey the teachings that God gave my ancestors through Moses. [31]You've come up with all kinds of terrible things to do to the Hebrews, but you'll never escape God's punishment. [32]We, the Hebrew people, are suffering because of our sins. [33]Even though our living Lord has been angry with us for a little while and is punishing and disciplining us, he will certainly restore our relationship with him again. [34]You wicked man! You're the most disgusting person that ever lived. Don't be a fool and arrogantly believe that you can oppose the LORD's children. [35]You'll never escape the judgment of the Almighty, who sees everything. [36]My brothers, who suffered for a little while, are now enjoying everlasting life because of God's promise.[a] But you will receive the punishment you deserve for your arrogance because God will judge you. [37]I'm about to give up my body and my life, as my brothers did, for the sake of our ancestors' traditions. I pray that God will show mercy to our nation quickly and that he will use trials and plagues to force you to acknowledge that he is the only God. [38]I also pray that, through my brothers and me, the Almighty will put and end to his anger, anger which our entire nation deserved."

[39]The king became bitter and furious. He treated the young man worse than his brothers because the young man treated him with contempt. [40]The young man, trusting the Lord completely, died without becoming unclean.[b]

[41]The mother died last, after her sons.

[42]This should completely clear up matters about the severe tortures the Jews faced and about how rulers tried to force them to eat meat that was sacrificed to false gods.

Judas Organizes an Army—1 Maccabees 3:1-26

8 [1]Judas Maccabeus and his followers secretly entered villages. They asked their relatives and those who had remained faithful to the Jewish religion to join them and help them. As a result, they recruited about 6,000 men. [2]Then they prayed to the Lord. They asked him to watch over his people, whom all the nations despised, to have pity on his temple, which evil people had dishonored, [3]and to have mercy on Jerusalem, which was being destroyed and was about to be leveled. They also asked

---

[a] 7:36 Or "covenant."

[b] 7:40 "Unclean" refers to anything that Moses' Teachings say is not presentable to God.

him to hear those who were being murdered and were calling to him for help, ⁴to remember the innocent babies who had died violent deaths, to take revenge on those who had insulted his name, and to show his hatred of evil.

⁵As soon as Judas organized his army, the foreigners were unable to defeat him, because the Lord now showed his mercy instead of his anger to the Jewish people. ⁶Judas would sneak into enemy cities and villages and set them on fire. He regained control of important locations and soundly defeated many enemy troops. ⁷He found that the best time for him to attack was at night. People everywhere talked about his courage.

Nicanor Invades Judea—*1 Maccabees 3:38-41*

⁸Philip saw that Judas was gradually making progress and that Judas was winning battles more frequently. So Philip wrote a letter to Ptolemy, who was the governor of Coelesyria and Phoenicia. He requested military help for the king's government. ⁹Ptolemy quickly appointed Nicanor to help Philip. Nicanor was Patroclus' son and one of those who held the title "Most Important Friend of the King." Ptolemy sent Nicanor to Judea with an army made up of more than 20,000 foreign soldiers from every nation. Nicanor's mission was to get rid of every Jew in Judea. Ptolemy also appointed Gorgias to go with him. Gorgias was a general who had a lot of military experience. ¹⁰Nicanor planned to sell Jewish prisoners as slaves so that he could pay off the 150,000 pounds of silver that the king owed the Romans in taxes. ¹¹So he immediately sent the cities along the coast an invitation to come and buy Jewish slaves. He promised to sell 90 slaves for 75 pounds of silver. However, he had no idea that the Almighty was about to punish him.

¹²Judas heard that Nicanor was coming to Judea with an army. When he shared this information with his soldiers, ¹³those who were cowards and didn't believe that God would punish their enemies left camp and ran away. ¹⁴The rest sold everything they owned. Then they got together and prayed to the Lord, "Rescue us! Before the fighting has even started, that evil man Nicanor has sold us as slaves. ¹⁵If you're not willing to rescue us for our sake, rescue us for the sake of the promises*a* that you made to our ancestors and for the sake of your awe-inspiring name by which they were called."

¹⁶Judas gathered the 6,000 men he had recruited and encouraged them not to panic when they saw the enemy soldiers or to become afraid of the large number of foreigners who were about to attack them for no reason. Instead, he encouraged them to fight bravely ¹⁷and to focus on

---

a 8:15 Or "covenants."

how their enemies had dishonored the holy place, how they had mocked and tortured the citizens of Jerusalem, and especially how they had tried to destroy the Jewish way of life. [18]Then he said, "Our enemies trust their weapons and their courage. But we trust the Almighty God. With a single command, the Almighty God can defeat the enemy that is coming to attack us and even the entire world."

[19]In addition, Judas reminded them about some of the times when God helped their ancestors. In the time of Sennacherib, 185,000 enemy soldiers were killed. [20]In the battle against the Galatians that took place in Babylonia, 8,000 Jews and 4,000 Macedonians fought the Galatians. Yet, when the Macedonians were having difficulties, the Lord[a] helped those 8,000 Jews to destroy 120,000 Galatians and to take a lot of loot besides.

Judas Defeats Nicanor—1 Maccabees 3:55–4:27

[21]By saying these things to his soldiers, Judas made them courageous and willing to die for their traditions and their country. Then he divided his army into four divisions. [22]He appointed his brothers Simon, Joseph, and Jonathan as commanders. Each of them was in charge of one division and was assigned 1,500 soldiers. [23](In addition, Eleazar was present.)[b] After Judas had read to his soldiers from the holy book, he gave them this password: "God will help us." Then, as commander of the first division, Judas attacked Nicanor.

[24]The Almighty fought for Judas and his soldiers, and they slaughtered more than 9,000 enemy troops. They wounded and disabled many of Nicanor's troops and forced the rest of them to flee. [25]They took the money from the very people who had come to buy them as slaves. After they had chased the enemy far away, they returned because it was getting late. [26]It was the evening before a day of worship, so they didn't continue to chase the enemy. [27]After they had collected weapons from the enemy soldiers who were dead and had stripped them of their valuables, they observed the day of worship. They praised the Lord and thanked him for guiding them safely through that day and showing his mercy to them again. [28]After the day of worship was over, they gave some of the valuables they had taken to widows, orphans, and those who had been tortured. Then they divided what was left among themselves and their children. [29]When they had finished doing this, they prayed together and asked their merciful Lord to restore their relationship with him.

---

[a] 8:20 Greek "Heaven." The author of 2 Maccabees uses the word *Heaven* in place of God's name, the Lord.

[b] 8:23 Greek meaning of this sentence uncertain.

Judas Defeats Timothy and Bacchides

³⁰Later, Judas and his troops fought against the soldiers of Timothy and Bacchides. They killed more than 20,000 enemy soldiers and gained control of some very strong fortifications. They divided a lot of loot and gave shares equal to their own to orphans, widows, old people, and those who had been tortured. ³¹They collected the enemy's weapons and carefully stored all of them in important locations, but they took the rest of the loot to Jerusalem. ³²They killed one of Timothy's commanding officers. This officer was a very wicked man who had caused the Jewish people a lot of suffering.

³³While people were celebrating the victory throughout the country, those who had set fire to the temple gates were burned to death by Judas and his soldiers. One of the men who was burned to death was Callisthenes, who had hidden in a small house. So he received the punishment he deserved for the evil thing he had done.

³⁴So Nicanor, the disgusting man who had brought 1,000 slave traders to buy Jewish prisoners, ³⁵was humiliated with the Lord's help by the very people he looked down on. He took off his official uniform and escaped through the open country all by himself like a runaway slave until he reached the city of Antioch. The only thing he did successfully was to destroy his own army. ³⁶This man once thought he could raise enough money to pay Roman taxes by selling Jewish prisoners in Jerusalem. Instead, he ended up spreading the news that the Jews had a God who defended them, and that because the Jews followed the teachings their God gave them, they couldn't be defeated.

The Lord Punishes Antiochus IV—*1 Maccabees 6:1-7; 2 Maccabees 1:11-17*

9 ¹About this same time, Antiochus made a disorderly retreat from Persia. ²Here's the reason he retreated: Antiochus had entered a city called Persepolis. He tried to rob its temples and take over the city. But large mobs of citizens armed themselves and attacked him. The citizens defeated Antiochus and his army and forced them to retreat in shame. ³While Antiochus was near the city of Ecbatana, he heard what had happened to Nicanor and Timothy's troops. ⁴He became absolutely furious. So he decided to take out his anger on the Jews for the defeat he had just suffered. He ordered his chariot driver not to stop until they had reached Jerusalem. He said arrogantly, "When I arrive in Jerusalem, I'll turn it into a Jewish cemetery." But the Lord*ᵃ* wasn't about to let him go unpunished.

ᵃ 9:4 Greek "Heaven." The author of 2 Maccabees uses the word *Heaven* in place of God's name, the Lord.

⁵The Lord, the God of Israel, sees everything. He struck Antiochus with an incurable disease that no one could see. As soon as Antiochus finished speaking, he suffered intense cramps and severe stomach pains. ⁶This was the perfect punishment for a man who had caused many people so much pain. ⁷Yet, that didn't stop him from being conceited. He was as arrogant as ever and began threatening to do violent things to the Jews. He even ordered his chariot driver to go faster. But as the chariot raced along, he fell out. He fell so hard that his entire body was in pain. ⁸A few seconds earlier, this man thought he could order around the waves in the sea, and he bragged that he was more than a mere human. He even thought that he could weigh the peaks of mountains on a scale. But when he fell to the ground and was carried off on a stretcher, God's power became clear to everyone. ⁹This evil man's body crawled with worms. He lived in pain and agony, and his skin rotted away. The entire army became sick because of the smell that came from his body. ¹⁰No one could stand to carry him because he smelled so bad. This was the man who, only a short time earlier, thought that he could take hold of the stars.

Antiochus Makes a Vow to the Lord—*1 Maccabees 6:8-17*

¹¹At this point Antiochus became humble. He became less arrogant and came to his senses because he was in constant pain due to God's punishment. ¹²When he couldn't stand the smell of his own body anymore, he said, "It's right for people to place themselves under God's authority. Mortals shouldn't think that they are God's equal." ¹³Then this disgusting man made vows to the Lord, who would no longer show him mercy. Antiochus vowed ¹⁴that he would declare Jerusalem, the holy city, to be a free city. This is the city he was in a hurry to level and make into a Jewish cemetery. ¹⁵He also vowed that he would give all the Jewish citizens the same rights as the Athenian citizens. Previously, he thought that the Jews didn't deserve to be buried and planned to leave their bodies and their children's bodies for the wild animals and birds to eat. ¹⁶Antiochus, who had looted the holy temple, vowed that he would make it even more beautiful than it had been, that he would give back many more holy utensils than he had taken, and that he would fund the sacrifices out of his own money. ¹⁷In addition to all this, he vowed to follow the Jewish way of life and to travel all over the world and tell everyone about God's power.

Antiochus Writes a Letter to the Jews

¹⁸Antiochus' pain wouldn't go away because God was giving him the punishment he deserved. Antiochus lost all hope of recovering, so he wrote the following letter to the Jews to win their favor:

[19] "From Antiochus, king and general.
To the honorable Jewish people.
Greetings, good health, and prosperity!

[20] "I hope that you and your children are in good health and
that everything is going well for you. I have confidence in the
LORD, [21] and I warmly remember the way you have honored me
and have shown me your loyalty.

"As I was returning from Persia, I became seriously ill. So I
think I should make arrangements for the general well-being of
everyone. [22] I haven't given up hope of recovering. Actually, I'm
confident that I will recover from my illness. [23] Nevertheless, I
remember that my father used to appoint a successor whenever
he marched inland [24] so that people would know who was left in
charge of the government. So if anything unexpected happened
or if some terrible news came back, the people throughout the
kingdom wouldn't be worried. [25] In addition, I know very well
that the rulers along the borders of my kingdom are watching
for an opportunity to take over my kingdom and are waiting
to see what will happen to me. That's why I've appointed my
son Antiochus V to be king. On a number of occasions, I have
officially put him in charge of the kingdom to serve most of
you when I traveled to the inland territories. (I've enclosed a
copy of a letter that I wrote to him.) [26] So I encourage you to
talk in public and in private about the good things I have done
for you. Also, I ask each of you to continue to be loyal to me
and my son. [27] I'm certain that he will be kind and fair to you
and will follow my policies closely."

[28] So this murderer, who slandered God, suffered as intensely as he
made other people suffer. He died a miserable death in the mountains of
a foreign country. [29] Philip, who had been his friend since childhood, was
going to carry his body home. But because Philip was afraid of Antiochus'
son, he went to Egypt and stayed with Ptolemy Philometor.

Judas and His Soldiers Cleanse the Temple—*1 Maccabees 4:36-61*

10 [1] With the Lord guiding them, Judas and his soldiers regained
control of the temple and the city of Jerusalem. [2] They tore down
the altars and the worship sites that the foreigners[a] had built in the marketplace. [3] They cleansed the temple and made another altar. Then they
made a fire, offered sacrifices, and burned incense for the first time in
two years. They lit the lights on the lamp stand and set out the bread of

---

[a] 10:2 Greek "the Philistines."

the presence. ⁴After they had done these things, they bowed with their faces touching the ground and prayed to the Lord. They asked him never to allow these terrible things to happen to them again. They asked him not to punish them so severely if they ever sinned again or to hand them over to uncivilized foreigners who would ridicule them.

⁵The temple was cleansed on the twenty-fifth day of the month of Chislev. This was the same day and the same month in which the foreigners had dishonored it. ⁶People joyfully celebrated for eight days, as they did during the Festival of Booths. They remembered how only a short time ago they had spent the Festival of Booths living in mountains and caves like wild animals. ⁷That's why they held leafy tree branches, other beautiful branches, and palm branches as they offered hymns of praise to God, who had successfully cleansed his own temple. ⁸The people took a vote and unanimously passed a law that required the entire Jewish nation to observe these days every year.

⁹So Antiochus IV, who was also called Epiphanes, died under these circumstances.

Ptolemy Macron Commits Suicide

¹⁰Now I'll tell you about what took place while Antiochus V, who was also called Eupator, was king. I'll give a brief summary of the main disasters that resulted from his wars. Antiochus Eupator was the son of that evil man Antiochus Epiphanes. ¹¹When Eupator became king, he appointed a man named Lysias to be chief of state and a man named Protarchus to be governor of Coelesyria and Phoenicia. ¹²This is the reason that Protarchus was appointed governor: Ptolemy, who was called Macron, was the first governor to treat the Jewish people fairly. He managed them peacefully to make up for the terrible things that had been done to them. ¹³Because of this, the king's friends brought accusations against him to Eupator. Everywhere that Ptolemy went, people called him a traitor because he deserted the island of Cyprus, which Philometor had put him in charge of, and went to serve Antiochus Epiphanes. Because he lost the people's respect,ᵃ he committed suicide by drinking poison.

Judas Defeats the Idumeans—*1 Maccabees 5:1-8*

¹⁴When Gorgias became governor of the region north of Judea, he always kept an army of hired soldiers ready for battle and attacked the Jews every chance he could. ¹⁵At the same time, the Idumeans had control of important fortifications ⌊south of Judea⌋ and continually harassed the Jews. They tried to start wars by taking in Jewish traitors who had fled from Jerusalem. ¹⁶But Judas and his soldiers prayed to God and asked

---

ᵃ 10:13 Greek meaning uncertain.

him to fight for them. Then they attacked the Idumean fortifications [17]with such force that they gained control of them. They forced those who were stationed on the wall to retreat and slaughtered everyone who got in their way. They killed more than 20,000 people.

[18]At least 9,000 men fled into two well-fortified towers, which were equipped to withstand any attack. [19]Judas had to go to some other places that needed him more urgently. So he left Simon and Joseph behind, along with Zacchaeus and his troops. These men had enough soldiers to carry out an attack on the fortified towers. [20]But Simon had some soldiers who would do anything for money. They accepted bribes from some of the enemy soldiers in the towers. After they had received 70,000 silver coins from these soldiers, they let them get away. [21]When someone told Judas what had happened, he held a meeting with the Jewish leaders. At this meeting he accused these men of selling their brothers for money because they had allowed their enemies to go free and to fight them another day. [22]So he killed these men because they had betrayed their people. Then he immediately captured the two towers. [23]Judas was always successful in war, and in his attack against the two fortifications, he killed more than 20,000 soldiers.

Judas Defeats Timothy

[24]Now Timothy, whom the Jews had defeated once before, recruited a very large army and brought together many cavalrymen from Syria. Then he marched toward Judea, intending to attack it. [25]As he was getting closer, Judas and his soldiers sprinkled dust on their heads, put on sackcloth, and prayed to God. [26]They faced the altar and knelt in front of it. They asked God to be merciful to them and to be an enemy to their enemies and an opponent to their opponents as he promised in Moses' Teachings.

[27]After they had finished praying, they grabbed their weapons and marched a long distance from the city. When they got close to the enemy, they stopped. [28]Then, just as the sun was coming up, the two armies attacked each other. The Jewish soldiers trusted the Lord to give them courage and success because he had promised to protect them and give them victory. But the enemy soldiers trusted their own fury to lead them into battle.

[29]When the battle became fierce, the enemy saw five distinguished men in the sky. The five men were riding on horses that had gold bridles, and they were leading the Jews into battle. [30]These men surrounded Judas, shielded him with their weapons, and kept him from getting wounded. They shot arrows and thunderbolts at the enemy, and the enemy became confused and blinded. Because they were thrown into confusion,

many enemy soldiers were killed. ³¹A total of 20,500 enemy soldiers were slaughtered as well as 6,000 cavalrymen.

³²Timothy fled to a fortification called Gazara. Gazara was a very strong fort, where Chaereas was the commander. ³³Judas and his soldiers were very happy that Timothy fled there, and they surrounded the fort for four days. ³⁴The troops inside the fort were confident that it was secure. So they insulted Judas and his soldiers and said terrible things to them. ³⁵On the fifth day, when the sun came up, 20 of Judas' young soldiers, who were very angry because of the insults, bravely attacked the troops stationed on the wall. With the fury of a wild animal, they killed everyone who got in their way. ³⁶While the troops inside the fort were distracted, some of Judas' other soldiers climbed the wall just as the 20 had done. They set the towers on fire, started other fires, and burned to death those who had insulted them. Another group of soldiers broke through the gates, let the rest of the soldiers in, and took over the city. ³⁷Some of Judas' soldiers found Timothy hiding in a cistern and killed him, his brother Chaereas, and Apollophanes. ³⁸When the attack was over, Judas and his soldiers sang hymns of praise and thanksgiving to the Lord, who had been very kind to the people of Israel and had given them the victory.

Judas Defeats Lysias—*1 Maccabees 4:26-35*

11 ¹A short time later, Lysias became very angry when he learned what had happened to Timothy. Lysias was the king's guardian and the chief of state, and he held the title "Relative of the King." ²He gathered about 80,000 soldiers and all his cavalry and went to fight the Jews. He intended to make Jerusalem a Greek settlement, ³to tax the temple (as he did the temples in other nations), and to put the office of chief priest up for sale every year. ⁴But he had no idea how powerful God was. He was arrogant because he had tens of thousands of infantrymen, thousands of cavalrymen, and 80 elephants. ⁵So Lysias invaded Judea. When he arrived at Beth Zur, he began a series of attacks against it. Beth Zur was a fortified city about 20 miles from Jerusalem.

⁶Judas and his soldiers heard that Lysias was attacking their fortifications. So Judas, his soldiers, and the people of Israel prayed to the Lord. They asked him to send an angel to rescue Israel. They were mourning and crying as they prayed. ⁷Judas was the first man to grab his weapons. He encouraged the others to risk their lives with him to help the Jewish people in Beth Zur. Then they eagerly left Jerusalem together. ⁸While they were still near Jerusalem, a horseman miraculously appeared and began to lead them. The horseman wore white clothes and was waving weapons that were made of gold. ⁹All of the soldiers praised God for his mercy. They became courageous and ready to fight not only humans but also wild animals. They were also ready to attack walls, even if the walls were made

of iron. [10]Now that the Lord had shown his mercy to them, they marched in battle formation and were confident that God would fight for them from heaven. [11]They charged the enemy like ferocious lions and killed 11,000 soldiers and 1,600 cavalrymen. They forced the rest of the enemy soldiers to flee. [12]Most of the soldiers who escaped left their weapons behind and were wounded. Lysias escaped by running away in disgrace.

Lysias Makes an Agreement With the Jews—*1 Maccabees 6:56-61*

[13]Lysias wasn't stupid. As he thought over the defeat he had just suffered, he realized that the Hebrews couldn't be beaten because the mighty God fought for them. So Lysias sent a message to the Jews. [14]He tried to persuade them to agree to a fair settlement. He promised that he would pressure the king and try to persuade him to become their friend. [15]Since Judas was concerned about what was best for everyone, he agreed to all the proposals that Lysias made. Eventually, the king granted every written request that Judas submitted to Lysias about the Jews.

Lysias' Letter to the Jewish People

[16]This is a copy of the letter that Lysias wrote to the Jews:

> "On the twenty-fourth day of the month of Dioscorinthius, in the year 164 B.C.
> From Lysias.
> To the Jewish people.
> Greetings!

> [17]"Your messengers, John and Absalom, have delivered your signed document, and they've asked me to comment on the items contained in it. [18]I have informed the king about everything that needed to be brought to his attention. He has agreed to do whatever he can. [19]So if you continue to be loyal to the government, I'll try in the future to help you get everything you want. [20]I have asked your messengers and my representatives to discuss the details with you."

[21]Sincerely,

Lysias

The King's Letters

[22]This is a copy of King Antiochus' letter:

> From King Antiochus V.
> To my dear friend Lysias.
> Greetings!

²³"Now that my father King Antiochus IV has gone to be with the gods, I don't want to disturb the citizens in my kingdom by telling them how to live their private lives. ²⁴I've heard that the Jewish people don't approve of my father's demand that they must live like Greeks. They prefer their own way of life and are asking for my permission to live by their own customs. ²⁵Since I don't want to disturb these people, I have decided to restore their temple and to allow them to follow their ancestors' customs. ²⁶It would be a good idea for you to tell them about my decision and to reach an agreement with them. Then they'll know what my policy is, and they'll gladly live the way they want to."

²⁷This is a copy of the letter that the king sent to the Jewish nation:

> "On the fifteenth day of the month of Xanthicus, in the year 164 B.C.
> From King Antiochus V.
> To the Jewish council and to the rest of the Jewish people.
> Greetings!

²⁸"I hope that you're well. I'm in good health. ²⁹Menelaus has told me that you want to return home. ³⁰So I'll agree to pardon all those who return by the thirtieth of this month. ³¹Then you can enjoy your own food and customs as you used to do. None of you will be bothered in any way for the mistakes you made in the past. ³²I have sent Menelaus to reassure you."

³³Sincerely,

King Antiochus

The Romans' Letter to the Jewish People

³⁴This is a copy of the letter that the Romans sent to the Jewish people:

> "On the fifteenth day of the month of Xanthicus, in the year 164 B.C.
> From the Roman ambassadors Quintus Memmius and Titus Manius.
> To the Jewish people.
> Greetings!

³⁵"We approve of everything that Lysias, who holds the title 'Relative of the King,' has agreed to do for you. ³⁶Review the matters that Lysias has decided to bring to the king's attention. Then send someone immediately to tell us how you would like

us to resolve these matters with the king. We're about to leave for Antioch to see the king. ³⁷So send messengers quickly so that we can find out what you want us to do."

³⁸Sincerely,

Ambassadors Memmius and Manius

Judas Attacks the Cities of Joppa and Jamnia

12 ¹When Lysias and the Jews had reached an agreement, Lysias went back to the king, and the Jews went back to farming. ²But many of the region's military leaders—Apollonius, who was Gennaeus' son, Timothy, Hieronymous, Demophon, and Nicanor, the commander of the troops from Cyprus—wouldn't allow the Jews to live in peace.

³Even the people who lived in the city of Joppa did something terrible to the Jews. They invited the Jews who lived in Joppa to go sailing on boats that they had provided. The Jews took their wives and children along because they didn't think the people of Joppa intended to do something bad to them. ⁴The Jews didn't suspect anything because the people of Joppa had voted to extend this invitation to them. So the Jews accepted the invitation because they wanted to live peacefully with the people of Joppa. While they were out at sea, the people of Joppa drowned more than 200 of the Jews.

⁵When Judas heard about the cruel way his people were treated, he summoned his soldiers. ⁶After they had prayed to God, who judges fairly, they went to Joppa and attacked those who had murdered his people. During the night, Judas set fire to the harbor, burned boats, and killed everyone who fled to the harbor for safety. ⁷The city's gates were closed, so he left. But he intended to return and kill everyone who lived in Joppa.

⁸Later, Judas heard that the people in the city of Jamnia wanted to get rid of the Jews there in the same way. ⁹So he attacked the people of Jamnia during the night and set their harbor and fleet on fire. The fire was so bright that it could be seen in Jerusalem, which was 30 miles away.

Judas Attacks the City of Caspin—*1 Maccabees 5:9-54*

¹⁰Judas and his soldiers left Jamnia and marched to meet Timothy in battle. When they were about a mile away from Jamnia, they were attacked by more than 5,000 Arabs and 500 cavalrymen. ¹¹The battle was fierce, but with God's help Judas and his soldiers won the battle. The Arabs asked Judas to make a peace treaty with them. They promised to give Judas cattle and to help him and his soldiers in other ways. ¹²Judas thought that the Arabs could be useful in many ways, so he agreed to make a peace treaty with them. After both sides shook hands, the Arabs returned to their tents.

¹³ Judas also attacked Caspin. Caspin was a heavily fortified city that was surrounded by walls. The population of Caspin was made up of people from many races. ¹⁴The people inside the city were confident that the city walls would protect them and that the food supply wouldn't run out. So they treated Judas and his soldiers cruelly. They shouted at them, insulted them, and used obscene language. ¹⁵But Judas and his soldiers prayed to God, who is the great ruler of the universe and who tore down Jericho's walls at the time of Joshua without using battering rams or large weapons. Then they fiercely attacked the city walls ¹⁶and captured the city because that was what God wanted. They slaughtered so many people that a nearby lake, which was about a quarter of a mile wide, appeared to be overflowing with blood.

Judas Defeats Timothy's Army—*1 Maccabees 5:37-44*

¹⁷From Caspin, Judas and his soldiers marched 95 miles until they arrived at a camp where a group of Jews called the Toubiani lived. ¹⁸They didn't find Timothy there because he had already left the region. Timothy had failed in his mission there, but in one place he did leave behind some soldiers in a strong fortification. ¹⁹So Dositheus and Sosipater, two of Judas' commanders, marched to the fortification and killed more than 10,000 soldiers whom Timothy had stationed there. ²⁰Meanwhile, Judas divided his army into divisions, appointed one commander for each division, and went to attack Timothy, who had 120,000 soldiers and 2,500 cavalrymen with him. ²¹When Timothy heard that Judas was coming, he sent the women, the children, and their personal belongings to a place called Karnaim. Karnaim was hard to attack and difficult to get to because every path that led to it was narrow. ²²As soon as Judas' first division appeared at Karnaim, the enemy soldiers became terrified because God, who sees everything, made a miraculous sight appear. As a result, the enemy soldiers scattered wildly in every direction and even wounded each other with their own swords. ²³Judas pursued those sinners with a vengeance and slaughtered about 30,000 of them.

²⁴Timothy was captured by the soldiers of Dositheus and Sosipater. But he cleverly demanded to be released unharmed. He told them that he held most of their parents and relatives as prisoners and that, if he wasn't released, all of them would be killed. ²⁵Timothy promised several times to release their parents and relatives unharmed. So the soldiers let him go free because they wanted to save their relatives.

Judas Defeats Other Enemies—*1 Maccabees 5:45-54*

²⁶Then Judas attacked Karnaim, destroyed the temple of the goddess Atargatis, and slaughtered 25,000 people. ²⁷After he had destroyed Karnaim and the temple, he attacked Ephron. Ephron was a fortified city

where many foreign people lived. Strong young soldiers were stationed in front of the city walls and fought bravely. Inside the city there were large supplies of weapons. ²⁸The Jews prayed to God, the ruler who can destroy the enemy's confidence. They captured the city and killed about 25,000 people.

²⁹Judas and his army left Ephron and marched to the city of Scythopolis, which was 75 miles from Jerusalem. ³⁰The Jews who lived there assured Judas that the citizens of Scythopolis were kind to them and had helped them in times of trouble. ³¹So Judas and his soldiers thanked the citizens of Scythopolis and encouraged them to continue to be kind to the Jews. Then Judas and his army went to Jerusalem. They arrived when the Festival of Weeks was about to begin.

Judas Defeats Gorgias

³²When the Festival of Weeks (which is also called Pentecost) was over, Judas and his army attacked Gorgias, the governor of Idumea. ³³Gorgias met them with 3,000 soldiers and 400 cavalrymen. ³⁴When the battle began, a few Jews were killed. ³⁵A strong cavalryman named Dositheus, who was one of the Toubiani, caught up with Gorgias. He grabbed Gorgias' cape and began to drag him away forcefully because he wanted to take that disgusting man alive. But a Thracian cavalryman attacked Dositheus and cut off his arm, and Gorgias escaped to the city of Marisa.

³⁶Judas prayed to the Lord for a man named Esdris and for his soldiers because they had been fighting a long time and were tired. Judas prayed that the Lord would appear and lead them in the battle. ³⁷He sang hymns in his native language as a battle cry. Then he made a surprise attack on Gorgias' troops and defeated them.

³⁸Then Judas and his soldiers went to the city of Adullam. The day of worship was about to begin. So they cleansed themselves, in keeping with the Jewish custom, and observed the day of worship.

Judas Prays and Offers a Sacrifice for the Dead

³⁹The next day, when Jewish law allowed them to work, Judas' soldiers went to get the bodies of the men who had been killed in battle. They wanted to place them with their relatives in their ancestors' tombs. ⁴⁰But they found religious objects inside the clothes of each dead man, objects used by those who worship the gods of Jamnia. Moses' Teachings don't allow Jewish people to possess these kinds of objects. Now everyone knew why these men were killed in battle. ⁴¹Judas and his soldiers praised the Lord for what he had done. The Lord had been a fair judge and had revealed what these men had tried to hide. ⁴²They prayed to the Lord and asked him to forgive the sin that these men had committed. Judas, who was an honorable man, encouraged his soldiers to be sure not to commit

any sins. After all, they had seen with their own eyes what had happened to the men who had sinned. ⁴³In addition, Judas took up a collection from all his soldiers. He collected about 2,000 silver coins and sent them to Jerusalem. The money was used to pay for a sacrifice for the sin these men had committed. He did this honorable thing because he believed that dead people would come back to life. ⁴⁴If he didn't believe that dead people would come back to life, it wouldn't have made any sense to pray for them. ⁴⁵Because Judas was holy and devout, he focused on the wonderful reward that is waiting ˪in heaven˩ for devout people who die. So he made a peace offering to the Lord for the men who had died in battle so that they might be forgiven for the sin they had committed.

Menelaus Is Executed

13 ¹In the year 163 B.C., Judas and his soldiers heard that King Antiochus V, who was also called Eupator, was coming with a large army to attack Judea. ²They also heard that Lysias, who was the king's guardian and the chief of state, was with him. Antiochus and Lysias were coming with a Greek army made up of 110,000 infantrymen, 5,300 cavalrymen, 22 elephants, and 300 chariots with sharp blades attached to the wheels.

³Menelaus, thinking only of himself, met with Antiochus and Lysias and encouraged Antiochus to attack Judea. Menelaus didn't care about his country's safety. He cared only about being appointed to office. ⁴But God, the King of kings, made Antiochus angry at this sinner. Lysias explained to the king that all of the troubles in Judea were Menelaus' fault. So the king ordered some of his soldiers to take Menelaus to the city of Beroea and to kill him by the regular method of execution used there. ⁵Beroea had a tower that was 75 feet high and was filled with ashes. A platform went around the top of the tower and sloped steeply into the ashes. ⁶People who were guilty of stealing from a temple or of other serious crimes were taken to the top of the tower and pushed into the ashes, where they died. ⁷That's how Menelaus, a man who didn't follow Moses' Teachings, died. He ˪sank into the pile of ashes, suffocated, and˩ didn't even reach the ground. ⁸Menelaus got exactly what he deserved. Because he had committed many sins against the altar, whose fire and ashes are holy, he died in ashes.

Judas Attacks the King's Headquarters

⁹As King Antiochus and his army marched toward Judea, the king became more arrogant and hostile. He intended to show the Jews that he could treat them much worse than his father had ever done. ¹⁰When Judas heard about this, he ordered the people to pray day and night that the Lord would help them now more than ever because they were about

to have their laws, their country, and their holy temple taken away. [11]Judas also ordered them to pray that the Lord would not let his people, who were starting to recover, fall under the control of those evil foreigners. [12]For three days everyone prayed the same prayer together. They cried, fasted, and prayed to the merciful Lord with their faces touching the ground. Then Judas encouraged them and ordered them to be ready for battle.

[13]After meeting privately with the Jewish leaders, Judas decided to settle the matter with God's help by fighting the king's army before it invaded Judea and took control of Jerusalem. [14]He left the outcome of the battle to God, the creator of the universe, and encouraged his soldiers to fight bravely and to be willing to die for their laws, temple, city, country, and way of life. Then they set up camp near the city of Modein. [15]He gave his soldiers this password: "God will give us the victory." After he had chosen the best young fighting men, he attacked the king's headquarters at night. Judas and his soldiers killed about 2,000 enemy troops there. They even stabbed to death the lead elephant and its driver. [16]As a result, the enemy troops became terrified and confused. Because Judas and his soldiers had successfully completed their mission, they left. [17]All this happened before sunrise because the Lord helped and protected Judas.

King Antiochus V Makes a Peace Treaty With the Jews—
1 Maccabees 6:48-63

[18]King Antiochus got a taste of how bold the Jews could be. So he tried various ways to take over the positions they held. [19]For example, the city of Beth Zur was a strong Jewish fortification. So he attacked Beth Zur over and over again. But every time he attacked, he was defeated. He kept making raids against Beth Zur. But every time he made a raid, he lost the battle. [20]Judas sent supplies to the soldiers inside the fort. [21]But a Jewish soldier named Rhodocus passed on some secret information to the enemy. Some of Judas' soldiers searched for Rhodocus, caught him, and executed him. [22]Because the soldiers in Beth Zur outfought King Antiochus, Antiochus offered them a peace treaty, which they accepted. Then he left there, attacked Judas and his soldiers, and lost the battle. [23]Afterward, he heard that Philip, his chief of state, had rebelled against him in Antioch. The king was stunned. He had peace talks with the Jews, agreed to their demands, and swore an oath to uphold their rights. After an agreement was reached, he offered a sacrifice and honored the temple with generous gifts. [24]He gave Judas his approval and left Hegemonides as governor of the territory extending from Ptolemais to Gerar. [25]Then he went to Ptolemais. The citizens of Ptolemais were angry about the agreement Antiochus had made with the Jews. In fact, they were so mad that they wanted the agreement to be canceled. [26]Lysias spoke in public

and defended the king's actions as well as he could. Because he was so convincing, he calmed the people down and gained their support. Then the king left for Antioch.

So this ends the story of the king's attack on Judea and his return to Antioch.

King Demetrius Sends Nicanor to Attack Judea—*1 Maccabees 7:1-21*

14 ¹Three years later, Judas and his soldiers heard that Seleucus' son Demetrius had sailed into the harbor at Tripolis with a fleet and a powerful army. ²They also heard that Demetrius had killed King Antiochus V and his guardian Lysias and had gained control of the country.

³A man named Alcimus was a former chief priest who had willingly made himself unclean*ᵃ* during a time of war. He realized that the Jews wanted to kill him and that he would never be able to approach the holy altar again. ⁴So he went to King Demetrius in the year 161 B.C. and presented the king with a gold crown, a palm branch, and some customary gifts from the temple. Alcimus said nothing to the king that day.

⁵But later, Alcimus got a chance to work out a foolish plan that he had. Demetrius invited him to an official meeting and asked him what he thought about the situation in Judea. Alcimus replied, ⁶"Judas Maccabeus is the leader of a group of Jewish people called the Hasidim. These are the people who keep fighting, rebelling, and preventing your kingdom from having peace. ⁷Because of them, I no longer hold the honored position of chief priest, which I am entitled to by birth. I have two reasons for being here today: ⁸First, I'm genuinely concerned about your interests, Your Majesty. Secondly, I'm concerned about my own people. The whole Jewish nation is in an unfortunate position because of the foolish actions of Judas and his followers, whom I mentioned earlier. ⁹But I'm sure you are fully aware of all these things, Your Majesty. So please treat my nation and its troubled people with the same kindness that you show to everyone. ¹⁰As long as Judas is alive, your government will never have peace."

¹¹When Alcimus finished speaking, the king's friends, who hated the things that Judas was doing, quickly got Demetrius even more irritated with Judas. ¹²So Demetrius immediately appointed Nicanor, who was in charge of his army's elephants, as the governor of Judea. Demetrius sent Nicanor to Judea ¹³and ordered him to kill Judas, scatter Judas' troops, and appoint Alcimus as chief priest of the world's greatest temple. ¹⁴The foreigners whom Judas had banished from Judea joined Nicanor in large numbers. They thought that a defeat to the Jewish nation would be to their advantage.

ᵃ 14:3 "Unclean" refers to anything that Moses' Teachings say is not presentable to God.

Nicanor Makes a Peace Treaty With the Jews

¹⁵ When the Jewish troops heard that Nicanor was coming to attack them and that the banished foreigners had joined him, they sprinkled dust on their heads. They prayed to God, who had made them his own people forever, because he had helped them by showing his miraculous power. ¹⁶ Then Judas, their commander, ordered the troops to leave immediately and attack the enemy near the village of Dessau. ¹⁷ Simon, Judas' brother, was already fighting Nicanor. But Simon was slowly losing the battle because the enemy had made a surprise attack on him.

¹⁸ When Nicanor heard how brave Judas and his soldiers were and how courageously they were fighting, he was afraid to let the battle continue. ¹⁹ So he sent Posidonius, Theodotus, and Mattathias to make a peace treaty with the Jews. ²⁰ After the terms of the peace treaty were examined in detail, Judas, the Jewish leader, discussed the terms with his soldiers. When both sides accepted all the terms, they agreed to sign the peace treaty. ²¹ The leaders set aside a day when they could have a private meeting together. On the day of the meeting, a chariot came from each side, and chairs were set up. ²² In strategic locations Judas placed armed men who were ready to fight, because he was afraid that the enemy might suddenly double-cross him. However, the meeting went well for both leaders.

²³ Nicanor spent some time in Jerusalem. He did nothing that made people suspicious. He even sent away the mobs of foreigners that had joined him. ²⁴ He always had Judas with him because he truly liked him. ²⁵ He urged Judas to get married and start a family. So Judas got married, settled down, and led a normal life.

Nicanor Turns Against Judas

²⁶ When Alcimus saw how well Judas and Nicanor were getting along with each other, he got a copy of the peace treaty and went to see King Demetrius. He told the king that Nicanor was undermining the government because he had appointed Judas, who was plotting against the kingdom, to take his place. ²⁷ The false charges brought against Nicanor by that corrupt man Alcimus made the king furious. So the king wrote a letter to Nicanor. In the letter he stated that he was displeased with the terms of the peace treaty, and he ordered Nicanor to arrest Judas and bring him as quickly as possible to Antioch.

²⁸ When Nicanor read the king's letter, he was upset. He hated to break an agreement with a man who had done nothing wrong. ²⁹ But since he couldn't disobey the king, he looked for a way to capture Judas by surprise. ³⁰ Judas noticed that Nicanor was beginning to treat him harshly and was becoming rude during their regular meetings. Judas knew that something was wrong. So he gathered many of his followers and hid from Nicanor.

³¹When Nicanor realized that Judas had outsmarted him, he went to the world's greatest and holiest temple. While the priests were offering the regular sacrifices, he ordered them to hand over Judas. ³²The priests swore with an oath that they didn't know where Judas was. ³³So Nicanor held out his hand, pointed at the temple, and swore this oath: "If you don't hand over Judas to me, I'll level God's temple, tear down the altar, and build a magnificent temple to Dionysus in this place."

³⁴After Nicanor said these terrible things, he left. The priests stretched out their hands toward heaven and prayed to God, who had always defended the Jewish nation. They prayed, ³⁵"Lord, you rule everything. Even though you've never needed anything, you chose to live among us in your temple. ³⁶Holy One, Lord of everything that is holy, keep this temple, which has just been cleansed, from ever being dishonored again."

The Story of Razis

³⁷Someone told Nicanor about a man named Razis, who was one of Jerusalem's leaders. Razis loved his people, had a very good reputation, and was called "the Father of the Jews" because of his loyalty. ³⁸In the early days of the war, someone had accused him of following the Jewish religion, because he had risked his life out of devotion to it. ³⁹Nicanor wanted everyone to see how much he hated the Jews. So he sent more than 500 soldiers to arrest Razis. ⁴⁰Nicanor thought that by arresting Razis, he could destroy the morale of the Jews. ⁴¹Nicanor's soldiers were about to capture the house where Razis lived. They were trying to force the courtyard gate open and were calling for someone to make a fire to burn down the doors of his house. Razis realized that he was surrounded, so he tried to commit suicide by falling on his sword. ⁴²He wanted to die with honor rather than be arrested by these sinners and have them humiliate him. ⁴³But because everything was happening so quickly, he failed to fall directly on his sword and kill himself. As the soldiers were rushing through the doorway, Razis ran up onto the roof of his house and bravely jumped off toward the soldiers below. ⁴⁴But the soldiers quickly stepped back, and he landed in the open space they had created. ⁴⁵Still alive and very angry, Razis got up. Even though blood was spurting out of his body and he was badly wounded, he ran through the crowd of soldiers and climbed on top of a high rock. ⁴⁶Having lost a lot of blood, he tore out his intestines with both hands and threw them at the soldiers. As he did this, he prayed that the Lord of life and breath would give these body parts back to him someday. That's the way Razis died.

Nicanor's Cruel Plan

15 ¹Nicanor heard that Judas and his soldiers were in the region of Samaria. So he planned to attack them on a day of worship so that his own army wouldn't suffer any casualties. ²Nicanor had forced some Jews to accompany his army. These Jews told Nicanor not to be cruel and uncivilized by attacking on a day of worship, but to honor the day of worship, the day that God, who sees everything, has specially chosen and set apart as holy.

³Nicanor, who was a disgusting man, asked them, "Is there actually a ruler in heaven who has ordered the Jews to observe the day of worship?"

⁴The Jews replied, "Yes! The Lord, who lives in heaven, is the ruler who has ordered us to worship on the seventh day of the week."

⁵Nicanor said, "I am a ruler on earth, and I order you to grab your weapons and do what the king wants." Despite everything he said, Nicanor didn't carry out his cruel plan.

Judas Encourages His Soldiers

⁶Nicanor, carried away by his arrogance, planned to set up a monument after his victory over Judas. ⁷But Judas never stopped believing that the Lord would help him. ⁸He continually encouraged his soldiers not to be afraid when the enemy attacked. He told them to remember that the LORD[a] had helped them in the past and to expect the Almighty to give them a victory now. ⁹He motivated his soldiers by reading from Moses' Teachings and the Prophets and by reminding them of the battles they had already won. ¹⁰After he got them ready to fight, he gave them their orders. At the same time, he reminded them that the foreigners had broken their promises and couldn't be trusted. ¹¹With the things he said, Judas armed each of his soldiers with courage. In addition, he told them about one of his dreams, a dream that made the soldiers happy and confident.

¹²This is Judas' dream: Judas saw the former chief priest Onias, who was a perfect gentleman, modest, gentle, and a good speaker and who had been trained from childhood to lead a devout life. Onias was stretching out his hands toward heaven and praying for the entire Jewish nation. ¹³Then Judas saw another man in his dream. The man had gray hair, looked very impressive, and had a lot of authority. ¹⁴Onias said, "This is Jeremiah, God's prophet. He loves the people of Israel and prays constantly for them and for Jerusalem, the holy city."

¹⁵Jeremiah held out his right hand and presented Judas with a gold sword. As Jeremiah was giving the sword to Judas, he said, ¹⁶"Take this sword. It's a holy gift from God. With this sword you will destroy your enemies."

---

[a] 15:8 Greek "Heaven." The author of 2 Maccabees uses the word *Heaven* in place of God's name, the LORD.

[17] Judas encouraged his soldiers with powerful words, so the soldiers were determined to do their best. The boys had as much courage as the men. Because Jerusalem, the holy place, and the temple courtyards were in danger, his soldiers decided not to march into battle. Instead, they decided to charge the enemy bravely and to settle the battle by engaging in hand-to-hand combat. [18] Their biggest concern was no longer their families and relatives but the holy temple. [19] The people left in Jerusalem were terrified. They were worried about the battle that was going to take place in the open country.

Nicanor Is Killed in Battle

[20] Everyone was waiting to see how the battle would turn out. The enemy forces were approaching. The troops were in battle formation, the elephants were placed in strategic positions, and the cavalry was riding at each end of the battle line. [21] As the large enemy forces approached, Judas noticed the different kinds of weapons they had and how fierce their elephants were. Then he stretched out his hands toward heaven and prayed to the Lord, who performs miracles. He knew that battles weren't decided by weapons but by the Lord and that the Lord gives the victory to those who deserve it. [22] Judas prayed, "Lord, when Hezekiah was king of Judea, you sent your angel to Sennacherib's camp and your angel killed 185,000 of his soldiers. [23] Ruler of heaven, send an angel ahead of us now to make our enemies tremble with fear. [24] Use your mighty power to strike down those who have insulted you and have come to attack your holy people." Then Judas ended his prayer.

[25] As Nicanor's army advanced, his soldiers blew trumpets and sang battle songs. [26] But the soldiers in Judas' army prayed as they went into battle. [27] They prayed to God, engaged in hand-to-hand combat, and killed more than 35,000 enemy soldiers. Afterward, they were very happy that God had appeared and helped them.

[28] When the battle was over and Judas and his soldiers were celebrating on their way home, they found Nicanor lying dead on the ground with all his armor on. [29] So they praised the ruler of heaven in their native language with loud shouts. [30] Their leader Judas had dedicated his entire life to defending his people and had been devoted to them ever since he was young. He ordered his soldiers to cut off Nicanor's head and right hand and to take them to Jerusalem. [31] When Judas arrived in Jerusalem, he called the Jewish people together. He made the priests stand in front of the altar, and he summoned the men who were in the fortress. [32] Then Judas showed them the head of that disgusting man Nicanor and the hand which that evil man had held out so arrogantly against the holy temple of the Almighty God. [33] In addition, Judas cut out Nicanor's tongue since Nicanor had said so many terrible things. Judas promised to feed

Nicanor's tongue piece by piece to the birds and to hang Nicanor's hand in front of the temple as a punishment for Nicanor's senseless behavior. ³⁴All the people praised the Lord, who had appeared and helped them, and the sky echoed with their praise. They said, "Praise the Lord because he didn't allow his temple to be dishonored."

³⁵Judas hung Nicanor's head from the fortress wall. Everyone who saw it knew that it was a sign of the Lord's help. ³⁶No one wanted this day to be forgotten. So the people took a vote and unanimously passed a law to celebrate the thirteenth day of the twelfth month every year. (The twelfth month is called Adar in the Aramaic language.) This new holiday fell on the day before Mordecai's Day, which is the Festival of Purim. ³⁷This is how everything turned out for Nicanor. From that time on, the Hebrew people remained in control of Jerusalem. So here is where I'll end my book.

The Writer's Conclusion

³⁸If my book is cleverly organized and well-written, that's what I tried to do. If the book is only average or poorly-written, that's the best I could do. ³⁹Drinking only wine or only water can make a person sick. But when wine and water are mixed together, a sweet and pleasant flavor is produced. In the same way, a book that is cleverly organized with interesting stories pleases those who read it. This is the end of my book.